Lecture Notes Series on Computing - Vol. 16

Parallel Algorithms

T0338561

LECTURE NOTES SERIES ON COMPUTING

Editor-in-Chief: D T Lee (*Academia Sinica, Taiwan*)

Published

Lecture Notes Series on Computing - Vol. 16

Parallel Algorithms

M. H. Alsuwaiyel

King Fahd University of Petroleum & Minerals (KFUPM), Saudi Arabia

NEW JERSEY • LONDON • SINGAPORE • BEIJING • SHANGHAI • HONG KONG • TAIPEI • CHENNAI • TOKYO

Published by

World Scientific Publishing Co. Pte. Ltd.
5 Toh Tuck Link, Singapore 596224
USA office: 27 Warren Street, Suite 401-402, Hackensack, NJ 07601
UK office: 57 Shelton Street, Covent Garden, London WC2H 9HE

Library of Congress Cataloging-in-Publication Data
Names: Alsuwaiyel, M. H., author.
Title: Parallel algorithms / M. H. Alsuwaiyel, King Fahd University of
    Petroleum & Minerals (KFUPM), Saudi Arabia.
Description: [Hackensack] New Jersey : World Scientific, [2022] |
    Series: Lecture notes series on computing, 1793-1223 ; vol. 16 |
    Includes bibliographical references and index.
Identifiers: LCCN 2022008953 | ISBN 9789811252976 (hardcover) |
    ISBN 9789811252983 (ebook for institutions) | ISBN 9789811252990 (ebook for individuals)
Subjects: LCSH: Parallel algorithms. | Parallel processing (Electronic computers)
Classification: LCC QA76.642 .A47 2022 | DDC 005.2/75--dc23/eng/20220429
LC record available at https://lccn.loc.gov/2022008953

British Library Cataloguing-in-Publication Data
A catalogue record for this book is available from the British Library.

For any available supplementary material, please visit
https://www.worldscientific.com/worldscibooks/10.1142/12744#t=suppl

Desk Editors: Balasubramanian Shanmugam/Amanda Yun

Typeset by Stallion Press
Email: enquiries@stallionpress.com

Printed in Singapore

To my wife Noura and my daughter Sara

Preface

In the last few decades, there has been an explosion of interest in the field of parallel computation. From the computer scientist's point of view, this has provided a challenging range of problems with new ground rules for the design and analysis of parallel algorithms.

This text is meant to be an introduction to the field of parallel algorithms and to techniques for efficient parallelization. The emphasis is upon designing algorithms within the timeless and abstract context of a high-level programming language, rather than depending upon highly detailed machine architectures.

Although the main theme of the book is algorithm design using different models of computation, it also emphasizes the other major component in algorithmic design: the analysis of parallel algorithms. It covers the analysis of most of the algorithms presented in detail. The focus of the presentation is on practical applications of algorithm design using different models of parallel computation. Each model is illustrated by providing an adequate number of algorithms to solve some problems that quite often arise in many applications in science and engineering.

The style of presentation of algorithms is straightforward, and uses pseudocode that is similar to the syntax of structured programming languages, e.g., **if-then-else**, **for** and **while** constructs. The pseudocode is sometimes intermixed with English whenever necessary. Describing a portion of an algorithm in English is indeed instructive; it conveys the idea with minimum effort on the part of the reader. However, sometimes it is both easier and more formal to use a pseudocode statement.

The book is largely self-contained, presuming no special knowledge of parallel computers or particular mathematics. However, the reader familiar with elementary ideas from the areas of discrete mathematics, data structures and sequential algorithms will be at an advantage. Most chapters include examples and illustrations. In addition, the solutions to all exercises are included at the end of each chapter.

The book is intended as a text in the field of the design and analysis of parallel algorithms. It includes adequate material for a course in parallel algorithms in the undergraduate or graduate levels.

The author would like to thank those who have critically offered suggestions, including the students of the parallel algorithms course at KFUPM. Special thanks go to Wasfi Al-Khatib and Sultan Almuhammadi for their valuable discussions and comments.

M. H. Alsuwaiyel

Khobar, Saudi Arabia

About the Author

Muhammad Hamad (M. H.) Alsuwaiyel is a retired Professor of the Information and Computer Science Department at King Fahd University of Petroleum and Minerals (KFUPM), Dhahran, Saudi Arabia. He was a member of KFUPM's faculty from 1991 to 2014. Dr Alsuwaiyel taught both undergraduate and graduate courses on design and analysis of algorithms, computer networks, discrete structures, theory of computing, automata and formal languages, foundations of computer science, mathematical logic, design and theory of algorithms, combinatorial algorithms optimization, parallel algorithms, theory of automata and formal languages, computational complexity, and computational geometry. He has publications in the design and analysis of algorithms. He holds a B.S. in Systems Engineering from KFUPM, an M.S. in Computer Science from University of Colorado at Boulder, USA and a Ph.D. in Computer Science from Northwestern University, Illinois, USA. M. H. Alsuwaiyel is the author of *Algorithms: Design Techniques and Analysis.*

Contents

Chapter 1

Introduction

With the growing number of areas in which computers are being used, there is an ever-increasing demand for more computing power. A means to attain very high computational speeds is to use a parallel computer, meaning, a computer that possesses several processing units, or processors. In this case, the problem is broken down into smaller parts, which are solved simultaneously, each by a different processor.

A parallel algorithm, as opposed to a traditional sequential algorithm, is an algorithm which can do multiple operations in a given time. In sequential algorithms, an algorithm is described and analyzed using the random-access machine (RAM) as a model of computation. By contrast, in parallel algorithms, an algorithm is described and analyzed using different models, one of which is the so-called parallel random-access machine (PRAM). The purpose of this chapter is to introduce parallel architectures and models, and illustrate parallel algorithms through simple examples.

1.1 Classifications of Parallel Architectures

There are four classifications of parallel architectures based upon the number of concurrent instruction streams and data streams available in the architecture.

(a) Single instruction stream, single data stream (SISD): Most conventional computers with one central processing unit (CPU) belong to this class. Examples of SISD architecture are the traditional uniprocessor machines like older personal computers and mainframe computers. By 2010, many personal computers had multiple cores.

(b) Single instruction stream, multiple data streams (SIMD): This category includes machines with a single program and multiple CPUs. In this class, a parallel computer consists of p identical processors. All processors operate under the control of a single instruction stream issued by a central control unit. Processors communicate among themselves during computation in order to exchange data or intermediate results in two ways, giving rise to two subclasses: SIMD computers where communication is effected through a shared memory, and those where it is done via an interconnection network.

(c) Multiple instruction streams, single data stream (MISD): This architecture is uncommon and unrealistic.

(d) Multiple instruction streams, multiple data streams (MIMD): This class of computers is the most general and most powerful. In this class, there are p processors, p streams of instructions, and p streams of data. The machines that fall into this category are capable of executing several programs independently. They include multi-core superscalar processors, and distributed systems, using either one shared memory space or a distributed memory space. In MIMD, processors may have multiple processing cores that can execute different instructions on different data. Most parallel computers, as of 2013, are MIMD systems.

1.2   Shared-Memory Computers

This class is also known in the literature as the Parallel Random-Access Machine (PRAM) model. It assumes that there is a random-access shared memory, such that any processor can access any variable with unit cost. This assumption of unit-cost access (regardless of the size of the memory) is unrealistic, but it makes the analysis of parallel algorithms easier. The programs written on these machines are, in general, of type SIMD. These kinds of algorithms are useful for understanding the exploitation of concurrency, for they divide the original problem into similar subproblems and then solve them in parallel. The introduction of the formal PRAM model had the aim of quantifying analysis of parallel algorithms in a way analogous to the RAM model. The structure of the PRAM is shown in Fig. 1.1. Here, multiple processors are attached to a single block of memory.

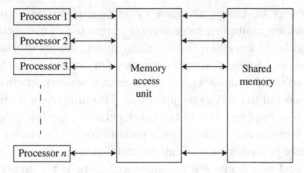

Fig. 1.1.   Parallel random access machine (PRAM).

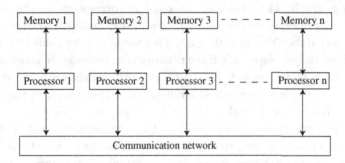

Fig. 1.2.   Interconnection network.

The processors can communicate among themselves through the shared memory only. A memory access unit connects the processors with the shared memory block.

1.3   Interconnection-Network Computers

Interconnection networks or distributed memory machines are constructed as processor-memory pairs and connected to each other in a well-defined pattern. These processor-memory pairs are often referred to as *processing elements* or PEs, or sometimes just as *processors*. An interconnection network may be viewed as an undirected graph $G = (V, E)$, where V is the set of nodes or processors, and E is the set of two-way links. Processors communicate between each other by sending messages. The structure of the interconnection network is shown in Fig. 1.2.

The topology of a network refers to its general infrastructure — the pattern in which multiple processors are connected. This pattern could either be regular or irregular, though many multi-core architectures today use highly regular interconnection networks. On one extreme, there is the complete graph, which models an interconnection network where every processor is connected to every other processor. This kind of connection is prohibitive, as it is impractical. On the other extreme, the line graph, which models the linear array, connects each node to one or two other nodes. In between, there is a multitude of interconnection networks that have both advantages and disadvantages. For instance, there is the hypercube, the mesh, the tree and the pyramid, to mention a few.

The degree of a network is the maximum degree of any vertex in the underlying graph. The degree of processor P corresponds to the number of processors directly connected to P. Naturally, networks of high degree become very difficult to manufacture. Therefore, it is desirable to use networks of low degree, especially if the network is to be scaled to an extremely large number of processors. In a network with n processors, a constant degree is preferable to one that is a function of n. For example, the degree of the mesh network is 4, while that of the hypercube is $\log n$.

The network diameter is defined as the maximum shortest path distance between any two processors. A low communication diameter is highly desirable, because it allows for efficient communication between arbitrary processors. For instance, the diameter of the hypercube with n processors is $\log n$, while the diameter of a mesh with the same number of processors is $2\sqrt{n} - 2$.

The bisection width of an interconnection network is the minimum number of links that have to be removed in order to disconnect the network into two approximately equal-sized subnetworks. In general, machines with a high bisection width are difficult to build, but they provide users with the possibility of moving large amounts of data efficiently. The bisection width implies a lower bound on the computations in an interconnection network, especially in algorithms that require massive data movements. For instance, in the problem of sorting n elements, $\Omega(n)$ data items may have to be moved from one half of the network to the other. For example, the bisection width of the hypercube is $\Theta(n)$, and it admits sorting algorithms in the order of $\Theta(\log^2 n)$ and $\Theta(\log n \log \log n)$, while the bisection width of the mesh is $\Theta(\sqrt{n})$, which explains why sorting on the mesh is $\Omega(\sqrt{n})$.

1.4   Two Simple Examples

Now, we present two simple examples of parallel algorithms, and define and illustrate some of the performance measures that are used in the analysis of parallel algorithms.

Example 1.1   Consider the problem of adding n numbers $s = a_1 + a_2 + \cdots + a_n$, where $n = 2^k$ for some nonnegative integer k. Sequentially, the expression can be computed by scanning the input from left to right in the obvious way using $n - 1$ additions. In parallel, $b_1 = a_1 + a_2, b_2 = a_3 + a_4, \ldots, b_{n/2} = a_{n-1} + a_n$ are computed in one parallel step using $n/2$ processors to produce a new expression $b_1 + b_2 + \cdots + b_{n/2}$ consisting of $n/2$ operands. Then $c_1 = b_1 + b_2, c_2 = b_3 + b_4, \ldots, c_{n/4} = b_{n/2-1} + b_{n/2}$ are computed in one parallel step using $n/4$ processors to produce a new expression $c_1 + c_2 + \cdots + c_{n/4}$ consisting of $n/4$ operands. This process continues until there is only one value left. The total number of parallel steps is $k = \log n$ using $n/2$ processors. $\square$

Example 1.2   Recall the search problem: Given a set $X = \{x_1, x_2, \ldots, x_n\}$ of n unordered and distinct elements, and an element y, determine j such that $y = x_j$ if $y \in X$ and $j = 0$ otherwise. n comparisons are needed in the worst case to solve this problem sequentially. In parallel, assume there are n processors $P_1, P_2, \ldots, P_n$, and that x_i is stored in P_i, $1 \leq i \leq n$. Initially, P_1 sets $j = 0$. Then all processors P_i compare y with x_i simultaneously. If $y \in X$, only one processor P_k will succeed in setting $j = k$. It follows that the problem can be solved in two parallel steps using n processors. Notice that concurrent read capability is required, as all processors need to read y at the same time. $\square$

Unlike in sequential algorithms, the performance measures include the number of processors and communication cost. Let n be the input size, and p the number of processors. Then, $T(n, p)$, or simply $T(n)$ if p is known from the context, denotes the *running time* of the algorithm using p processors. If the algorithm has two parameters, n and m, then we write $T(n, m, p)$. We may also write $T(n, p)$ or $T(n, m)$ if m or p are known from the context. In Example 1.1, $T(n, n/2) = \Theta(\log n)$, while in Example 1.2, $T(n, n) = \Theta(1)$. The *cost* of an algorithm is the product of the running time and number of processors, e.g., $C(n, p) = pT(n, p)$. In Example 1.1,

$C(n, n/2) = \Theta(n \log n)$, while in Example 1.2, $C(n, n) = \Theta(n)$. The *work* done by an algorithm is the total number of operations done by individual processors. It is less than or equal to the cost of the algorithm. In Example 1.1, $W(n, n/2) = n/2 + n/4 + \cdots + 1 = n - 1 = \Theta(n)$, while in Example 1.2, $W(n, n) = \Theta(n)$, since there are n comparisons.

The ratio $S(p) = T(n, 1)/T(n, p)$ is called the *speedup* of the algorithm, where $T(n, 1)$ should be taken from the best sequential algorithm. An algorithm achieves a *perfect speedup* if $S(p) = p$. In Example 1.1, $S(n/2) = \Theta(n/\log n)$, while in Example 1.2, $S(n) = \Theta(n)$. A useful measure of the utilization of the processors is the *efficiency* of a parallel algorithm, which is defined as $E(n, p) = S(p)/p = T(n, 1)/pT(n, p)$. The efficiency is the ratio of the time used by one processor with a sequential algorithm and the total time used by p processors, which is the cost of the algorithm. The efficiency indicates the percentage of the processors' time that is not wasted, compared to the sequential algorithm. If $E(n, p) = 1$, then the amount of work done by all processors throughout the execution of the algorithm is equal to the amount of work required by the sequential algorithm. In this case, we get optimal usage of the processors. All in all, the goal is to maximize efficiency. In Example 1.1, $E(n, n/2) = \Theta(1/\log n)$, while in Example 1.2, $E(n, n) = \Theta(n)/n\Theta(1) = \Theta(1)$.

Chapter 2

Shared-memory Computers (PRAM)

2.1 Introduction

The parallel random-access machine (PRAM) was intended as the parallel-computing analogy to the random-access machine (RAM). It is used to model parallel algorithmic performance such as time complexity, where the number of processors assumed is typically also stated. As in the RAM, the PRAM model neglects issues such as synchronization and communication, but includes the number of processors. Algorithm cost, for instance, is estimated using two parameters: time × number of processors. Read/write conflicts are resolved by one of the following models:

- Exclusive read exclusive write (EREW): In this strategy, every processor can read or write to a memory cell at a time.
- Concurrent read exclusive write (CREW): Here, multiple processors can read a memory cell but only one can write to it at a time.
- Exclusive read concurrent write (ERCW): This is never considered.
- Concurrent read concurrent write (CRCW): In this strategy, multiple processors can read from or write to the same memory cell at the same time.

In the CRCW model, the writes cause some discrepancies, and hence the write is further defined as:

- COMMON: If all processors write the same value, it is successful; otherwise it is illegal.

7

- ARBITRARY: Only one arbitrary attempt by an arbitrary processor is successful.
- PRIORITY: Processors are ranked, and the processor with the maximum rank can write.

Array reduction uses associative binary operations (e.g., SUM, Logical AND or MAX) of processor contents. Only either the maximum of processors' contents, or the sum of all contents in all processors can be written.

In the PRAM, there is no limit on the number of processors in the machine. Any memory location is accessible from any processor, and there is no limit on the amount of shared memory in the system.

2.2   The Balanced Tree Method

The balanced tree method is one of the parallel algorithmic design techniques usually implemented either as the main component or as a subtask of the parallel algorithm. Let $\circ$ be a binary associative operation (e.g., $+, \times, \min, \max$), and consider computing the expression

$$s = a_1 \circ a_2 \circ \cdots \circ a_n,$$

where $n = 2^k$ for some nonnegative integer k (see Example 1.1). Sequentially, the expression can be computed by scanning the input from left to right. In parallel, $b_1 = a_1 \circ a_2, b_2 = a_3 \circ a_4, \ldots, b_{n/2} = a_{n-1} \circ a_n$ are computed in one parallel step to produce a new expression $s = b_1 \circ b_2 \circ \cdots \circ b_{n/2}$ consisting of $n/2$ operands. This process continues until there is only one value to compute. This procedure defines a complete binary tree where the input is initially at its leaves, and each internal node corresponds to a subproblem, while the root corresponds to the overall problem. Each leaf node is assigned a processor $P_i, 1 \leq i \leq n$. The internal nodes at level $j, 0 \leq j \leq k - 1$, are assigned processors $P_1, P_2, \ldots, P_{2^j}$. The computations at the internal nodes of the same level are performed in one parallel step. Figure 2.1 depicts a typical complete binary tree for $n = 8$. It has $2n - 1$ nodes. Note that it is represented by the array $B[1..2n - 1]$, where the children for $B[j], 1 \leq j \leq n - 1$, are stored at $B[2j]$ and $B[2j + 1]$. For $j, 1 \leq j \leq n - 1$, if $B[2j] = x$ and $B[2j + 1] = y$, then $B[j] = x \circ y$.

Algorithm PARADDITION performs the operation of addition on n numbers stored initially in array $A[1..n]$. The first **for** loop copies the

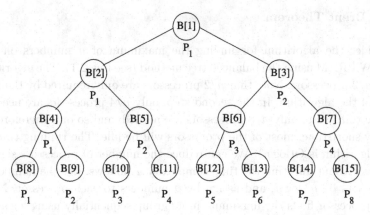

Fig. 2.1. The computation of $s = a_1 \circ a_2 \circ \cdots \circ a_n$.

numbers in A into $B[n], B[n+1], \ldots, B[2n-1]$, which correspond to the leaves of the binary tree. The **for** loop in Line 3 is repeated $k = \log n$ times, once for each internal level of the tree. The **for** loop at line 4 is for performing 2^i additions in parallel, $i = k - 1, k - 2, \ldots, 0$.

Algorithm 2.1 PARADDITION
Input: $A[1..n]$, an array of n numbers, where $n = 2^k$.
Output: $A[1] + A[2] + \cdots + A[n]$.

1. **for** $j \leftarrow 1$ **to** n **do in parallel**
2. $B[j + n - 1] \leftarrow A[j]$
3. **for** $i \leftarrow k - 1$ **downto** 0 **do**
4.   **for** $j \leftarrow 2^i$ **to** $2^{i+1} - 1$ **do in parallel**
5. $B[j] \leftarrow B[2j] + B[2j + 1]$
6.   **end for**
7. **end for**
8. **return** $B[1]$

The running time of the algorithm is equal to the depth of the binary tree, which is $\Theta(\log n)$. The work done by the algorithm is proportional to the number of additions performed in the internal nodes, which is $n - 1$. The cost of the algorithm is $n \times \Theta(\log n) = \Theta(n \log n)$.

2.3   Brent Theorem

Consider the algorithm for finding the maximum of n numbers on the
EREW PRAM using the balanced tree method (see Fig. 2.1). The algorithm
uses $n/2$ processors. Note that $n/2$ processors are only required by the first
step of the algorithm. In the second step, only $n/4$ processors are needed.
In the third step, only $n/8$ processors are needed, and so on. Therefore, in
a very short time, most of the processors will be idle. The running time of
the algorithm is $\Theta(\log n)$. We can reduce the number of processors signifi-
cantly without affecting the time complexity as follows. Let the number of
processors be $n/\log n$, and assign $\log n$ numbers to each processor. Now,
each processor finds the maximum in its group sequentially using $\log n - 1$
comparisons, and the parallel algorithm continues to find the maximum of
the $n/\log n$ group maxima. Thus, the running time is still $\Theta(\log n)$, while
the cost of the algorithm is reduced from $\Theta(n \log n)$ to $\Theta(n)$. The following
theorem, known as Brent's theorem, generalizes the above discussion.

Theorem 2.1   Suppose an algorithm A_p performs t_p parallel steps using p
processors on the PRAM such that the total number of operations over all
processors is s, and let $q = s/t_p$. Then, there exists an algorithm A_q that
performs at most $2t_p$ parallel steps using q processors. Moreover, if the
sequential time complexity is $O(s)$, then the cost of A_q is optimal.

Proof.   Let $s_i, 1 \leq i \leq t_p$, be the number of operations performed by
all p processors in step i of Algorithm A_p. Let Algorithm A_q emulate A_p
by replacing each parallel step i of A_p by $\lceil s_i/q \rceil$ parallel steps. The total
number of parallel steps performed by algorithm A_q is thus

$$t_q = \sum_{i=1}^{t_p} \left\lceil \frac{s_i}{q} \right\rceil$$

$$= \sum_{i=1}^{t_p} \left\lceil \frac{s_i \times t_p}{s} \right\rceil$$

$$\leq \sum_{i=1}^{t_p} \left(\frac{s_i \times t_p}{s} + 1 \right)$$

$$= t_p + \frac{t_p}{s} \sum_{i=1}^{t_p} s_i$$

$$= 2t_p,$$

since $\sum_{i=1}^{t_p} s_i = s$. The new cost of the algorithm is $\leq 2t_p \times \frac{s}{t_p} = 2s = O(s)$. Hence, if the sequential time complexity is $O(s)$, then Algorithm A_q is cost-optimal. $\qquad\square$

Thus, in O-notation, if the original running time is $O(t_p)$, and the work is $O(s)$, then the number of processors can be reduced to $O(s/t_p)$ without increasing the running time. Recall Algorithm PARADDITION in Section 2.2 for the addition of n numbers using n processors. The running time of the algorithm is $\Theta(\log n)$ and it performs a total of $O(n)$ operations. Its cost is $\Theta(n \log n)$. By Brent Theorem, the number of processors can be reduced to $n/\log n$ without changing the time complexity. The new cost is $\Theta(n)$, which is optimal.

2.4 Sorting in $\Theta(1)$ Time on the CRCW PRAM Model

Let $A[1..n]$ be an array of n elements to be sorted on the CRCW PRAM model with n^2 processors. We use the SUM criterion for resolving write conflicts. In other words, if k processors need to write $x_1, x_2, \ldots, x_k$ simultaneously in the same memory location, then the sum $x_1 + x_2 + \cdots + x_k$ is written in that memory location. Assume for simplicity that the elements are distinct. The rank of element $A[i]$ is defined to be the number of elements in A less than $A[i]$. Algorithm SORTINGCRCW performs the operation of sorting on A. There are concurrent writes in Line 3, as more than one processor may attempt to write to the same memory location. For instance, $A[1]$ will be compared with $A[1], A[2], A[3], \ldots, A[n]$ simultaneously, and many processors may attempt to execute the statement $r[i] \leftarrow 1$ at the same time. These concurrent writes are resolved using the sum operation. Specifically, the sum of all 1's will be assigned to $r[i]$, which is the rank of $A[i]$. Note that there are no write conflicts in the assignment in Line 7. Clearly, the running time of the algorithm is $\Theta(1)$, and its cost is $\Theta(n^2)$. The above algorithm is also sometimes referred to as *enumeration sort*.

Algorithm 2.2 SORTINGCRCW
Input: $A[1..n]$, an array of n elements.

Output: $A[1..n]$ sorted in ascending order.

1. **for** $i \leftarrow 1$ **to** n **do in parallel**
2.   **for** $j \leftarrow 1$ **to** n **do in parallel**
3.   **if** $A[i] > A[j]$ **then** $r[i] \leftarrow 1$ **else** $r[i] \leftarrow 0$
4.   **end for**
5. **end for**
6. **for** $i \leftarrow 1$ **to** n **do in parallel**
7. $A[r[i] + 1] \leftarrow A[i]$
8. **end for**

2.4.1 *Implementation on the CREW PRAM model*

The above algorithm can be implemented to run on the CREW PRAM with n processors only, but the running time will increase substantially. The CREW algorithm is shown as Algorithm SORTINGCREW.

Algorithm 2.3 SORTINGCREW
Input: $A[1..n]$, an array of n elements.

Output: $A[1..n]$ sorted in ascending order.

1. **for** $i \leftarrow 1$ **to** n **do in parallel**
2. $r[i] \leftarrow 0$
3. **for** $i \leftarrow 1$ **to** n **do in parallel**
4.   **for** $j \leftarrow 1$ **to** n **do**
5.   **if** $A[i] > A[j]$ **then** $r[i] \leftarrow r[i] + 1$
6.   **end for**
7. **end for**
8. **for** $i \leftarrow 1$ **to** n **do in parallel**
9. $B[r[i] + 1] \leftarrow A[i]$
10. **end for**
11. **return** B

The difference between this algorithm and Algorithm SORTINGCRCW for the CRCW PRAM is that the **for** loop in Line 4 is now sequential. There are no concurrent writes, but there are concurrent reads. For instance, comparing $A[1]$ with any pair of $A[1], A[2], A[3], \ldots, A[n]$ will not take place simultaneously, and hence the statement $r[1] \leftarrow r[1] + 1$ will not be executed more than once at the same time. However, $A[1]$, for example, will be fetched n times simultaneously when comparing $A[1], A[2], \ldots, A[n]$

with $A[1]$. Clearly, the running time is $\Theta(n)$, and the cost is $\Theta(n^2)$. We will see later in this chapter that sorting n elements on the CREW PRAM can be effected in optimal $\Theta(\log n)$ time using n processors.

2.4.2 *Implementation on the EREW PRAM model*

The above CREW algorithm can be implemented to run on the EREW PRAM with n processors without increasing the running time or cost; we only need to take care of concurrent reads. The EREW algorithm is given as Algorithm SORTINGEREW. In this algorithm, $A[j]$ is compared starting with

---

Algorithm 2.4 SORTINGEREW
Input: $A[1..n]$, an array of n elements.

Output: $A[1..n]$ sorted in ascending order.

1. **for** $j \leftarrow 1$ **to** n **do in parallel**
2. $r[j] \leftarrow 0$
3. $C[j] \leftarrow A[j]$
4. **end for**
5. **for** $i \leftarrow 1$ **to** $n-1$ **do**
6.   **for** $j \leftarrow 1$ **to** n **do in parallel**
7. $k \leftarrow i + j \pmod{n}$ **if** $k = 0$ **then** $k \leftarrow n$
8.   **if** $A[j] > C[k]$ **then** $r[j] \leftarrow r[j] + 1$
9.   **end for**
10. **end for**
11. **for** $i \leftarrow 1$ **to** n **do in parallel**
12. $B[r[i] + 1] \leftarrow A[i]$
13. **end for**
14. **return** B

---

the element at distance i. Figure 2.2 depicts an example of the comparisons performed by the algorithm on 8 elements. In this figure, comparing x and y is shown by an arrow from x to y. As is evident from the figure, there are no concurrent reads or concurrent writes. In the first iteration of the outer **for** loop, $A[1]$ is compared with $C[2] = A[2]$, $A[2]$ is compared with $C[3] = A[3]$, etc. (see Fig. 2.2(a)). In the second iteration, that is, when $i = 2$, $A[1]$ is compared with $C[3] = A[3]$, $A[2]$ is compared with $C[4] = A[4]$, etc. (see Fig. 2.2(b)). In the third iteration, that is, when $i = 3$, $A[1]$ is compared with $C[4] = A[4]$, $A[2]$ is compared with $C[5] = A[5]$, etc. (see Fig. 2.2(c)). Finally, in the last iteration, when $i = n - 1$, $A[1]$ is compared with $C[n] = A[n]$, $A[2]$ is compared with $C[1] = A[1]$, and so

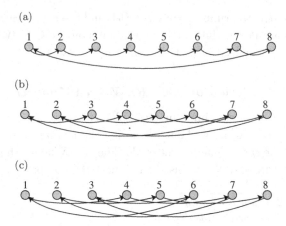

Fig. 2.2.   Example of the action of Algorithm SORTINGEREW.

forth. Clearly, the running time is $\Theta(n)$, and the cost is $\Theta(n^2)$. We will see later in this chapter that sorting n elements on the EREW PRAM can be achieved in optimal $\Theta(\log n)$ time using n processors.

2.5   Parallel Prefix

Let $X = \langle x_1, x_2, \ldots, x_n \rangle$ be a sequence of n numbers, where $n = 2^k$ for a nonnegative integer k. Let $\circ$ be a binary associative operation defined on X. The *prefix sums* problem is to compute the n partial sums: $s_1 = x_1$, $s_2 = x_1 \circ x_2, \ldots, s_i = x_1 \circ x_2 \circ \cdots \circ x_i, \ldots, s_n = x_1 \circ x_2 \circ \cdots \circ x_n$. It is also called the *scan* or the *scan operation*. We will call $s_1, s_2, \ldots, s_n$ the *prefix sums*. Algorithm PARPREFIX is a simple iterative procedure to compute the prefix sums. The algorithm uses n processors. There are $k = \log n$ iterations in the outer loop in Step 5. Since the time needed for the loop in Step 6 is $\Theta(1)$, the running time of the algorithm is $\Theta(\log n)$. Its cost is $n \times \Theta(\log n) = \Theta(n \log n)$, which is not optimal in view of the $\Theta(n)$ time complexity for the sequential algorithm. The work can be computed as follows. The number of operations done by Step 6 in the first iteration is $n - 1$, and in the jth iteration it is $n - 2^{j-1}$. Thus, $W(n) = \sum_{j=1}^{k} (n - 2^{j-1}) = \Theta(n \log n)$. The cost can be reduced to $\Theta(n)$ by reducing the number of processors to $n/\log n$, and making some simple modifications.

Algorithm 2.5 PARPREFIX
Input: $X = \langle x_1, x_2, \ldots, x_n \rangle$, a sequences of n numbers, where $n = 2^k$.
Output: $S = \langle s_1, s_2, \ldots, s_n \rangle$, the prefix sums of X.

1. **for** $i \leftarrow 1$ **to** n **do in parallel**
2. $s_i \leftarrow x_i$
3. **end for**
4. $t \leftarrow 1$
5. **for** $j \leftarrow 1$ **to** k **do**
6.   **for** $i \leftarrow t + 1$ **to** n **do in parallel**
7. $s_i \leftarrow s_{i-t} \circ s_i$
8.   **end for**
9. $t \leftarrow 2t$
10. **end for**
11. **return** S

Another algorithm for computing the prefix sums is shown as Algorithm PARPREFIXREC, which is recursive. First, it recursively computes the prefix sums $s_2, s_4, s_6 \ldots, s_n$. It then computes $s_1, s_3, s_5, \ldots, s_{n-1}$ using the combined divide-and-conquer step. Except for the recursive call, the parallel time is $\Theta(1)$. Hence, $T(n) = \Theta(\log n)$. We compute the work done by the algorithm as follows. There are $n/2$ and $n/2 - 1$ iterations in the loops in Steps 3 and 7, respectively. Therefore $W(n) = W(n/2) + \Theta(n) = \Theta(n)$. The cost, however, is not optimal since the number of processors needed is $n/2$ for a total cost of $\Theta(n \log n)$.

Algorithm 2.6 PARPREFIXREC
Input: $X = \langle x_1, x_2, \ldots, x_n \rangle$, a sequences of n numbers, where $n = 2^k$.
Output: $S = \langle s_1, s_2, \ldots, s_n \rangle$, the prefix sums of X.

1. $s_1 \leftarrow x_1$
2. **if** $n = 1$ **then return** $S = \langle x_1 \rangle$
3. **for** $i \leftarrow 1$ **to** $n/2$ **do in parallel**
4. $x_{2i} \leftarrow x_{2i-1} \circ x_{2i}$
5. **end for**
6. Recursively compute the prefix sums of $\langle x_2, x_4, \ldots, x_n \rangle$ and store them in $\langle s_2, s_4, \ldots, s_n \rangle$
7. **for** $i \leftarrow 2$ **to** $n/2$ **do in parallel**
8. $s_{2i-1} \leftarrow s_{2(i-1)} \circ x_{2i-1}$
9. **end for**
10. **return** $S = \langle s_1, s_2, \ldots, s_n \rangle$

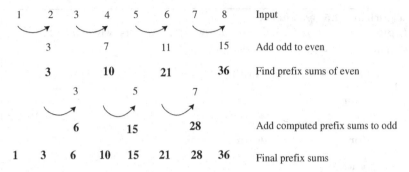

Fig. 2.3.   Example of recursive parallel prefix, Algorithm PARPREFIXREC.

There are no concurrent reads or writes in the above two algorithms, and hence they run on the EREW PRAM.

Example 2.1   Figure 2.3 shows an example of the recursive parallel prefix algorithm, PARPREFIXREC. We will use addition as the binary operation. The input is given in Line 1. In Line 2, the odd-indexed numbers are added to the even-indexed numbers. In Line 3, the prefix sums are computed recursively for the even-indexed numbers. These prefix sums are shown in boldface: 3, 10, 21, 36. These prefixes are added to the odd-indexed numbers, which results in the odd-indexed prefix sums. These prefix sums are shown in Line 5 in boldface: 6, 15, 28. The last line shows the final prefix sums.   □

2.5.1   *Array packing*

Let $A = \langle a_1, a_2, \ldots, a_n \rangle$ be an array of n elements such that t of them are "marked" and the remaining $n - t$ elements are "unmarked". The *array packing* problem consists of creating another array D where all the marked elements are moved to the lower part of D and the unmarked ones to the upper part of the array D without changing their relative order. One method of packing consists of assigning a value of 1 to each of the marked elements and a value of 0 to each of the unmarked elements. A new array $B = \langle b_1, b_2, \ldots, b_n \rangle$ is used to hold the 0–1 values, with $b_i = 1$ if and only if a_i is marked. Now, if we apply the prefix sums algorithm to the array B and store the prefix sums in $C = \langle c_1, c_2, \ldots, c_n \rangle$, the ranks of the marked elements will be computed in C. Specifically, if a_i is marked, then it is stored in D at position c_i. So, the marked elements are moved to the first t cells of array D. Likewise, the ranks of the unmarked elements are computed by interchanging 0's and 1's in array B. Finally, the prefix computation is run again and the unmarked elements are moved to the last $n - t$ cells of array D.

Example 2.2 We now illustrate array packing explained above. Referring to Fig 2.4, the problem requires us to pack the even elements to the left. The first row, part (a), contains the input array A. The second row, part (b), contains the 0–1 values in array B. Array C in part (c) of the figure contains the result of applying parallel prefix on array B. Array D in part (d) contains the even numbers packed in their positions as given in array C. If we now interchange 0's and 1's in B, then we can pack the odd numbers using the same procedure to pack the even numbers. This is shown in Figs. 2.4(e)–(g).

□

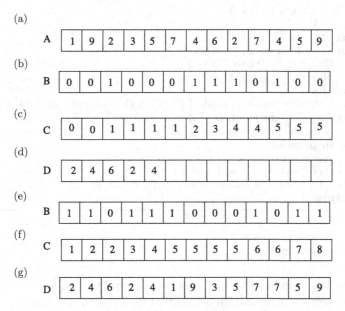

Fig. 2.4. Example of array packing.

2.5.2 *Parallel quicksort*

A parallel version of the quicksort algorithm for the EREW PRAM with n processors is shown as Algorithm PARQUICKSORT. As in the sequential quicksort algorithm, the pivot v is chosen as $A[1]$. First, the pivot is copied n times to avoid concurrent reads. This can be done by a broadcasting procedure in time $\Theta(\log n)$(see Exercise 2.5). Next, array packing is used to partition the array A into two parts, one with elements less than v and one with elements greater than v. This takes $\Theta(\log n)$ time as explained in Section 2.5.1. Next, these two parts are sorted recursively into A_1 and A_2, whose concatenation together with v is returned as the sorted array. In the worst case, the recursion depth can be as large as $\Theta(n)$, causing the running time to be $\Theta(n \log n)$. However, the average recursion depth is $\Theta(\log n)$, for a total running time of $\Theta(\log^2 n)$.

Algorithm 2.7 PARQUICKSORT

Input: An array $A[1..n]$ of n distinct numbers.

Output: A sorted in ascending order.

1. **if** $n = 1$ **then** return A
2. $v \leftarrow A[1]$
3. Let $B[i] = v$ for $1 \leq i \leq n$
4. **for** $i \leftarrow 1$ **to** n **do in parallel**
5.   **if** $A[i] < B[i]$ **then** $C[i] \leftarrow 1$
6.   **else if** $A[i] > B[i]$ **then** $C[i] \leftarrow 0$
7. **end for**
8. Pack the numbers in A marked 1 in C at the beginning of A followed by v followed by the numbers in A marked 0 in C
9. Let w be the position of v in A
10. **do in parallel**
11. $A_1 \leftarrow$ PARQUICKSORT$(A, 1, w - 1)$
12. $A_2 \leftarrow$ PARQUICKSORT$(A, w + 1, n)$
13. $A \leftarrow A_1 || v || A_2$, the concatenation of A_1, v and A_2
14. **return** A

2.6 Parallel Search

Consider the search problem: Given a sequence $S = \langle a_1, a_2, \ldots, a_n \rangle$ of n distinct elements drawn from a linearly ordered set such that $a_1 < a_2 < \cdots < a_n$, and an element x, find the index $k, 1 \leq k \leq n$, such that $x = a_k$

if $x \in S$ and 0 otherwise. Assume that we have a CREW PRAM with p processors, $1 \le p < n$. For convenience, let $n = (p+1)q$. First, the sequence S is divided into $p+1$ subsequences of q elements each, and x is compared to the elements at the p internal boundaries of these subsequences. That is, the algorithm compares x with p elements simultaneously; processor P_i compares x with a_{iq} for $1 \le i \le p$. We have the following cases:

(1) If for some i, $1 \le i \le p$, $x = a_{iq}$, the algorithm returns $k = iq$ and halts.
(2) $x < a_q$, and hence only the elements less than a_q are kept for the next stage. This is shown as the shaded area in Fig. 2.5(a). In this case, the algorithm returns the index of x in $\langle a_1, a_2, \ldots, a_{q-1} \rangle$.
(3) $x > a_{pq}$, and hence only the elements greater than a_{pq} are kept for the next stage. This is shown as the shaded area in Fig. 2.5(b). In this case, the algorithm returns pq plus the index of x in $\langle a_{pq+1}, a_{pq+2}, \ldots, a_n \rangle$.
(4) There exists an i, $1 \le i < p$, such that $x > a_{iq}$ and $x < a_{(i+1)q}$. The next stage performs the search on $\langle a_{iq+1}, a_{iq+2}, \ldots, a_{(i+1)q-1} \rangle$. This is shown as the shaded area in Fig. 2.5(c). In this case, the algorithm returns iq plus the index of x in $\langle a_{iq+1}, a_{iq+2}, \ldots, a_{(i+1)q-1} \rangle$.

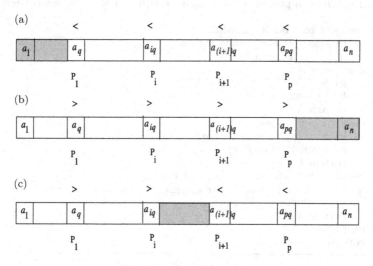

Fig. 2.5.   Parallel search.

The above discussion is summarized in Algorithm PARSEARCH. In Step 1, all processors read x simultaneously in one step. Step 2 is the stopping condition for recursion, which happens when the number of remaining elements drops as or below the number of processors. In this case, n processors are allocated, and each processor tests one element for equality against x. If one processor finds element $a_i = x$, it sets $k = i$. The remaining steps are as explained above.

The size of the recursive call is approximately $\frac{n}{p+1}$. Hence, the running time is given by the recurrence $T(n) = T(n/(p+1)) + \Theta(1)$ whose solution is $T(n) = \Theta(\log_{p+1} n) = \Theta(\frac{\log n}{\log(p+1)})$. There are at most p element comparisons in each stage for a total of $\Theta(p \log_{p+1} n)$. Hence, the work done by the algorithm is $W(n) = \Theta(p \log_{p+1} n)$. If $p = n^\epsilon, 0 < \epsilon < 1$, then $T(n) = \Theta(1)$ and $W(n) = \Theta(n^\epsilon)$.

Algorithm 2.8 PARSEARCH

Input: A sequence $S = \langle a_1, a_2, \ldots, a_n \rangle$ of n distinct elements such that
  $a_1 < a_2 < \cdots < a_n$, and an element x.

Output: The index $k, 1 \leq k \leq n$, such that $x = a_k$ if $x \in S$ and 0 otherwise.

1. Initialize: $k \leftarrow 0$, All processors read x
2. **if** $n \leq p$ use n processors to compare x with $a_i, 1 \leq i \leq n$, and **return** k.
3. $q \leftarrow n/(p+1)$
4. **for** $i \leftarrow 1$ **to** p **do in parallel**
5.   Processor P_i compares x with a_{iq}
6.   **if** $x = a_{iq}$ **return** $k = iq$
7. **if** $x < a_q$ **then**
8.   let $S' = \langle a_1, a_2, \ldots, a_{q-1} \rangle$
9. $k \leftarrow$ PARSEARCH(S', x)
10.   **return** k
11. **else if** $x > a_{pq}$ **then**
12.   let $S' = \langle a_{pq+1}, a_{pq+2}, \ldots, a_n \rangle$
13. $k \leftarrow$ PARSEARCH(S', x)
14.   **return** $k + pq$
15. **else** let i be such that $x > a_{iq}$ and $x < a_{(i+1)q}$. **do**
16.   let $S' = \langle a_{iq+1}, a_{iq+2}, \ldots, a_{(i+1)q-1} \rangle$
17. $k \leftarrow$ PARSEARCH(S', x)
18.   **return** $k + iq$
19. **end if**
20. **return** $k = 0$

Example 2.3 We apply Algorithm PARSEARCH for parallel search using two processors on the sequence $S = \langle 1, 3, 4, 6, 9, 12, 14, 15, 20 \rangle$ and $x = 8$. Initially, the algorithm divides S into three subsequences

$$\langle 1, 3, 4 \rangle, \quad \langle 6, 9, 12 \rangle, \quad \langle 14, 15, 20 \rangle.$$

The two processors compare x with elements at the internal boundaries, that is, 4 and 12. Since $8 > 4$ and $8 < 12$, the search area is reduced to $\langle 6, 9 \rangle$. Finally, the two processors perform two comparisons simultaneously and both of them return 0 indicating that x is not found. The number of parallel steps is 2. $\qquad\Box$

Example 2.4 We apply Algorithm PARSEARCH for parallel search using two processors on the same sequence in Example 2.3 and $x = 14$. Initially, the algorithm divides S into three subsequences

$$\langle 1, 3, 4 \rangle, \quad \langle 6, 9, 12 \rangle, \quad \langle 14, 15, 20 \rangle.$$

The two processors compare x with elements at the internal boundaries, that is, 4 and 12. $14 > a_6 = 12$, so the search area is reduced to $\langle 14, 15, 20 \rangle$. Now, the number of remaining elements is greater than p, so the algorithm performs one more iteration and divides these elements into three subsequences $\langle 14 \rangle, \langle 15 \rangle$ and $\langle 20 \rangle$. In this iteration, $q = n/(p+1) = 3/3 = 1$. Since $x = a_q = a_1 = 14$, the algorithm returns $6 + 1 = 7$. The number of parallel steps is 3. $\qquad\Box$

2.7 Pointer Jumping

Let L denote a linked list of n elements, and let us associate a processor with each element in the list. Each element x has two fields: $succ(x)$ and $dist(x)$. $succ(x)$ is a pointer that points to the next element in the list. The $succ$ field of the last element points to itself, that is, $succ(L(n)) = L(n)$. The other field $dist$ is initially 1 if $succ(x) \neq x$ and 0 if $succ(x) = x$. An algorithm is required to be developed to compute: for each element x — its distance from the end of the list and to store it in $dist(x)$. Algorithm PJUMPING computes the distances from each node to the end of the list using a technique called *pointer jumping* or *doubling*.

Algorithm 2.9 PJUMPING

Input: A Linked list $L = (dist(x), succ(x))$, $1 \leq x \leq n$.

Output: $dist(x), 1 \leq x \leq n$, the distance of x from the end of the list.

1. **for** $x \leftarrow 1$ **to** n **do in parallel**
2. $\quad s(x) \leftarrow succ(x)$
3. $\quad$ **while** $s(x) \neq s(s(x))$ **do**
4. $\quad\quad dist(x) \leftarrow dist(x) + dist(s(x))$
5. $\quad\quad s(x) \leftarrow s(s(x))$
6. $\quad$ **end while**
7. **end for**

Pointer jumping consists of updating the successor of each node by that node successor's successor. Thus, the distance between a node and its successor doubles unless it is its own successor. Hence, after k iterations, the distance between a node x and its successor is 2^k unless $succ(x)$ is the last element in the list. It follows that the **while** loop is executed $\lceil \log n \rceil$ times, which means the parallel time complexity of the algorithm is $T(n) = \Theta(\log n)$. Its cost, however, is $\Theta(n \log n)$ since there are n processors.

Example 2.5   Figure 2.6 illustrates the algorithm for a list of seven elements. Each pointer $s(x)$ is shown as an arc from one element to another, and the arc from element x is labelled with the current value of $dist(x)$. The original list is shown on the top of the figure, and the rest of the figure shows the lists after each of the three iterations.   □

2.8   Euler Tour

The Euler tour technique on trees is a very powerful tool when designing parallel algorithms for trees. Let G be a directed graph. An *Euler circuit* in G is a cycle that visits each edge exactly once. G is said to be *Eulerian* if it has an Euler circuit. It is well-known that G is Eulerian if and only if the indegree of each vertex is equal to its outdegree. Let $T = (V, E)$ be a given tree, and let $T' = (V, E')$ be obtained from T by replacing each edge (u, v) of T by two directed edges (u, v) and (v, u) in opposite directions. Then, T' is Eulerian since the indegree of each vertex is equal to its outdegree (see Fig. 2.7). We now show how to construct an Euler circuit in T, which is commonly known as *Euler tour*.

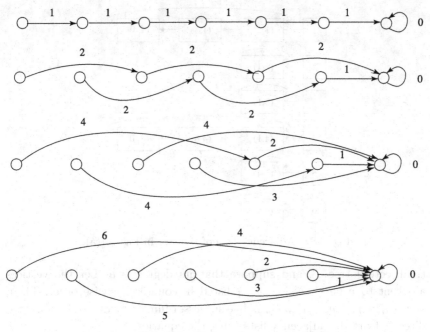

Fig. 2.6. Pointer jumping.

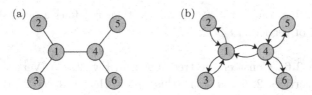

Fig. 2.7. (a) A tree. (b) A directed tree.

A tree T is represented by its adjacency lists as shown in Fig. 2.8 for the adjacency lists of the graph shown in Fig. 2.7(a). The edges in each list are listed in a counterclockwise order. We define the function $next(e)$ to be the edge following edge e in the adjacency lists. Note that the lists are circular, so if e is the last edge in its list, then $next(e)$ is the first edge in the list. Each edge (i, j) in the adjacency lists has two pointers, one to the next edge and the other to the edge (j, i).

An Euler tour can be defined by specifying the successor function $succ(e)$, which gives the next edge in the tour. Let v be a vertex in the

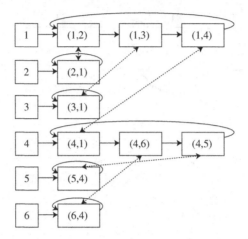

Fig. 2.8.   Adjacency lists of the tree in Fig. 2.7(a).

(undirected) tree T, and suppose that its degree is d. Let the vertices adjacent to v be $u_0, u_1, \ldots, u_{d-1}$ listed in counterclockwise order. Then, $succ((u_i, v)) = (v, u_{(i+1)\bmod d})$. The successor function can also be obtained directly from the adjacency lists using the equation

$$succ((i, j)) = next((j, i)).$$

If the resulting tour is $\tau = e_1, e_2, \ldots, e_k$, then τ defines a depth-first order on the set of vertices.

Example 2.6   Consider the tree shown in Fig. 2.7(a). Vertex 1 has the adjacent vertices $2, 3$ and 4, in this order. Hence, $succ((2, 1)) = (1, 3)$, $succ((3, 1)) = (1, 4)$, and $succ((1, 2)) = (2, 1)$. Using the *next* function, $succ((2, 1)) = next((1, 2)) = (1, 3)$, and so on. The *next* and *succ* functions for all edges in the tree are shown in Table 2.1. It follows that the Euler tour starting from edge $(1, 2)$ is

$$\tau = (1, 2), (2, 1), (1, 3), (3, 1), (1, 4), (4, 6), (6, 4), (4, 5), (5, 4), (4, 1), (1, 2).$$

The above Euler tour τ defines the following depth-first ordering on the set of vertices: $1, 2, 1, 3, 1, 4, 6, 4, 5, 4, 1$.   □

Clearly, using the two pointers in each node of the adjacency lists, it takes $\Theta(1)$ time to find $succ(e)$, and hence, the Euler tour can be computed in $\Theta(1)$ steps using $O(n)$ processors on the EREW PRAM.

Table 2.1.   The next and successor functions.

edge e	$next(e)$	$succ(e)$
(1,2)	(1,3)	(2,1)
(1,3)	(1,4)	(3,1)
(1,4)	(1,2)	(4,6)
(2,1)	(2,1)	(1,3)
(3,1)	(3,1)	(1,4)
(4,1)	(4,6)	(1,2)
(4,6)	(4,5)	(6,4)
(4,5)	(4,1)	(5,4)
(5,4)	(5,4)	(4,1)
(6,4)	(6,4)	(4,5)

2.8.1   *Directing a tree*

The Euler tour technique on trees can be used to make a tree directed. The first step is to assign a root, which we will assume to be the first vertex in the tour r. This can be done by deleting the last edge in the tour, which converts the Euler circuit into an Euler path. Next, we assign 1 to every edge in the resulting tour, and apply the prefix sums algorithm on the set of edges defined by the tour. Finally, for each edge (u, v) assign the parent of v $p(v) = u$ whenever the prefix sum of (u, v) is smaller than the prefix sum of (v, u). The algorithm is given as Algorithm DIRECTINGTREE. Clearly, the algorithm runs in $O(\log n)$ time using $O(n)$ processors on the EREW PRAM.

Algorithm 2.10   DIRECTINGTREE
Input: A tree T and a vertex r in T.

Output: Assign parents to all nodes in T except r.

1. Find an Euler tour τ for the tree T.
2. Remove the last edge (x, r) from τ.
3. Assign 1 to every edge of the tour τ.
4. Apply parallel prefix on the set of edges of τ.
5. Assign $p(r) = 0$, $p(x) = r$, and for each other edge (u, v) assign $p(v) = u$ whenever the prefix sum of (u, v) is smaller than the prefix sum of (v, u).

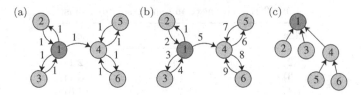

Fig. 2.9. Directing the tree in Fig. 2.7(a).

Example 2.7 We convert the tree shown in Fig. 2.7(a) into a directed tree rooted at vertex 1. Consider the tree shown in Fig. 2.9(a), which is the tree in Fig. 2.7(b) with assigned weights of 1 to all edges. The last edge in the tour τ has been deleted. The prefix sums are shown in Fig. 2.9(b), and the rooted tree is shown in Fig. 2.9(c). Note, for example, that 4 is the parent of 6 since the prefix sum on edge $(4, 6)$ is smaller than the prefix sum on edge $(6, 4)$ in Fig. 2.9(b).   □

2.8.2 *Computing vertex levels in a tree*

Let T be a tree rooted at vertex r. The *vertex level* of a vertex v is the distance between v and the root r measured in the number of edges. Note that we have assumed here that T is rooted. Let τ be the Euler path starting at r. On this path, assign the weights $w(p(v), v) = 1$ and $w(v, p(v)) = -1$, and perform parallel prefix on τ. Finally, set $level(v)$ to the prefix sum of the edge $(p(v), v)$. The algorithm is given as Algorithm TREELEVELS. Clearly, the algorithm runs in $O(\log n)$ time using $O(n)$ processors on the EREW PRAM.

Algorithm 2.11 TREELEVELS
Input: A tree T rooted at r.

Output: Assign levels to all nodes in T.

 1. Find an Euler tour τ for the tree T.
 2. Remove the last edge from τ.
 3. Assign the weights $w(p(v), v) = 1$ and $w(v, p(v)) = -1$.
 4. Apply parallel prefix on the set of edges of τ.
 5. Set $level(v)$ to the prefix sum of the edge $(p(v), v)$.

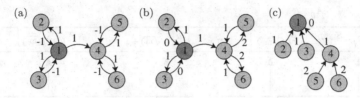

Fig. 2.10. Computing levels of the vertices in the tree shown in Fig. 2.7(a).

Example 2.8 We compute the levels of the vertices in the tree shown in Fig. 2.7(a), where vertex 1 is the root. Consider the tree shown in Fig. 2.10(a), which is the tree in Fig. 2.7(b) with assigned weights of 1 and -1 as explained above. The last edge in the tour τ has been deleted. The prefix sums are shown in Fig. 2.10(b), and the tree with levels of the vertices is shown in Fig. 2.10(c). □

2.9 Merging by Ranking

Given a sequence S and an element x, let $\operatorname{rank}(x, S)$ be the number of elements in S less than x. It is not hard to modify Algorithm PARSEARCH given in Section 2.6 so that on input S and x, it returns $\operatorname{rank}(x, S)$. We will refer to the modified algorithm as Algorithm MODPARSEARCH.

2.9.1 *Computing ranks*

Let $A = \langle a_1, a_2, \ldots, a_n \rangle$ and $B = \langle b_1, b_2, \ldots, b_m \rangle$ be two sequences of $n+m$ distinct numbers, each sorted in increasing order. The problem of merging A and B into a new sequence $C = \langle c_1, c_2, \ldots, c_{m+n} \rangle$ may be solved in parallel by computing for each $x \in A \cup B, r_A = \operatorname{rank}(x, A)$ and $r_B = \operatorname{rank}(x, B)$, and setting $c_k = x$, where $k = r_A + r_B + 1$. The ranks of all items in B are found in parallel, where a processor P_i is assigned to each element $b_i \in B$. To find $\operatorname{rank}(b_i, A)$, P_i performs binary search on A, and this is done for all $b_i \in B$ in parallel. To compute the rank of b_i in B, we use the identity $\operatorname{rank}(b_i, B) = i - 1$. Next, we repeat the above procedure for all items $a_j \in A$ to find $\operatorname{rank}(a_j, B)$ and set $\operatorname{rank}(a_j, A) = j - 1$. The above algorithm works on the CREW PRAM in time $O(\max\{\log n, \log m\})$.

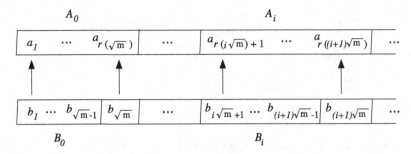

Fig. 2.11.   Computing rank(B, A).

In the following, we present a faster algorithm that runs in time $O(\log \log n)$ for the case $m = n$. First, we develop an algorithm for computing rank$(B, A) = \{\text{rank}(b, A) \mid b \in B\}$; finding rank$(A, B)$ can be achieved in a similar fashion. For clarity, let $s = \sqrt{m}$. First, use Algorithm MOD-PARSEARCH to compute in parallel the ranks of $b_s, b_{2s}, \ldots, b_m$, using $\sqrt{n}$ processors for each rank. Call these ranks $r(s), r(2s), \ldots, r(m)$. This divides the remaining elements in B into s subsequences $B_0, B_1, \ldots, B_{s-1}$ of $s - 1$ elements each, where $B_0 = \{b_1, b_2, \ldots, b_{s-1}\}$, $B_1 = \{b_{s+1}, b_{s+2}, \ldots, b_{2s-1}\}$, and in general $B_i = \{b_{is+1}, b_{is+2}, \ldots, b_{(i+1)s-1}\}$. This induces a partition of $\{a_1, a_2, \ldots, a_{r(m)}\}$ into s subsequences $A_0, A_1, \ldots, A_{s-1}$, where $A_0 = \{a_1, a_2, \ldots, a_{r(s)}\}$, $A_1 = \{a_{r(s)+1}, a_{r(s)+2}, \ldots, a_{r(2s)}\}$, and in general $A_i = \{a_{r(is)+1}, a_{r(is)+2}, \ldots, a_{r((i+1)s)}\}$ (see Fig 2.11).

Note that $|A_i|$ may vary; it may be 0 or n. Let $b_{is+j} \in B_i$. Then, we should search for rank(b_{is+j}, A_i) in A_i, and compute rank(b_{is+j}, A) from the equation

$$\text{rank}(b_{is+j}, A) = \text{rank}(b_{is}, A) + \text{rank}(b_{is+j}, A_i). \qquad (2.1)$$

Note that this means

If rank$(b_{(i+1)s}, A) = \text{rank}(b_{is}, A)$, then rank$(b_{is+j}, A_i) = 0$.

Thus, the problem of computing the ranks of B in A reduces to computing the ranks of B_i in A_i, $0 \leq i \leq s - 1$. Call the algorithm recursively on (A_i, B_i) to compute rank(B_i, A_i) for $0 \leq i \leq s-1$. For $b_{is+j} \in B_i$, let $r_i(j) = \text{rank}(b_{is+j}, A_i)$. Thus, as stated in Eq. 2.1, rank$(b_{is+j}, A) = r(is) + r_i(j)$.

The above discussion is outlined in Algorithm PARRANK. The algorithm returns $R = \{r(1), r(2), \ldots, r(m)\}$, a set of m ranks, where

$r(i) = \text{rank}(b_i, A)$. In Line 8, the algorithm returns $R_i = \{r_i(1), r_i(2), \ldots,$ $r_i(s-1)\}$, a set of $s-1$ ranks corresponding to $\text{rank}(B_i, A_i)$.

Algorithm 2.12 PARRANK
Input: $A = \langle a_1, a_2, \ldots, a_n \rangle$ and $B = \langle b_1, b_2, \ldots, b_m \rangle$ are two sequences of $n + m$ distinct numbers, each sorted in increasing order.
Output: $\text{rank}(B, A) = \{\text{rank}(b_i, A) \mid b_i \in B\}$.

1. **if** $m < 4$ **then for** $i \leftarrow 1$ **to** m **do in parallel**
2.   Use Algorithm MODPARSEARCH to compute
        $r(i) = \text{rank}(b_i, A)$ using n processors.
3. **for** $i \leftarrow 1$ **to** s **do in parallel**
4.   Use Algorithm MODPARSEARCH to compute
        $r(is) = \text{rank}(b_{is}, A)$ using $\sqrt{n}$ processors.
5. **end for**
6. $r(0) \leftarrow 0$
7. **for** $i \leftarrow 0$ **to** $s-1$ **do in parallel**
8.   **if** $r(is) = r((i+1)s)$ **then** $R_i \leftarrow \{0, 0, \ldots, 0\}$
9.   **else**
10. $R_i \leftarrow$ PARRANK(A_i, B_i)
11.   **for** $j \leftarrow 1$ **to** $s-1$ **do in parallel**
12. $r(is + j) \leftarrow r(is) + r_i(j)$
13.   **end for**
14.   **end if**
15. **end for**
16. **return** $R = \{r(1), r(2), \ldots, r(m)\}$

It is easy to see that the number of processors used by the algorithm is $O(\sqrt{m}\sqrt{n}) = O(m + n)$ as required by Steps 3 and 4 of the algorithm. Steps 1–4 take constant time. Step 10 takes at most $T(n, \sqrt{m})$ time since $|A_i|$ can be as large as n. Hence, the running time is given by the recurrence

$$T(n, m) \leq \begin{cases} O(1) & \text{if } m < 4 \\ T(n, \sqrt{m}) + O(1) & \text{if } m \geq 4, \end{cases}$$

whose solution is $T(n, m) = O(\log \log m)$. The work done by Steps 1–2 of the algorithm is $O(n)$. The number of operations done by Steps 3 and 4 is $O(\sqrt{m}\sqrt{n}) = O(m + n)$ since the call to Algorithm MODPARSEARCH performs $O(\sqrt{n}) \times O(1) = O(\sqrt{n})$ operations. The work done by Steps 7–16 of the algorithm except for the recursive calls is $O(m)$. It follows that the overall work done by the algorithm is $W(n, m) = O((n + m) \log \log m)$.

Example 2.9   Let $A = \langle 10, 30, 40, 60, 70, 90, 110, 120 \rangle$ and $B = \langle 20, 50, 80, 100 \rangle$, so $m = 4$ and $n = 8$. $s = 2$, $b_2 = 50$ and $b_4 = 100$. First, the ranks of b_2 and b_4 are computed: $r(2) = 3$ and $r(4) = 6$. Next, B_0, B_1, A_0 and A_1 are computed: $B_0 = \{20\}, B_1 = \{80\}, A_0 = \{10, 30, 40\}$ and $A_1 = \{60, 70, 90\}$. Now, the algorithm recursively computes the ranks of B_0 in A_0 and B_1 in A_1: $r_0(1) = 1$ (which is the rank of 20 in A_0), so $R_0 = \{1\}$, and $r_1(1) = 2$ (which is the rank of 80 in A_1), so $R_1 = \{2\}$. Finally, we compute the ranks of B_0 in A and B_1 in A: $r(1) = r(0) + r_0(1) = 0 + 1 = 1$ and $r(3) = r(2) + r_1(1) = 3 + 2 = 5$. It follows that $R = R(B, A) = \{1, 3, 5, 6\}$.   □

Example 2.10   Suppose we change B in Example 2.9 to $B = \langle 7, 8, 80, 100 \rangle$. Then, $b_2 = 8$, $r(2) = 0$ and $B_0 = \{7\}$. Also, $A_0 = \{\}$ and $A_1 = \{10, 30, 40, 60, 70, 90\}$. By Step 8 of the algorithm, since $r(0) = r(2)$, $R_0 = \{0\}$ and thus the algorithm will not be called recursively on A_0 and B_0. Consequently, $r(1) = r(0) + r_0(1) = 0 + 0 = 0$.   □

2.9.2   *Merging*

To merge A and B, we only need to compute rank(B, A) and rank(A, B). Algorithm PARMERGE merges A and B into a sequence C. It is assumed here that $|A| = |B| = n$. Let $b_i \in B$. Then, the index of b_i in C is equal to rank(b_i, B) + rank$(b_i, A) + 1 = (i - 1) + r(i) + 1 = r(i) + i$. Similarly, for $a_j \in A$, the index of a_j in C is equal to rank(a_j, A) + rank$(a_j, B) + 1 = (j - 1) + r(j) + 1 = r(j) + j$.

Algorithm 2.13 PARMERGE
Input: $A = \langle a_1, a_2, \ldots, a_n \rangle$ and $B = \langle b_1, b_2, \ldots, b_n \rangle$ are two sequences of $2n$ distinct numbers each sorted in increasing order.
Output: A sequence $C = \langle c_1, c_2, \ldots, c_{2n} \rangle$ which is the merge of A and B.

1. $\{r(1), r(2), \ldots, r(n)\} \leftarrow$ PARRANK(A, B) (Find rank(B, A))
2. $\{r'(1), r'(2), \ldots, r'(n)\} \leftarrow$ PARRANK(B, A) (Find rank(A, B))
3. **for** $i \leftarrow 1$ **to** n **do in parallel**
4. $\quad c_{i+r(i)} \leftarrow b_i$
5. $\quad c_{i+r'(i)} \leftarrow a_i$
6. **end for**
7. **return** C

Clearly, the running time of Algorithm PARMERGE is $T(n) = O(\log \log n)$. The cost of the algorithm is $C(n) = O(n \log \log n)$.

2.9.3 *Parallel bottom-up merge sorting*

The algorithm for bottom-up sorting works by merging pairs of consecutive elements, then merging consecutive pairs to form 4-element sequences, and so on. This algorithm can easily be parallelized as shown in Algorithm PARBOTTOMUPSORT. Note here that $n = 2^k$ for some positive integer k.

Algorithm 2.14 PARBOTTOMUPSORT
Input: $A = \langle a_1, a_2, \ldots, a_n \rangle$, a sequences of n distinct numbers, where $n = 2^k$.
Output: A sorted in increasing order.

1. **for** $j \leftarrow 1$ **to** n **do in parallel**
2. $\quad S_{0,j} \leftarrow a_j$
3. **end for**
4. **for** $i \leftarrow 1$ **to** k **do**
5. $\quad t \leftarrow n/2^i$
6. $\quad$ **for** $j \leftarrow 1$ **to** t **do in parallel**
7. $\quad\quad S_{i,j} \leftarrow$ PARMERGE$(S_{i-1,2j-1}, S_{i-1,2j})$
8. $\quad$ **end for**
9. **end for**
10. $A \leftarrow S_{k,1}$
11. **return** A

Algorithm PARBOTTOMUPSORT defines a (conceptual) complete binary tree whose nodes are the sequences $S_{i,j}$, $0 \le i \le k, 1 \le j \le 2^{k-i}$. Initially, the elements are stored at the leaves $S_{0,j}, 1 \le j \le n$. Subsequently, the sequence $S_{i,j}$ corresponding to an internal node is computed by merging its children $S_{i-1,2j-1}$ and $S_{i-1,2j}$. Now, we compute the running time of the algorithm. Algorithm PARMERGE is called in Step 7, and it takes $O(\log \log |S_{i-1,2j-1}|) = O(\log \log 2^{i-1})$. This is repeated in the **for** loop in Step 4 k times, for sizes $1, 2, 4, \ldots, n/2$. Hence, the running time is

$$T(n) = \sum_{i=1}^{k} O(\log \log 2^{i-1})$$

$$= \sum_{i=1}^{k} O(\log(i-1))$$

$$= \sum_{i=1}^{k} O(\log k)$$

$$= O(k \log k)$$

$$= O(\log n \log \log n).$$

2.10 The Zero-one Principle

A sorting algorithm is called *oblivious* if it consists of comparison-exchange operations that are prescribed and independent of the input elements and results of comparisons between them. The zero-one principle states that if a comparison-based oblivious algorithm sorts any sequence of zeros and ones, then it sorts any sequence of arbitrary values. It really simplifies the proofs of correctness of many oblivious sorting algorithms.

Lemma 2.1   If an oblivious comparison-exchange algorithm sorts any sequence of zeros and ones, then it sorts any sequence of arbitrary values.

Proof.   Suppose for the sake of contradiction that an oblivious comparison-exchange algorithm sorts all sequences of zeros and ones, but fails to sort the input sequence $\langle x_1, x_2, \ldots, x_n \rangle$ of arbitrary numbers. Let π be a permutation such that $x_{\pi(1)} \le x_{\pi(2)} \le \cdots \le x_{\pi(n)}$, and for some permutation $\sigma \ne \pi$, let the output of the algorithm be $x_{\sigma(1)}, x_{\sigma(2)}, \ldots, x_{\sigma(n)}$. Then, there exists some integer j such that $x_{\sigma(i)} = x_{\pi(i)}$ for $i < j$ and $x_{\sigma(j)} > x_{\pi(j)}$. Hence, there must exist $k > j$ such that $x_{\sigma(k)} = x_{\pi(j)}$. For $1 \le i \le n$, define $y_i = 0$ if $x_i \le x_{\pi(j)}$, and $y_i = 1$ if $x_i > x_{\pi(j)}$. Now, consider the action of the algorithm on input $\langle y_1, y_2, \ldots, y_n \rangle$ of 0's and 1's. The algorithm will perform the same set of comparison-exchange operations as it did for the original input $\langle x_1, x_2, \ldots, x_n \rangle$. In particular, the output of the algorithm on the y_i's input will be

$$y_{\sigma(1)}, y_{\sigma(2)}, \ldots, y_{\sigma(j-1)}, y_{\sigma(j)}, \ldots, y_{\sigma(k)} \cdots = 0, 0, \ldots, 0, 1, \ldots, 0, \ldots,$$

which is not sorted. This contradicts the assumption that the algorithm sorts all sequences of zeros and ones. $\square$

2.11   Odd–Even Merging

Let $A = \langle a_0, a_1, \ldots, a_{n-1} \rangle$ and $B = \langle b_0, b_1, \ldots, b_{n-1} \rangle$ be two sorted sequences of $2n$ distinct numbers, where n is a power of 2. The odd–even merging method is summarized in Algorithm ODDEVENMERGE.

Algorithm 2.15 ODDEVENMERGE
Input: Two sorted sequences $A = \langle a_0, a_1, \ldots, a_{n-1} \rangle$ and
      $B = \langle b_0, b_1, \ldots, b_{n-1} \rangle$ of n elements each sorted in ascending order,
      where $n = 2^k$.
Output: The elements in $S = A \cup B$ in sorted order.

1. **if** $n \leq 2$ **return** the merge of A and B, and exit.
2. Let $A_{\text{even}} = \langle a_0, a_2, \ldots, a_{n-2} \rangle$ and $A_{\text{odd}} = \langle a_1, a_3, \ldots, a_{n-1} \rangle$ be the even and odd subsequences of A, respectively.
3. Let $B_{\text{even}} = \langle b_0, b_2, \ldots, b_{n-2} \rangle$ and $B_{\text{odd}} = \langle b_1, b_3, \ldots, b_{n-1} \rangle$ be the even and odd subsequences of B, respectively.
4. Recursively merge A_{even} and B_{odd} to obtain $C = \langle c_0, c_1, \ldots, c_{n-1} \rangle$.
5. Recursively merge A_{odd} and B_{even} to obtain $D = \langle d_0, d_1, \ldots, d_{n-1} \rangle$.
6. Let E be the shuffle of C and D, that is,
   $E = \langle c_0, d_0, c_1, d_1, \ldots, c_{n-1}, d_{n-1} \rangle$.
7. Traverse the pairs (c_i, d_i) in E, $0 \leq i \leq n - 1$, and interchange the elements in each pair if they are out of order to obtain the sorted sequence $S = \langle s_0, s_1, \ldots, s_{2n-1} \rangle$
8. **return** S

After the execution of Step 6, we have $s_0 = \min\{c_0, d_0\}$, $s_1 = \max\{c_0, d_0\}$, $s_2 = \min\{c_1, d_1\}$, $s_3 = \max\{c_1, d_1\}, \ldots, s_{2n-2} = \min\{c_{n-1}, d_{n-1}\}$, $s_{2n-1} = \max\{c_{n-1}, d_{n-1}\}$.

The algorithm uses $2n$ processors on the EREW PRAM. Obviously, the time needed in each recursive call is $\Theta(1)$. Hence, the running time of the algorithm is governed by the recurrence $T(n) = T(n/2) + \Theta(1)$, whose solution is $T(n) = \Theta(\log n)$. The work done by the algorithm is given by the recurrence $W(n) = 2W(n/2) + \Theta(n)$, and hence $W(n) = \Theta(n \log n)$.

Example 2.11   Let $A = \langle 1, 3, 4, 7 \rangle$ and $B = \langle 2, 5, 6, 8 \rangle$. Then, $A_{\text{even}} = \{1, 4\}$, $A_{\text{odd}} = \{3, 7\}$, $B_{\text{even}} = \{2, 6\}$, $B_{\text{odd}} = \{5, 8\}$, $C = \langle 1, 4, 5, 8 \rangle$ and $D = \langle 2, 3, 6, 7 \rangle$. $E = \langle 1, 2, 4, 3, 5, 6, 8, 7 \rangle$. The pair $(4, 3)$ is out of order, so 4 and 3 are exchanged. The same applies to the pair $(8, 7)$. The sorted sequence is $S = \langle 1, 2, 3, 4, 5, 6, 7, 8 \rangle$. See Fig. 2.12. $\square$

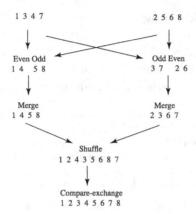

Fig. 2.12.   An example of odd–even merging.

Theorem 2.2 Algorithm ODDEVENMERGE correctly merges A and B into S.

Proof. Let A, B, C, D and E be as defined in Algorithm ODDEVENMERGE, and assume the elements in $A \cup B$ are distinct. By the zero-one principle (Lemma 2.1, we may assume that A and B consist of zeros and ones. Let x and y be the number of zeros in A and B, respectively. Then, A_{even} has $\lceil \frac{x}{2} \rceil$ zeros, A_{odd} has $\lfloor \frac{x}{2} \rfloor$ zeros, B_{even} has $\lceil \frac{y}{2} \rceil$ zeros, and B_{odd} has $\lfloor \frac{y}{2} \rfloor$ zeros. Consequently, C has $w = \lceil \frac{x}{2} \rceil + \lfloor \frac{y}{2} \rfloor$ zeros and D has $z = \lfloor \frac{x}{2} \rfloor + \lceil \frac{y}{2} \rceil$ zeros. Clearly, w and z differ by at most 1, and hence we have the following three cases. If $w = z$ or $w = z + 1$, then

$$E = \underbrace{0, 0, \ldots, 0}_{w+z}, 1, 1, \ldots, 1,$$

and E is sorted. If, however, $w = z - 1$, then

$$E = \underbrace{0, 0, \ldots, 0}_{2w}, 1, 0, 1, \ldots, 1,$$

and E will be sorted after making one exchange of 0 and 1.   □

The algorithm for sorting is given as Algorithm ODDEVENMERGESORT. The running time of the algorithm is $\Theta(\log^2 n)$. Its work is $\Theta(n \log^2 n)$.

Algorithm 2.16 ODDEVENMERGESORT
Input: A sequence $S = \langle a_0, a_1, \ldots, a_{n-1} \rangle$ where n is a power of 2.
Output: The elements in S in sorted order.

1. $S_1 \leftarrow \langle a_0, a_1, \ldots, a_{n/2-1} \rangle$.
2. $S_2 \leftarrow \langle a_{n/2}, a_{n/2+1}, \ldots, a_{n-1} \rangle$.
3. $S_1' \leftarrow$ ODDEVENMERGESORT(S_1)
4. $S_2' \leftarrow$ ODDEVENMERGESORT(S_2)
5. $S \leftarrow$ ODDEVENMERGE(S_1', S_2')
6. **return** S

2.12 Bitonic Merging and Sorting

A sequence $S = \langle a_1, a_2, \ldots, a_n \rangle$ is *monotonically increasing* if $a_1 \leq a_2 \leq \cdots \leq a_n$, and is *monotonically decreasing* if $a_1 \geq a_2 \geq \cdots \geq a_n$. A sequence is *monotone* if it is monotonically increasing or monotonically decreasing. A monotone sequence can be represented pictorially as shown in Fig. 2.13(a), where there is a point for each item in the sequence. The sequence corresponding to this diagram is $T = \langle a_1, \ldots, a_i, \ldots, a_j, \ldots, a_n \rangle$, where $1 < i < j < n$. However, if we are not interested in the actual values of the items in the sequence, but only in their relative order, then we can simply represent a monotone sequence by a line segment. An example is shown in Fig. 2.13(b) for the monotonically increasing sequence T above. Figure 2.13(c) shows a generic monotone sequence in which the items and their number are immaterial. Thus, the diagram shown in Fig. 2.13(c) is the representation of any monotonically increasing sequence. Similarly, a monotonically decreasing sequence can be represented by a line segment with negative slope.

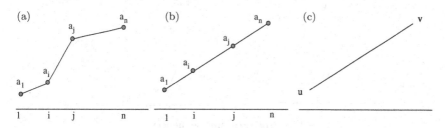

Fig. 2.13.   A monotone sequence.

A sequence $S = \langle a_1, a_2, \ldots, a_n \rangle$ is *bitonic* if it monotonically increases and then monotonically decreases, that is, there is an i, $1 \leq i \leq n$, such that

$$a_1 \leq a_2 \leq \cdots \leq a_i \geq a_{i+1} \geq a_{i+2} \geq \cdots \geq a_n,$$

or can be circularly shifted to become monotonically increasing and then monotically decreasing. Thus, a sequence is also bitonic if it is monotone. For example, the sequence $\langle 1, 3, 5, 7, 4, 2 \rangle$ is bitonic, while $\langle 1, 3, 1, 2 \rangle$ is not. The sequence $\langle 7, 8, 3, 1, 0, 4 \rangle$ is also a bitonic sequence, because it is a cyclic shift of $\langle 0, 4, 7, 8, 3, 1 \rangle$. We will represent a bitonic sequence by a diagram consisting of a polygonal chain composed of line segments intersecting at their internal endpoints, with at most one local maximum and one local minimum. Each line segment represents a monotone sequence. Figure 2.14 shows the diagrams of two bitonic sequences. In part (a) there is one local maximum, and in part (b) there is one local maximum and one local minimum. If the number of line segments is 1 or 2, then the diagram is a bitonic sequence. If the number of line segments is more than 2, then the diagram is a bitonic sequence if and only if there does not exist a horizontal line that intersects the polygonal chain at more than 2 points. To see this, consider Fig. 2.15, which shows the diagram of a sequence with three intersections of the polygonal chain with a horizontal line.

The sequence corresponding to this diagram is $\langle a_1, \ldots, a_i, \ldots, a_j, \ldots, a_n \rangle$, where $1 < i < j < n$, with the following inequalities: $a_1 > a_i, a_i < a_j, a_j > a_n$ and $a_n < a_1$. If this sequence is bitonic, then the sequence $\alpha = \langle a_1, a_i, a_j, a_n \rangle$ such that $a_1 > a_i < a_j > a_n < a_1$ is bitonic. Then, it is possible through circular shifts to transform α into two monotonic

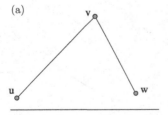
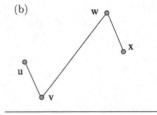

Fig. 2.14.   Bitonic sequences.

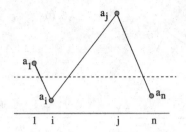

Fig. 2.15.   A non-bitonic sequences.

sequences, one increasing followed by one decreasing. It can be shown, however, that α cannot be converted to such a sequence. Hence, the sequence is not bitonic.

Now, consider the sequence α' obtained from α by increasing the value of a_n so that $a_n > a_1$. Then, we have $a_1 > a_i < a_j > a_n > a_1$, and thus α' is bitonic, as it can be transformed into $\alpha'' = \langle a_i, a_j, a_n, a_1 \rangle$, which consists of two monotonic sequences. The diagram of α' is similar to the one shown in Fig. 2.14(b); there does not exist a horizontal line that intersects this diagram at more than 2 points. The diagram of α'' is similar to the one shown in Fig. 2.14(a).

Example 2.12 Consider the sequence $\alpha = \langle 4, 1, 6, 3 \rangle$. Its diagram is the one shown in Fig. 2.15. In this sequence, $4 > 1 < 6 > 3 < 4$, so α is obviously not a bitonic sequence. However, if we change 3 to 5 to obtain $\alpha' = \langle 4, 1, 6, 5 \rangle$, the new sequence is bitonic since in this case $4 > 1 < 6 > 5 > 4$. Its diagram is similar to the one shown in Fig. 2.14(b). With one cyclic shift, α' is converted to $\alpha'' = \langle 1, 6, 5, 4 \rangle$, which consists of two monotonic sequences — one increasing and one decreasing. Its diagram is similar to the one shown in Fig. 2.14(a). □

Let $S = \langle a_1, a_2, \ldots, a_n \rangle$ be a bitonic sequence. Define

$$S_1 = \langle \min(a_1, a_{n/2+1}), \min(a_2, a_{n/2+2}), \ldots, \min(a_{n/2}, a_n) \rangle, \qquad (2.2)$$

and

$$S_2 = \langle \max(a_1, a_{n/2+1}), \max(a_2, a_{n/2+2}), \ldots, \max(a_{n/2}, a_n) \rangle. \qquad (2.3)$$

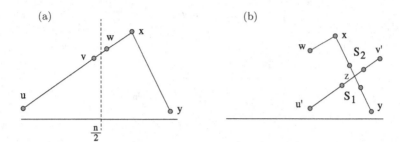

Fig. 2.16.   Bitonic sequences.

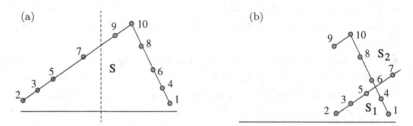

Fig. 2.17.   Bitonic sequences example.

Then, both S_1 and S_2 are bitonic sequences. Moreover,

$$\max(S_1) \le \min(S_2). \tag{2.4}$$

Consider, for example, the bitonic sequence u, v, w, x, y shown in Fig. 2.16(a). Here, the line segment $\overline{u, v}$ accounts for approximately half the elements in the sequence. Shift the line segment $\overline{u, v}$ to the right until the vertex u is aligned vertically with w. The resulting line segment $\overline{u', v'}$ intersects the line segment $\overline{x, y}$ at the vertex z. Then, $S_1 = u', z, y$ and $S_2 = w, x, z, v'$ as shown in Fig. 2.16(b) are bitonic. It is clear from the figure that $\max(S_1) \le \min(S_2)$.

Example 2.13 Consider the bitonic sequence $S = \langle 2, 3, 5, 7, 9, 10, 8, 6, 4, 1 \rangle$ shown in Fig. 2.17(a). If we apply the procedure described above for splitting this sequence, we obtain the two bitonic sequences $S_1 = \langle 2, 3, 5, 4, 1 \rangle$ and $S_2 = \langle 9, 10, 8, 6, 7 \rangle$ shown in Fig. 2.17(b). S_2 is a cyclic shift of the sequence $\langle 10, 8, 6, 7, 9 \rangle$. Furthermore, $\max(S_1) = 5 \le 6 = \min(S_2)$.   □

By Eq. (2.4), every element of the sequence S_1 is less than or equal to every element of the sequence S_2. Thus, the problem of sorting the elements in S is reduced to sorting the elements in S_1 and S_2 separately. This is summarized in Algorithm BITONICMERGE. It is important to note that the input to the algorithm is a bitonic sequence S of length n, where n is a power of 2, and the output is the elements in S in sorted order. The algorithm first computes S_1 and S_2 as in Eqs. 2.2 and 2.3. Now, S_1 and S_2 are bitonic sequences, so the algorithm recursively computes the two sorted sequences S_1' and S_2', and returns their concatenation sequence $S_1' \| S_2'$.

Algorithm 2.17 BITONICMERGE

Input: A bitonic sequence $S = \langle a_1, a_2, \ldots, a_n \rangle$, where n is a power of 2.

Output: The elements in S in sorted order.

1. **if** $|S| = 1$ **then return** S
2. **for** $i \leftarrow 1$ **to** $n/2$ **do in parallel**
3.   **if** $a_i > a_{i+n/2}$ **then** interchange a_i and $a_{i+n/2}$
4. **end for**
5. $S_1 = \langle a_1, a_2, \ldots, a_{n/2} \rangle$
6. $S_2 = \langle a_{n/2+1}, a_{n/2+2}, \ldots, a_n \rangle$
7. $S_1' \leftarrow$ BITONICMERGE(S_1)
8. $S_2' \leftarrow$ BITONICMERGE(S_2)
9. **return** $S_1' \| S_2'$, the concatenation of S_1' and S_2'

Algorithm BITONICMERGE works on the EREW PRAM with n processors. The running time is $\Theta(\log n)$ and the total amount of work is $\Theta(n \log n)$, which is not optimal in view of the $O(n)$ time sequential algorithm.

Example 2.14 Consider the instance given in Fig. 2.18. Line 1 is the input bitonic sequence. Line 2 shows the first split into two bitonic sequences. Lines 3 and 4 show the second and third splits, respectively. $\square$

$$2\ 5\ 7\ 8\ 6\ 4\ 3\ 1$$
$$2\ 4\ 3\ 1 \mid 6\ 5\ 7\ 8$$
$$2\ 1 \mid 3\ 4 \mid 6\ 5 \mid 7\ 8$$
$$1 \mid 2 \mid 3 \mid 4 \mid 5 \mid 6 \mid 7 \mid 8$$

Fig. 2.18. Bitonic merge example for $n = 8$.

(a)   (b)

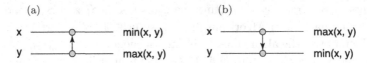

Fig. 2.19.   (a) Increasing comparator. (b) Decreasing comparator.

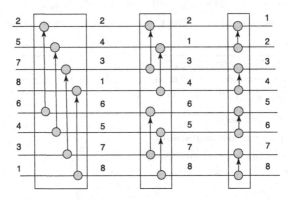

Fig. 2.20.   Bitonic merge network for $n = 8$.

A *comparator* is a devise with two inputs x and y, and two outputs $\min(x, y)$ and $\max(x, y)$. It is either an *increasing* comparator, shown in Fig. 2.19(a), or *decreasing* comparator, shown in Fig. 2.19(b). A *network of comparators* is composed solely of wires and comparators. Algorithm BITONICMERGE can be implemented on a network of comparators, also called a *merging network*, as illustrated in Fig. 2.20. A sample input of a bitonic sequence OR bitonic sequences are shown on the wires. The merging network with n inputs consists of $\log n$ columns, called stages.

2.12.1   *Bitonic sorting*

Bitonic sorting essentially works like Algorithm MERGESORT in that it divides the input into two halves, sorts each half recursively and uses Algorithm BITONICMERGE to merge the two sorted sequences. It is given in Algorithm BITONICSORT. To merge two monotonic sequences S_1' and S_2' sorted in ascending order, first reverse S_2' and form the bitonic sequence S_3 obtained by concatenating S_1' and S_2'', where S_2'' is the reverse of S_2'. Finally, apply Algorithm BITONICMERGE to S_3.

Algorithm 2.18 BITONICSORT
Input: A sequence S of n elements, where n is a power of 2.

Output: The elements in S in sorted order.

1. **if** $|S| > 1$ **then**
2. $\quad S_1 \leftarrow \langle a_1, a_2, \ldots, a_{n/2} \rangle$
3. $\quad S_2 \leftarrow \langle a_{n/2+1}, a_{n/2+2}, \ldots, a_n \rangle$
4. $\quad S_1' \leftarrow$ BITONICSORT(S_1)
5. $\quad S_2' \leftarrow$ BITONICSORT(S_2)
6. $\quad S_2'' \leftarrow$ Reverse of S_2'
7. $\quad S_3 \leftarrow S_1' \| S_2''$, the concatenation of S_1' and S_2''
8. $\quad S \leftarrow$ BITONICMERGE(S_3)
9. $\quad$ **return** S
10. **end if**

The algorithm uses n processors on the EREW PRAM. Obviously, the time needed in each recursive call is $\Theta(\log n)$. Hence, the running time of the algorithm is governed by the recurrence

$$T(n) = \begin{cases} c & \text{if } n = 1 \\ T(n/2) + \Theta(\log n) & \text{if } n \geq 2, \end{cases}$$

whose solution is $T(n) = \Theta(\log^2 n)$. The work done by the algorithm is $W(n) = \Theta(n \log^2 n)$, which is not optimal.

Theorem 2.3 Algorithm BITONICSORT correctly sorts a given sequence of numbers in ascending order.

Proof. By the zero-one principle (Lemma 2.1, we may assume that the input consists of 0's and 1's. Let A and B be two strings of 0's and 1's such that $|A| + |B| = n$, and assume without loss of generality that $n = 2^m \geq 2$. The proof is by induction on m. If $m = 1$, then clearly the input will be sorted, so assume that the algorithm correctly sorts its input for all powers h, $1 \leq h < m$, and let $|A| + |B| = 2^m$. First, A and B will be sorted separately, and B will be reversed, and so they will look like the following:

$$A = 0^i 1^j, \quad B = 1^k 0^l.$$

Next, some 1's in A will be swapped with 0's in B by Step 3 of Algorithm BITONICMERGE. Let A' and B' be A and B after swapping, respectively.

If $j \leq l$, all 1's in A will be swapped with 0's in B, and A' will consist of 0's only. In this case, A' and B' will look like:

$$A' = 0^{i+j}, \quad B' = 1^k 0^{l-j} 1^j.$$

If, however, $j > l$, then l 1's in A will be swapped with l 0's in B, and A' and B' will look like the following:

$$A' = 0^i 1^{j-l} 0^l, \quad B' = 1^{k+l}.$$

Finally, A' and B' will be merged separately and concatenated by Algorithm BITONICMERGE to produce $A''||B''$, which is sorted in ascending order. $\square$

We can derive a sorting network by unrolling recursion as follows: Starting from $n = 1$, any sequence of length 1 is monotonic, and hence any sequence of length 2 is bitonic. In the first stage of bitonic sort, bitonic sequences of size 2 are merged to create ordered lists of size 2. If these sequences alternate between being ordered into increasing and decreasing order, then at the end of this stage of merging, we have $n/4$ bitonic sequences of size 4. In the next stage, bitonic sequences of size 4 are merged into sorted sequences of size 4, alternately into increasing and decreasing orders so as to form $n/8$ bitonic sequences of size 8. Given an unordered sequence of size n, exactly $\log n$ stages of merging are required to produce a completely ordered sequence. Figure 2.21 shows a bitonic sorting

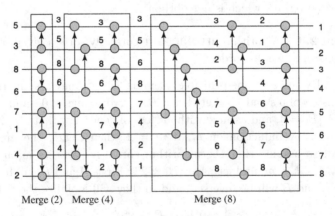

Fig. 2.21. Bitonic sort network for $n = 8$.

network with sample input of size 8. This network has three stages labeled Merge(2), Merge(4) and Merge(8). Stage 3 in the figure is identical to the merging network of Fig. 2.20.

2.13 Pipelined Mergesort

Recall the parallel bottom-up merge sorting algorithm, Algorithm PAR-BOTTOMUPSORT, discussed in Section 2.9.3. The algorithm works by merging pairs of consecutive elements, then merging consecutive pairs to form 4-element sequences, and so on. The running time of the algorithm was shown to be $O(\log n \log \log n)$. In fact, there is a $\Omega(\log \log n)$-time-lower bound for merging two sorted sequences of n elements using n processors on the CREW PRAM. In this section, we sketch an optimal $\Theta(\log n)$ time algorithm for sorting n items on the CREW PRAM with $\Theta(n)$ processors. The algorithm can be modified to work on the EREW PRAM with the same time complexity. It is a modification of Algorithm PARBOTTOMUPSORT, in which merges are pipelined efficiently. We will assume in this section that the elements to be sorted are all distinct and that n is a power of 2.

Let a, b and c be three numbers such that $a < c$. We say that b is *between* a and c if $a \leq b < c$. We also say that a and c *straddle* b. Given a sequence A and an element a, recall that $\text{rank}(a, A)$ denotes the number of elements in A less than a. We will assume that all sequences and arrays are implicitly augmented with $-\infty$ and ∞, so the rank of the minimum element is 1, not 0. Given two arrays A and B, the cross rank $R(A, B) = \langle \text{rank}(a, B) \mid a \in A \rangle$. Let a and b be two adjacent items in B (if necessary, we let $a = -\infty$ or $b = \infty$). We define the range $[a, b)$ to be the interval induced by item a (including the cases $a = -\infty$ and $b = \infty$). Let C be a sorted sequence of numbers. C will be called a *3-cover* or simply a *cover* of A if each interval induced by consecutive elements of C contains at most three elements from A. More precisely, for any two consecutive elements a and c in C_∞, the set $\{b \in A \mid a \leq b < c\}$ has at most 3 elements, where $C_\infty = \{-\infty\} \cup C \cup \{+\infty\}$. For example, if C contains the numbers 9, 18 and 30 while A contains 1, 5, 20, 23, 25 and 35, then C is a 3-cover for A. If, however, A also contains 28, then C is not a 3-cover for A, since in this case the number of elements between 18 and 30 is more than 3.

2.13.1   *The algorithm*

The sorting algorithm is described in terms of a complete binary tree T with
n leaves. Initially, the n elements to be sorted are placed at the leaves of T,
one element per leaf, and the internal nodes contain empty sequences. Let v
be an internal node in the tree. L_v will denote the sequence of leaves of the
subtree T_v rooted at v. In the course of the algorithm, the internal nodes
of T will contain sorted sequences of elements. The task of node v is to sort
the sequence L_v. The algorithm goes through stages $t, 1 \leq t \leq 3 \log n - 2$.
By $A_v(t)$ we denote the sequence associated with node v at stage t. The
items in $A_v(t)$ will be a rough sample of the items in L_v. As the algorithm
proceeds, the size of $A_v(t)$ increases, and $A_v(t)$ becomes a more accurate
approximation of L_v, and it will always be a sorted subsequence of L_v. We
say that node v is *complete* at stage t if and only if $A_v(t) = L_v$; otherwise v
is said to be *active*. Throughout the algorithm, node v from its left son x
a sorted sequence $B_x(t)$, and from its right son y a sorted sequence $B_y(t)$
hence producing the sequence $B_v(t+1)$, which is sent to the parent of v.
In each of these sequences, the size of the next object is twice as big as the
size of the preceding one. That is, for all nodes v,

$$|A_v(t+1)| = 2|A_v(t)|, \quad \text{and} \quad |B_v(t+1)| = 2|B_v(t)|.$$

We explain the processing performed in one stage at an arbitrary internal
node v of the tree. The array $A_v(t)$ is the array at hand at the start of
the stage; $A_v(t+1)$ is the array at hand at the start of the next stage, and
$A_v(t-1)$ is the array at hand at the start of the previous stage, if any. Also,
in each stage, we will create an array $B_v(t)$ at node v; $B_v(t+1)$, $B_v(t-1)$
are the corresponding arrays in respectively, the next, and previous, stage.
$B_v(t)$ is a sorted array comprising every fourth item in $A_v(t)$, for the active
node v.

The computation performed during each stage at each internal node v
comprises the following two phases:

(1) Compute $B_v(t) \leftarrow \alpha(A_v(t))$ and send it to the parent of v, where
    $\alpha(A_v(t))$ is computed as follows: If v is active, then $\alpha(A_v(t))$ consists
    of every fourth element of $A_v(t)$. During the first stage after v becomes
    complete, $\alpha(A_v(t))$ consists of every fourth element of $A_v(t)$. During
    the second stage after v becomes complete, $\alpha(A_v(t))$ consists of every

second element of $A_v(t)$, while in the third stage $\alpha(A_v(t))$ consists of every element of $A_v(t)$.

(2) If v is active, then merge $B_x(t)$ with $B_y(t)$ using the cover $A_v(t)$ to obtain $A_v(t+1)$. That is, $A_v(t+1) \leftarrow B_x(t) \cup B_y(t)$, where $\cup$ denotes merging. If v is complete, then v ignores its inputs $B_x(t)$ and $B_y(t)$.

By (1) above, three stages after node v becomes complete, its parent becomes complete too. The exception is in stage 1 in which the nodes at the level before the last merge their inputs and become complete in one stage. Hence, the total number of stages of the algorithm is $3 \log n - 2$.

Figure 2.22 illustrates the flow of the algorithm with $n = 8$ by depicting stages 2–7, that is, after nodes d, e, f and g become complete. Note that the total number of stages is $3 \log 8 - 2 = 7$. In part (c) of this figure, we have $A_a(4) = \{\}, B_b(4) = \langle 8 \rangle$ and $B_c(4) = \langle 6 \rangle$. In part (d) of this figure, we have $A_a(5) = \langle 6, 8 \rangle, B_b(5) = \langle 5, 8 \rangle$ and $B_c(5) = \langle 3, 6 \rangle$.

The proof of the following theorem is omitted.

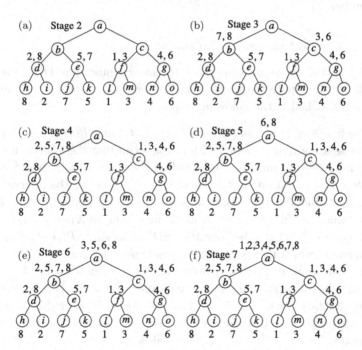

Fig. 2.22. The flow of the algorithm with $n = 8$.

Theorem 2.4 $B_v(t)$ is a 3-cover of $B_v(t+1)$.

We will need the following observation to show that the merge can be performed in $O(1)$ time.

Observation 2.1 Let A and C be two sorted sequences such that C is a cover for A. Then, for any sorted sequence D, $C \cup D$ is a cover for A, where $\cup$ denotes the merge operation.

By the above theorem, $B_x(t-1)$ is a 3-cover for $B_x(t)$ for each node x. By the above observation, since $A_v(t) = B_x(t-1) \cup B_y(t-1)$, we deduce $A_v(t)$ is a 3-cover for $B_x(t)$; similarly, $A_v(t)$ is a 3-cover for $B_y(t)$. Since $A_v(t+1) = B_x(t) \cup B_y(t)$, it follows that $A_v(t)$ is a 3-cover for $A_v(t+1)$.

We will assume that $R(A_v(t), B_x(t))$ and $R(A_v(t), B_y(t))$ are available. Let a be an item in $B_x(t)$; the rank of a in $A_v(t+1) = B_x(t) \cup B_y(t)$ is equal to the sum of its ranks in $B_x(t)$ and $B_y(t)$. So to perform the merge we compute the cross ranks $R(B_x(t), B_y(t))$ and $R(B_y(t), B_x(t))$ (the method is given below).

2.13.2 *Computing and maintaining ranks*

In order for the algorithm to perform the merges quickly in $\Theta(1)$ time, we show how to compute the ranks in $\Theta(1)$ time. We compute and maintain ranks as described in the following steps.

(1) The first step is to compute $R(B_x(t), A_v(t))$ and $R(B_y(t), A_v(t))$. For two adjacent items a and b with $a < b$, recall that the interval induced by item a is the range $[a, b)$ (including the cases $a = -\infty$ and $b = \infty$). Let u be an item in $A_v(t)$; u may be $-\infty$. Consider the interval $I(u)$ in $A_v(t)$ induced by u, and consider the set of items $X(u)$ in $B_x(t)$ contained in $I(u)$ (there are at most three items in $X(u)$ by the 3-cover property). $X(u)$ can be found in $\Theta(1)$ time since $R(A_v(t), B_x(t))$ is available, which means rank(u, B_x) is known. Each item a in $X(u)$ is given its rank in $A_v(t)$ as rank$(a, A_v(t)) = $ rank$(u, A_v(t)) + 1$ (note that all elements are distinct, which means $a > u$). For example, in Fig. 2.22(d), with $t = 5$, we have $A_a(5) = \{6, 8\}, B_b(5) = \{5, 8\}$. If we let $u = -\infty$, then $I(u) = (-\infty, 6)$ and $X(u) = \{5\}$. Hence, rank$(5, A_a(5)) = 0 + 1 = 1$. This takes care of $R(B_x(t), A_v(t))$. We repeat the symmetrical procedure to compute $R(B_y(t), A_v(t))$. These

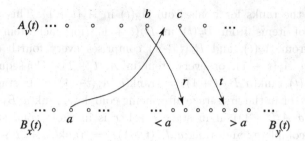

Fig. 2.23. Computing $R(B_x(t), B_y(t))$.

ranks are needed for computing $R(B_x(t), B_y(t))$ and $R(B_y(t), B_x(t))$, which are required by the merge step $A_v(t+1) \leftarrow B_x(t) \cup B_y(t)$.

(2) Now, we show how to compute $R(B_x(t), B_y(t))$; $R(B_y(t), B_x(t))$ can be found in a similar fashion. Let a be an item in $B_x(t)$; we show how to compute its rank in $B_y(t)$. (See Fig. 2.23.) We determine the two items b and c in $A_v(t)$ that straddle a, using rank$(a, A_v(t))$ computed above. Suppose that b and c have ranks r and t, respectively, in $B_y(t)$. Then, all items of rank r or less are smaller than item a (recall we assumed that all the inputs were distinct), while all items of rank greater than t are larger than item a; thus the only items about which there is any doubt as to their sizes relative to a are the items with rank $s, r < s \leq t$. But there are at most three such items by the 3-cover property. By means of at most two comparisons, the relative order of a and these (at most) three items can be determined.

(3) At this point, we find the value for each item a in $B_x(t)$, using its rank in $B_y(t)$ computed above, the two items b and c in $B_y(t)$ that straddle a, and the ranks of b and c in $A_v(t+1)$. Similarly, we find the value for each item d in $B_y(t)$, using its rank in $B_x(t)$, the two items e and f in $B_x(t)$ that straddle d, and the ranks of e and f in $A_v(t+1)$. This information is needed for computing $R(A_v(t+1), B_x(t+1))$ and $R(A_v(t+1), B_y(t+1))$.

(4) Now, we show how to compute $R(A_v(t+1), B_x(t+1))$ and $R(A_v(t+1), B_y(t+1))$ can be found by a similar means. For each item a in $A_v(t+1)$, we want to determine its rank in $B_x(t+1)$. Given the ranks for an item from $A_v(t)$ in both $B_x(t)$ and $B_y(t)$, we can immediately deduce the rank of this item in $A_v(t+1) = B_x(t) \cup B_y(t)$ (the new rank is just the sum of the two old ranks). Similarly, we

obtain the ranks for items from $A_x(t)$ in $A_x(t+1)$. This yields the ranks of items from $B_x(t)$ in $B_x(t+1)$ (for each item in $B_x(t)$ came from $A_x(t)$, and $B_x(t+1)$ comprises every fourth or second item in $A_x(t+1)$, or every item in $A_x(t+1)$). Consequently, for $a \in B_x(t), \text{rank}(a, B_x(t+1)) = \frac{1}{4}\text{rank}(a, A_x(t+1))$, if in stage $t+1$ x is active or in the first stage after being complete, $\text{rank}(a, B_x(t+1)) = \frac{1}{2}\text{rank}(a, A_x(t+1))$, if in stage $t+1$ x is in the second stage after being complete, and $\text{rank}(a, B_x(t+1)) = \text{rank}(a, A_x(t+1))$, if in stage $t+1$ x is in the third stage after being complete. For example, in Fig. 2.22, if $t = 4$, then we have $A_b(4) = \{2, 5, 7, 8\}$, $B_b(4) = \{8\}, A_b(5) = A_b(4), B_b(5) = \{5, 8\}$, and $\text{rank}(8, B_b(5)) = \frac{1}{2}\text{rank}(8, A_b(5)) = 2$ (note that stages 4 and 5 are in parts (c) and (d) of the figure). Thus, for every item in $A_v(t+1)$ that came from $B_x(t)$ we have its rank in $B_x(t+1)$; it remains to compute the rank for those items in $A_v(t+1)$ that came from $B_y(t)$.

Let a be an item in $B_y(t)$. We compute $\text{rank}(a, B_x(t+1))$ as follows: Recall that for each item a from $B_y(t)$, we computed the straddling items b and c from $B_x(t)$. (See Fig. 2.24.) We know the ranks r and t of b and c, respectively, in $B_x(t+1)$ (as asserted in the previous paragraph). Every item of rank r or less in $B_x(t+1)$ is smaller than a, while every item of rank greater than t is larger than a. Thus, the only items about which there is any doubt concerning their size relative to a are the items with rank $s, r < s \le t$. But there are at most three such items by the 3-cover property. As before, the relative order of a and these (at most) three items can be determined by means of at most two comparisons.

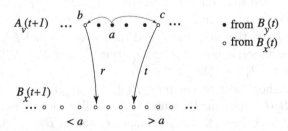

Fig. 2.24. Computing $\text{rank}(a, B_x(t+1))$ for $a \in B_y(t)$.

2.13.3 *Analysis of the algorithm*

It is not difficult to prove that the merge step takes $\Theta(1)$ time at each stage of the algorithm, given that we assign a processor to every array element. Hence, the total running time is $\Theta(\log n)$. Now, we estimate the number of processors needed, which is equal to the total array elements at any stage of the algorithm. First, we compute the total number of items in the $A(t)$ arrays. Let v be an internal node, and assume, as before, that x and y are the children of v. If $|A_v(t)| \neq 0$ and x is not complete, then

$$2|A_v(t)| = |A_v(t+1)| = |B_x(t)| + |B_y(t)| = \frac{1}{4}(|A_x(t)| + |A_y(t)|) = \frac{1}{2}|A_x(t)|,$$

that is, $|A_v(t)| = \frac{1}{4}|A_x(t)|$. So the total size of the $A(t)$ arrays at v's level is $\frac{1}{8}$ the size of the $A(t)$ arrays at x's level, if x is not complete (the number of nodes at v's level is $\frac{1}{2}$ of that at x's level). This need not be true at complete nodes x. It is true for the first stage in which x is complete; but for the second stage, $|A_v(t)| = \frac{1}{2}|A_x(t)|$, and so the total size of the $A(t)$ arrays at v's level is $\frac{1}{4}$ of the total size of the arrays at x's level; likewise, for the third stage, $|A_v(t)| = |A_x(t)|$, and so the total size of the $A(t)$ arrays at v's level is $\frac{1}{2}$ of the total size of the $A(t)$ arrays at x's level.

Thus, on the first stage in which x is complete, the total size of the $A(t)$ arrays is bounded above by $n + n/8 + n/64 + \cdots = n + n/7$; on the second stage, by $n + n/4 + n/32 + \cdots = n + 2n/7$; on the third stage, by $n + n/2 + n/16 + \cdots = n + 4n/7$. Using a similar argument, it can be shown that on the first stage, the total size of the $B(t)$ arrays is bounded above by $2n/7$; on the second stage, by $4n/7$; on the third stage, by $8n/7$. We conclude that the algorithm needs $\Theta(n)$ processors (so as to have a processor standing by each item in the $A(t)$ and $B(t)$ arrays) and takes constant time for the merge step.

The following theorem summarizes the main result. Its proof follows from Theorem 2.4 and the algorithm's description and timing analysis. Recall that the algorithm can be modified to run on the EREW PRAM with the same complexities.

Theorem 2.5 The pipelined mergesort algorithm sorts a sequence of n elements in $\Theta(\log n)$ time using $\Theta(n)$ processors on the EREW PRAM.

2.14   Selection

The problem of selection is defined as follows: Given a sequence $A = \langle a_1, a_2, \ldots, a_n \rangle$ of n elements and a positive integer $k, 1 \leq k \leq n$, find the kth smallest element in A. A straightforward solution would be to sort A in $\Theta(\log n)$ time and return the kth smallest element. However, the work done by this approach is $\Theta(n \log n)$, which is not optimal. There is an optimal sequential algorithm that runs in $\Theta(n)$ time. It can be shown that this sequential algorithm can be parallelized to run on the PRAM in $\Theta(\log^2 n)$ time using $n / \log n$ processors. In this section, we present an algorithm, which is shown as Algorithm PARSELECT, to solve the selection problem, that runs in time $O(\log n \log \log n)$ and uses $n / \log n$ processors. This algorithm is a modification of the parallel version of the sequential selection algorithm.

Algorithm 2.19 PARSELECT
Input: A sequence $A = \langle a_1, \ldots, a_n \rangle$ of elements and an integer k, $1 \leq k \leq n$.
Output: The kth smallest element in A

1. $c \leftarrow 1/\log(4/3)$
2. **for** $j \leftarrow 1$ **to** $\lfloor c \log \log n \rfloor$
3.   Divide A into $|A|/\log|A|$ groups of $\log|A|$ elements each.
4.   Find the median of each group individually.
         Let the set of medians be M.
5.   Sort M and find its median m.
6.   Partition A into three sequences:
   $$A_1 = \{a \mid a < m\}$$
   $$A_2 = \{a \mid a = m\}$$
   $$A_3 = \{a \mid a > m\}$$
7.   **case**
             $|A_1| \geq k$: $A \leftarrow A_1$
             $|A_1| + |A_2| \geq k$: **return** m
             $|A_1| + |A_2| < k$:
8. $A = A_3$
9. $k \leftarrow k - |A_1| - |A_2|$
10.   **end case**
11. **end for**
12. Sort A and **return** the kth smallest element in A.

The **for** loop is executed $c \log \log n$ times, where $c = 1/\log(4/3)$, after which the number of elements in A drops to $O(n/\log n)$. The algorithm then sorts A using the pipelined mergesort algorithm and the kth smallest element is returned in $O(\log n)$ time, using $O(n/\log n)$ processors. Within the **for** loop, first A is partitioned into $|A|/\log|A|$ blocks of $\log|A|$ elements each. The median of each block is found using one processor in $\Theta(|A|)$ sequential time, and the median of medians m is computed by sorting the set M using the pipelined mergesort algorithm in $\Theta(\log(|A|/\log|A|)) = O(\log n)$ time, using $\Theta(|A|/\log|A|)$ processors. A is then partitioned to A_1, of elements smaller than m, A_2 of elements equal to m and A_3 of elements greater than m. If $|A_1| < k \leq |A_1| + |A_2|$, the algorithm terminates and returns m. Else, if $|A_1| \geq k$, A is set to A_1. Otherwise, if $|A_1| + |A_2| < k$, then A is set to A_3 and k is set to $k - |A_1| - |A_2|$.

Partitioning A can be achieved by labeling the elements in A with numbers $1, 2$ and 3 according to whether $a < m, a = m$ or $a > m$, respectively. Then, the parallel prefix algorithm can be used to extract and compact the arrays A_1, A_2 and A_3. This can be achieved in $\Theta(\log|A|)$ time using $O(|A|/\log|A|) = O(n/\log n)$ processors. It follows that the **for** loop takes $O(\log n)$ time in each iteration.

If we let s denote the group size, then the median of medians m is smaller than (and greater than) at least $(|A|/2s)(s/2) = |A|/4$ elements. That is, it is greater than (and smaller than) at most $3|A|/4$ elements (Exercise 2.17). Thus, in the second iteration, $|A| \leq 3n/4$, and in the jth iteration $|A| \leq (3/4)^j n$. Consequently, after $\lfloor c \log \log n \rfloor$ iterations, the size of A is at most

$$\left(\frac{3}{4}\right)^{c \log \log n} \times n$$
$$= (\log n)^{c \log(3/4)} \times n$$
$$= \frac{n}{(\log n)^{c \log(4/3)}}$$
$$= \frac{n}{(\log n)^{\log(4/3)/\log(4/3)}}$$
$$= \frac{n}{\log n}$$
$$= p.$$

Therefore, in Step 12, there will be enough processors to sort A in $O(\log p) = O(\log n)$ time. Since the time required in each iteration is

$O(\log n)$, the running time of the algorithm is $O(\log n \log \log n)$. The work done in each iteration is $O(|A|)$. Hence, the total work done is at most

$$n + (3/4)n + (3/4)^2 n + \cdots + (3/4)^{\lfloor c \log \log n \rfloor} n = \Theta(n),$$

which is optimal. However, the cost, which is $O(n \log \log n)$, is not optimal.

2.15   Multiselection

Let $A = \langle a_1, a_2, \ldots, a_n \rangle$ be a sequence of n elements drawn from a linearly ordered set, and let $K = \langle k_1, k_2, \ldots, k_r \rangle$ be a sorted sequence of positive integers between 1 and n. The *multiselection* problem is to select the k_ith smallest element for all values of $i, 1 \le i \le r$. To make the presentation simple, we will assume that all elements in A are distinct. Consider Algorithm PARMULTISELECT1. The algorithm initially uses $n/\log n$ processors. In the two recursive calls, it uses $p|A_1|/|A|$ and $p|A_2|/|A|$ processors, where p is the current number of processors. The recurrence for the running time of this divide and conquer algorithm is $T(n,r) = T(n, r/2) + O(\log n \log \log n)$ since we used the parallel algorithm for selection, Algorithm PARSELECT, of Section 2.14. As the recursion depth is $\log r$, the solution to this recurrence is $T(n,r) = O(\log n \log \log n \log r)$.

Algorithm 2.20 PARMULTISELECT1
Input: A sequence $A = \langle a_1, a_2, \ldots, a_n \rangle$ of n elements, and a sorted sequence
  of r positive integers $K = \langle k_1, k_2, \ldots, k_r \rangle$. The number of processors p.
Output: The k_ith smallest element in A, $1 \le i \le r$.

1. $r \leftarrow |K|$
2. If $r > 0$ **then**
3.   Set $k = k_{\lceil r/2 \rceil}$.v
4.   Use Algorithm PARSELECT to find a, the kth smallest element in A.
5.   Output a.
6.   Let $A_1 = \langle a_i \mid a_i < a \rangle$ and $A_2 = \langle a_i \mid a_i > a \rangle$.
7.   Let $K_1 = \langle k_1, k_2, \ldots, k_{\lceil r/2 \rceil - 1} \rangle$ and
       $K_2 = \langle k_{\lceil r/2 \rceil + 1} - k, k_{\lceil r/2 \rceil + 2} - k, \ldots, k_r - k \rangle$.
8.   PARMULTISELECT1($A_1, K_1, p|A_1|/|A|$).
9.   PARMULTISELECT1($A_2, K_2, p|A_2|/|A|$).
10. **end if**

In the remaining of this section, we present an efficient algorithm to solve this problem that runs in time

$$T(n, p) = O((n/p + t_s(p, p))(\log r + \log(n/p)))$$

on the PRAM with p processors, $r \leq p < n$, where $t_s(p, p)$ is the time needed to sort p elements using p processors. If $p = n/\log n$, the running time becomes $T(n, n/\log n) = O(\log n(\log r + \log \log n))$.

In the algorithm to be presented, we will use the following notation to repeatedly partition A into smaller subsets: Let $a \in A$ with rank k_a. Partition A into two subsets $A' = \{x \in A \mid x \leq a\}$ and $A'' = \{x \in A \mid x > a\}$. This partitioning of A induces the following bipartitioning of K: $B' = \{k \in K \mid k \leq k_a\}$ and $B'' = \{k - k_a \mid k \in K \text{ and } k > k_a\}$. In this case, we will call each of (A', B') and (A'', B'') a *selection pair*. Let (A', B') be a selection pair. We will label (A', B') as "active" if $|B'| > 0$; otherwise it will be called "inactive". The algorithm is given as Algorithm PARMULTISELECT2.

We turn to the analysis of the algorithm. First, we allocate a number of processors for each active set. Specifically, we assign $p' = (|A|/s)p$ processors for active set (A, B), where s is the number of remaining elements computed in Line 15. There are enough processors for all active sets. The set A is partitioned into p' groups of $w = |A|/p' = s/p$ elements each. Note that $w \leq n/p = q$. The median of medians m is smaller than (and greater than) at least $(|A|/2w)(w/2) = |A|/4$ elements. That is, it is greater than (and smaller than) at most $3|A|/4$ elements (Exercise 2.17). Hence, after $c \log r$ iterations, the size of each subset is at most

$$\left(\frac{3}{4}\right)^{c \log r} \times n$$

$$= r^{c \log (3/4)} \times n$$

$$= \frac{n}{r^{c \log (4/3)}}$$

$$= \frac{n}{r^{\log (4/3)/ \log (4/3)}}$$

$$= \frac{n}{r}.$$

Algorithm 2.21 PARMULTISELECT2

Input: A sequence $A = \langle a_1, \ldots, a_n \rangle$ of elements and a sorted sequence of positive integers $B = \langle k_1, k_2, \ldots, k_r \rangle$, $1 \leq k_i \leq n$. The number of processors p.

Output: The k_ith smallest element in A, $1 \leq i \leq r$.

1. $\mathcal{L} \leftarrow \{(A, B)\}$; Mark (A, B) "active"; $s \leftarrow n$; $q \leftarrow n/p$.

2. $c \leftarrow 1/\log(4/3)$

3. Repeat Steps 4–16 $c(\log r + \log q)$ times.

4. **for each** active pair $(A, B) \in \mathcal{L}$ **do in parallel**

5.   Assign $p' = (|A|/s)p$ processors for active set (A, B).

6.   **if** $|A| \leq p'$ **then** sort A and return the k_ith smallest element for $1 \leq i \leq |B|$.

7.   **else do**

8. $w \leftarrow |A|/p' = s/p$. Partition A into p' subsequences $A_1, A_2, \ldots, A_{p'}$ of size at most $w \leq q$ each. Find the median m_i of each A_i. Sort these medians to obtain the median of medians m.

9.   Find k, the rank of m in A.

10.   Partition A into A' and A'', where A' (resp. A'') is the set of elements in A less than or equal to (resp. greater than) m.

11.   Partition B into B' and B'', where B' (resp. B'') is the set of elements in B less than or equal to (resp. greater than) k. Subtract k from each rank in B''.

12.   Replace (A, B) in $\mathcal{L}$ by (A', B') and (A'', B'').

13.   If B' is empty, then mark (A', B') as "inactive"; otherwise mark it as "active". If B'' is empty, then mark (A'', B'') as "inactive"; otherwise mark it as "active". Discard inactive pairs.

14.   **end if**

15.   Let s be the number of all remaining elements.

16. **end for**

17. Sort all partitions A in all active pairs $(A, B) \in \mathcal{L}$, and for each element in B return its corresponding element in A.

We observe that if A is partitioned into more than r subsets, then *at most r of these subsets are active*, and the rest are inactive, since the number of ranks in B is $\leq r$. Consequently, after $c \log r$ iterations, there are at most r subsets of size at most n/r each. Clearly, after $c \log q$ additional iterations, the size of active subsets in the first stage will be reduced further by a factor of q, so that the size of each subset is upperbounded by $n/rq = p/r$. In other words, after $c \log q$ additional iterations, there are at most r subsets of size at most p/r each.

Now, we compute the overall time needed by the algorithm in the first $\log r$ iterations. Consider an arbitrary iteration where there are a number of subsets of total size less than or equal to n. We analyze the running time taken by a pair (A, B) of maximum size, that is, $|A| \le n$ is maximum among all active pairs. Finding the medians m_i takes $O(q)$ sequential time. Sorting the medians can be done in $t_s(|A|/w, p') = t_s(p', p') \le t_s(p, p)$ parallel time. Computing k, the rank of m in A, and the sets A' and A'' can be achieved in $O(w + \log p') = O(q + \log p)$ parallel time using parallel prefix and compaction. Since K is sorted, both B' and B'' are computed using parallel p'-search in $O(\log_{p'} r) = O(\log r / \log p')$ time. Hence, the time needed by the first $\log r$ iterations is

$$O\left((q + t_s(p, p) + \log p) \log r + \frac{\log^2 r}{\log p'}\right).$$

Observe that $t_s(p, p) \ge \log p$ and since $r \le p$, we have

$$\frac{\log^2 r}{\log p'} \le \frac{\log p \log r}{\log p'} \le \log p \log r.$$

Hence, the above expression reduces to

$$O((q + t_s(p, p)) \log r) = O((n/p + t_s(p, p)) \log r).$$

The time taken by the next $\log q$ iterations is asymptotically the same as that taken by the first $\log r$ iterations, except that the number of iterations $\log r$ is replaced by $\log q$. Hence, the remaining iterations can be completed in time $O((q + t_s(p, p)) \log q) = O((n/p + t_s(p, p)) \log(n/p))$.

As to the sorting step in Line 17 of the algorithm, we have at most r subsets of size at most $n/rq = p/r$ each to be sorted. If we allocate p/r processors to each of the r subsets, the time needed for sorting is $t_s(p/r, p/r)$, which is negligible.

It follows that the time complexity of the algorithm is

$$T(n, p) = O((n/p + t_s(p, p))(\log r + \log(n/p))).$$

If, for example, we set $p = n^{1-\epsilon}$, $0 < \epsilon < 1$, we may use a simple $O(\log^2 p)$ sorting algorithm, and the above expression reduces to

$$T(n, n^{1-\epsilon}) = O((n^\epsilon + \log^2 p)(\log r + \log(n^\epsilon)))$$
$$= O(n^\epsilon(\log r + \log(n^\epsilon))),$$

which is optimal for $r \geq n^\epsilon$, since the cost of the algorithm will be $O(n \log r)$. If, on the other hand, we set $p = n/\log n$ and use the pipelined mergesort algorithm of Section 2.13, the time complexity becomes

$$T(n, n/\log n) = O((\log n + \log(n/\log n))(\log r + \log \log n))$$
$$= O(\log n(\log r + \log \log n)),$$

which is optimal for $r \geq \log n$. This is superior to the running time of Algorithm PARMULTISELECT1. If we let $r = O(\log n)$, the time complexity becomes $O(\log n \log \log n)$, which is the same as the running time for the classical selection of one element presented in Section 2.14. In the special case when $r = 1$ and $p = n/\log n$, the running time reduces to that of the $O(\log n \log \log n)$ parallel selection algorithm of Section 2.14.

2.16 Matrix Multiplication

Given two $n \times n$ matrices A and B, consider the problem of computing the product $C = AB$, where $n = 2^k$ for some positive integer k. Assume that there are n^3 processors available, labeled $P_{i,j,l}, 1 \leq i, j, l \leq n$. Each entry $c_{i,j}$ of C is the dot product of two vectors: row i of A and column j of B. First we present an algorithm for the dot product. Algorithm DOTPRODUCT computes the dot product of two given vectors row i of A and column j of B of dimension n each using n processors. Lines 1 and 2 compute $W = A[i, *]B[*, j]$ in $\Theta(1)$ time. The rest of the algorithm is similar to Algorithm PARADDITION in Section 2.2. The second **for** loop copies the numbers in W into $V[n], V[n+1], \ldots, V[2n-1]$, which correspond to the leaves of the binary tree. The **for** loop in Line 5 is repeated $k = \log n$ times, once for each internal level of the tree. The **for** loop at line 6 is for performing 2^r additions in parallel, $r = k-1, k-2, \ldots, 0$. (See Section 2.2).

Algorithm 2.22 DOTPRODUCT

Input: Two $n \times n$ matrices A and B and two indices i and j, $n = 2^k$.

Output: The dot product of row i of A and column j of B.

1. **for** $l \leftarrow 1$ **to** n **do in parallel**
2. $W[l] \leftarrow A[i,l] * B[l,j]$
3. **end for**
4. **for** $l \leftarrow 1$ **to** n **do in parallel**
5. $V[l + n - 1] \leftarrow W[l]$
6. **end for**
7. **for** $r \leftarrow k - 1$ **downto** 0 **do**
8.   **for** $t \leftarrow 2^r$ **to** $2^{r+1} - 1$ **do in parallel**
9. $V[t] \leftarrow V[2t] + V[2t+1]$
10.   **end for**
11. **end for**
12. **return** $V[1]$

The algorithm for matrix multiplication is a parallelization of the traditional $\Theta(n^3)$ time sequential algorithm. It is shown as Algorithm PARMATRIXMULT. It uses n^3 processors. The n processors $P_{i,j,1}, P_{i,j,2}, \ldots, P_{i,j,n}$ compute $C[i,j]$ using Algorithm DOTPRODUCT.

Algorithm 2.23 PARMATRIXMULT

Input: Two $n \times n$ matrices A and B, $n = 2^k$.

Output: The product $C = AB$.

1. **for** $i \leftarrow 1$ **to** n **do in parallel**
2.   **for** $j \leftarrow 1$ **to** n **do in parallel**
3. $C[i,j] \leftarrow$ DOTPRODUCT(A, B, i, j)
4.   **end for**
5. **end for**
6. **return** C

Thus, the running time of the algorithm is dominated by the call to Algorithm DOTPRODUCT, which takes $\Theta(\log n)$ time. The work done by the algorithm can be computed as follows. Line 3 is executed n^2 times, and in each call to Algorithm DOTPRODUCT, it performs $\Theta(n)$ operations. Hence, the work done by the algorithm is $\Theta(n^3)$. Notice that the algorithm requires concurrent read capability, and hence it runs on the CREW PRAM.

2.17   Transitive Closure

Assume that an $n \times n$ adjacency matrix representation of a directed graph $G = (V, E)$ is given, where $|V| = n$. In such a representation, $A(i, j) = 1$ if and only if there is an edge from v_i to v_j in E, and $A(i, j) = 0$ if $(v_i, v_j) \notin E$. The *transitive closure* of A is represented as an $n \times n$ Boolean matrix A^* in which $A^*(i, j) = 1$ if and only if there is a path in G from v_i to v_j. $A^*(i, j) = 0$ if no such path exists. One way to obtain the transitive closure of A is to compute A^n by performing $\lceil \log n \rceil$ operations of squaring the matrix: $A \times A = A^2, A^2 \times A^2 = A^4$, and so on until a matrix A^m is obtained where $m \geq n$. Here, we use the Boolean matrix multiplication method, in which the operations of scalar multiplication and addition in the standard matrix multiplication are replaced by the logical "AND" and "OR" operations, respectively. Since there are $\lceil \log n \rceil$ matrix multiplications, $A^* = A^n$ can be obtained in time $\Theta(\log^2 n)$ with $\Theta(n^3)$ processors on the CREW PRAM using Boolean matrix multiplication (see Section 2.16). The total number of operations is $\Theta(n^3 \log n)$.

2.18   Shortest Paths

Let $G = (V, E)$ be a weighted directed graph on n vertices, in which each edge (i, j) has a weight $w[i, j]$. If there is no edge from vertex i to vertex j, then $w[i, j] = \infty$. For simplicity, we will assume that $V = \{1, 2, \ldots, n\}$. We assume that G does not have negative weight cycles, that is, cycles whose total weight is negative. The problem is to find the *distance* from each vertex to all other vertices, where the distance from vertex i to vertex j is the length of a shortest path from i to j. Let i and j be two different vertices in V. Define $d_{i,j}^k$ to be the length of a shortest path from i to j that contains at most k edges, $1 \leq k \leq n - 1$. Thus, for example, $d_{i,j}^1 = w[i, j]$, $d_{i,j}^2$ is the length of a shortest path from i to j that contains at most two edges, and so on. Then, by definition, $d_{i,j}^{n-1}$ is the length of a shortest path from i to j, i.e., the distance from i to j. Given this definition, we can compute $d_{i,j}^k$ recursively as follows.

$$
d_{i,j}^k = \begin{cases} 0 & \text{if } i = j \\ w[i, j] & \text{if } k = 1 \\ \min_l \{d_{i,l}^{k/2} + d_{l,j}^{k/2}\} & \text{if } k \geq 2. \end{cases}
$$

Let D^k be the matrix whose entries are $d_{i,j}^k$, $1 \le i, j \le n$. Then, D^k can be obtained from $D^{k/2}$ by squaring, except that the operations "+" and "min" replace the usual matrix operations "×" and "+", respectively. Letting $D^1 = (d_{i,j}^1)$, we can use the operations "+" and "min" to evaluate $D^2, D^4, \ldots, D^m$, where m is the smallest power of $2 \ge n - 1$. This takes $\lceil \log(n - 1) \rceil$ matrix multiplications. Hence, the running time is $\Theta(\log^2 n)$ using $\Theta(n^3)$ processors on the CREW PRAM (see Section 2.16). The total number of operations is $\Theta(n^3 \log n)$.

2.19   Minimum Spanning Trees

Let $G = (V, E)$ be a weighted undirected graph on n vertices, in which each edge (i, j) has a weight $w[i, j]$. If there is no edge from vertex i to vertex j, then $w[i, j] = \infty$. We will assume that $V = \{1, 2, \ldots, n\}$. A *spanning tree T* of G is a subgraph $T = (V, E')$ such that T is a tree. In what follows, we present an algorithm to construct a minimum spanning tree for a graph that is denoted by its weight matrix. We will assume without loss of generality that the weights are distinct. If they are not distinct, each weight of an edge e can be appended by the label of that edge. The algorithm to be presented is based on the following theorem whose proof is easy.

Theorem 2.6   Let $G = (V, E)$ be a weighted undirected graph. Partition the set of vertices into $\{V_1, V_2\}$. Let e be the edge of minimum weight connecting V_1 and V_2. Then e belong to the minimum weight spanning tree.

A *rooted directed tree* of G is a tree in which every edge is directed and every vertex has outdegree 1. A *rooted star* is a rooted directed tree in which every vertex is directly connected to the root. Figure 2.25(a) shows a directed rooted tree, and Fig. 2.25(b) shows a rooted star.

The algorithm for finding a minimum spanning tree is given as Algorithm PRAMMST. The algorithm proceeds through stages. In the beginning, there is a forest of trees consisting of all vertices and no edges. Each tree consists of exactly one vertex. Subsequently, during each stage, the edge with the minimum weight incident on each tree is selected. The newly selected edges are added to the current forest to yield a new forest. This continues until there is only one tree in the forest, that is, the minimum spanning tree.

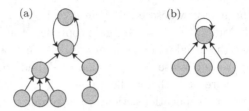

Fig. 2.25.   (a) A directed rooted tree. (b) A rooted star.

Algorithm 2.24 PRAMMST

Input: A graph G represented by its $n \times n$ weight matrix W.

Output: A minimum spanning tree T of G.

1. $T \leftarrow \{\};$ $m = n$.
2.   **while** $m > 1$ **do**
3.   **for** all vertices $v \in V(G)$ **do**
4.   let $C(v) = u$, where $W(v,u) = \min\{W(v,x) \mid x \neq v\}$.
5. $T \leftarrow T \cup \{(u,v)\}$
6.   **end for**
7.   Shrink each directed tree of the forest defined by C to a
         rooted star. Set $m \leftarrow$ Number of rooted stars.
8.   Compress each rooted star to a supervertex. Assign the
         labels (numbers) $1, 2, 3, \ldots, m$ to these supervertices.
9.   Let W' be the reduced $m \times m$ adjacency matrix of the graph
         whose rows and columns correspond to the newly created
         supervertices.
10.   Set $W \leftarrow W'$. Let G be the corresponding graph.
11. **end while**

In the algorithm, the vector C defined by the newly selected edges
defines directed rooted trees. These rooted trees are converted to rooted
stars. Every star is then compressed into a *supervertex*. In other words,
replace each star by a new vertex. Label these new vertices as $1, 2, \ldots, m$,
where m is the number of stars. Let W' be the reduced $m \times m$ adjacency
matrix of the graph whose rows and columns correspond to the newly created supervertices. We store the edge (x,y) of the original graph next to the
$W'(i,j)$ entry, where (x,y) is the edge of minimum weight connecting the
trees corresponding to supervertices i and j. This will enable us to recover
an edge in the original graph quickly. It can be shown that the construction
of the matrix W' from W takes $O(\log n)$ time using $O(n^2)$ processors on

the CREW PRAM (Exercise 2.49). The foregoing procedure of compressing nodes, finding minimum-weight incident edges, and reducing the adjacency matrix is continued until there is only one tree spanning all the vertices of G.

Example 2.15 Consider the graph shown in Fig. 2.26(a). During the first iteration of the **while** loop, the adjacency vector C is given by $C(1) = 2$, $C(2) = 1$, $C(3) = 1$, $C(4) = 8$, $C(5) = 7$, $C(6) = 3$, $C(7) = 5$, and $C(8) = 4$, and the following edges are added to T: $(1, 2), (1, 3), (4, 8), (5, 7), (3, 6)$. Hence, there are three rooted directed trees as shown in Fig. 2.26(b). By Step 7, the rooted trees are converted to rooted stars as shown in Fig. 2.26(c), and m is set to 3. The new matrix W with the newly assigned labels, and augmented with the minimum weight edges is then given by

$$\begin{bmatrix} \infty & 5, (2, 4) & 10, (4, 5) \\ 5, (2, 4) & \infty & 12, (3, 7) \\ 10, (4, 5) & 12, (3, 7) & \infty \end{bmatrix}.$$

The corresponding graph is shown in Fig. 2.26(d). The vertices in this graph were labeled as 1, 2, and 3. Thus, vertex 1 represents the set $\{4, 8\}$, vertex 2 represents the set $\{1, 2, 3, 6\}$, and vertex 3 represents the set $\{5, 7\}$.

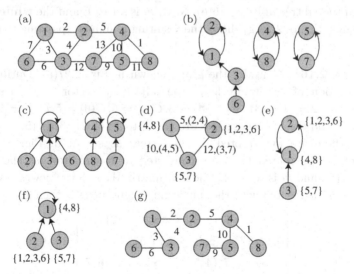

Fig. 2.26.   Example of the construction of minimum spanning tree.

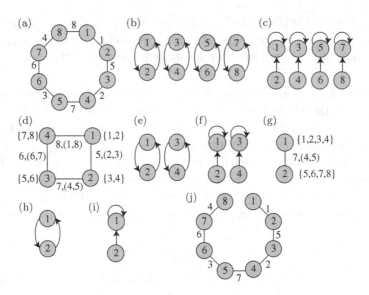

Fig. 2.27.   Example of the construction of minimum spanning tree.

Hence, during the second iteration, $C(1) = 2, C(2) = 1$ and $C(3) = 1$, and the following edges are added to T: $(2,4), (4,5)$. Figure 2.26(e) shows the new rooted tree. Figure 2.26(f) shows the new star formed from the directed rooted tree in Fig. 2.26(e). Next, m is set to 1, and the **while** loop terminates. Figure 2.26(g) shows the resulting minimum spanning tree.   □

Example 2.16   Consider the graph shown in Fig. 2.27(a). During the first iteration of the **while** loop, the adjacency vector C is given by $C(1) = 2, C(2) = 1, C(3) = 4, C(4) = 3, C(5) = 6, C(6) = 5, C(7) = 8$, and $C(8) = 7$, and the following edges are added to T: $(1,2), (3,4), (5,6), (7,8)$. Hence, there are four rooted directed trees as shown in Fig. 2.27(b). By Step 7, the rooted trees are converted to rooted stars as shown in Fig. 2.27(c), and m is set to 4. The new matrix W with the newly assigned labels, and augmented with the minimum weight edges is then given by

$$\begin{bmatrix} \infty & 5,(2,3) & \infty & 8,(1,8) \\ 5,(2,3) & \infty & 7,(4,5) & \infty \\ \infty & 7,(4,5) & \infty & 6,(6,7) \\ 8,(1,8) & \infty & 6,(6,7) & \infty \end{bmatrix}.$$

The corresponding graph is shown in Fig. 2.27(d). The vertices in this graph were labeled as 1, 2, 3 and 4. Thus, vertex 1 represents the set $\{1,2\}$, vertex 2 represents the set $\{3,4\}$, vertex 3 represents the set $\{5,6\}$ and vertex 4 represents the set $\{7,8\}$. Hence, during the second iteration, $C(1) = 2, C(2) = 1, C(3) = 4$ and $C(4) = 3$, and the edges $(2,3)$ and $(6,7)$ are added to T. Thus, there are two rooted directed trees as shown in Fig. 2.27(e). By Step 7, the rooted trees are converted to rooted stars as shown in Fig. 2.27(f), and m is set to 2. The new matrix W with the newly assigned labels, and augmented with the minimum weight edges is then given by

$$\begin{bmatrix} \infty & 7, (4,5) \\ 7, (4,5) & \infty \end{bmatrix}.$$

The corresponding graph is shown in Fig. 2.27(g). During the third iteration, the vector C is given by $C(1) = 2$ and $C(2) = 1$, and the edge $(4,5)$ is added to T. Figure 2.27(h) shows the new rooted tree. Figure 2.27(i) shows the new star formed from the directed rooted tree in Fig. 2.27(h). Next, m is set to 1, and the **while** loop terminates. Figure 2.27(j) shows the resulting minimum spanning tree. $\square$

The running time is computed as follows. Step 4 of computing C takes $O(\log m) = O(\log n)$ time using $O(m^2) = O(n^2)$ processors, since it computes m minima; one minimum per row. Step 7 of shrinking trees into stars takes $O(\log m) = O(\log n)$ using $O(n)$ processors by the technique of pointer jumping. As noted above, the construction of the $m \times m$ matrix in Step 9 takes $O(\log n)$ time using $O(n^2)$ processors. Steps 7 and 9 require simultaneous memory access, and hence the algorithm works on the CREW model. After each iteration of the **while** loop, the number of stars is reduced by at least a half, and hence there are at most $\log n$ iterations. It follows that the overall running time of the algorithm is $O(\log^2 n)$ using a total of $O(n^2)$ processors.

2.20   Computing the Convex Hull of a Set of Points

Let $S = \{p_1, p_2, \ldots, p_n\}$ be a set of n points in the plane, where n is a power of 2. The *convex hull* of S, denoted by $CH(S)$, is the smallest convex polygon containing all the points of S. The convex hull is usually represented

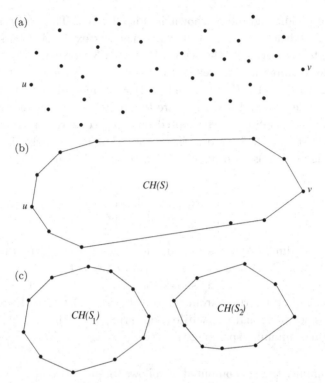

Fig. 2.28.   (a) The set of points S. (b) Convex hull of S. (c) Convex hulls of S_1 and S_2.

by a list of points, called vertices, ordered clockwise (or counterclockwise). See Figs. 2.28(a) and (b) for an example, in which S consists of 32 points. In what follows, we present a divide-and-conquer parallel algorithm to find $CH(S)$ in $\Theta(\log n)$ time using $O(n)$ processors on the CREW PRAM.

As a preprocessing step, the points in S are first sorted in ascending order of their x-coordinates in $\Theta(\log n)$ time using the pipelined merge-sort algorithm. So, assume that $x(p_1) \leq x(p_2) \leq \cdots \leq x(p_n)$, where $x(p_i)$ denotes the x-coordinate of point p_i. We will assume for simplicity that no three points of S are collinear, and no two points have the same x-coordinate. Next, the set of points S is divided into two halves $S_1 = \langle p_1, p_2, \ldots, p_{n/2} \rangle$ and $S_2 = \langle p_{n/2+1}, p_{n/2+2}, \ldots, p_n \rangle$. Now, we recursively determine the two convex hulls of the two halves $CH(S_1)$ and

$CH(S_2)$. Figure 2.28(c) shows the two convex hulls of the points in part (a) of the figure.

Consider the convex hull $CH(S)$ shown in Fig. 2.28(b). Here, u and v are the two points with minimum and maximum x-coordinates, respectively (recall that no two points have the same x-coordinate). These two points are clearly part of $CH(S)$. The polygonal chain defined by the edges from u to v in clockwise traversal is called the *upper hull* $UH(S)$. The *lower hull*, $LH(S)$, is defined similarly as the polygonal chain defined by the edges from v to u in clockwise traversal. The algorithm, after determining $CH(S_1)$ and $CH(S_2)$, proceeds by constructing the upper and lower hulls of S. The upper hull of S, $UH(S)$, is constructed by joining $UH(S_1)$ and $UH(S_2)$ by a line segment, called a *tangent*, such that $CH(S_1)$ and $CH(S_2)$ are below it. The lower hull $LH(S)$ is constructed in a similar manner to obtain the desired $CH(S)$. In what follows, we compute the upper tangent and upper hull $UH(S)$.

Let $\langle x_1, x_2, \ldots, x_r \rangle$ and $\langle y_1, y_2, \ldots, y_s \rangle$ be the upper hulls $UH(S_1)$ and $UH(S_2)$ of S_1 and S_2, respectively. We now show how to find the line of the tangent $\overline{x^* y^*}$ with the property that both of $UH(S_1)$ and $UH(S_2)$ are below it. That is, $\overline{x^* y^*}$ is a tangent to both $UH(S_1)$ and $UH(S_2)$. The most crucial phase of the algorithm is the identification of the upper and lower tangents. We outline the steps of the algorithm for determining $\overline{x^* y^*}$ in the following two observations.

Observation 2.2 *If x_i is a vertex of $UH(S_1)$, its tangent line $\overline{x_i v_i}$ with $UH(S_2)$ can be found in $\Theta(1)$ time using $\sqrt{s}$ processors.*

Proof. We find the vertex v_i in $UH(S_2)$ such that $\overline{x_i v_i}$ is a tangent of $UH(S_2)$ as follows. Let y_j be any vertex in $UH(S_2)$, and let y_{j-1} and y_{j+1} be the two vertices to the left and right of y_j, respectively. If $x_i y_j y_{j-1}$ is a right turn and $x_i y_j y_{j+1}$ is a left turn, then v_i is to the right of y_j (see Fig. 2.29(a)). If $x_i y_j y_{j-1}$ is a left turn and $x_i y_j y_{j+1}$ is a right turn, then v_i is to the left of y_j (see Fig. 2.29(b)). If both $x_i y_j y_{j-1}$ and $x_i y_j y_{j+1}$ are right turns, then $v_i = y_j$ (see Fig. 2.29(c)). Hence, we do parallel search on the set of vertices of $UH(S_2)$ using $\sqrt{s}$ processors to identify the vertex y_k such that $v_i = y_k$. There are $\log_{\sqrt{s}} s = 2$ iterations in this search, which implies that the running time is $\Theta(1)$. $\qquad\square$

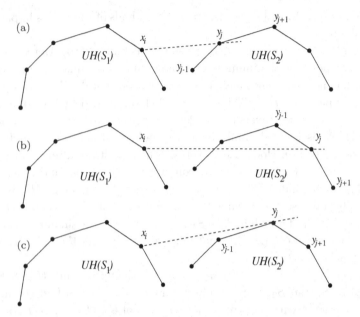

Fig. 2.29.   Tangents to $UH(S_2)$.

Observation 2.3   The common tangent $\overline{x^*y^*}$ of $UH(S_1)$ and $UH(S_2)$ can be determined in $\Theta(1)$ time using $\sqrt{r}\sqrt{s}$ processors.

Proof.   Let $\overline{x_i v_i}$ be a tangent to $UH(S_2)$ at v_i determined as described in Observation 2.2, and let x_{i-1} and x_{i+1} be the two vertices to the left and right of x_i, respectively. If $\overline{x_i v_i}$ is also a tangent to $UH(S_1)$, then $x^* = x_i$. If $x_{i-1}x_i v_i$ is a left turn, then x^* is to the left of x_i (see Fig. 2.30(a)). If $x_{i-1}x_i v_i$ is a right turn, then x^* is to the right of x_i (see Fig. 2.30(b)). This allows us to determine, for any given vertex x_i of $UH(S_1)$, whether the vertex x^* appears to the left of, to the right of, or equal to x_i in $\Theta(1)$ time. Thus, to locate x^*, we do double parallel search, the outer search is on the vertices of $UH(S_1)$, and for each vertex x_i in $UH(S_1)$, we do the inner parallel search on the vertices of $UH(S_2)$. The parallel search performed on the set of vertices of $UH(S_2)$ is done as outlined in Observation 2.2 to obtain the tangent $\overline{x_i v_i}$ and next, we the test for the location of x^* relative to x_i as stated above. We will use $\sqrt{r}$ processors for the outer search on the vertices of $UH(S_1)$, and so there are $\log_{\sqrt{r}} r = 2$ iterations in this search. We use $\sqrt{s}$ processors for the inner search on the vertices of $UH(S_2)$, which amounts

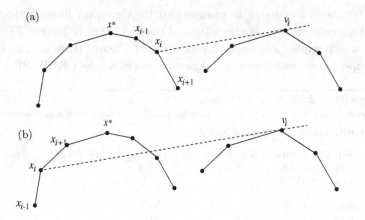

Fig. 2.30.   Tangents to $UH(S_1)$.

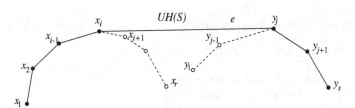

Fig. 2.31.   Upper hull of S, $UH(S)$.

to two iterations for the inner search. Thus, the total number of processors used is $\sqrt{r}\sqrt{s} \leq n$, that is, $\sqrt{s}$ processors for every vertex considered in $UH(S_1)$. It follows that the overall running time to find the upper tangent is $\Theta(1)$ using $\sqrt{r}\sqrt{s} \leq n$ processors. $\qquad\square$

Observations 2.2 and 2.3 provide the steps for finding the upper common tangent $\overline{x^*y^*}$. The lower common tangent can be found in a similar fashion. It remains to finish the construction of $CH(S)$. Let $x_i = x^*$ and $y_j = y^*$. To construct $UH(S)$, first, we remove the vertices $x_{i+1}, x_{i+2}, \ldots, x_r$ from $UH(S_1)$ and remove the vertices $y_1, y_2, \ldots, y_{j-1}$ from $UH(S_2)$ to obtain $UH'(S_1)$ and $UH'(S_2)$, respectively. That is, $UH'(S_1) = \langle x_1, x_2, \ldots, x_i \rangle$ and $UH'(S_2) = \langle y_j, y_{j+1}, \ldots, y_s \rangle$. Next, connecting x_i in $UH'(S_1)$ to y_j in $UH'(S_2)$ by the edge $e = \overline{x^*y^*} = \overline{x_i y_j}$ yields the desired upper hull $UH(S)$ (see Fig. 2.31). Finally, the problem of computing $LH(S)$ can be solved in a similar fashion.

The above discussion is summarized in Algorithm PARCONVEXHULL. The recurrence for the running time of the algorithm is $T(n) = T(n/2) + \Theta(1)$, which implies a running time of $\Theta(\log n)$. Clearly, there are concurrent read operations, and hence the algorithm works on the CREW PRAM.

Algorithm 2.25 PARCONVEXHULL

Input: A set $S = \{p_1, \ldots, p_n\}$ of n points in the plane, where n is a power of 2.

Output: The convex hull of S, $CH(S)$.

1. Sort The points in S in nondecreasing order of their x-coordinates.
2. $CH(S) \leftarrow ch(S)$
3. **return** $CH(S)$

Procedure $ch(S)$

1. **if** $|S| \leq 4$ **then**
2.   compute $CH(S)$ by a straightforward method.
3.   **return** (CH(S))
4. **end if**
5. Divide S into two halves $S_1 = \langle p_1, p_2, \ldots, p_{n/2} \rangle$ and $S_2 = \langle p_{n/2+1}, p_{n/2+2}, \ldots, p_n \rangle$.
6. $CH(S_1) \leftarrow ch(S_1)$; $CH(S_2) \leftarrow ch(S_2)$
7. Let $UH(S_1) \leftarrow \langle x_1, x_2, \ldots, x_r \rangle$ and $UH(S_2) \leftarrow \langle y_1, y_2, \ldots, y_s \rangle$ be the upper hulls of S_1 and S_2, respectively.
8. Find the common upper tangent $\overline{x_i y_j}$.
9. $UH'(S_1) \leftarrow \langle x_1, x_2, \ldots, x_i \rangle$ and $UH'(S_2) \leftarrow \langle y_j, y_{j+1}, \ldots, y_s \rangle$.
10. $UH(S) \leftarrow UH'(S_1) \cup UH'(S_2) \cup \overline{x_i y_j}$.
11. Repeat Steps 7 to 10 to find the lower hull of S, $LH(S)$.
12. $CH(S) \leftarrow UH(S) \cup LH(S)$
13. **return** $CH(S)$

2.21 Bibliographic Notes

There are a number of books on parallel algorithms on the PRAM. These include Akl [4], Akl [5], Akl [6], Akl and Lyons [8], Chaudhuri [21], Cosnard and Trystram [29], Gibbons and Rytter [37], Grama, Gupta, Karypis and Kumar [39], Horowitz, Sahni and Rajasekaran [43], JáJá [44], Lakshmivarahan and Dhall [53], Miller and Boxer [66], Roosta [77], and Xavier and Iyengar [104]. Prefix computations are described in Lakshmivarahan and Dhall [53], which is a book devoted to parallel prefix computations. The $O(\log \log n)$ time algorithm for merging on the PRAM is due to Kruscal [49]. The $O(\log \log n)$ time algorithm for computing the maximum as well as algorithms for merging and sorting were given in Shiloach and Vishkin [87]. Bitonic and odd–even sorting networks were described in Batcher [15]. Multiselection on the PRAM is a modification of an algorithm in Alsuwaiyel [11]. The pipelined mergesort algorithm is due to Cole [26]. A survey of parallel sorting and selection algorithms can be found in Rajasekaran [75]. The ideas for selection on the PRAM are from Akl([7] and Vishkin [102]. The algorithm for the minimum spanning tree problem is due to Sollin, and was inspired by the one presented in JáJá [44]. Parallel algorithms for graph problems on the PRAM can be found in Gibbons and Rytter [37]. Parallel algorithms for problems in computational geometry on the PRAM can be found in Akl and Lyons [8]. The divide-and-conquer approach for computing the planar convex hull is due to Shamos [82]. For more references on parallel algorithms on the PRAM, see for instance JáJá [44].

2.22   Exercises

2.1. Give a parallel algorithm to compute the maximum of n numbers in the sequence $\langle x_1, x_2, \ldots, x_n \rangle$ on the EREW PRAM. What is the running time of your algorithm?

2.2. Consider Algorithm SORTINGCREW presented in Section 2.4.1. Suppose we change the outer loop in Line 3 to sequential and change the inner loop in Line 4 to parallel, will the algorithm still work on the CREW PRAM? Explain.

2.3. Use parallel prefix to compute the sequence of maximums $x_1, \max\{x_1, x_2\}, \max\{x_1, x_2, x_3\}, \ldots, \max\{x_1, x_2, \ldots, x_n\}$ for the sequence $S = \langle x_1, x_2, \ldots, x_n \rangle$.

2.4. Let $S = \langle x_1, x_2, \ldots, x_n \rangle$ be a sequence of integers. Give an algorithm to rearrange the elements of S so that all negative integers precede all positive integers. For example, if $S = \langle 3, -2, 1, -5, 4, -6, 7 \rangle$, the result should be $\langle -2, -5, -6, 3, 1, 4, 7 \rangle$.

2.5. Give an algorithm to broadcast an item x stored in processor P_0 to all other processors in the EREW PRAM with $n = 2^k$ processors. What is the running time of your algorithm?

2.6. Consider Algorithm PARQUICKSORT in Section 2.5.2 for parallel quicksort. What is the cost of the algorithm on average? How about in the worst case?

2.7. What is the number of parallel steps in Algorithm PARSEARCH for parallel search discussed in Section 2.6?

2.8. Apply Algorithm PARSEARCH for parallel search using two processors on the sequence

$$S = \langle 1, 2, 5, 7, 8, 11, 12, 15, 19 \rangle \quad \text{and} \quad x = 8.$$

How many parallel steps are there?

2.9. Illustrate the operation of Algorithm PARRANK in Section 2.9.1 for computing the ranks of B in A on the input:

$$A = \langle 1, 4, 7, 10, 12, 14, 19, 20 \rangle \quad \text{and} \quad B = \langle 5, 11, 15, 18 \rangle.$$

2.10. Illustrate the operation of Algorithm ODDEVENMERGE in Section 2.11 for odd–even merging on the input:

$$A = \langle 2, 5, 6, 8 \rangle \quad \text{and} \quad B = \langle 1, 3, 7, 9 \rangle.$$

2.11. Do Exercise 2.10 with the following modification. Merge A_{odd} with B_{odd} and A_{even} with B_{even}. (See Exercise 2.46).

2.12. Let A, B, C, D and E be as defined in Algorithm ODDEVENMERGE discussed in Section 2.11, and assume the elements in $A \cup B$ are distinct. Given a sequence X and an element x, recall that $\text{rank}(x, X)$ is the number of elements in X less than x. Express $\text{rank}(x, C)$ and $\text{rank}(x, D)$ in terms of $\text{rank}(x, A)$ and $\text{rank}(x, B)$.

2.13. Use the result of Exercise 2.12 to show that for $c \in C$, either c is in its correct position in E or to the left of it.

2.14. Use the result of Exercise 2.12 to show that for $d \in D$, either d is in its correct position in E or to the right of it.

2.15. Illustrate the operation of the bitonic sort network shown in Fig. 2.21 on the input sequence $\langle 6, 7, 1, 4, 2, 5, 8, 3 \rangle$.

2.16. Give an example of a bitonic sequence with one local maximum and one local minimum.

2.17. In Algorithm PARSELECT for selection discussed in Section 2.14, show that in each iteration, the median of medians m is greater than and smaller than at most $3|A|/4$ elements.

2.18. Consider Algorithm PARMULTISELECT1 for multiselection discussed in Section 2.15. Compare the algorithm given with direct application of Algorithm PARSELECT given in Section 2.14.

2.19. Repeat Exercise 2.18 with the second algorithm for multiselection for the PRAM, Algorithm PARMULTISELECT2.

2.20. Suggest an algorithm for sorting using multisession. What is the time complexity of your algorithm?

2.21. Consider the algorithm for matrix multiplication discussed in Section 2.16. What is the cost of the algorithm? What modification should be done in order to make the total cost $O(n^3)$?

2.22. Let P be a simple polygon (that is not necessarily convex) with n vertices, and let x be a point. Assume that there are n processors, each assigned to one edge. Give an *efficient* parallel algorithm to decide whether x is in the interior of P. (*Hint*: Draw a horizontal line L such that x lies on L. Count how many times L intersects with the edges of P).

2.23. Let $x_1, x_2, \ldots, x_n$ be n Boolean variables. Show how to find the logical OR of these variables in $O(1)$ time on the COMMON CRCW PRAM with n processors.

2.24. Let $\langle x_1, x_2, \ldots, x_n \rangle$ be a sequence of n distinct numbers. Show how to find the maximum of these numbers in $O(1)$ time on the CRCW PRAM with n^2 processors.

2.25. Let $\langle x_1, x_2, \ldots, x_n \rangle$ be a sequence of n distinct numbers. Show how to find the maximum of these numbers in $O(\log \log n)$ time on the CRCW PRAM with n processors. *Hint*: Partition the input into $\sqrt{n}$ parts and recursively find the maximum in each part. Use Exercise 2.24.

2.26. Let S be a sequence of n distinct numbers and $x \in S$. The rank of x in S is the number of elements in S less than x. Show how to compute the rank of x in S in $O(\log n)$ time on the CREW PRAM with n processors.

2.27. Let S be a sequence of n integers, and x an integer. Show how to compute $\text{rank}(x, S)$ and the rank of x in S, in $O(\log n)$ time on the EREW PRAM using $O(n)$ operations.

2.28. Let $S = \{x_1, x_2, \ldots, x_n\}$ be n numbers and k an integer, $1 \le k \le n$. Show how to find the kth smallest element in S in $O(\log n)$ time on the CREW PRAM with n^2 processors.

2.29. Let $S = \langle x_1, x_2, \ldots, x_n \rangle$ be a sequence of n numbers. Consider the simple recursive algorithm for parallel prefix that divides the sequence S into two halves: $S_1 = \langle x_1, x_2, \ldots, x_{n/2} \rangle$ and $S_2 = \langle x_{n/2+1}, x_{n/2+2}, \ldots, x_n \rangle$, and then calls the algorithm recursively on each of S_1 and S_2.

  (a) Write down the detailed algorithm.
  (b) Will the algorithm work on the EREW PRAM?
  (c) What is the total work done by the algorithm?
  (d) Will Brent's Theorem (Theorem 2.1) help in reducing the number of processors without increasing the running time complexity?

2.30. Let $\langle x_1, x_2, \ldots, x_n \rangle$ be a sequence of n numbers. The *prefix minima* is to compute for each i, $1 \le i \le n$, the minimum among the elements $\{x_1, x_2, \ldots, x_i\}$. Develop an algorithm to compute the prefix minima that runs in time $O(\log n)$ on the EREW PRAM.

2.31. Do Exercise 2.30 using *suffix minima* instead, that is, compute for each i, $1 \leq i \leq n$, the minimum among the elements $\{x_i, x_{i+1}, \ldots, x_n\}$.

2.32. Let $\langle x_1, x_2, \ldots, x_n \rangle$ be a sequence of n numbers. The *suffix computation problem* is to compute the suffixes $x_n, x_{n-1} \circ x_n, \ldots, x_1 \circ x_2 \circ \cdots \circ x_n$. Give an $O(\log n)$ time algorithm to solve this problem on the CREW PRAM with n processors.

2.33. Do Exercise 2.32 for the case of EREW PRAM.

2.34. Let $T_1, T_2, \ldots, T_m$ be m directed and rooted binary trees on n vertices. Each node has a pointer to its parent, except the root which points to itself. Design a parallel algorithm to allow each vertex to know the identity of the tree to which it belongs (The trees are identified by their roots. The roots are numbered $1, 2, \ldots, m$).

2.35. Compute the *next* and *succ* functions as describe in Table 2.1 (page 25) for all vertices in the tree shown in Fig. 2.32. Use the obtained values to derive an Euler tour.

2.36. Use the Euler tour technique to direct the tree shown in Fig. 2.32, where vertex 1 is to be set as the root.

2.37. Use the Euler tour technique to assign levels to the vertices in the tree shown in Fig. 2.32.

2.38. In a *postorder* traversal of a tree T at the root r, the subtrees of r are traversed from left to right in postorder followed by r. Develop an algorithm to determine the postorder numbering of the vertices in a rooted tree. What is the time complexity of your algorithm?

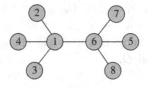

Fig. 2.32.   A tree.

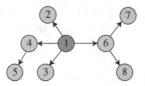

Fig. 2.33.   A rooted tree.

2.39. Apply the algorithm developed in Exercise 2.38 on the tree shown in Fig. 2.33.

2.40. Parallelize Horner's rule to evaluate a polynomial of degree n under the EREW PRAM in time $O(\log n)$.

2.41. Let $\langle x_1, x_2, \ldots, x_n \rangle$ be a sequence of n distinct numbers. Design a parallel algorithm for the CREW PRAM to sort this sequence in time $O(\log n)$. Assume an unlimited number of processors.

2.42. Let n be a positive integer. Consider the problem of computing the polynomials $x'_i = x^i$, for $1 \le i \le n$. Show how to compute the x'_i's in $O(\log n)$ time. Specify the PRAM model used.

2.43. Consider Algorithm PARQUICKSORT presented in Section 2.5.2. Suppose we always select the median as the pivot (see Section 2.14). What will be the running time of the algorithm?

2.44. Let A and B be two sequences of distinct number sorted in ascending order, where $|A| = |B| = n$. Design an $O(1)$ time algorithm to merge A and B on the CREW PRAM. Assume an unlimited number of processors.

2.45. Apply Brent's theorem on Algorithm PARMERGE presented in Section 2.9.2.

2.46. In Algorithm ODDEVENMERGE in Section 2.11, A_{even} is merged with B_{odd} and A_{odd} is merged with B_{even}. Rewrite the algorithm with the modification so that it merges A_{odd} with B_{odd} and A_{even} with B_{even}. It is important to know that this will change the step of traversing the shuffle of C and D.

2.47. Let $G = (V, E)$ be an undirected graph with n vertices. Give an algorithm to decide whether G contains a triangle, that is, three mutually adjacent vertices. Assume that G is represented by its adjacency matrix. Your algorithm should run in $O(\log n)$ time on the CRCW PRAM with n^3 processors.

2.48. Prove Theorem 2.6.

2.49. Show that the reduced adjacency matrix in the minimum spanning tree algorithm of Section 2.18 can be constructed in time $O(\log n)$ using $O(n^2)$ processors on the CREW PRAM.

2.50. Show the steps of computing a minimum spanning tree on the graph shown in Fig. 2.34.

2.51. Show the steps of computing a minimum spanning tree on the graph shown in Fig. 2.35.

2.52. Let $G = (V, E)$ be an undirected graph. G is bipartite if and only if V can be partitioned into two parts V_1 and V_2, such that every edge connects a vertex in V_1 with a vertex in V_2. Equivalently, G is bipartite if and only if it contains no odd-length cycles. Develop an algorithm to test whether G is bipartite.

2.53. Illustrate the operation of the bitonic sort network shown in Fig. 2.21 on the input $\langle 6, 7, 1, 4, 2, 5, 8, 3 \rangle$.

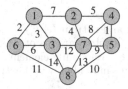

Fig. 2.34.   An undirected graph.

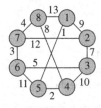

Fig. 2.35.   An undirected graph.

2.54. Let A, A', C and C' be sorted sequences such that C is a 3-cover for A and C' is a 3-cover for A'. Is $C \cup C'$ necessarily a 3-cover for $A \cup A'$? See Section 2.13 for the definition of 3-cover.

2.55. Illustrate the operation of the pipelined mergesort algorithm on the input $\langle 6, 7, 1, 4, 2, 5, 8, 3 \rangle$.

2.56. Prove Observation 2.1.

2.57. Let W, X and Y be three sorted sequences such that $Y = W \cup X$, and $W \cap X = \phi$. Assume that $R(S, S)$ is known for any sequence S, where $R(A, B)$ is the cross ranks of A in B as defined in Section 2.13. Show how to compute $R(W, X)$ and $R(X, W)$ in $O(1)$ time using $O(|Y|)$ processors.

2.58. Parallelize the $\Theta(n)$ time sequential algorithm for selection using $n/\log n$ processors on the PRAM. Analyze your algorithm.

Algorithm 2.26 SELECT
Input: An array $A[1..n]$ of n elements and an integer k, $1 \leq k \leq n$.
Output: The kth smallest element in A.

1. $select(A, k)$

Procedure $select(A, k)$
1. $n \leftarrow |A|$
2. **if** $n < 44$ **then** sort A and **return** $(A[k])$
3. Let $q = \lfloor n/5 \rfloor$. Divide A into q groups of 5 elements each. If 5 does not divide p, then discard the remaining elements.
4. Sort each of the q groups individually and extract its median. Let the set of medians be M.
5. $mm \leftarrow select(M, \lceil q/2 \rceil)$ $\{mm$ is the median of medians$\}$
6. Partition A into three arrays:
   $A_1 = \{a \mid a < mm\}$
   $A_2 = \{a \mid a = mm\}$
   $A_3 = \{a \mid a > mm\}$
7. **case**
   $|A_1| \geq k$: **return** $select(A_1, k)$
   $|A_1| + |A_2| \geq k$: **return** mm
   $|A_1| + |A_2| < k$: **return** $select(A_3, k - |A_1| - |A_2|)$
8. **end case**

2.59. Let $A = \langle a_1, a_2, \ldots, a_n \rangle$ be a sequence of numbers and let k be a given integer between 1 and n. Design and analyze a parallel algorithm to find all k smallest items in A. Do not use multiselection. What model of computation did you use?

2.23 Solutions

2.1. Give a parallel algorithm to compute the maximum of n numbers in the sequence $\langle x_1, x_2, \ldots, x_n \rangle$ on the EREW PRAM. What is the running time of your algorithm?

Similar to Algorithm PARADDITION for parallel addition discussed in Section 2.2.

2.2. Consider Algorithm SORTINGCREW presented in Section 2.4.1. Suppose we change the outer loop in Line 3 to sequential and change the inner loop in Line 4 to parallel, will the algorithm still work on the CREW PRAM? Explain.

No, since there will be concurrent writes. For instance, comparing $A[1]$ with $A[2]$ and comparing $A[1]$ with $A[3]$ will take place simultaneously, and hence the statement $r[1] \leftarrow r[1] + 1$ may be executed at least twice at the same time.

2.3. Use parallel prefix to compute the sequence of maximums $x_1, \max\{x_1, x_2\}, \max\{x_1, x_2, x_3\}, \ldots, \max\{x_1, x_2, \ldots, x_n\}$ for the sequence $S = \langle x_1, x_2, \ldots, x_n \rangle$.

Similar to Algorithm PARPREFIX for parallel prefix discussed in Section 2.5.

2.4. Let $S = \langle x_1, x_2, \ldots, x_n \rangle$ be a sequence of integers. Give an algorithm to rearrange the elements of S so that all negative integers precede all positive integers. For example, if $S = \langle 3, -2, 1, -5, 4, -6, 7 \rangle$, the result should be $\langle -2, -5, -6, 3, 1, 4, 7 \rangle$.

Use array packing; — similar to Example 2.2.

2.5. Give an algorithm to broadcast an item x stored in processor P_0 to all other processors in the EREW PRAM with $n = 2^k$ processors. What is the running time of your algorithm?

First, P_0 writes x to global memory, and P_1 reads x. P_0 and P_1 then broadcast x to P_2 and P_3 simultaneously. P_0, P_1, P_2 and P_3 then broadcast x to P_4, P_5, P_6 and P_7, and so on. The running time is $\Theta(\log n)$.

2.6. Consider Algorithm PARQUICKSORT in Section 2.5.2 for parallel quicksort. What is the cost of the algorithm on average? How about in the worst case?

The cost of the algorithm on average is $\Theta(n \log^2 n)$, and $\Theta(n^2 \log n)$ in the worst case.

2.7. What is the number of parallel steps in Algorithm PARSEARCH for parallel search discussed in Section 2.6?

The number of parallel steps is at most $\log_{p+1} n + 1$.

2.8. Apply Algorithm PARSEARCH for parallel search using two processors on the sequence

$$S = \langle 1, 2, 5, 7, 8, 11, 12, 15, 19 \rangle \quad \text{and} \quad x = 8.$$

How many parallel steps are there?

Initially, the algorithm divides S into three subsequences

$$\langle 1, 2, 5 \rangle, \quad \langle 7, 8, 11 \rangle, \quad \langle 12, 15, 19 \rangle.$$

The two processors compare x with elements at the internal boundaries, that is, 5 and 11. Since $8 > 5$ and $8 < 11$, the search area is reduced to $\langle 7, 8 \rangle$. Finally, the two processors perform two comparisons simultaneously and one of them returns $3 + 2 = 5$. The number of parallel steps is 2.

2.9. Illustrate the operation of Algorithm PARRANK in Section 2.9.1 for computing the ranks of B in A on the input:

$$A = \langle 1, 4, 7, 10, 12, 14, 19, 20 \rangle \quad \text{and} \quad B = \langle 5, 11, 15, 18 \rangle.$$

Similar to Examples 2.9 and 2.10.

2.10. Illustrate the operation of Algorithm ODDEVENMERGE in Section 2.11 for odd–even merging on the input:

$$A = \langle 2, 5, 6, 8 \rangle \quad \text{and} \quad B = \langle 1, 3, 7, 9 \rangle.$$

Similar to Example 2.11.

2.11. Do Exercise 2.10 with the following modification. Merge A_{odd} with B_{odd} and A_{even} with B_{even}. (See Exercise 2.46).

Similar to Exercise 2.10.

2.12. Let A, B, C, D and E be as defined in Algorithm ODDEVENMERGE discussed in Section 2.11, and assume the elements in $A \cup B$ are distinct. Given a sequence X and an element x, recall that $\text{rank}(x, X)$ is the number of elements in X less than x. Express $\text{rank}(x, C)$ and $\text{rank}(x, D)$ in terms of $\text{rank}(x, A)$ and $\text{rank}(x, B)$.

Let $x \in A \cup B$. Then,

$$\text{rank}(x, C) = \left\lceil \frac{\text{rank}(x, A)}{2} \right\rceil + \left\lfloor \frac{\text{rank}(x, B)}{2} \right\rfloor,$$

and

$$\text{rank}(x, D) = \left\lfloor \frac{\text{rank}(x, A)}{2} \right\rfloor + \left\lceil \frac{\text{rank}(x, B)}{2} \right\rceil.$$

2.13. Use the result of Exercise 2.12 to show that for $c \in C$, either c is in its correct position in E or to the left of it.

For $x \in X$, let $\text{pos}(x, X)$ be the position of x in the sequence X, where $\text{pos}(x, X) \geq 0$. For $c \in C$, let $r_1 = \text{rank}(c, A)$ and $r_2 = \text{rank}(c, B)$, and $r_c = r_1 + r_2$. Either $c \in A$ or $c \in B$. If $c \in A$, then r_1 is even since $\text{pos}(c, A)$ is even, and it follows that the position of c in E is

$$\text{pos}(c, E) = 2\,\text{rank}(c, C) = 2\left\lceil \tfrac{r_1}{2} \right\rceil + 2\left\lfloor \tfrac{r_2}{2} \right\rfloor$$
$$\leq r_1 + (r_2) \text{ since } r_1 \text{ is even}$$
$$= r_c.$$

Since $r_c - 1 = r_1 + (r_2 - 1) \leq 2\left\lceil \tfrac{r_1}{2} \right\rceil + 2\left\lfloor \tfrac{r_2}{2} \right\rfloor = \text{pos}(c, E)$, we have

$$r_c - 1 \leq \text{pos}(c, E) \leq r_c. \tag{2.5}$$

Thus, either $\text{pos}(c, E) = r_c - 1$ or $\text{pos}(c, E) = r_c$. That is, either c is in its correct position in E or to the left of it.

On the other hand, if $c \in B$, then r_2 is odd since $\text{pos}(c, B)$ is odd, and we get the same inequalities.

2.14. Use the result of Exercise 2.12 to show that for $d \in D$, either d is in its correct position in E or to the right of it.

For $x \in X$, let $\text{pos}(x, X)$ be the position of x in the sequence X, where $\text{pos}(x, X) \geq 0$. For $d \in D$, let $r_3 = \text{rank}(d, A), r_4 = \text{rank}(d, B)$ and $r_d = r_3 + r_4$. If $d \in A$ then r_3 is odd since $\text{pos}(d, A)$ is odd. It follows that if $d \in A$, then the position of d in E is

$$\begin{aligned}
\text{pos}(d, E) = 2 \, \text{rank}(d, D) + 1 &= 2\left\lfloor \tfrac{r_3}{2} \right\rfloor + 2\left\lceil \tfrac{r_4}{2} \right\rceil + 1 \\
&\leq (r_3 - 1) + (r_4 + 1) + 1 \text{ since } r_3 \text{ is odd} \\
&= r_d + 1.
\end{aligned}$$

Since $r_d = (r_3 - 1) + (r_4) + 1 \leq 2\left\lfloor \tfrac{r_3}{2} \right\rfloor + 2\left\lceil \tfrac{r_4}{2} \right\rceil + 1 = \text{pos}(d, E)$, we have

$$r_d \leq \text{pos}(d, E) \leq r_d + 1. \tag{2.6}$$

Thus, either $\text{pos}(d, E) = r_d$ or $\text{pos}(d, E) = r_d + 1$. That is, either d is in its correct position in E or to the right of it.

If $d \in B$, then r_4 is even, and we get the same inequalities.

2.15. Illustrate the operation of the bitonic sort network shown in Fig. 2.21 on the input sequence $\langle 6, 7, 1, 4, 2, 5, 8, 3 \rangle$.

Similar to Fig. 2.21.

2.16. Give an example of a bitonic sequence with one local maximum and one local minimum.

The sequence $\langle 2, 1, 4, 3 \rangle$ is such an example.

2.17. In Algorithm PARSELECT for selection discussed in Section 2.14, show that in each iteration, the median of medians m is greater than and smaller than at most $3|A|/4$ elements.

Let $r = |A| / \log |A|$ be the number of groups, and $s = \log |A|$ be the size of each group. Let the groups be $g_1, g_2, \ldots, g_r$ with medians

$m_1, m_2, \ldots m_r$, where $m_i \leq m_{i+1}$, $1 \leq i \leq r-1$. Then, the median of medians $m \geq m_i$ for $1 \leq i \leq r/2$. Hence, m is greater than or equal to at least $\frac{s}{2}$ elements in groups $g_1, g_2, \ldots, g_{r/2}$. Thus, $m \geq$ at least $\frac{r}{2} \times \frac{s}{2} = \frac{|A|}{4}$ elements. It follows that $m \leq$ at most $\frac{3|A|}{4}$ elements. Similarly, $m \geq$ at most $\frac{3|A|}{4}$ elements.

2.18. Consider Algorithm PARMULTISELECT1 for multiselection discussed in Section 2.15. Compare the algorithm given with direct application of Algorithm PARSELECT given in Section 2.14.

Direct application of Algorithm PARSELECT r times takes

$$r \times O(\log n \log\log n) = O(r \log n \log\log n),$$

using $n/\log n$ processors. On the other hand, Algorithm PARMULTI-SELECT1 takes

$$O(\log r \log n \log\log n).$$

which is less than direct application for any r that is asymmetrically more than constant.

2.19. Repeat Exercise 2.18 with the second algorithm for multiselection for the PRAM, Algorithm PARMULTISELECT2.

Direct application of Algorithm PARSELECT r times takes

$$r \times O(\log n \log\log n) = O(r \log n \log\log n),$$

using $n/\log n$ processors. On the other hand, Algorithm PARMULTI-SELECT2 takes

$$O(\log n (\log r + \log\log n)).$$

which is less than direct application for any r that is asymmetrically more than constant.

2.20. Suggest an algorithm for sorting using multisession. What is the time complexity of your algorithm?

Use Algorithm PARMULTISELECT2 on the PRAM with $n/\log n$ processors. Setting $r = n$, its running time becomes

$$O(\log n(\log r + \log\log n)) = O(\log^2 n),$$

which is cost optimal.

2.21. Consider the algorithm for matrix multiplication discussed in Section 2.16. What is the cost of the algorithm? What modification should be done in order to make the total cost $O(n^3)$.

The cost is $\Theta(n^3 \log n)$. To make the total cost $O(n^3)$, reduce the number of processors to $O(n^3/\log n)$.

2.22. Let P be a simple polygon (that is not necessarily convex) with n vertices, and let x be a point. Assume that there are n processors, each assigned to one edge. Give an *efficient* parallel algorithm to decide whether x is in the interior of P. (*Hint:* Draw a horizontal line L such that x lies on L. Count how many times L intersects with the edges of P).

As suggested by the hint. Assign one edge of the polygon to each processor. Each processor stores a 1 if its assigned edge intersects the line L and 0 otherwise. Finally, perform the sum of these stored values and test whether it is even or odd. The total time is $\Theta(\log n)$.

2.23. Let $x_1, x_2, \ldots, x_n$ be n Boolean variables. Show how to find the logical OR of these variables in $O(1)$ time on the COMMON CRCW PRAM with n processors.

Let y hold the output. Initially, set $y = 0$. Each processor P_i executes the command: **if** $x_i = 1$ **then** $y = 1$. Then all processors P_j with $x_j = 1$ will write the same value. Hence, the output is $y = 1$ using the COMMON PRAM if and only if at least one x_i is 1.

2.24. Let $\langle x_1, x_2, \ldots, x_n \rangle$ be a sequence of n distinct numbers. Show how to find the maximum of these numbers in $O(1)$ time on the CRCW PRAM with n^2 processors.

Label the n^2 processors as $P_{i,j}$, $1 \leq i,j \leq n$. Let processors $P_{i,1}, P_{i,2}, \ldots, P_{i,n}$ define group i, $1 \leq i \leq n$. Then, group i will compute y_i, which is the OR of $x'_{i,1}, x'_{i,2}, \ldots, x'_{i,n}$, where $x'_{i,j} = (x_i < x_j)$, as shown in the solution of Exercise 2.23. Clearly, y_i is 0 if and only if x_i is the maximum. Each processor P_i executes the command: **if** $y_i = 0$ **then** output x_i. Only one processor will succeed and output its element. The reason concurrent writes are needed is the computation of the OR's.

2.25. Let $\langle x_1, x_2, \ldots, x_n \rangle$ be a sequence of n distinct numbers. Show how to find the maximum of these numbers in $O(\log \log n)$ time on the CRCW PRAM with n processors. *Hint*: Partition the input into $\sqrt{n}$ parts and recursively find the maximum in each part. Use Exercise 2.24.

Partition the input into $\sqrt{n}$ parts and recursively find the maximum in each part. Each part is assigned $\sqrt{n}$ processors to find the maximum recursively (number of elements equals number of processors). Let the maximums be $x'_1, x'_2, \ldots, x'_{\sqrt{n}}$. Use Exercise 2.24 to find the maximum of $x'_1, x'_2, \ldots, x'_{\sqrt{n}}$ using n processors in $O(1)$ time. The running time is given by the recurrence $T(n) = T(\sqrt{n}) + O(1)$ whose solution is $T(n) = O(\log \log n)$.

2.26. Let S be a sequence of n distinct numbers and $x \in S$. The rank of x in S is the number of elements in S less than x. Show how to compute the rank of x in S in $O(\log n)$ time on the CREW PRAM with n processors.

Let $S = \langle a_1, a_2, \ldots, a_n \rangle$. Compute $A[i] = (a_i < x)$ for $1 \leq i \leq n$. Let r be the sum of 1's in array A. Output r: r can be found by addition or parallel prefix in $O(\log n)$ time. The reason concurrent reads are required is so that all processors read x at the same time.

2.27. Let S be a sequence of n integers, and x an integer. Show how to compute $\text{rank}(x, S)$, the rank of x in S, in $O(\log n)$ time on the EREW PRAM using $O(n)$ operations.

To adapt the solution of Exercise 2.26 to the EREW PRAM, first broadcast x to all processors, say $B[i] = x$ for $1 \leq i \leq n$, then compute $(A[i] < B[i])$ for $1 \leq i \leq n$. To broadcast x, first P_1 copies $B[1] = x$ to $B[2]$. Next, P_1 and P_2 copy $B[1]$ and $B[2]$ to $B[3]$ and $B[4]$, respectively. Next, P_1, P_2, P_3 and P_4 copy $B[1], B[2], B[3]$ and $B[4]$ to $B[5], B[6], B[7]$ and $B[8]$, respectively, and so on. The number of writes is equal to $1 + 2 + 4 + \cdots + 2^k = 2n - 1$, where $k = \log n$. The number of comparisons $(A[i] < B[i])$ is n, which is equal to the number of assignments. Hence, the total number of operations is $\Theta(n)$.

2.28. Let $S = \{x_1, x_2, \ldots, x_n\}$ be n numbers and k an integer, $1 \leq k \leq n$. Show how to find the kth smallest element in S in $O(\log n)$ time on the CREW PRAM with n^2 processors.

Assume the x_i's are distinct. Label the n^2 processors as $P_{i,j}$, $1 \leq i, j \leq n$. Let processors $P_{i,1}, P_{i,2}, \ldots, P_{i,n}$ define group i, $1 \leq i \leq n$. For $i = 1, 2, \ldots, n$, we use Exercise 2.26 to find the rank of x_i in group i, and store it in $B[i]$, $1 \leq i \leq n$. Now, for $i = 1, 2, \ldots, n$, processor $P_{i,1}$ outputs x_i if its rank $B[i]$ is equal to $k - 1$. Note that exactly one processor will output the kth smallest element, so there are no concurrent writes. The running time is $O(\log n)$ and the fact that it runs on the CREW PRAM follows from Exercise 2.26.

2.29. Let $S = \langle x_1, x_2, \ldots, x_n \rangle$ be a sequence of n numbers. Consider the simple recursive algorithm for parallel prefix that divides the sequence S into two halves: $S_1 = \langle x_1, x_2, \ldots, x_{n/2} \rangle$ and $S_2 = \langle x_{n/2+1}, x_{n/2+2}, \ldots, x_n \rangle$, and then calls the algorithm recursively on each of S_1 and S_2.

(a) Write down the detailed algorithm.
(b) Will the algorithm work on the EREW PRAM?
(c) What is the total work done by the algorithm?
(d) Will Brent's Theorem (Theorem 2.1) help in reducing the number of processors without increasing the running time complexity?

(a) The algorithm is shown as Algorithm PARPREFIX2.
(b) The algorithm will not work on the EREW PRAM. There are concurrent reads of $s_{n/2}$.

Algorithm 2.27 PARPREFIX2
Input: $X = \langle x_1, x_2, \ldots, x_n \rangle$, a sequences of n numbers, where $n = 2^k$.
Output: $S = \langle s_1, s_2, \ldots, s_n \rangle$, the prefix sums of X.

1. **if** $n = 1$ **then return** x_1
2. **else do**
3. $X_1 = \langle x_1, x_2, \ldots, x_{n/2} \rangle$
4. $X_2 = \langle x_{n/2+1} x_{n/2+2}, \ldots, x_n \rangle$
5. $S_1 \leftarrow$ PARPREFIX2(X_1)
6. $S_2 \leftarrow$ PARPREFIX2(X_2)
7.   **for** $j \leftarrow (n/2 + 1)$ **to** n **do in parallel**
8. $s_j \leftarrow s_j + s_{n/2}$
9.   **end for**
10. **return** $S_1 \cup S_2$

    (c) The total number of operations (additions) done by the algorithm is given by the recurrence $W(n) = 2W(n/2) + n/2$, whose solution is $W(n) = \Theta(n \log n)$, which is the total work performed by the algorithm.

    (d) Brent's Theorem does not help in reducing the number of processors, since the total number of operations is $\Theta(n \log n)$.

2.30. Let $\langle x_1, x_2, \ldots, x_n \rangle$ be a sequence of n numbers. The *prefix minima* is to compute for each i, $1 \leq i \leq n$, the minimum among the elements $\{x_1, x_2, \ldots, x_i\}$. Develop an algorithm to compute the prefix minima that runs in time $O(\log n)$ on the EREW PRAM.

This is the parallel prefix problem using the associative binary operation MIN.

2.31. Do Exercise 2.30 using *suffix minima* instead, that is, compute for each i, $1 \leq i \leq n$, the minimum among the elements $\{x_i, x_{i+1}, \ldots, x_n\}$.

The algorithm is similar to Algorithm PARPREFIXREC. It is shown as Algorithm PSMINIMA.

2.32. Let $\langle x_1, x_2, \ldots, x_n \rangle$ be a sequence of n numbers. The *suffix computation problem* is to compute the suffixes $x_n, x_{n-1} \circ x_n, \ldots, x_1 \circ x_2 \circ \cdots \circ x_n$. Give an $O(\log n)$ time algorithm to solve this problem on the CREW PRAM with n processors.

Algorithm 2.28 PSMINIMA

Input: $X = \langle x_1, x_2, \ldots, x_n \rangle$, a sequences of n numbers, where $n = 2^k$.

Output: $S = \langle s_1, s_2, \ldots, s_n \rangle$, where $s_i = \min\{x_i, x_{i+1}, \ldots, x_n\}$ are the suffix minima.

1. $s_n \leftarrow x_n$
2. **if** $n = 1$ **then return** $S = \langle x_n \rangle$
3. **for** $i \leftarrow 1$ **to** $n/2$ **do in parallel**
4. $x_{2i-1} \leftarrow \min\{x_{2i-1}, x_{2i}\}$
5. **end for**
6. Recursively compute the prefix minima of $\langle x_1, x_3, \ldots, x_{n-1} \rangle$ and store them in $\langle s_1, s_3, \ldots, s_{n-1} \rangle$
7. **for** $i \leftarrow 1$ **to** $(n/2) - 1$ **do in parallel**
8. $s_{2i} \leftarrow \min\{x_{2i}, s_{2i+1}\}$
9. **end for**
10. **return** $S = \langle s_1, s_2, \ldots, s_n \rangle$

The algorithm is similar to Algorithm PARPREFIX2 in the solution of Exercise 2.29. It is shown as Algorithm PARSUFFIX.

Algorithm 2.29 PARSUFFIX

Input: $X = \langle x_1, x_2, \ldots, x_n \rangle$, a sequences of n numbers, where $n = 2^k$.

Output: $S = \langle s_1, s_2, \ldots, s_n \rangle$, where $s_i = x_i \circ x_{i+1} \circ \cdots \circ x_n$.

1. **if** $n = 1$ **then return** x_1
2. **else do**
3. $X_1 = \langle x_1, x_2, \ldots, x_{n/2} \rangle$
4. $X_2 = \langle x_{n/2+1} x_{n/2+2}, \ldots, x_n \rangle$
5. $S_1 \leftarrow$ PARSUFFIX(X_1)
6. $S_2 \leftarrow$ PARSUFFIX(X_2)
7.   **for** $j \leftarrow 1$ **to** $n/2$ **do in parallel**
8. $s_j \leftarrow s_j \circ s_{(n/2)+1}$
9.   **end for**
10. **return** $S_1 \cup S_2$

2.33. Do Exercise 2.32 for the case of EREW PRAM.

The algorithm is a generalization of Algorithm PSMINIMA in the solution of Exercise 2.31. Replace the MIN operator with $\circ$.

2.34. Let $T_1, T_2, \ldots, T_m$ be m directed and rooted binary trees on n vertices. Each node has a pointer to its parent, except the root which

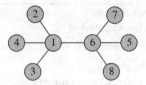

Fig. 2.36. A tree.

points to itself. Design a parallel algorithm to allow each vertex to know the identity of the tree to which it belongs. The trees are identified by their roots. The roots are numbered $1, 2, \ldots, m$.

Use pointer jumping to let each node point to its root. Then assign $root(s) \leftarrow succ(s)$ for all nodes s.

2.35. Compute the *next* and *succ* functions as describe in Table 2.1 (page 25) for all vertices in the tree shown in Fig. 2.36. Use the obtained values to derive an Euler tour.

Similar to Example 2.6.

2.36. Use the Euler tour technique to direct the tree shown in Fig. 2.36, where vertex 1 is to be set as the root.

Similar to Example 2.7.

2.37. Use the Euler tour technique to assign levels to the vertices in the tree shown in Fig. 2.36.

Similar to Example 2.8.

2.38. In a *postorder* traversal of a tree T at the root r, the subtrees of r are traversed from left to right in postorder followed by r. Develop an algorithm to determine the postorder numbering of the vertices in a rooted tree. What is the time complexity of your algorithm?

Construct an Euler tour τ. Then, τ visits each vertex v several times, and we only need to record the last visit, which happens when the edge $(v, p(v))$ is visited. The detailed algorithm is given as Algorithm TREEPOSTORDER.

The time complexity is dominated by computing the prefix sums, which is $\Theta(\log n)$ using $O(n)$ processors on the EREW PRAM.

Algorithm 2.30 TREEPOSTORDER

Input: A tree T on n vertices rooted at r.

Output: Assign postorder numbers to all vertices in T.

1. Find an Euler tour τ for the tree T.
2. Assign the weights $w(p(v), v) = 0$ and $w(v, p(v)) = 1$, $v \neq r$.
3. Apply parallel prefix on the set of edges of τ.
4. Set $postorder(v)$ to the prefix sum of the edge $(v, p(v))$.
5. Set $postorder(r)$ to n.

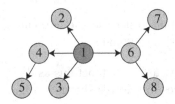

Fig. 2.37.   A rooted tree.

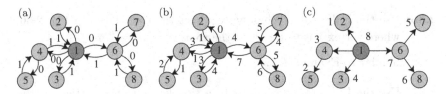

Fig. 2.38.   Postorder numbering of the vertices in a rooted tree.

2.39. Apply the algorithm developed in Exercise 2.38 on the tree shown in Fig. 2.37.

See Fig. 2.38. The edges in the tour are assigned 0 and 1 in Fig. 2.38(a). Parallel prefix is applied in Fig. 2.38(b), and the postorder numbers are shown in Fig. 2.38(c).

2.40. Parallelize Horner's rule to evaluate a polynomial of degree n under the EREW PRAM in time $O(\log n)$.

$$f(x) = a_0 + a_1 x + a_2 x^2 + \cdots + a_{n-1} x^{n-1}$$

$$= a_0 + x(a_1 + x(a_2 + x((\ldots x(a_{n-2} + a_{n-1} x) \ldots))))$$

$$= a_0 + x(a_1 + x(a_2 + x((\ldots x(a_{n/2-2} + a_{n/2-1}x)\ldots))))$$
$$+ x^{n/2}(a_{n/2} + x(a_{n/2+1} + x(a_{n/2+2} + x((\ldots x(a_{n-2}$$
$$+ a_{n-1}x)\ldots)))).$$

Thus, recursively compute the two halves, and multiply the right half by $x^{n/2}$, which is computed by doubling in each recursive call: $x \leftarrow x * x$.

2.41. Let $\langle x_1, x_2, \ldots, x_n \rangle$ be a sequence of n distinct numbers. Design a parallel algorithm for the CREW PRAM to sort this sequence in time $O(\log n)$. Assume an unlimited number of processors.

Use n groups of processors. Each group g_k, $1 \leq k \leq n$, consists of n^2 processors, and uses Exercise 2.28 to find the kth smallest element on the CREW PRAM.

2.42. Let n be a positive integer. Consider the problem of computing the polynomials $y_i = x^i$, for $1 \leq i \leq n$. Show how to compute the y_i's in $O(\log n)$ time.

Use parallel prefix.

2.43. Consider Algorithm PARQUICKSORT presented in Section 2.5.2. Suppose we always select the median as the pivot (see Section 2.14). What will be the running time of the algorithm?

We will use $n/\log n$ processors. The running time for finding the median is that for selection, which is $O(\log n \log \log n)$. Since there are $\log n$ levels, the overall running time is $O(\log^2 n \log \log n)$.

2.44. Let A and B be two sequences of distinct number sorted in ascending order, where $|A| = |B| = n$. Design an $O(1)$ time algorithm to merge A and B on the CREW PRAM. Assume an unlimited number of processors.

Let C be the array that will hold the merge of A and B. We will use n-ary search (parallel search using n processors for each element-search). Associate n processors with each element of A and B. Let $P_{i,1}, P_{i,2}, \ldots, P_{i,n}$ be the n processors associated with $A[i]$. Processor

$P_{i,j}$ tests whether $B[j] < A[i]$ and $B[j+1] > A[i]$. If this is the case, then $\text{rank}(A[i], B) = j$, and we set $C[i + j] = A[i]$. This is done for each element of A. We repeat the procedure for array B. The total number of processors needed is $2n^2$.

2.45. Apply Brent's theorem on Algorithm PARMERGE presented in Section 2.9.2.

The amount of work done by Algorithm PARMERGE is $O(n \log \log n)$, assuming $n = m$. Since the work is equal to the cost, Brent's theorem is of no help in reducing the cost by reducing the number of processors.

2.46. In Algorithm ODDEVENMERGE in Section 2.11, A_{even} is merged with B_{odd} and A_{odd} is merged with B_{even}. Rewrite the algorithm with the modification that it merges A_{odd} with B_{odd} and A_{even} with B_{even}. It is important to know that this will change the step of traversing the shuffle of C and D.

In this case, we traverse E starting from d_0. Thus, we compare d_0 with c_1, d_1 with c_2, and so on.

2.47. Let $G = (V, E)$ be an undirected graph with n vertices. Give an algorithm to decide whether G contains a triangle, that is, three mutually adjacent vertices. Assume that G is represented by its adjacency matrix. Your algorithm should run in $O(\log n)$ time on the CRCW PRAM with n^3 processors.

Let A be the $n \times n$ adjacency matrix. There is a triangle in G if and only if there is a 1 in the diagonal of A^3. Thus, to test for the presence of a triangle, compute A^3 in $\Theta(\log n)$ time, and test its diagonal for the occurrence of 1 by taking the OR of the diagonal elements in $O(1)$ time as explained in Exercise 2.23.

2.48. Prove Theorem 2.6.

Let T be a spanning tree, and let $\{V_1, V_2\}$ be a partition of the vertices. Let e be an edge connecting V_1 and V_2 in T. Suppose there is another edge e' connecting V_1 and V_2 in G such that $w(e') < w(e)$. Consider the tree T' obtained from T by replacing edge e by edge e', that is, $T' = T - \{e\} \cup \{e'\}$. Then, the total cost of T' is less than that of T.

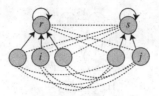

Fig. 2.39. Connections between two rooted stars. Some of the weights may be ∞.

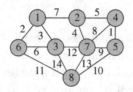

Fig. 2.40. An undirected graph.

2.49. Show that the reduced adjacency matrix in the minimum spanning tree algorithm of Section 2.18 can be constructed in time $O(\log n)$ using $O(n^2)$ processors on the CREW PRAM.

If r and s are the roots of two stars, then the (r, s) entry of the reduced matrix W' is computed as

$$W'(r, s) = \min\{W(i, j) \mid C(i) = r \quad \text{and} \quad C(j) = s\}.$$

See Fig. 2.39. Let n_1 and n_2 be the number of nodes in stars r and s, respectively. The edge of minimum weight can be determined in time $O(\log(n_1 + n_2)) = O(\log n)$ using $O(n_1 n_2)$ processors by computing n_1 minima using parallel prefix, and then computing the minimum of these minima. The total number of processors used is $\sum n_1 n_2$, which is less than or equal to the total number of edges = $O(n^2)$. Since all $W'(r, s)$'s can be computed in parallel, the construction of the matrix W' from W takes $O(\log n)$ time using $O(n^2)$ processors on the CREW PRAM.

2.50. Show the steps of computing a minimum spanning tree on the graph shown in Fig. 2.40.

Similar to Examples 2.15 and 2.16.

2.51. Show the steps of computing a minimum spanning tree on the graph shown in Fig. 2.41.

Similar to Examples 2.15 and 2.16.

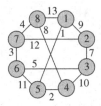

Fig. 2.41.   An undirected graph.

2.52. Let $G = (V, E)$ be an undirected graph. G is bipartite if and only
if V can be partitioned into two parts V_1 and V_2 such that every
edge connects a vertex in V_1 with a vertex in V_2. Equivalently, G is
bipartite if and only if it contains no odd-length cycles. Develop an
algorithm to test whether G is bipartite.

First, find a spanning tree T for G. Next, make T directed, and find
the level of each vertex. Let V_1 be the set of vertices at even levels,
and let V_2 be the set of vertices at odd levels. Test whether two
adjacent vertices (in G) are both in V_1 or in V_2. If there exists an
edge (u, v) in E such that u and v are both in V_1 or both in V_2,
then G is not bipartite.

2.53. Illustrate the operation of the bitonic sort network shown in Fig. 2.21
on the input $\langle 6, 7, 1, 4, 2, 5, 8, 3 \rangle$.

Similar to the example shown in the Fig. 2.21.

2.54. Let A, A', C and C' be sorted sequences such that C is a 3-cover
for A and C' is a 3-cover for A'. Is $C \cup C'$ necessarily a 3-cover for
$A \cup A'$? See Section 2.13 for the definition of 3-cover.

No, as evident from the following counterexample: Let $A = \langle 2, 5, 6, 7 \rangle$,
$A' = \langle 1, 3, 4, 8 \rangle$, $C = \langle 2, 7 \rangle$ and $C' = \langle 1, 8 \rangle$. Then, $C \cup C' = \langle 1, 2, 7, 8 \rangle$
and $A \cup A' = \langle 1, 2, 3, 4, 5, 6, 7, 8 \rangle$. There are 5 elements in $A \cup A'$
between 2 and 7.

2.55. Illustrate the operation of the pipelined mergesort algorithm on the
input $\langle 6, 7, 1, 4, 2, 5, 8, 3 \rangle$.

Similar to the example shown in Fig. 2.22.

2.56. Prove Observation 2.1.

Let $C = \langle c_1, c_2, \ldots \rangle$ and $D = \langle d_1, d_2, \ldots \rangle$. Let d_i and d_{i+1} be two adjacent elements in D, and assume that there are no elements in C between them. Let c_j be the element in C immediately before d_i, and c_{j+1} the element in C immediately following d_{i+1} (including $-\infty$ and $+\infty$). Since C is a 3-cover for A, there are at most three elements in A between c_i and c_{i+1}. It follows that there are at most three elements in A between d_i and d_{i+1}. The other case where there are elements in C between d_i and d_{i+1} is similar.

2.57. Let W, X and Y be three sorted sequences such that $Y = W \cup X$, and $W \cap X = \phi$. Assume that $R(S, S)$ is known for any sequence S, where $R(A, B)$ is the cross ranks of A in B as defined in Section 2.13. Show how to compute $R(W, X)$ and $R(X, W)$ in $O(1)$ time using $O(|Y|)$ processors.

For any $a \in X$, $r(a, X) = r(a, Y) - r(a, W)$, where $r(a, W)$ is the rank of a in W. This takes care of $R(W, X)$. Computing $R(X, W)$ is similar.

2.58. Parallelize the $\Theta(n)$ time sequential algorithm for selection using $n/\log n$ processors on the PRAM. Analyze your algorithm.

Each step of the sequential algorithm is done in parallel using the available processors. Dividing the inputs into groups of 5 elements will meaning unclear. Sorting the $\log n$-element groups takes $\Theta(\log n)$ sequential time (each group is assigned one processor). Computing A_1, A_2 and A_3 takes $\Theta(\log n)$ time using parallel prefix and packing as explained in the parallel quicksort algorithm in Section 2.5.2. The recursive calls take $T(n/\log n)$ and $T(3n/4)$. Hence the running time is given by the recurrence $T(n) \leq T(3n/4) + T(n/\log n) + \Theta(\log n)$, whose solution is $T(n) = O(\log^2 n)$.

2.59. Let $A = \langle a_1, a_2, \ldots, a_n \rangle$ be a sequence of numbers and let k be a given integer between 1 and n. Design and analyze a parallel algorithm to find all k smallest items in A. Do not use multiselection. What model of computation did you use?

Use Exercise 2.28 to find the kth smallest element on the CREW PRAM with n^2 processors and call it x. For $1 \leq i \leq n$, let $B[i] = 1$

if $a_i \leq x$ and $B[i] = 0$ otherwise. Now use parallel prefix and packing to move the k smallest elements to the beginning of A or to any other location. The model used is the CREW. To solve this problem more efficiently, use the parallel selection algorithm discussed in Section 2.14 on the EREW PRAM using $n/\log n$ processors only.

Chapter 3

The Hypercube

3.1 Introduction

The hypercube is one of the most popular, versatile and efficient topological structures of interconnection networks. It has many excellent features, and thus became the first choice of topological structure in parallel processing and computing systems. Let $d \geq 0$. The d-dimensional hypercube H_d has $n = 2^d$ nodes and $d2^{d-1}$ edges. Each node corresponds to a d-bit binary string, and two nodes are linked by an edge if and only if their binary strings differ in precisely one bit. Each node is incident to $d = \log n$ other nodes, one for each bit position. Figure 3.1 shows the d-dimensional hypercubes for $d = 1, 2, 3$.

An edge in the hypercube is called a *dimension k edge* if it links two nodes that differ in their kth bit position.

In the d-dimensional hypercube H_d, for any $k \leq d$, the removal of the dimension k edges leaves two disjoint copies of a $(d-1)$-dimensional hypercube. Conversely, a d-dimensional hypercube H_d can be constructed from two $(d-1)$-dimensional hypercubes H_{d-1} by simply connecting the ith node of one H_{d-1} to the ith node of the other H_{d-1}. Thus, a hypercube has a simple recursive structure. For example, see Fig. 3.2. The d-dimensional hypercube H_d has a diameter d, which is low, and a high bisection width of 2^{d-1}.

Let $G_1 = (V_1, E_1)$ and $G_2 = (V_2, E_2)$ be two undirected graphs. The *Cartesian product* of G_1 and G_2 is an undirected graph, denoted by $G_1 \times G_2$, where $V(G_1 \times G_2) = V_1 \times V_2$. There are two distinct vertices $x_1 x_2$ and

95

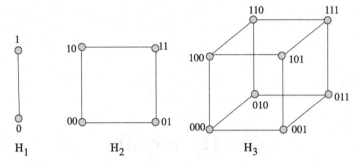

Fig. 3.1. d-dimensional hypercube for $d = 1, 2, 3$.

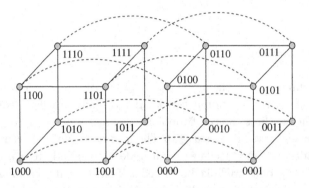

Fig. 3.2.   The construction of H_4 from two H_3's.

$y_1 y_2$, where $x_1, y_1 \in V(G_1)$ and $x_2, y_2 \in V(G_2)$, are linked by an edge in $G_1 \times G_2$ if and only if either $x_1 = y_1$ and $(x_2, y_2) \in E(G_2)$, or $x_2 = y_2$ and $(x_1, y_1) \in E(G_1)$. Examples of Cartesian products are shown in Figs. 3.1 and 3.2, where $H_2 = H_1 \times H_1$, $H_3 = H_2 \times H_1$ and $H_4 = H_3 \times H_1$. Let K_2 be the complete graph on two vertices. Then, H_d can be defined recursively as follows:

$$H_1 = K_2, \quad H_d = H_{d-1} \times H_1 = \underbrace{H_1 \times H_1 \times \cdots \times H_1}_{d}, \quad d \geq 2.$$

3.2   The Butterfly

The butterfly interconnection network is closely related to the hypercube. Th d-dimensional butterfly B_d consists of $n = (d+1)2^d$ processors and

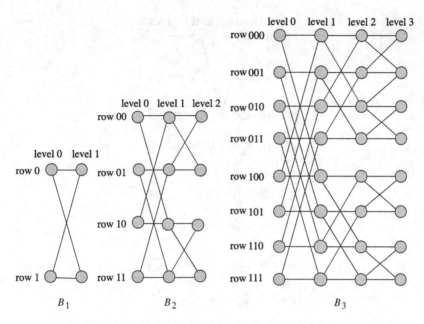

Fig. 3.3. d-dimensional butterfly for $d = 1, 2, 3$.

$d2^{d+1}$ links. Each processor in B_d is represented by the pair (u, i), where i is the *level* or *dimension* of the processor, $0 \le i \le d$, and u is a d-bit binary number that denotes the row of the processor. Two processors (u, i) and (v, j) are connected by a link if and only if $j = i + 1$ and either u and v are identical, or u and v differ in exactly the jth bit. Figure 3.3 shows the d-dimensional butterfly for $d = 1, 2, 3$. If u and v are identical, the link is said to be a *straight* link, otherwise it is called a *cross* link. Edges connecting processors on levels i and $i + 1$ are called *level $i + 1$* edges.

There are structural similarities between the hypercube and the butterfly. In particular, the ith node of H_d corresponds naturally to the ith row of B_d, and the ith dimension edge (u, v) of H_d corresponds to cross edges $((u, i - 1), (v, i))$ and $((v, i - 1), (u, i))$ in level i of B_d. We can obtain the hypercube H_d from the butterfly B_d by merging all nodes in the same row in B_d, and then removing the extra copy of each edge.

The butterfly has a simple recursive structure. Figure 3.4 shows a 3-dimensional butterfly with level 3 nodes removed. The result is two 2-dimensional butterflies, one consisting of even rows (solid edges), and

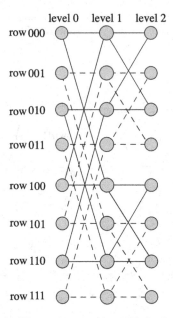

Fig. 3.4.   Recursive structure of the butterfly.

the other of odd rows (dashed edges). Alternatively, we could remove the
level 0 nodes of B_d to obtain two identical B_{d-1}'s.

A useful property of the d-dimensional butterfly is that the level 0 processor in any row u is linked to the level d processor in any row v by a
unique path of length d. The path traverses each level exactly once, using
the cross edge from level i to level $i + 1$ if and only if u and v differ in the
$(i + 1)$th bit. We will call this path the *greedy path*. Figure 3.5(a) shows
the greedy path from $(000, 0)$ to $(110, 3)$. It follows that the diameter of the
d-dimensional butterfly is $2d = \Theta(\log n)$. Figure 3.5(b) shows a 2^d-leaf complete binary tree contained within the d-dimensional butterfly. The leaves
of the tree are the level d nodes of the butterfly.

An algorithm that runs on the butterfly is called a *normal butterfly algorithm* if no two processors at different levels are active at the same time.
That is, at any given time, only processors in the same level are participating in the computation. A single step of a normal butterfly algorithm can
be simulated in one step of the hypercube.

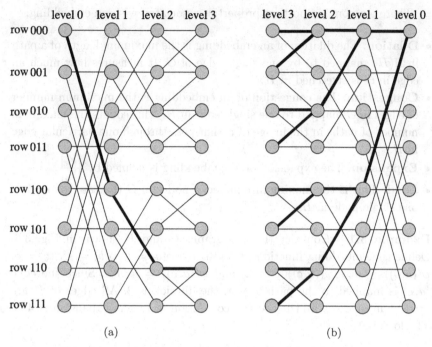

Fig. 3.5. (a) The greedy path from $(000, 0)$ to $(110, 3)$. (b) A complete binary tree contained within B_3.

3.3 Embeddings of the Hypercube

There is an ever-growing interest in the portability of algorithms developed for architectures based on other topologies, such as linear arrays, rings, two-dimensional meshes, and complete binary trees, into the hypercube. Let $G = (V_g, E_g)$ and $H = (V_h, E_h)$ be two undirected graphs, called the *guest* and *host* graphs, respectively. An *embedding* of G into H is defined by two mappings: $\phi : V_g \to V_h$ from the set of vertices of G to the set of vertices of H, and $\psi : E_g \to \Pi(H)$ from the set of edges of G to the set of paths in H. Note that a path may consist of one edge, so in some embeddings, the mapping is $\psi : E_g \to E_h$ in which edges in G are mapped to edges in H.

There are some important properties associated with an embedding:

- **Dilation.** The dilation of an embedding is the maximum length of a path in $\Pi(H)$ mapped to by one single edge of G. It measures how much an edge in G is stretched in H.
- **Congestion.** The congestion of an embedding is the maximum number of edges in G mapped to one single edge in H. This counts the maximum number of paths in the image of ψ that pass through one particular edge in H.
- **Expansion.** The expansion of an embedding is defined by $\frac{|V_h|}{|V_g|}$.
- **Load.** This is the maximum number of nodes in G that are mapped to one single node in H.

Example 3.1 Consider the two graphs G and H shown in Fig. 3.6. Define the embedding functions ϕ and ψ by: $\phi(a) = w, \phi(b) = x, \phi(c) = z$, $\psi((a,b)) = w, x, \psi((b,c)) = x, z$, and $\psi((a,c)) = w, y, z$. Since the edge (a,c) is mapped to the path w, y, z, the dilation is 2. All edges of H are used at most once, and hence the congestion is 1. The expansion is $4/3$. The load is 1.   □

3.3.1   *Gray codes*

A Gray code is an ordering of all possible d-bit binary sequences so that for all $k \geq 0$, k and $k + 1$ differ in exactly one bit. The sequence of 3-bit numbers corresponding to $0, 1, \ldots, 7$ is $000, 001, 011, 010, 110, 111, 101, 100$. The Gray code of d bits is denoted by G_d, which is defined recursively as

$$G_1 = \{0, 1\} \quad \text{and} \quad G_{k+1} = \{0G_k, 1G_k^R\},$$

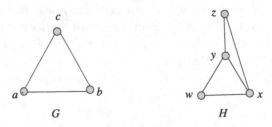

Fig. 3.6.   Example of graph embedding.

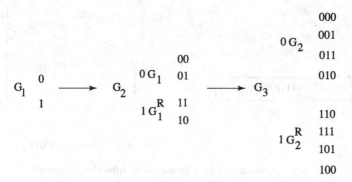

Fig. 3.7.   Construction of G_3.

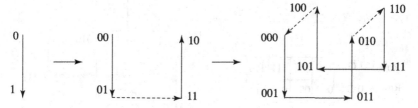

Fig. 3.8.   Pictorial illustration of the construction of G_3.

where $0G_k$ and $1G_k$ denote prefixing each element in the sequence G_k with 0 and 1, respectively, and G_k^R denotes G_k in reverse order. Thus, for example, to construct the sequence G_3, we do the following steps (see Fig. 3.7):

(1) Write down the sequence for G_1 columnwise, that is $\begin{smallmatrix} 0 \\ 1 \end{smallmatrix}$.
(2) Next, construct G_2 as $\begin{smallmatrix} 0G_1 \\ 1G_1^R \end{smallmatrix}$.
(3) Repeat step 2 to get G_3 as $\begin{smallmatrix} 0G_2 \\ 1G_2^R \end{smallmatrix}$.

Figure 3.8 shows the recursive construction of G_3 pictorially. Note that this is a Hamiltonian cycle in H_3.

3.3.2   *Embedding of a linear array into the hypercube*

The embedding of a linear array with $n = 2^d$ processors into H_d is straightforward (see Fig. 3.9). As we saw above, renumbering the hypercube processors using the Gray code induces a Hamiltonian cycle. Hence, a linear array or a ring with $n = 2^d$ processors can be embedded into H_d with dilation 1 and congestion 1.

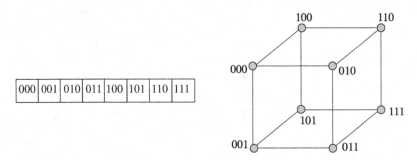

Fig. 3.9. Embedding of a linear array into the hypercube.

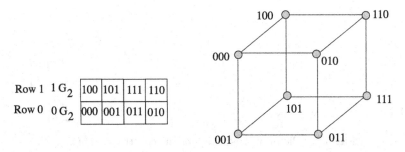

Fig. 3.10. Embedding of a mesh into the hypercube.

3.3.3   *Embedding of a mesh into the hypercube*

The linear array is really a 1-dimensional mesh. Although the word mesh usually refers to the 2-dimensional mesh, there are d-dimensional meshes in general with dimensions $r_1, r_2, \ldots, r_d$. A d-dimensional mesh is the cross product (Cartesian product) of d arrays. This is similar to the hypercube in which a d-dimensional hypercube is the cross product of d hypercubes of dimension 2. A 2-dimensional mesh can be embedded by extending the idea discussed above for the case of linear arrays to two dimensions. Let M be a mesh with 2^r rows and 2^c columns. We treat each row independently as a linear array. Next, we generate the numbers $0, 1, \ldots, 2^c - 1$ in Gray code and prefix each processor number in row j with the number j in Gray code. Figure 3.10 provides an example of embedding a mesh with $2^1 \times 2^2$ nodes into H_3. First, label each node in row 0 with the numbers

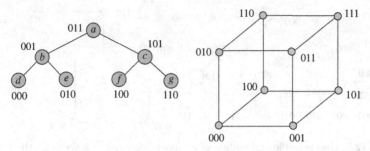

Fig. 3.11. An example of embedding of a binary tree with 7 nodes into the hypercube with 8 nodes.

$0, 1, 2, 3(00, 01, 11, 10)$ using G_2 code. Do the same for row 1. Finally, prefix each node label in rows 0 and 1 with 0 and 1, respectively.

3.3.4 *Embedding of a binary tree into the hypercube*

There are several embeddings of binary trees into hypercubes.

Example 3.2   Consider the embedding of a complete binary tree with 7 nodes into a hypercube with 8 nodes shown in Fig. 3.11. The embedding shown is inorder since the nodes of the binary tree are labeled inorder. Since the edge (a, c) is mapped to the path $011, 111, 101$, whose length is 2 (which is maximum) the dilation is 2. In fact, the dilation can be found from the binary labels on the tree by computing the Hamming distance between adjacent nodes in the binary tree. For instance, the Hamming distance between 001 and 010 in the tree is 2. All edges of the hypercube are used at most twice, and hence the congestion is 2. The expansion is $8/7$, and the load is 1. □

Theorem 3.1   It is impossible to embed a complete binary tree T with $n - 1$ nodes into a hypercube H with $n \geq 8$ nodes with dilation 1.

Proof.   Assume $n = 2^d$. Since T has $n - 1$ nodes, the number of leaves in T is $n/2$. Suppose for the sake of contradiction that a complete binary tree with $n - 1$ nodes is a subgraph of the d-dimensional hypercube H_d. A node in H_d has even parity if the number of ones in its binary string is even;

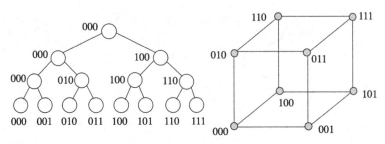

Fig. 3.12.   One possible embedding of a binary tree with n leaves into the hyper-cube with n nodes with dilation 1.

otherwise it has odd parity. It is easy to see that the number of nodes of even parity is $n/2$, and the number of nodes of odd parity is $n/2$. Assume without loss of generality that the hypercube node that contains the root of T has even parity. Since the neighbors of this node have odd parity, the children of the root of T are contained in odd parity hypercube nodes. Similarly, the grandchildren of the root of T are contained in even parity hypercube nodes, and so on. Hence, the leaves and their grandparents, which account for $n/2 + n/8 = 5n/8$ nodes, must all be contained in hypercube nodes of the same parity. This is impossible, as there are only $n/2$ nodes with the same parity in H_d. It follows that T is not a subgraph of H_d. □

It is possible, however, to embed a complete binary tree T with n leaves into a hypercube H with n nodes with dilation 1. Note that the tree has a total of $2n$-1 nodes. In this embedding, the ith leaf of the binary tree T is mapped to the ith node of the hypercube, and each internal node of T is mapped to the same hypercube node as its leftmost descendant leaf. See Fig. 3.12.

3.4   Broadcasting in the Hypercube

Broadcasting a datum x from processor P_0 to all other processors in the d-dimensional hypercube can be achieved as follows. In the first step, P_0 sends x to P_1. In step 2, P_0 and P_1 send in parallel x to P_2 and P_3. In step 3, P_0, P_1, P_2 and P_3 send in parallel x to P_4, P_5, P_6 and P_7. The formal algorithm is shown as Algorithm HCBROADCAST. The notation $j^{(i)}$ denotes j with the ith bit complemented, $0 \le i \le d - 1$. For example, $101^2 = 001$. The total number of steps in the algorithm is d.

Algorithm 3.1 HCBROADCAST
Input: x.
Output: Broadcast x from P_0 to all other processors.

1. **for** $i \leftarrow 0$ **to** $d - 1$ **do**
2.   **for all** $j < 2^i$ **and** $j < j^{(i)}$ **do in parallel**
3.   Processor P_j sends x to processor $P_{j^{(i)}}$
4.   **end for**
5. **end for**

3.5 Semigroup Operations

The hypercube is ideal for semigroup operations, e.g., addition and finding the maximum. Assume that n numbers are distributed, one per processor. Then, in order to compute a semigroup operation over this set of numbers, the technique of *reduction* is used as shown in Algorithm HCSUM for the case of the binary operation of addition. The notation $i^{(l)}$ means i with the lth bit complemented. After d steps, the final result will be known to processor P_0. The instruction $A[i] \leftarrow A[i] + A[i^{(l)}]$ involves two substeps; in the first substep, $A[i]$ is copied from processor P_i to processor $P_{i^{(l)}}$, and in the second substep, the addition operation is performed. Clearly, the number of parallel steps in the algorithm is $d = \Theta(\log n)$.

Algorithm 3.2 HCSUM
Input: A sequence of numbers $A[j], 0 \leq j \leq n - 1$, stored in $P_0, P_1, \ldots, P_{n-1}$.
      where $n = 2^d$.
Output: $\sum_{j=0}^{n-1} A[j]$ stored in P_0.

1. **for** $l \leftarrow d - 1$ **downto** 0 **do**
2.   **for all** $i, 0 \leq i \leq 2^l - 1$ **do in parallel**
3. $A[i] \leftarrow A[i] + A[i^{(l)}]$
4.   **end for**
5. **end for**

3.6 Permutation Routing on the Hypercube

Consider the problem of routing in the d-dimensional hypercube H_d with $n = 2^d$ processors. We consider this the problem of *permutation routing* in which every processor tries to send to a different destination. Processor i

wants to send a packet v_i to destination $\delta(i)$. We also assume *oblivious routing*, in which the route taken by packet v_i depends only on the destination $\delta(i)$, and not on any other packet's destination $\delta(j)$. A *collision* occurs when two packets arrive at the same processor at the same time, and try to leave along the same link. To deal with collisions, every processor has a queue and a prioritizing scheme for each incoming packet. If incoming packets try to leave along the same link, they are placed in a queue and then sent off in different time steps.

3.6.1 *The greedy algorithm*

A straightforward method for oblivious routing is called *bit fixing*, which works by taking the bit address of the source processor and changing one bit at a time to the address of the destination processor. Each time a bit is changed, the packet is forwarded to a neighboring processor. Clearly, bit fixing is an optimal routing scheme for a single packet. If the source i and destination j differ by k bits, then the packet must traverse at least k links in the hypercube to get to its destination. Bit fixing takes exactly k steps. However, the queue size can be as large as $O(\sqrt{n})$, as is evident from the following theorem.

Theorem 3.2   The maximum queue size of the greedy algorithm for permutation routing on the d-dimensional hypercube is $O(\sqrt{n})$.

Proof.   Notice that during bit fixing routing, an intermediate address is always of the form $z = y_1 \cdots y_k x_{k+1} \cdots x_d$, where x_i is a bit of the source address, and y_j is a bit of the destination address. If two packets collide, that means their destination addresses agree in their first k bits, and their source addresses agree in their last $d - k$ bits, where $1 \le k \le d$. There are 2^k packets with source addresses agreeing on $x_{k+1} \cdots x_d$, and 2^{d-k} packets with destination addresses agreeing on $y_1 \ldots y_k$ that may end up at processor P_z. Therefore, if we let S be the set of packets that collide at processor P_z, then $|S| \le \sum_{k=1}^{d} \min\{2^k, 2^{d-k}\}$, since k ranges between 1 and d. Assume without loss of generality that d is even. Then,

$$|S| \le \sum_{k=1}^{d} \min\{2^k, 2^{d-k}\}$$

$$= \sum_{k=1}^{d/2} 2^k + \sum_{k=d/2+1}^{d} 2^{d-k}$$

$$= \sum_{k=1}^{d/2} 2^k + \sum_{k=0}^{d/2-1} 2^k$$

$$= 3 \times 2^{d/2} - 3.$$

$$= O(2^{d/2})$$

$$= O(\sqrt{n}).$$

It follows that the maximum queue size is $O(\sqrt{n})$. $\qquad\square$

3.6.2 *The randomized algorithm*

If we have to route many packets, bit fixing can cause many collisions, as shown in Theorem 3.2. In fact, so can any deterministic oblivious routing strategy. We have the following theorem, which is quite general:

Theorem 3.3 Any deterministic oblivious permutation routing scheme for a parallel machine with n processors, each with d outward links requires $\Omega(\sqrt{n/d})$ steps.

Luckily, we can avoid this bad case by using a randomized routing scheme. In fact, most permutations cause very few collisions. So, the idea is to first route all the packets using a *random permutation*, and then from there to their final destination. That is,

(a) Phase 1. Choose a random permutation σ of $\{1, 2, \ldots, n\}$. Route packet v_i to destination $\sigma(i)$ using bit fixing.
(b) Phase 2. Route packet v_i from $\sigma(i)$ to destination $\delta(i)$ using bit fixing.

The following observation about bit fixing during one of the two phases above is important.

Observation 3.1 Two packets can come together along a route and then separate, but only once. That is, a pair of routes can look like Fig 3.13(a), but part (b) of the figure is impossible.

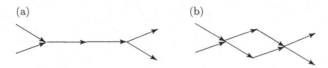

Fig. 3.13.   Packets collision.

To see this, notice that during bit fixing routing, an intermediate address is always of the form $y_1 \ldots y_k x_{k+1} \ldots x_d$, where x_i is a bit of the source address, and y_j is a bit of the destination address. If two routes collide at the kth step, that means their destination addresses agree in their first k bits, and the source addresses agree in their $d-k$ bits. At each time step, we add one more bit of the destination address, which means we increment k. Eventually, the destination bits must disagree since the destinations are different. Let k_0 be the value of k at which this happens. Then, the y_{k_0} destination bit is different for the two packets. At this point, the two packets separate, and they will never collide again, because all the later intermediate destinations will include the y_{k_0} bit. Observation 3.1 is the crux of the proof of the following theorem:

Theorem 3.4 Let S be the set of packets whose routes intersect v_i's route. Then, the delay of packet v_i is $\leq |S|$.

Notice that whenever the routes of two packets intersect, one of the packets may be delayed by one time step. Once that packet is delayed by one time step at the first shared node, it will flow along the shared route behind the other packet, and will not be delayed any more by that packet. If the same route intersects other routes, each of them may add a delay of one time step. This happens either because another packet collides with the current packet along a shared route, or because another packet collides with a packet that is ahead of the current packet along a part of the route which is shared by all three. In either case, an extra delay of at most one results.

To get the running time of this scheme, we compute the expected value of the size of the set S above. Define the indicator random variable $X_{i,j}$ which is 1 when the routes of packets v_i and v_j share at least one edge, and $X_{i,j}$ is 0 otherwise. Then, by the above theorem, the expected delay of packet v_i is the expected size of S, which is $\mathbf{E}\left[\sum_{j=1}^{n} X_{i,j}\right]$. It is rather difficult to get an estimate of this quantity. It is easier to think of $Y(e)$, which is the number of routes that pass through a given edge e. Now, suppose the route of packet v_i consists of the edges $(e_1, e_2, \ldots, e_k)$. Then, we have $\sum_{j=1}^{n} X_{i,j} \leq \sum_{l=1}^{k} Y(e_l)$. Hence,

$$\mathbf{E}\left[\sum_{j=1}^{n} X_{i,j}\right] \leq \mathbf{E}\left[\sum_{l=1}^{k} Y(e_l)\right].$$

To use this bound, we next compute $\mathbf{E}[Y(e)]$. Notice that

$\mathbf{E}[Y(e)] = $ (sum of lengths of all routes)/(total edges in the network).

The sum of lengths of all routes is the expected length of a route times n (the number of all routes). The average length of a route is $d/2$ because a d-bit source differs from a random destination address in $d/2$ bits on average. So, the sum of route lengths is $nd/2$. The total number of edges in the network is the number of nodes times the number of outbound links, which is nd. So, $\mathbf{E}[Y(e)] = (nd/2)/(nd) = 1/2$. Thus, if the path for packet v_i has k edges along it, then

$$\mu = \mathbf{E}\left[\sum_{j=1}^{n} X_{i,j}\right] \leq \mathbf{E}\left[\sum_{l=1}^{k} Y(e_l)\right] = \sum_{l=1}^{k} \mathbf{E}[Y(e_l)] = \frac{k}{2} \leq d \times \frac{1}{2} = \frac{d}{2}.$$

Now, we can apply Chernoff bound in Theorem A.3 to the probability of there being a substantial number of paths intersecting v_i's path. The Chernoff bound is

$$\mathbf{Pr}\left[\sum_{j=1}^{n} X_{i,j} > (1+\delta)\mu\right] < 2^{-\delta\mu}.$$

We now compute the probability that v_i is delayed at least $3d$ steps. So, we require that $(1+\delta)\mu = 3d$. Notice that we do not actually know what μ is, but we have a bound for it of $\mu \leq d/2$. It follows that $\mu\delta \geq 2.5d$. Thus, the probability that v_i is delayed by at least $3d$ steps is bounded above by $2^{-2.5d}$.

This is a bound for the probability that a given packet is delayed more than $3d$ steps. But we want to get a bound for the probability that no packet gets delayed more than $3d$ steps. For that it is enough to use Boole's inequality for probabilities as a bound:

Boole's inequality: For any finite sequence of events $\mathcal{E}_1, \mathcal{E}_2, \ldots, \mathcal{E}_n$,

$$\mathbf{Pr}[\mathcal{E}_1 \cup \mathcal{E}_2 \cup \cdots \cup \mathcal{E}_n] \leq \mathbf{Pr}[\mathcal{E}_1] + \mathbf{Pr}[\mathcal{E}_2] + \cdots + \mathbf{Pr}[\mathcal{E}_n]. \qquad (3.1)$$

There are $n = 2^d$ routes in total, and the probability that one of these takes more than $3d$ steps is bounded above by $2^d 2^{-2.5d} = 2^{-1.5d}$. So we can make the following assertion: With probability at least $1 - 2^{-1.5d}$ every packet reaches its destination $\sigma(i)$ in $4d$ or fewer steps. The $4d$ comes from the delay time $3d$ plus the time for bit fixing steps, which is $\leq d$. Notice that all of this applies to just one phase of the algorithm. So, the full algorithm(two phases) routes all packets to their destinations with high probability in $8d$ or fewer steps.

3.7 Permutation Routing on the Butterfly

Consider the problem of sending packets from level 0 to level d in the d-dimensional butterfly B_d. Processor $(i, 0)$ in level 0 wants to send a packet v_i to destination $(\delta(i), d)$ in level d. We consider the problem of *permutation routing* in which every processor in level 0 tries to send to a different destination in level d. That is, the function $\delta(i)$ is a permutation.

A simple process for routing a single packet obliviously is called bit fixing. For definitions of bit fixing, its lower bound, collision and oblivious routing, see Section 3.6. Next we discuss in detail a randomized routing scheme for the butterfly. This scheme consists of three phases.

(a) Phase 1. Choose a random permutation σ of $\{1, 2, \ldots, 2^d\}$. Route packet v_i to destination $(\sigma(i), d)$ using the greedy path.
(b) Phase 2. Route packet v_i from $(\sigma(i), d)$ to destination row but in level 0 $(\delta(i), 0)$ using the greedy path.
(c) Phase 3. Route packet v_i from $(\delta(i), 0)$ in level 0 to $(\delta(i), d)$ in level d through direct links.

In what follows, we analyze Phase 1; Phase 2 is the reverse of Phase 1, and Phase 3 takes d steps.

Let S be the set of packets whose routes intersect v_i's route. Define the indicator random variable $X_{i,j}$ which is 1 when the routes of packets v_i

and v_j share at least one edge, and $X_{i,j}$ is 0 otherwise. Then, by Theorem 3.4, the expected delay of packet v_i is the expected size of S, which is $\mathbf{E}\left[\sum_{j=1}^{2^d} X_{i,j}\right]$. It is rather difficult to get an estimate of this quantity. It is easier to think of $Y(e)$, which is the number of routes that pass through a given edge e. Now, suppose the route of packet v_i consists of the edges $(e_1, e_2, \ldots, e_d)$. Then, we have $\sum_{j=1}^{2^d} X_{i,j} \le \sum_{l=1}^{d} Y(e_l)$. Hence,

$$\mathbf{E}\left[\sum_{j=1}^{2^d} X_{i,j}\right] \le \mathbf{E}\left[\sum_{l=1}^{d} Y(e_l)\right].$$

To use this bound, we next compute $\mathbf{E}[Y(e_l)]$. Consider the link e_l at level l, which connects level $l-1$ node to level l node. The number of packets that can potentially go through e_l is 2^{l-1} since there are only 2^{l-1} processors at level 0 for which there are greedy paths through this link. In fact, if $e_l = ((u, l-1), (v, l))$, then u is the root of a complete binary tree with 2^{l-1} leaves in level 0. Now, we compute the probability that packet v_i will go through link e_l. Consider what happens to packet v_i in level 0, when it wants to move to level 1. There are two links to choose from to go to level 1, either the direct link or the cross link. Thus, it takes one of these two links with probability $1/2$. It follows that in order for packet v_i to go through link e_l, it has to go through l links with probability $(1/2)^l$. Clearly, $Y(e_l)$ has the binomial distribution with parameters 2^{l-1} and $(1/2)^l$ (see Section A.4.3). Hence, $\mathbf{E}[Y(e_l)] = 2^{l-1} \times (1/2)^l = 1/2$. Thus,

$$\mathbf{E}\left[\sum_{j=1}^{2^d} X_{i,j}\right] \le \mathbf{E}\left[\sum_{l=1}^{d} Y(e_l)\right] = \sum_{l=1}^{d} \mathbf{E}[Y(e_l)] = \frac{d}{2}.$$

Now, we can apply Chernoff bound in Theorem A.3 to the probability of there being a substantial number of paths intersecting v_i's path. The Chernoff bound is

$$\mathbf{Pr}\left[\sum_{j=1}^{2^d} X_{i,j} > (1+\delta)\mu\right] < 2^{-\delta\mu}.$$

We compute the probability that v_i is delayed at least $3d$ steps. So, we require that $(1+\delta)\mu = 3d$. Notice that we do not actually know what μ is, but we have a bound for it of $\mu \le d/2$. It follows that $\mu\delta \ge 2.5d$. Thus, the probability that v_i is delayed by at least $3d$ steps is bounded above by $2^{-2.5d}$.

This is a bound for the probability that a given packet is delayed more than $3d$ steps. But we want to get a bound for the probability that no packet gets delayed more than $3d$ steps. For that, it is enough to use Boole's inequality for probabilities as a bound (Eq. (3.1)): There are 2^d routes in total, and the probability that one of these takes more than $3d$ steps is bounded above by $2^d 2^{-2.5d} = 2^{-1.5d}$. So we can make the following assertion: With probability at least $1 - 2^{-1.5d}$, every packet v_i reaches its phase 1 destination $(\sigma(i), d)$ in $4d$ or fewer steps. The $4d$ comes from the delay time $3d$ plus the time for bit fixing steps, which is d. Notice that all of this applies to just one phase of the algorithm. So, the full algorithm(three phases) routes all packets to their destinations with high probability in $4d + 4d + d = 9d$ or fewer steps.

3.8   Computing Parallel Prefix on the Hypercube

The parallel prefix problem was defined in Section 2.5. In this section, we show how to compute it on the hypercube. Let H_d be a d-dimensional hypercube, where each processor P_i contains item x_i, $0 \le i \le n-1 = 2^d - 1$. Assume that each processor has two registers: s and z. The algorithm is shown as Algorithm HCPARPREFIX. The notation $j^{(i)}$ means j with the ith bit complemented, $0 \le i \le d - 1$, where $i = 0$ corresponds to the rightmost least significant binary digit. For example, $100^1 = 110$. s_j computes the sum $x_0 \circ x_2 \circ \cdots \circ x_j$, and z_j is a temporary variable. Initially, $s_i = z_i = x_i$, $0 \le i \le n - 1$.

Algorithm 3.3 HCPARPREFIX

Input: $X = \langle x_0, x_1, \ldots, x_{n-1} \rangle$, a sequences of n numbers, where $n = 2^d$.

Output: $S = \langle s_0, s_1, \ldots, s_{n-1} \rangle$, the prefix sums of X.

1. **for** $i \leftarrow 0$ **to** $d - 1$ **do**
2.   **for all** $j < j^{(i)}$ **do in parallel**
3. $z_{j^{(i)}} \leftarrow z_{j^{(i)}} \circ z_j$
4. $s_{j^{(i)}} \leftarrow s_{j^{(i)}} \circ z_j$
5. $z_j \leftarrow z_{j^{(i)}}$
6.   **end for**
7. **end for**

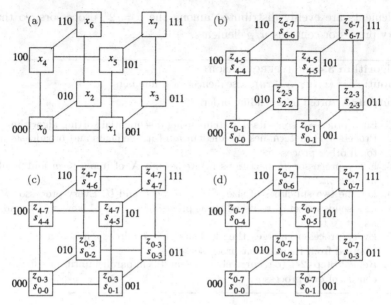

Fig. 3.14. Example of computing parallel prefix on the 3-dimensional hypercube.

Figure 3.14 illustrates the operation of the algorithm on the 3-dimensional hypercube. For clarity, the intermediate calculations have been shown with indices of the form s_{i-j}, which is equal to $x_i \circ x_{i+1} \circ \cdots \circ x_j$, $0 \le i \le j \le n-1$. The same thing applies to z_{i-j}. Figure 3.14(b) shows the contents of registers after the computations in the first iteration ($i = 0$). Parts (c) and (d) show the contents of registers after the computations in the second and third iterations ($i = 1$ and 2). There are $d = \log n$ iterations in the algorithm, each takes $\Theta(1)$ time. Hence, its running time is $\Theta(\log n)$.

3.9   Hyperquicksort

Quicksort is a very popular sorting algorithm. There have been numerous attempts to parallelize it for a variety of machines and models of computation; see Section 2.5.2 for an example. One attempt is hyperquicksort, which is targeted for the case of hypercubes with $p < n$, where n is the number of items and p is the number of processors. The algorithm is shown as Algorithm HCHYPERQUICKSORT. Initially, it is assumed that the

n elements are evenly distributed among the $p = 2^d$ processors, so that every processor contains n/p elements.

Algorithm 3.4 HCHYPERQUICKSORT

Input: $X = \langle x_1, x_2, \ldots, x_n \rangle$, a sequences of n numbers.

Output: X sorted in ascending order.

1. Each processor sorts its n/p items using a sequential sorting algorithm.
2. Processor P_0 determines the median m of its elements and broadcasts it to all other processors.
3. Every processor P_i partitions its items into X of items $\leq m$ and Y of items $> m$.
4. Let the two subcubes of size 2^{d-1} each be L and U. Every processor P_i in L sends its set Y to its adjacent processor P_j in U. Likewise, P_j sends its set X to P_i.
5. Every processor merges the elements that it already has with those it received from its adjacent processor.
6. Repeat Steps 2–5 to recursively sort L and U in parallel until the subcubes consist of one processor.

Clearly, Algorithm HCHYPERQUICKSORT sorts its input. What remains is to find its running time. Assume that the data is balanced, so that after Step 5 is executed, each processor has $\Theta(n/p)$ elements. In this case, the recursion depth is $O(\log p) = O(d)$. Step 1 takes $\Theta((n/p) \log(n/p))$ time. Determining the median in Step 2 takes $\Theta(1)$ time since the items in each processor are sorted. Broadcasting m takes $\Theta(d)$ time in one recursive call for a total of $d + (d - 1) + (d - 2) + \cdots = \frac{d(d+1)}{2} = \Theta(d^2)$ in all recursive calls. Step 3 takes $\Theta(n/p)$ time. Step 4 of data transmission takes $\Theta(n/p)$ time. By the end of this step, every element in L is $\leq$ every element in U. Step 5 of merging the two sets takes $\Theta(n/p)$ time.

It can be shown that if the data is initially distributed in a random fashion, the expected running time of the algorithm is

$$\Theta\left((n/p) \log(n/p) + d^2 + dn/p\right).$$

The $(n/p) \log(n/p)$ term represents the sorting step. The d^2 term represents broadcasting as stated above, and the dn/p term represents the time required for exchanging and merging sets of elements in all recursive calls. One disadvantage of the algorithm is that the elements may not be evenly distributed after the algorithm terminates.

3.10 Sample Sort

Sample sort is a generalization of quicksort, in which a sample of size s is selected, and the input is partitioned into $s + 1$ parts, where all elements in one part are less than all elements in the next part. Each part is then sorted separately. Let n be the number of elements, and p the number of processors, where $n \geq p^2$. Let $S = \{a_1, a_2, \ldots, a_n\}$ be the sequence of elements to be sorted, and assume they are distinct.

Parallel sample sort consists of the following steps: In the beginning, it is assumed that each processor has a list of $w = \frac{n}{p}$ items, which it sorts using a sequential sorting algorithm. Define a *regular sample* $X = X_0 \cup X_1 \cup \cdots X_{p-1}$ to be a set of $p(p-1)$ elements, where

$$X_j = \{a_{(w/p)+jw}, a_{(2w/p)+jw}, \ldots, a_{((p-1)w/p)+jw}\}, \quad 0 \leq j \leq p - 1.$$

In other words, from each of the p lists, $p - 1$ samples are chosen, evenly spaced throughout the list. Next, X is sorted using a sequential sorting algorithm. This can be achieved by letting each processor send its sample of $p - 1$ elements to processor P_0, which then sorts the whole sample of $p(p-1)$ elements (Exercise 3.9). Let this *ordered* sample be

$$b_1, b_2, \ldots, b_{p(p-1)}.$$

Next, choose

$$Y = b_{(p/2)}, b_{p+(p/2)}, \ldots, b_{(p-2)p+(p/2)}$$

as the $p - 1$ pivots for partitioning S, which we will refer to as

$$y_1, y_2, \ldots, y_{(p-1)}.$$

In other words, the $p(p-1)$ samples are sorted and $p - 1$ elements evenly spaced throughout the sorted list, are chosen to be the pivots.

The partitioning of S is accomplished as follows. Each processor finds where each of the $p - 1$ pivots divides its list using binary search, after which each of the p sorted lists of S have been divided into p sorted sublists with the property that every item in every list's ith sorted sublist is greater than any item in any list's $(i - 1)$th sorted sublist, for $2 \leq i \leq p$.

Finally, each processor P_i, $1 \leq i \leq p$, performs a p-way mergesort to merge all the ith sorted sublists of p lists. Note that, unlike in the first step, in which each processor sorts a contiguous block of items, each processor merges p sublists stored in p different areas. Because of the demarcations established before, their merges are completely independent of each other. The above description is summarized in Algorithm SAMPLESORT.

Algorithm 3.5 SAMPLESORT
Input: $S = \langle a_1, a_2, \ldots, a_n \rangle$, a sequences of n numbers.
Output: S sorted in ascending order.

1. Set $w \leftarrow \frac{n}{p}$.
2. Each processor sorts its list of size w.
3. Each processor chooses evenly spaced $p - 1$ samples from its list. Let X be the set of $p(p - 1)$ samples.
4. Sort X using a sequential sorting algorithm. Let this *ordered* sample be $b_1, b_2, \ldots, b_{p(p-1)}$.
5. Choose $Y = b_{(p/2)}, b_{p+(p/2)}, \ldots, b_{(p-2)p+(p/2)}$ as the $p - 1$ pivots.
6. Each processor P_i finds where each of the $p-1$ pivots divides its list using binary search, and divides its list into p sublists.
7. Each processor P_i, $1 \leq i \leq p$, performs a p-way mergesort to merge all the ith sorted sublists of p lists.

Example 3.3   Figure 3.15 provides an illustration of Algorithm SAMPLE-SORT for the case $n = 24$ and $p = 3$. The input is given in Fig. 3.15(a), which is divided into three parts, one part per processor. The set X of

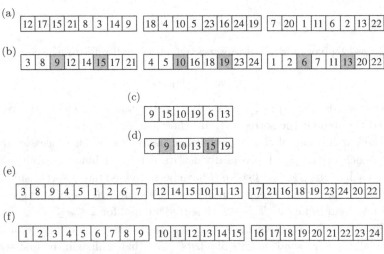

Fig. 3.15.   Illustration of Algorithm SAMPLESORT.

sample elements is shown as the shaded items in Fig. 3.15(b). These items are shown in Fig. 3.15(c). Sorting this sample and choosing $p - 1 = 2$ pivots is shown in Fig. 3.15(d). Figure 3.15(e) shows the contents of each processor after merging the sublists, and Fig. 3.15(f) shows the sorted items. $\square$

Theorem 3.5 In the last step of Algorithm SAMPLESORT, each processor merges less than or equal to $2w = \frac{2n}{p}$ elements.

Proof. Consider any processor P_i, $1 \leq i \leq p$. There are three cases.

Case 1: $i = 1$. All the items to be merged by processor P_1 must be $\leq y_1$. Since there are $p^2 - p - \frac{p}{2}$ samples which are $> y_1$, there are at least $(p^2 - p - \frac{p}{2})\frac{w}{p}$ elements of S which are $> y_1$. In other words, there are at most $n - (p^2 - p - \frac{p}{2})\frac{w}{p} = (p + \frac{p}{2})\frac{w}{p} < 2w$ elements of S which are $\leq y_1$.

Case 2: $i = p$. All the items to be merged by processor P_p must be $> y_{p-1}$. Since there are $(p-2)p + \frac{p}{2}$ samples which are $\leq y_{p-1}$, there are at least $(p^2 - 2p + \frac{p}{2})\frac{w}{p}$ elements of S which are $\leq y_{p-1}$. In other words, there are at most $n - (p^2 - 2p + \frac{p}{2})\frac{w}{p} = (2p - \frac{p}{2})\frac{w}{p} < 2w$ elements of S which are $> y_{p-1}$.

Case 3: $1 < i < p$. All the items to be merged by processor P_i must be $> y_{i-1}$ and $\leq y_i$. Since there are $(i - 2)p + \frac{p}{2}$ samples which are $\leq y_{i-1}$, there are at least $((i - 2)p + \frac{p}{2})\frac{w}{p}$ elements of S which are $\leq y_{i-1}$. On the other hand, there are $(p - i)p - \frac{p}{2}$ samples which are $> y_i$. Thus, there are at least $((p-i)p - \frac{p}{2})\frac{w}{p}$ elements of S which are $> y_i$. Combining these two inequalities, there are at most

$$n - \left((i - 2)p + \frac{p}{2}\right)\frac{w}{p} - \left((p - i)p - \frac{p}{2}\right)\frac{w}{p} = 2p\frac{w}{p} = 2w$$

elements of S for processor P_i to merge.

It follows that no processor merges more than $2w = \frac{2n}{p}$ elements in the last step of the algorithm. $\square$

Now, we analyze the running time of the algorithm. Step 2 of sequential sorting takes $\Theta(w \log w)$. Step 4 of sorting the sample takes $\Theta(p^2 \log p^2)$. In Step 5, each processor performs $p - 1$ binary searches in $O(p \log w)$ time. By Theorem 3.5, in the last step of merging the sublists, the size of data to be merged by any processor is less than or equal to $2w$, and hence the time needed by this step is $O(w \log p)$. Hence, the total running time is

$$T(n,p) = \Theta(w \log w + w \log p + p \log w + p^2 \log p^2) = \Theta(w \log w + p^2 \log p^2),$$

since $n \geq p^2$. When $n \geq p^3$, the running time becomes

$$T(n) = \Theta(w \log w) = \Theta\left(\frac{n}{p} \log \frac{n}{p}\right).$$

3.11   Selection on the Hypercube

Recall the problem of selection discussed in Section 2.14: Given a sequence $A = \langle a_1, a_2, \ldots, a_n \rangle$ of n elements and a positive integer $k, 1 \leq k \leq n$, find the kth smallest element in A. In this section, we develop an algorithm that runs on the hypercube with $p < n$ processors. The algorithm is shown as Algorithm HCSELECT.

Algorithm 3.6 HCSELECT

Input: A sequence $A = \langle a_1, \ldots, a_n \rangle$ of elements and an integer k, $1 \leq k \leq n$.

Output: The kth smallest element in A.

1. **if** $|A| \leq p$ **then** sort A and return the kth smallest element.
2. **for** $i \leftarrow 0$ to $p - 1$ **do in parallel**
3.   Processor P_i computes the median m_i of its local n/p elements using an optimal sequential algorithm for selection. Let the set of medians be M.
4. **end for**
5. Sort M and find its median m.
6. Broadcast m to all p processors.
7. Partition A into three sequences:
$A_1 = \{a \mid a < m\}$
$A_2 = \{a \mid a = m\}$
$A_3 = \{a \mid a > m\}$
8. **case**
9. $|A_1| \geq k$:
10.   Distribute A_1 evenly over all processors
11.   HCSELECT(A_1, k)
12. $|A_1| + |A_2| \geq k$: **return** m
13. $|A_1| + |A_2| < k$:
14.   Distribute A_3 evenly over all processors
15. $k \leftarrow k - |A_1| - |A_2|$
16.   HCSELECT(A_3, k)
17. **end case**

The time complexity of the algorithm can be computed as follows: Step 3 of the algorithm takes $O(n/p)$ time using an optimal sequential algorithm for selection. The sorting step in Line 4 takes $t_s(p,p)$ time, which is the time needed to sort p elements using p processors. Broadcasting m in Step 5 requires $O(\log p)$ time. Partitioning A into A_1, A_2 and A_3 can be done by first each processor splitting its data, and then computing the global sizes of A_1, A_2 and A_3. This takes $O(n/p + \log p)$ time using parallel prefix and compaction. The load balancing problem (see Section 3.13) is to redistribute data items stored in a hypercube such that the number of items in different processors differ by at most one after the redistribution. We use a load balancing algorithm that has a time complexity of $O(M + \log p)$ where M is the maximum number of items at any processor before the redistribution. Thus, data distribution in Steps 10 and 14 takes $O(n/p + \log p)$ time.

The median of medians m is smaller than (and greater than) at least $(|A|/2p)(p/2) = |A|/4$ elements. That is, it is greater than (and smaller than) at most $3|A|/4$ elements (Exercise 2.17). Hence, the recursive call takes at most $T(3n/4)$. This implies the following recurrence for the running time:

$$T(n,p) = \begin{cases} O(n) & \text{if } p = 1 \\ O(t_s(p,p)) & \text{if } p \geq n \\ T(3n/4,p) + O(n/p + t_s(p,p)) & \text{if } 1 < p < n. \end{cases}$$

The recursion depth is $\log n - \log p$, since the recursion ceases when n becomes less than p. The solution to this recurrence is

$$T(n,p) = O(n/p + t_s(p,p)(\log n - \log p)) = O(n/p + t_s(p,p)\log(n/p)).$$

If, for example, we let $p = n/\log n$ and use the $O(\log p \log \log p)$ time sorting algorithm, then the time complexity becomes

$$\begin{aligned} T(n, n/\log n) &= O(\log n + \log p \log \log p \log(\log n)) \\ &= O(\log n + \log n (\log \log n)^2) \\ &= O(\log n (\log \log n)^2). \end{aligned}$$

3.12 Multiselection on the Hypercube

Let $A = \langle a_1, a_2, \ldots, a_n \rangle$ be a sequence of n distinct elements drawn from a linearly ordered set, and let $K = \langle k_1, k_2, \ldots, k_r \rangle$ be a sequence of positive integers between 1 and n. The *multiselection* problem is to select the k_ith smallest element for all values of $i, 1 \leq i \leq r$. The hypercube structure is ideal for parallel execution of balanced divide-and-conquer algorithms. This leads to the following idea of the multiselection algorithm: First, use Algorithm HCSELECT to find the median m of A. Use m as a splitter to partition A into A_1 of items smaller than or equal to m, and A_2 of items larger than m. This induces a bipartition of B into two subsequences — B_1 of items less than $k = \lceil n/2 \rceil$, and B_2 of items greater than k. The algorithm is then recursively called in parallel with (A_1, B_1) and (A_2, B_2). Note that since the elements are distinct, $|A_1| = \lceil n/2 \rceil$ and $|A_2| = \lfloor n/2 \rfloor$. Following this idea, the algorithm is shown as Algorithm HCMULTISELECT. In $cube(s, d)$, s is the starting address of the cube and d is its dimension. Initially, the algorithm is called with HCMULTISELECT($A, B, cube(0, \log p)$).

In Step 13, A_1 is discarded, since $|B_1| = 0$. Similarly, in Step 16, A_2 is discarded, since $|B_2| = 0$. Let Q denote our hypercube with $p = 2^d$ processors. Q can be divided into two disjoint halves L and U, where L consists of processors with addresses $0x$, and U consists of processors with addresses $1x$. Now, we show how to move the elements in A_1 and A_2 to L and U, respectively, as stated in Steps 19 and 20. Every processor P in Q logically partitions its local set of data into two groups X and Y, where X contains those elements less than or equal to the median m, and Y contains those elements greater than m. This requires $O(n/p)$ sequential time. Now, each processor P_{0x} in L sends its set Y to its adjacent processor P_{1x} in U. Likewise, each processor P_{1x} in U sends its set X to its adjacent processor P_{0x} in L. Notice that when this step is complete, all elements less than or equal to m are in L, while all elements greater than m are in U. This step requires $O(n/p)$ time for the transmission of data. It is followed by load balancing (see Section 3.13). The load balancing problem is to redistribute data items stored in a hypercube such that the number of items in different processors differ by at most one after the redistribution. The load balancing algorithm that we will use has a time complexity of

---

Algorithm 3.7 HCMULTISELECT

Input: A sequence $A = \langle a_1, \ldots, a_n \rangle$ of elements and a sequence of positive integers $B = \langle k_1, k_2, \ldots, k_r \rangle$, $1 \leq k_i \leq n$. $cube(s, d)$, the starting address of the cube s and its dimension d.

Output: The k_ith smallest element in A, $1 \leq i \leq r$.

1. $p \leftarrow 2^d$.
2. **if** $p = 1$ **then** use a sequential multiselection algorithm and exit.
3. **else if** $|A| \leq p$ **then** sort A and return the k_ith smallest element, $1 \leq i \leq r$.
4. **else if** $|B| = 1$ **then** use Algorithm HCSELECT to find the k_1th smallest element.
5. **else do** Steps 6 to 24
6. Use Algorithm HCSELECT to find the median element m
7. Broadcast m to all p processors.
8. $k \leftarrow \lceil |A|/2 \rceil$.
9. Partition A into A_1 and A_2, where A_1 (resp. A_2) is the set of elements in A less than or equal to (resp. greater than) m.
10. Partition B into B_1 and B_2, where B_1 (resp. B_2) is the set of elements in B less than or equal to (resp. greater than) k. Subtract k from each item in B_2.
11. **case**
12. $|B_1| = 0$:
13.   Distribute A_2 evenly over all processors
14.   HCMULTISELECT(A_2, B_2, s, d)
15. $|B_2| = 0$:
16.   Distribute A_1 evenly over all processors
17.   HCMULTISELECT(A_1, B_1, s, d)
18. $|B_1| > 0$ and $|B_2| > 0$:
19.   Distribute A_1 evenly over all processors in $L = cube(, s)$ d-1
20.   Distribute A_2 evenly over all processors in $U = cube(, s + 2^{d-1})$ d-1
21.   **do in parallel**
22.   HCMULTISELECT$(A_1, B_1, cube(s, d - 1))$
23.   HCMULTISELECT$(A_2, B_2, cube(s + 2^{d-1}, d - 1))$
24. **end case**

$O(M + \log p)$ where M is the maximum number of items at any processor before the redistribution. Thus, it runs in time $O(n/p + \log p)$.

The time complexity of the algorithm can be computed as follows: finding the median m by Algorithm HCSELECT in Step 6 requires $O(n/p + t_s(p,p)\log(n/p))$ time, where $t_s(p,p)$ is the time needed to sort p elements using p processors. Partitioning A into A_1 and A_2 can be done by each processor splitting its data in time $O(n/p)$. Data redistribution takes $O(n/p + \log p)$ time. This implies the following recurrence for the running time:

$$T(n,r,p) \leq \begin{cases} O(n \log r) & \text{if } p = 1 \\ O(\frac{n}{p} + t_s(p,p)\log(\frac{n}{p})) & \text{if } r = 1 \\ O(t_s(p,p)) & \text{if } p \geq n \\ T(\frac{n}{2}, r-1, \frac{p}{2}) + O(\frac{n}{p} + t_s(p,p)\log(\frac{n}{p})) & \text{if } 1 < p,\, r < n. \end{cases}$$

In the worst case, the recursion depth is $\min\{r, \log p, \log n\} = \min\{r, \log p\}$ since $p < n$. It follows that the solution to this recurrence is

$$T(n,r,p) = O((n/p + t_s(p,p)\log(n/p)) \min\{r, \log p\}).$$

If we use the $O(\log p \log \log p)$ time sorting algorithm, then the time complexity becomes

$$T(n,r,p) = O((n/p + \log p \log \log p \log(n/p)) \min\{r, \log p\}).$$

If we let $p = n^{1-\epsilon}$ for $0 < \epsilon < 1$, then there is always a constant n_0 such that $n/p = n^\epsilon > \log p \log \log p \log(n/p)$ holds for all $n > n_0$. This shows that $T(n, r, n^{1-\epsilon}) = O(n^\epsilon \min\{r, \log n^{1-\epsilon}\})$.

3.13   Load Balancing on the Hypercube

The load balancing problem on the hypercube is to redistribute data items stored in a hypercube such that the number of items in different processors differ by at most one after the redistribution. In this section, we present a simple load balancing algorithm on the hypercube. Assume that it takes one time unit to move one item from one processor to a neighboring processor.

Thus, moving k units of load from one processor to a neighboring processor takes k units of time. Suppose we have a hypercube with $n = 2^d$ processors such that each processor P_i has L_i units of load. In the load balancing problem, it is requited to redistribute the load so that if L_i' is the load on processor P_i after the redistribution, then $|L_i' - L_j'| \leq 1$ for every pair of processors P_i and P_j. We are interested in balancing load as well as minimizing the load transfer time. The load can be balanced such that $|L_i' - L_j'| \leq 1$ for every pair of processors P_i and P_j by balancing across each of the d dimensions of the hypercube.

Now, we describe the algorithm in connection with the example shown in Fig. 3.16. Consider an eight-processor hypercube with the initial load distribution shown in Fig. 3.16(a). We consider the dimensions of the hypercube in the order $2, 1, 0$. When considering dimension 2, we ensure that the total loads of the two subhypercubes of size 4 differ by at most one. The total load in the subhypercube $\{P_0, P_1, P_2, P_3\}$ is 56, while that in the subhypercube $\{P_4, P_5, P_6, P_7\}$ is 48. After balancing across dimension 2, each of these subhypercubes will have a total load of 52. We use the embedding of a hypercube into a binary tree, as shown in Fig. 3.12. Thus, the processors will communicate using the binary tree of Fig. 3.16(b). Note that the tree levels are numbered 0, 1, 2, 3 such that the root is at level 0.

First, we perform an upward pass starting from level 2 (the level above the leaves) up to the root. During this pass, level 2 and level 1 nodes compute the total load in the leaves of the subtrees of which they are the root. This gives the numbers next to each node at levels 2 and 1. Now, at the root, we compute the load difference δ between the two subhypercubes of size 4. Since $\delta = 8$, 4 units of load have to be transferred from the hypercube $\{P_0, P_1, P_2, P_3\}$ to the hypercube $\{P_4, P_5, P_6, P_7\}$. To get the actual processor-to-processor load transfer, we make a pass down the tree as shown by the downward arrows in Fig. 3.16(b). P_0 on level 1 knows that its hypercube has to transfer 4 units of load to hypercube $\{P_4, P_5, P_6, P_7\}$. It attempts to do this by having each of its size-2 hypercubes transfer $4/2 = 2$ units. This is possible as one size-2 hypercube has 30 units and the other has 26. On level 2, P_0 has to allocate a 2-unit data transfer from $\{P_0, P_1\}$ and processor P_2 has to allocate a 2-unit transfer from $\{P_2, P_3\}$. This is accomplished by having each of the processors $\{P_0, P_1, P_2, P_3\}$ transfer 1

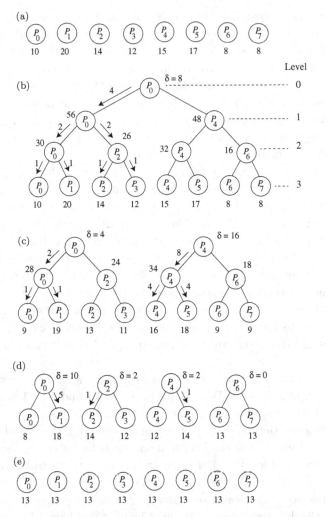

Fig. 3.16.   Load balancing algorithm on the 3-dimensional hypercube.

unit of load to their neighboring processors across dimension 2, i.e, processors P_0, P_1, P_2 and P_3 transfer 1 unit each to processors P_4, P_5, P_6 and P_7,
respectively. During the load allocation downward pass, we are repeatedly
in the situation shown in Fig. 3.17. Here, a and b are hypercube loads computed in the upward pass, w is the load to be allocated at this level by P_i,

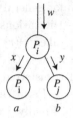

Fig. 3.17.   Load allocation downward pass.

Fig. 3.18.   The last iteration of the downward pass.

and $x + y = w$. From the nature of the downward pass, we have $w \leq a + b$. We would like to have $x \approx y$, i.e., $x = \lceil w/2 \rceil$ and $y = \lfloor w/2 \rfloor$. This is possible only if $a \geq \lceil w/2 \rceil$ and $b \geq \lfloor w/2 \rfloor$. In case $a < \lceil w/2 \rceil$, we set $x = a$, and $y = w - x$. In case $b < \lfloor w/2 \rfloor$, we set $y = b$, and $x = w - b$. In the last iteration of the downward pass, the situation is shown in Fig. 3.18. Here, a is the current load in processor P_i, and $w \leq a$. Processor P_i is to transfer w load units to its neighbor along the balancing dimension. Following this, the load in processor P_i is $a - w$.

Now, in our example, the numbers below the leaf nodes of Fig. 3.16(c) give the load in each processor following the dimension 2 balancing. Next, we balance across dimension 1. For this, pairs of hypercubes with two processors each are considered. The hypercubes $\{P_0, P_1\}$ and $\{P_2, P_3\}$ balance load as do the hypercubes $\{P_4, P_5\}$ and $\{P_6, P_7\}$. This is done in parallel. Figure 3.16(c) shows the two pass process. Processors P_0 and P_1 are to transfer one unit each to processors P_2 and P_3, respectively, and processors P_4 and P_5 are to transfer 4 units each to processors P_6 and P_7, respectively. The load in each processor after this load transfer is given below the leaves of Fig. 3.16(d). In the third and final load balancing iteration, load is balanced in pairs of processors that differ in bit 0. Figure 3.16(d) shows the computation. After the required load redistribution, each processor has 13 units of load (Fig. 3.16(e)).

The load balancing algorithm for general d is summarized in Algorithm HCLOADBALANCE. There are $d - 1$ iterations, and each upward and downward pass of a tree of height r takes $\Theta(r) = O(\log d)$ time. Hence, the overall running time of the algorithm is $O(d^2 + m)$. Here, $m = \sum_{i=0}^{d-1} m_i$, where m_i is the maximum load transferred between a pair of processors when balancing along dimension i. From the above discussion, it follows that $|L_i' - L_j'| \leq 1$ for all i and j. Finally, we note that the load balancing problem can be solved in time $O(\log p + M)$, where p is the number of processors and M is the maximum number of items at any processor before the distribution (see the bibliographic notes).

Algorithm 3.8 HCLOADBALANCE

Input: A d-dimensional hypercube with loads L_i, $0 \leq i \leq 2^d$.

Output: Perform load balancing on the hypercube.

1. **for** $r \leftarrow d - 1$ **downto** 0 **do**
2.   Perform an upward pass computing the sum of loads in the subtree leaves.
3.   Perform a downward pass to compute the load to be transferred.
4.   Transfer load.
5. **end for**

3.14   Computing Parallel Prefix on the Butterfly

The parallel prefix problem was defined in Section 2.5. In this section, we show how to compute this problem on the butterfly. For simplicity, we will assume addition as the binary operation. Recall from Section 3.2 that a complete binary tree with 2^d leaves corresponding to level 0 processors, and rooted at $(0, d)$ is a subgraph of the d-dimensional butterfly (see Fig. 3.5(b)). Assume that each processor has two registers: s and z. Register s at node v, denoted by $s(v)$, contains the sum of all items at the leaves of the subtree rooted at v, and $z(v)$ contains the sum of all items at the leaves of the subtree rooted at the left child of node v. Initially, the items $x_1, x_2, \ldots, x_n$ are input to the $n = 2^d$ processors at level 0 in registers z and s. The algorithm consists of two passes: Bottom-up and top-down. It is shown as Algorithm BFPARPREFIX.

Obtaining the running time is straightforward; it is $\Theta(d)$ in both the bottom-up phase and the top-down phase.

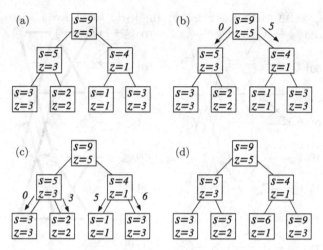

Fig. 3.19. Example of computing parallel prefix on the 2-dimensional butterfly.

Algorithm 3.9 BFPARPREFIX
Input: $X = \langle x_1, x_2, \ldots, x_n \rangle$, a sequences of n numbers, where $n = 2^d$.
Output: $S = \langle s_1, s_2, \ldots, s_n \rangle$, the prefix sums of X.

(a) Bottom-up phase. See Fig. 3.19(a). Each leaf node l sends its item $s(l)$ to its parent. Each internal node v upon receipt of two s-values $s(x)$ and $s(y)$ from its children x and y computes their sum and stores it in register $s(v)$. It also stores $s(x)$, the left child sum, in register $z(v)$.
(b) Top-down phase. See Figs. 3.19(b-d). Initially, the root sends 0 to its left child and z to its right child. Each node v upon receipt of value y from its parent does the following: If v is a leaf, it sets $s(v) = s(v) + y$; otherwise it sends y to its left child, and sends $y + z(v)$ to its right child. At the end, the s value at the ith leaf contains $s_i = x_1 + x_2 + \cdots + x_i$, $1 \leq i \leq n$.

3.15 Odd–Even Merging and Sorting on the Butterfly

In this section, we implement odd–even merging and sorting on the d-dimensional butterfly, where $n = 2^d$; odd–even merging and sorting on the PRAM were discussed in Section 2.11. Let $A = \langle a_0, a_1, \ldots, a_{n/2-1} \rangle$ and $B = \langle b_0, b_1, \ldots, b_{n/2-1} \rangle$ be two sorted sequences of $n/2$ elements each. Initially, A and B are input into level d of the d-dimensional butterfly, where

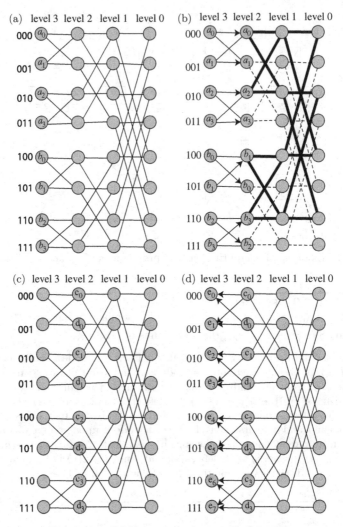

Fig. 3.20.   Odd–even merging on the butterfly.

the a_i's are input to the lower half, and the b_i's are input to the upper half (see Fig. 3.20(a)). The odd–even merging method is outlined in Algorithm BFODDEVENMERGE. It is important to note that the butterfly has a recursive structure; the even rows of the d-dimensional butterfly and the

---

Algorithm 3.10 BFODDEVENMERGE
Input: Two sorted sequences $A = \langle a_0, a_1, \ldots, a_{n/2-1} \rangle$ and
$B = \langle b_0, b_1, \ldots, b_{n/2-1} \rangle$ of $n/2$ elements each, where $n = 2^d$. A and B are stored in level d of the butterfly.
Output: The elements in $S = A \cup B$ in sorted order.

1. **if** $n = 2$ **then** merge the two elements and exit. e Move the a_i's to level $d-1$ along the straight edges and the b_i's to level $d-1$ along the cross edge as shown in Fig. 3.20(b). This is equivalent to partitioning the input into $A_{even}, A_{odd}, B_{even}$, and B_{odd}, and storing them in the $(d-1)$-dimensional butterflies.
2. Recursively merge A_{even} and B_{odd} to obtain $C = \langle c_0, c_1, \ldots, c_{n/2-1} \rangle$ using the even $(d-1)$-dimensional butterfly.
3. Recursively merge A_{odd} and B_{even} to obtain $D = \langle d_0, d_1, \ldots, d_{n/2-1} \rangle$ using the odd $(d-1)$-dimensional butterfly.
4. Let E' be the shuffle of C and D, that is,
   $E' = \langle c_0, d_0, c_1, d_1, \ldots, c_{n/2-1}, d_{n/2-1} \rangle$. Starting from c_0 in E', compare each c_i with the following d_i, and switch them if they are out of order to obtain the sorted sequence $E = \langle e_0, e_1, \ldots, e_{n-1} \rangle$.
5. **return** $S = E$.

---

odd rows contain a $(d-1)$-dimensional butterfly each (refer to Fig. 3.4). These two $(d-1)$-dimensional butterflies will henceforth be referred to as the even and odd butterflies. In Fig. 3.20(b), the even $(d-1)$-dimensional butterfly and the odd $(d-1)$-dimensional butterfly are shown with thick and dashed lines, respectively.

The first step in the algorithm is to move the a_i's to level $d-1$ along the straight edges and the b_i's to level $d-1$ along the cross edges in one step as shown in Fig. 3.20(b). This is equivalent to partitioning the input into $A_{even}, A_{odd}, B_{even}$, and B_{odd} and storing them in the $(d-1)$-dimensional butterflies. Next, the algorithm recursively merges A_{even} with B_{odd} to produce C, and recursively merges B_{even} with A_{odd} to produce D using the even and odd $(d-1)$-dimensional butterflies, respectively (see Figs. 3.20(b) and (c)). Here $C = \langle c_0, c_1, \ldots, c_{n/2-1} \rangle$ and $D = \langle d_0, d_1, \ldots, d_{n/2-1} \rangle$. Let E' be the shuffle of C and D, that is, $E' = \langle c_0, d_0, c_1, d_1, \ldots, c_{n/2-1}, d_{n/2-1} \rangle$ (see Fig. 3.20(c)). E' is scanned from left to right (in one step) for pairs that are out of order, which are ordered, if necessary. In other words, starting from c_0, compare each c_i with the following d_i, and switch them if they are out of order. This is accomplished by letting the even rows at level d compute $\min\{c_i, d_i\}$ and the odd rows at level d compute $\max\{c_i, d_i\}$. The result of the comparisons and exchanges, which is the sequence $E = \langle e_0, e_1, \ldots, e_{n-1} \rangle$ is then stored in level d of the d-dimensional butterfly as the desired sorted sequence (see Fig. 3.20(d)).

The analysis of the algorithm is straightforward. Step 1 takes $\Theta(1)$ time. Steps 2 and 3 take $T(n/2)$ time each. Step 4 takes $\Theta(1)$ time. Hence, the running time of the algorithm is governed by the recurrence $T(n) = T(n/2) + \Theta(1)$, whose solution is $T(n) = \Theta(\log n)$. The proof of correctness is given by Theorem 2.2 in Section 2.11.

Example 3.4   Consider merging the two sorted sequences $A = \langle 1, 3, 5, 8 \rangle$ and $B = \langle 2, 4, 6, 7 \rangle$ on the 3-dimensional butterfly shown in Fig. 3.21(a). The a_i's are first moved to level 2 along the straight edges and the b_i's are moved to level 2 along the cross edge as shown in Fig. 3.20(b). This is equivalent to partitioning the input into $A_{even}, A_{odd}, B_{even}$ and B_{odd} and storing them in the 2-dimensional butterflies. Thus, $A_{even} = \{1, 5\}$, $A_{odd} = \{3, 8\}$, $B_{even} = \{2, 6\}$ and $B_{odd} = \{4, 7\}$. A_{even} and B_{odd} are merged recursively as well as A_{odd} and B_{even} in the 2-dimensional butterflies, and the two sequences $C = \langle 1, 4, 5, 7 \rangle$ and $D = \langle 2, 3, 6, 8 \rangle$ are formed as shown in Figs. 3.21(b) and (c). Finally, the elements in each pair (c_i, d_i) in the sequence $E' = \langle 1, 2, 4, 3, 5, 6, 7, 8 \rangle$, which is the shuffle of C and D, are compared and exchanged if they are out of order as shown in Fig. 3.21(d). The pair (4, 3) is out of order, so 4 and 3 are interchanged. The sorted sequence is $E = \langle 1, 2, 3, 4, 5, 6, 7, 8 \rangle$ as shown in Fig. 3.21(d). $\square$

The algorithm for sorting is given as Algorithm BFODDEVENMERGE-SORT. It is similar to Algorithm ODDEVENMERGESORT for the PRAM in Section 2.11 Initially, the input sequence is input to level d of the butterfly.

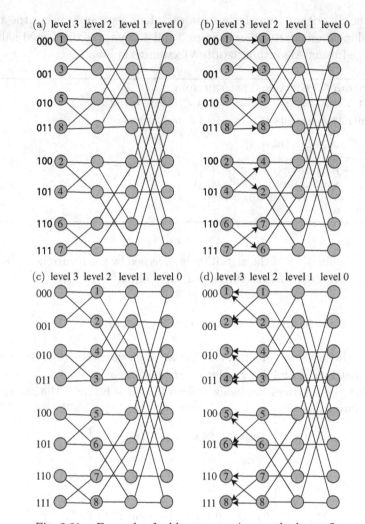

Fig. 3.21. Example of odd–even merging on the butterfly.

First, the algorithm recursively sorts each half separately using the two $(d-1)$-dimensional butterflies in Steps 3 and 4. Next, the two sorted halves are merged using Algorithm BFODDEVENMERGE in Step 5.

Algorithm 3.11 BFODDEVENMERGESORT
Input: A sequence $S = \langle a_0, a_1, \ldots, a_{n-1} \rangle$ where $n = 2^d$.
Output: The elements of S in sorted order.

1. $S_1 \leftarrow \langle a_0, a_1, \ldots, a_{n/2-1} \rangle$.
2. $S_2 \leftarrow \langle a_{n/2}, a_{n/2+1}, \ldots, a_{n-1} \rangle$.
3. $S_1' \leftarrow$ BFODDEVENMERGESORT(S_1)
4. $S_2' \leftarrow$ BFODDEVENMERGESORT(S_2)
5. $S \leftarrow$ BFODDEVENMERGE(S_1', S_2')
6. **return** S

The running time of the algorithm is governed by the recurrence $T(n) = T(n/2) + \Theta(\log n)$, whose solution is $T(n) = \Theta(\log^2 n)$.

3.16 Matrix Multiplication on the Hypercube

Consider the problem of matrix multiplication on the hypercube: Given two square matrices A and B of order $n \times n$, find their product $C = A \times B$. Note that the matrices are indexed from 0 to $n - 1$. Thus, the matrix A has the form:

$$A = \begin{bmatrix} a_{0,0} & a_{0,1} & \cdots & a_{0,n-1} \\ a_{1,0} & a_{1,1} & \cdots & a_{1,n-1} \\ \vdots & \vdots & & \vdots \\ a_{n-1,0} & a_{n-1,1} & \cdots & a_{n-1,n-1} \end{bmatrix}.$$

Assume that there are $n^3 = 2^{3r}$ processors $P_0, P_1, \ldots, P_{n^3-1}$. The processors will also be referred to by the triple (l, i, j), $0 \le l, i, j \le n - 1$. So, if the index of a processor has the binary representation $b_{3r-1}b_{3r-2}\ldots b_0$, then the binary representations of l, i and j are

$$b_{3r-1}b_{3r-2}\ldots b_{2r}, \quad b_{2r-1}b_{2r-2}\ldots b_r, \quad b_{r-1}b_{r-2}\ldots b_0,$$

respectively. In particular, if we fix any index l, i, or j, and vary the remaining indices over all its possible values, we obtain a subcube of dimension $2r$, and if we fix any pair of indices l, i, and j, and vary the remaining index over all its possible values, we obtain a subcube of dimension r.

Initially, the input elements of A and B are distributed over the n^2 processors $P(0, i, j)$, $0 \le i, j \le n - 1$, so that $A(0, i, j) = a_{i,j}$ and $B(0, i, j) = b_{i,j}$. There are three registers associated with every processor $P(l, i, j)$, namely $A(l, i, j), B(l, i, j)$ and $C(l, i, j)$. The desired final configuration is

$$C(0, i, j) = c_{i,j}, \quad 0 \le i, j \le n - 1,$$

where

$$c_{i,j} = \sum_{l=0}^{n-1} a_{i,l} b_{l,j}. \tag{3.2}$$

The algorithm computes the product matrix C by directly making use of (3.2). The algorithm has three phases. In the first phase, elements of A and B are redistributed over the n^3 processors so that we have $A(l, i, j) = a_{i,l}$ and $B(l, i, j) = b_{l,j}$. In the second phase, the products $C(l, i, j) = A(l, i, j) \times B(l, i, j) = a_{i,l} b_{l,j}$ are computed. Finally, in the third phase, the sums $\sum_{l=0}^{n-1} C_{l,i,j}$ are computed. An outline of the algorithm is shown as follows.

1. For $0 \leq l \leq n - 1$, set $A(l,i,j) \leftarrow A(0,i,j)$ and $B(l,i,j) \leftarrow B(0,i,j)$.
2. Set $A(l,i,j) \leftarrow A(l,i,l)$, $0 \leq j \leq n - 1$.
3. Set $B(l,i,j) \leftarrow B(l,l,j)$, $0 \leq i \leq n - 1$.
4. For each $0 \leq i,j \leq n - 1$, processor $P(l,i,j)$ computes the product $C(l,i,j) \leftarrow A(l,i,j) \times B(l,i,j)$.
5. For each $0 \leq i,j \leq n - 1$, processors $P(l,i,j)$, where $0 \leq l \leq n - 1$, compute the sum $C(0,i,j) = \sum_{l=0}^{n-1} C(l,i,j)$.

In Step 1, the contents of registers A and B in the processors of subcube $l = 0$ are broadcast to all other processors. In Step 2, a copy of the contents of register A of each processor in column l is sent to all processors in the same row, and in Step 3, a copy of the contents of register B of each processor in row l is sent to all processors in the same column. Thus, after Step 2 is completed, $A(l,i,j) = a_{i,l}$, and after Step 3 is completed, $B(l,i,j) = b_{l,j}$. Step 5 performs the sum $\sum_{l=0}^{n-1} C(l,i,j)$. This is a typical hypercube sum operation for each pair (i,j) applied on subcubes with processors $P(l,i,j)$, $0 \leq l \leq n - 1$ (see Algorithm HCSUM in Section 3.5).

Example 3.5 Consider multiplying the two 4×4 matrices on a hypercube with $n = 2^6 = 64$ processors, where

$$A = \begin{bmatrix} 1 & 2 & 3 & 4 \\ 5 & 6 & 7 & 8 \\ 9 & 10 & 11 & 12 \\ 13 & 14 & 15 & 16 \end{bmatrix} \quad \text{and} \quad B = \begin{bmatrix} -1 & -2 & -3 & -4 \\ -5 & -6 & -7 & -8 \\ -9 & -10 & -11 & -12 \\ -13 & -14 & -15 & -16 \end{bmatrix}.$$

Figure 3.22(a) shows the initial input stored in registers A and B (Only the first 16 processors are shown in the figure). Figure 3.22(b) shows the result of applying Step 2 of the algorithm's outline. As shown in the figure, the A registers in the first 16 processors contain the first column of matrix A, that is, $A(0,i,j) = a_{i,0}$. Figure 3.22(c) shows the result of applying Step 3 of the algorithm's outline. As shown in the figure, the B registers in the first 16 processors contain the first row of matrix A, that is, $B(0,i,j) = b_{0,j}$. □

The details of the algorithm are given as Algorithm HCMATRIXMULT. In the algorithm, $S(b_k = d)$ denotes the set of processor labels t, $0 \leq t \leq n^3 - 1$,

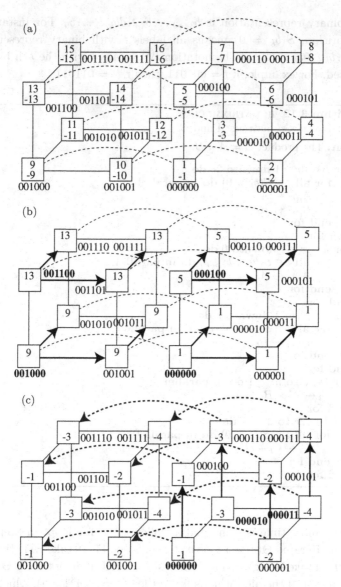

Fig. 3.22. Illustration of matrix multiplication on the hypercube.

whose binary representation is $b_{3r-1} \ldots b_{k+1} d b_{k-1} \ldots b_0$. For instance, in the algorithm, $S(b_k = 0)$ means all labels t with binary representation $b_{3r-1} \ldots b_{k+1} 0 b_{k-1} \ldots b_0$. The notation $t^{(k)}$ means t with the kth bit complemented. For example, if $t = 001011$, then $t^{(4)} = 011011$.

Algorithm 3.12 HCMATRIXMULT

Input: Two $n \times n$ matrices A and B.

Output: The product $C = A \times B$.

1. **for** $k \leftarrow 3r - 1$ **downto** $2r$ **do**
2.   **for all** $t \in S(b_k = 0)$ **do in parallel**
3. $A_{t^{(k)}} \leftarrow A_t$
4. $B_{t^{(k)}} \leftarrow B_t$
5.   **end for**
6. **end for**
7. **for** $k \leftarrow r - 1$ **downto** 0 **do**
8.   **for all** $t \in S(b_k = b_{2r+k})$ **do in parallel**
9. $A_{t^{(k)}} \leftarrow A_t$
10.   **end for**
11. **end for**
12. **for** $k \leftarrow 2r - 1$ **downto** r **do**
13.   **for all** $t \in S(b_k = b_{r+k})$ **do in parallel**
14. $B_{t^{(k)}} \leftarrow B_t$
15.   **end for**
16. **end for**
17. **for** $t \leftarrow 0$ **to** $n^3 - 1$ **do in parallel**
18. $C_t \leftarrow A_t \times B_t$
19. **end for**
20. **for** $k \leftarrow 2r$ **to** $3r - 1$ **do**
21.   **for all** $t \in S(b_k = 0)$ **do in parallel**
22. $C_t \leftarrow C_t + C_{t^{(k)}}$
23.   **end for**
24. **end for**

The running time is computed as follows: the **for** loops in Steps 1, 7, and 12 are iterated $\Theta(r) = \Theta(\log n)$ times. Steps 17–19 take $\Theta(1)$ time, and Steps 20–24 take $\Theta(\log n)$ time. Hence, the overall running time is $\Theta(\log n)$. The total cost of the algorithm is $n^3 \times \Theta(\log n) = \Theta(n^3 \log n)$, which is not optimal.

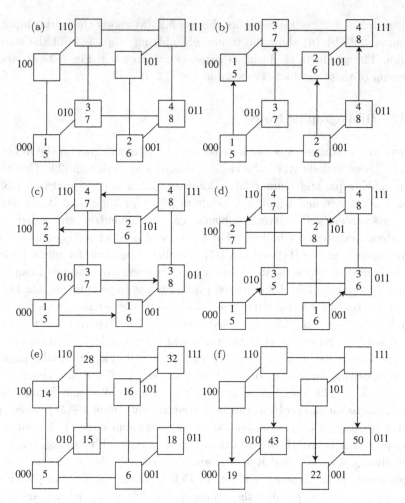

Fig. 3.23. Example of matrix multiplication on the hypercube.

Example 3.6 Figure 3.23 shows an example of running Algorithm HCMA-TRIXMULT on the two matrices

$$A = \begin{bmatrix} 1 & 2 \\ 3 & 4 \end{bmatrix} \quad \text{and} \quad B = \begin{bmatrix} 5 & 6 \\ 7 & 8 \end{bmatrix}.$$

There are $n = 2^3 = 8$ processors. Figure 3.23(a) shows the initial input. Figures. 3.23(b)–(d) show the results of applying Steps 1–14 of the algorithm. The products of A and B registers are shown in Fig. 3.23(e), and the sum of these products is shown in Fig. 3.23(f).   □

3.17 Bibliographic Notes

There are a number of books that cover parallel algorithms on the hypercube. These include Akl [4], Akl [5], Cosnard and Trystram [29], Grama, Gupta, Karypis and Kumar [39], Horowitz, Sahni and Rajasekaran [43], Lakshmivarahan and Dhall [52], Leighton [57], and Miller and Boxer [66]. An assortment of matrix problems can be found/is embedded in Lakshmivarahan and Dhall [52]. For a survey of parallel sorting and selection algorithms, see Rajasekaran [75]. Parallel algorithms for many problems, including problems in computational geometry on the mesh can be found in Leighton [57]. Randomized routing in the hypercube and the butterfly are based on Valiant[100] and Valiant and Brebner[101]. Selection on the hypercube is from Chandran and Rosenfeld [20]. Hyperquicksort is due to Wagar[93]. Sample sort is from Shi and Schaeffer [86]. Multiselection on the hypercube is from Shen [83] and Shen [84]. The $O(\log n \log \log n)$ time algorithm for sorting on the hypercube can be found in Cypher and Plaxton [30]. The load balancing algorithm is from Woo and Sahni [99]. The load balancing problem can be solved in time $O(\log p + M)$, where p is the number of processors and M is the maximum number of items at any processor before the distribution. For more on load balancing, see Jan and Huang [45], JáJá and Ryu [46], and Plaxton [74]. Parallel matrix multiplication on the hypercube is due to Dekel, Nassimi and Sahni [33]. For more references on parallel algorithms on the hypercube interconnection network, see for instance Leighton [57].

3.18 Exercises

3.1. Give an $O(d)$ time algorithm for broadcasting in the d-dimensional hypercube H_d if the origin of the message is an arbitrary processor.

3.2. Design a recursive algorithm to compute the sum of n numbers on the hypercube with $n = 2^d$ processors. What is the time complexity of your algorithm?

3.3. Design a recursive algorithm to compute the prefix sums of n numbers on the hypercube with $n = 2^d$ processors. What is the time complexity of your algorithm?

3.4. Describe how to implement the odd–even merge sort on a hypercube of dimension d.

3.5. Design an algorithm to rearrange a sequence of n numbers distributed one number per processor in a d-dimensional hypercube, where $n = 2^d$, so that all numbers smaller than or equal to the average precede all numbers greater than the average. Your algorithm should run in $\Theta(\log n)$ time.

3.6. Explain how to compute the prefix sums of n numbers on a hypercube with p processors, where $p < n$. What is the running time of your algorithm?

3.7. Explain how to run the algorithm for quicksort designed for the PRAM and discussed in Section 2.5.2 on the hypercube with n processors.

3.8. Illustrate the operation of Algorithm SAMPLESORT discussed in Section 3.10 on the input

$$18, 12, 23, 14, 15, 16, 7, 21, 20, 19, 11, 2, 24, 14, 5, 6, 17, 1,$$

where $n = 18$ and $p = 3$.

3.9. In Algorithm SAMPLESORT discussed in Section 3.10, each processor sends its sample of $(p - 1)$ elements to P_0, which in turn collects a sample of $p(p-1)$ elements. Explain how this data transmission can be achieved, and analyze its cost.

3.10. A sorting method known as BUCKETSORT works as follows. Let S be a sequence of n numbers within a reasonable range, say all numbers are between 1 and m, where m is not too large compared to n. The numbers are distributed into k buckets, with the first bucket containing those numbers between 1 and $\lfloor m/k \rfloor$, the second bucket containing those numbers between $\lfloor m/k \rfloor + 1$ to $\lfloor 2m/k \rfloor$, and so on.

The numbers in each bucket are then sorted using an optimal sorting algorithm. Show how to parallelize the algorithm.

3.11. Analyze the running time of Algorithm BUCKETSORT in the solution to Exercise 3.10.

3.12. Consider the algorithm for permutation routing in the hypercube discussed in Section 3.6. What is the probability that the algorithm will route all packets to their destinations in $8d$ steps or fewer?

3.13. Consider Algorithm HCSELECT for selection on the hypercube discussed in Section 3.11. For what values of p is the algorithm optimal?

3.14. Consider Algorithm PARSELECT for selection on the EREW PRAM presented in Section 2.14. Suppose we simulate this algorithm to run on the hypercube with $n/\log n$ processors. What will be the running time of the algorithm? Compare this with that of Algorithm HCSELECT for selection on the hypercube presented in Section 3.11. (See Exercise 3.21).

3.15. Outline an algorithm to find all the kth largest elements in a hypercube with $p < n$ processors. What is the running time of your algorithm?

3.16. Consider Algorithm HCMULTISELECT for multiselection on the hypercube discussed in Section 3.12. For what values of r is the algorithm cost optimal when the number of processors is $n^{1-\epsilon}$?

3.17. Consider Algorithm HCMULTISELECT for multiselection on the hypercube discussed in Section 3.12. Compare the algorithm given with direct application of Algorithm HCSELECT given in Section 3.11.

3.18. Construct the Gray code sequence G_4.

3.19. Consider the two graphs shown in Fig. 3.24. Find an embedding of G into H. What are the dilation, congestion, expansion and load of your embedding?

3.20. Give an embedding similar to the one given in Example 3.2, except that it is postorder, that is, the nodes of the binary tree are labeled

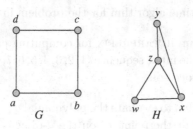

Fig. 3.24. Exercise 3.19.

in postorder traversal. What are the dilation, congestion, expansion and load of the embedding?

3.21. Explain how to simulate an EREW PRAM on a hypercube with n processors.

3.22. Compute the bisection width of the d-dimensional butterfly B_d.

3.23. Design an algorithm to compute the sum of n numbers on the hypercube with p processors, $1 \le p < n$. Is your algorithm always optimal?

3.24. Explain how to compute the maximum of 2^{d-1} numbers distributed arbitrarily in a hypercube with 2^d processors. What is the running time of your algorithm?

3.25. Consider the partial permutation routing problem on the hypercube in which every processor is the source of at most one packet and the destination of at most one packet. Will Theorem 3.2 hold for this routing problem?

3.26. Consider the many-to-many routing problem on the hypercube in which every processor is the source of r packets and the destination of r packets. Suppose we run the greedy algorithm for routing on the hypercube to solve this problem. What will be the maximum queue size?

3.27. Give an $O(nd)$ time algorithm for the problem of routing in the d-dimensional hypercube if every processor has a packet to be sent to every other processor, where $n = 2^d$. *Hint*: Use randomized routing n times.

3.28. Give an $O(n)$ time algorithm for the problem in Exercise 3.27.

3.29. Apply Algorithm HCPARPREFIX for computing parallel prefix on the hypercube on the input sequence $\langle 1, 2, 3, 4, 5, 6, 7, 8 \rangle$. Assume a hypercube with 8 processors.

3.30. Give an algorithm to evaluate the polynomial $a_{n-1}x^{n-1} + a_{n-2}x^{n-2} + \cdots + a_1 x + a_0$ at the point x_0 on the d-dimensional hypercube H_d with $n = 2^d$ processors. Assume that each a_i is stored in processor P_i, $0 \leq i \leq n - 1$.

3.31. Consider a hypercube with four processors $\{P_0, P_1, P_2, P_3\}$ with initial loads $8, 2, 6, 4$. Perform load balancing on the hypercube so that, at the end, each processor has the same load.

3.32. Redo Exercise 3.31 using the algorithm presented in Section 3.13.

3.33. Consider a hypercube with eight processors $\{P_0, P_1, \ldots, P_7\}$ with initial loads $8, 5, 6, 4, 7, 2, 5, 3$. Perform load balancing on the hypercube using the algorithm described in Section 3.13 so that, at the end, each processor has approximately the same load.

3.34. Suggest a heuristic to improve the performance of the load balancing algorithm discussed in Section 3.13.

3.35. Illustrate the operation of Algorithm BFODDEVENMERGE for merging on the butterfly to merge the two sorted sequences $A = \langle 1, 4, 6, 9 \rangle$ and $B = \langle 2, 5, 7, 8 \rangle$ on the 3-dimensional butterfly.

3.36. Use the matrix multiplication algorithm on the hypercube discussed in Section 3.16 to compute the product $C = A \times B$ of the two 2×2 matrices A and B shown below. Assume a hypercube with $n = 2^3 = 8$ processors.

$$A = \begin{bmatrix} 1 & 3 \\ 2 & 4 \end{bmatrix} \quad \text{and} \quad B = \begin{bmatrix} 2 & 1 \\ 4 & 3 \end{bmatrix}.$$

3.37. Suggest an algorithm for computing the transitive closure of an adjacency matrix A on the hypercube. What is the running time of the algorithm?

3.38. Suggest an algorithm for computing the shortest paths in a directed graph G represented by its adjacency matrix A on the hypercube. What is the running time of the algorithm?

3.39. Let $S = \langle x_0, x_1, \ldots, x_{n-1} \rangle$ be a sequence of numbers stored in a hypercube with n processors where x_i is stored in P_i, $0 \leq i < n$, and let y be stored in P_0. Give an algorithm to count the number of elements in S that are larger than y.

3.40. Following the example shown in Fig. 3.19, show how to compute the prefix sums of the sequence $\langle 1, 2, 3, 4 \rangle$ on the 2-dimensional butterfly.

3.41. The d-dimensional cube-connected cycles (CCC) is constructed from the d-dimensional hypercube by replacing each node with a cycle of length d (see Fig. 3.25). The nodes in the cycle corresponding to node x in the hypercube are labeled as $(x, 1), (x, 2), \ldots, (x, d)$. Node (x, i) is connected to node (y, j) if and only if $x = y$ and $|i - j| = 1$ (mod d) or $i = j$ and x and y are connected in the corresponding hypercube. The CCC has $d2^d$ nodes. Derive an algorithm to find the sum of $n = d2^d$ numbers stored in the CCC, one number per processor. The resulting sum should be stored in processor $P_{(0^d, 1)}$.

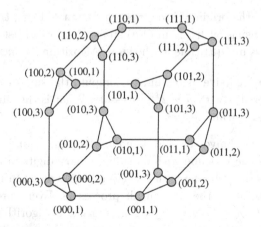

Fig. 3.25.   3-dimensional cube-connected cycles (CCC).

3.42. What are the degree and diameter of the d-dimensional cube-connected cycles described in Exercise 3.41?

3.43. What is the bisection width of the d-dimensional cube-connected cycles described in Exercise 3.41?

3.44. Give an algorithm for computing the prefix sums on the d-dimensional cube-connected cycles described in Exercise 3.41. Your algorithm should run in $O(d) = O(\log n)$ time.

3.45. Give an embedding function from the d-dimensional hypercube to the d-dimensional cube-connected cycles(CCC) network described in Exercise 3.41. What is the dilation of the embedding?

3.46. What is the congestion of the embedding in Exercise 3.45?

3.47. Explain how to simulate a hypercube with 2^d processors on the cube-connected cycles with $d2^d$ processors described in Exercise 3.41.

3.19 Solutions

3.1. Give an $O(d)$ time algorithm for broadcasting in the d-dimensional hypercube H_d if the origin of the message is an arbitrary processor.

Let P_i be the origin of broadcasting datum x. First, transfer x from P_i to P_0 using bit fixing in $O(d)$ steps, then broadcast it to all other processors in $O(d)$ time as shown in Algorithm HCBROADCAST.

3.2. Design a recursive algorithm to compute the sum of n numbers on the hypercube with $n = 2^d$ processors. What is the time complexity of your algorithm?

Let the two halves of the hypercube be $0H_{d-1}$ and $1H_{d-1}$, where $0H_{d-1}$ is the subcube with 0 leading binary digits in its labels, and $1H_{d-1}$ is the subcube with 1 leading binary digits in its labels. The idea is to store the sum in all processors. Every processor has a register t for storing the (partial) sums. See Algorithm HCSUMREC. The running time is given by the recurrence $T(n) = T(n/2) + \Theta(1) = \Theta(\log n)$.

Algorithm 3.13 HCSUMREC

Input: n numbers $x_1, x_2, \ldots, x_n$ stored in H_d, one element per processor.

Output: The sum of the numbers stored in all processors of H_d.

1. if $n = 1$ then set the t register to the x-value and exit
2. Recursively find the sum in each subcube
3. Each processor with label $0y$ in $0H_{d-1}$ adds the content of its t register to the t register of processor with label $1y$ in subcube $1H_{d-1}$.
4. Processor with label $1y$ in subcube $1H_{d-1}$ copies the content of its t register back to the t register of processor with label $0y$ in subcube $0H_{d-1}$.

3.3. Design a recursive algorithm to compute the prefix sums of n numbers on the hypercube with $n = 2^d$ processors. What is the time complexity of your algorithm?

The idea is similar to that in the solution to Exercise 3.2. We compute both the prefix sums and the sum of the numbers simultaneously. Define $0H_{d-1}$ and $1H_{d-1}$ as in the solution of Exercise 3.2. Every processor P_i has two registers s_i for storing the prefix sums and t_i for storing the (partial) sums. See Algorithm HCPREFIXSUMREC. After Step 4, all processors have the prefix sums and the same total. The running time is given by the recurrence $T(n) = T(n/2) + \Theta(1) = \Theta(\log n)$.

Algorithm 3.14 HCPREFIXSUMREC

Input: n numbers $x_1, x_2, \ldots, x_n$ stored in H_d, one element per processor.

Output: The prefix sums of $s_1, s_2, \ldots, s_n$.

1. if $n = 1$ then copy the x-value to registers s and t and exit
2. Recursively find the prefix sums in each subcube
3. Each processor P_i with label $0y$ adds the content of its t_i register to register s_j of processor P_j with label $1y$.
4. Each processor P_i with label $0y$ adds the content of its t_i register to register t_j of processor P_j with label $1y$.
5. Processor $1y$ in subcube $1H_{d-1}$ copies the content of its t register back to the t register of processor $0y$ in subcube $0H_{d-1}$.

3.4. Describe how to implement the odd–even merge sort on a hypercube of dimension d.

We adapt Algorithm BFODDEVENMERGE for the butterfly discussed in Section 3.15. The algorithm is normal for the butterfly since at any given time, only processors in the same level are participating in the computation, which means a single step of the butterfly algorithm can be simulated in one step of the hypercube. Hence, the algorithm can be implemented to run on the hypercube in time $\Theta(d^2) = \Theta(\log^2 n)$.

3.5. Design an algorithm to rearrange a sequence of n numbers distributed one number per processor in a d-dimensional hypercube, where $n = 2^d$, so that all numbers smaller than or equal to the average precede all numbers greater than the average. Your algorithm should run in $\Theta(\log n)$ time.

This is a direct application of parallel prefix. First, find the sum, divide it by n to obtain the average v. Next, broadcast v to all processors in the hypercube. Label all elements $\leq v$ with 1 and the others with 0. Finally, apply packing and route each element to its proper location.

3.6. Explain how to compute the prefix sums of n numbers on a hypercube with p processors, where $p < n$. What is the running time of your algorithm?

Divide the input into p groups of n/p elements each. Find the prefix sums individually and sequentially in each group in $\Theta(n/p)$ time. Let the final prefix sums (the totals of all groups) be $S = s_1, s_2, \ldots, s_p$. Apply parallel prefix on the sequence S in $\Theta(\log p)$ time. Finally, update the prefix sums in all groups sequentially in $\Theta(n/p)$ time. The overall running time is $\Theta(n/p + \log p)$ time.

3.7. Explain how to run the algorithm for quicksort designed for the PRAM and discussed in Section 2.5.2 on the hypercube with n processors.

The algorithm runs on the hypercube with no modifications.

3.8. Illustrate the operation of Algorithm SAMPLESORT discussed in Section 3.10 on the input

$$18, 12, 23, 14, 15, 16, 7, 21, 20, 19, 11, 2, 24, 14, 5, 6, 17, 1,$$

where $n = 18$ and $p = 3$.

Similar to Example 3.3.

3.9. In Algorithm SAMPLESORT discussed in Section 3.10, each processor sends its sample of $(p - 1)$ elements to P_0, which in turn collects a sample of $p(p - 1)$ elements. Explain how this data transmission can be achieved, and analyze its cost.

Each odd-numbered processor sends its sample to its (even-numbered) neighbor. Next, each even-numbered processor combines the sample it has received from its neighbor with its own sample. This process of sending to neighbors continues until processor P_0 receives all the $p(p - 1)$ samples. The total time taken is

$$(p - 1) + 2(p - 1) + 4(p - 1) + \cdots + 2^{\lceil \log p \rceil}(p - 1) = \Theta(p^2).$$

3.10. A sorting method known as BUCKETSORT works as follows. Let S be a sequence of n numbers within a reasonable range, say all numbers are between 1 and m, where m is not too large compared to n. The numbers are distributed into k buckets, with the first bucket containing those numbers between 1 and $\lfloor m/k \rfloor$, the second bucket containing those numbers between $\lfloor m/k \rfloor + 1$ to $\lfloor 2m/k \rfloor$, and so on. The numbers in each bucket are then sorted using an optimal sorting algorithm. Show how to parallelize the algorithm.

Let the number of processors be p, and set the number of buckets $k = p$. Assign n/p elements to each processor. Each processor partitions its assigned elements into p partitions, one for each of the p buckets. Next, each processor sends each part of its bucket to the appropriate processor, and retains its part. Each processor then combines the $p - 1$ parts received from the other $p - 1$ processors with its retained elements. Finally, each processor sorts its items using an optimal sequential sorting algorithm. Note that we have assumed that the processors know the interval $[1..m]$.

3.11. Analyze the running time of Algorithm BUCKETSORT in the solution to Exercise 3.10.

Initially, assume that each processor has n/p elements stored in its local memory. Partitioning the items in each bucket into p blocks takes $O(\frac{n}{p}\log m)$ time using binary search. Sending data to their processors can be achieved in $O(\frac{n}{p}\log p)$ time. The sorting step takes $\Theta(\frac{n}{p}\log\frac{n}{p})$ time. Hence, the total running time is

$$\Theta\left(\frac{n}{p}\log\frac{n}{p} + \frac{n}{p}\log m + \frac{n}{p}\log p\right).$$

If $m = O(n)$, then the running time becomes $\Theta(\frac{n}{p}\log n)$, since $p < n$.

3.12. Consider the algorithm for permutation routing in the hypercube discussed in Section 3.6. What is the probability that the algorithm will route all packets to their destinations in $8d$ steps or fewer?

With probability at least $1 - 2^{-1.5d}$, every packet v_i reaches its destination $\sigma(i)$ in $4d$ or fewer steps. So, the full algorithm (two phases) routes all packets to their destinations in $8d$ or fewer steps with probability $(1 - 2^{-1.5d}) \times (1 - 2^{-1.5d}) = (1 - 2^{-1.5d})^2$.

3.13. Consider Algorithm HCSELECT for selection on the hypercube discussed in Section 3.11. For what values of p is the algorithm optimal?

Since the lower bound for any sequential selection algorithm is $\Omega(n)$, the lower bound for the parallel version is $\Omega(n/p)$. Therefore, the algorithm is optimal for all values of $p = n^\epsilon$, $0 < \epsilon < 1$. In this case, the running time of the algorithm is $\Theta(n^{1-\epsilon})$.

3.14. Consider Algorithm PARSELECT for selection on the EREW PRAM presented in Section 2.14. Suppose we simulate this algorithm to run on the hypercube with $n/\log n$ processors. What will be the running time of the algorithm? Compare this with that of Algorithm HCSELECT for selection on the hypercube presented in Section 3.11. (See Exercise 3.21).

The running time will be

$$O(\log n \log \log n \log p) = O(\log^2 n \log \log n).$$

This is much slower than Algorithm HCSELECT, which runs in time $O(\log n (\log \log n)^2)$.

3.15. Outline an algorithm to find all the kth largest elements in a hypercube with $p < n$ processors. What is the running time of your algorithm?

First, find the kth smallest element x using the algorithm for selection. Next, broadcast x to all processors. Finally, each processor outputs all elements greater than or equal to x. The running time is $O(n/p + T_s(n, p) + \log p) = O(n/p + T_s(n, p))$, where $T_s(n, p)$ is the time required by the selection algorithm.

3.16. Consider Algorithm HCMULTISELECT for multiselection on the hypercube discussed in Section 3.12. For what values of r is the algorithm cost optimal when the number of processors is $n^{1-\epsilon}$?

When $p = n^{1-\epsilon}$, the running time is

$$T(n, r, n^{1-\epsilon}) = O(n^\epsilon \min\{r, \log n^{1-\epsilon}\}).$$

Since the lower bound for any sequential multiselection algorithm is $\Omega(n \log r)$, the lower bound for the parallel version is $\Omega((n/p) \log r)$. Hence, the algorithm is cost optimal for $r \geq p = n^{1-\epsilon}$.

3.17. Consider Algorithm HCMULTISELECT for multiselection on the hypercube discussed in Section 3.12. Compare the algorithm given with direct application of Algorithm HCSELECT given in Section 3.11.

Direct application of Algorithm HCSELECT r times takes

$$r \times O(n/p + t_s(p, p)(\log n - \log p)) = O(rn/p + rt_s(p, p) \log(n/p)).$$

On the other hand, Algorithm HCMULTISELECT takes

$$O((n/p + t_s(p, p) \log(n/p)) \min\{r, \log p\}),$$

which is less than direct application for $r > \log p$.

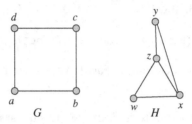

Fig. 3.26.   Exercise 3.19.

3.18. Construct the Gray code sequence G_4.

Similar to Fig. 3.7.

3.19. Consider the two graphs shown in Fig. 3.26. Find an embedding of G into H. What are the dilation, congestion, expansion and load of your embedding?

Define the embedding functions ϕ and ψ by: $\phi(a) = w, \phi(b) = x, \phi(c) = y, \phi(d) = z,$ $\psi((a,b)) = w, x, \psi((b,c)) = x, y,$ $\psi((c,d)) = y, z$ and $\psi((a,d)) = w, z$. Since each edge of G is mapped to exactly one edge of H, the dilation is 1. All edges of H are used at most once, and hence the congestion is 1. The expansion is $3/3 = 1$, and the load is 1.

3.20. Give an embedding similar to the one given in Example 3.2, except that it is postorder, that is, the nodes of the binary tree are labeled in postorder traversal. What are the dilation, congestion, expansion and load of the embedding?

Similar to Example 3.2.

3.21. Explain how to simulate an EREW PRAM on a hypercube with n processors.

The simulation is done using routing. PRAM processor local computation is done locally, while a read/write by PRAM processor i to PRAM memory j can be simulated by a packet going through the network from the node simulating i to the node simulating j. Thus, simulating a PRAM with p processors on a hypercube with the same number of processors is a packet routing problem. Since the hypercube can route a packets in $O(\log p)$ steps, it can simulate any EREW PRAM with p processors with an $O(\log p)$ factor delay.

3.22. Compute the bisection width of the d-dimensional butterfly B_d.

Figure 3.3 shows the d-dimensional butterfly for $d = 1, 2, 3$. From the figure, it is clear that for $j > 1$, B_j can be divided into two halves with $2 \times 2^{d-1} = 2^d$ connections between them. To construct a bisection width of this size, simply remove the cross edges from a single level.

3.23. Design an algorithm to compute the sum of n numbers on the hypercube with p processors, $1 \leq p < n$. Is your algorithm always optimal?

Assume that each processor P_i contains at least one number; if not then let P_i contain 0. First, compute the sum of the numbers in each processors. Next, compute the sum of the $p = 2^d$ resulting numbers using the technique of reduction, which is a method similar to the method used in broadcasting in the hypercube, but in reverse order. This is shown in Algorithm HCSUM. Here the notation $j^{(i)}$ means j with the ith bit complemented, $0 \leq i \leq d - 1$. If the numbers are distributed evenly among the p processors, so that each processor contains n/p numbers, then the running time is $O(\max\{\frac{n}{p}, d\})$, which is optimal. Otherwise, the algorithm is not optimal, as the running time may be as large as $\Theta(n)$. In this case, data redistribution may be helpful if it takes $o(m)$, where m is the maximum number of elements in all processors.

Algorithm 3.15 HCSUM
Input: $x_0, x_1, \ldots, x_{2^d - 1}$.

Output: The sum of the numbers $x_0, x_1, \ldots, x_{2^d - 1}$ stored in processors $P_0, P_1, \ldots, P_{2^d - 1}$ of H_d.

1. **for** $i \leftarrow d - 1, d - 2, \ldots, 1, 0$ **do**
2.   **for all** $j < 2^i$ and $j < j^{(i)}$ **do in parallel**
3. $x_j \leftarrow x_j + x_{j^{(i)}}$
4.   **end for**
5. **end for**

3.24. Explain how to compute the maximum of 2^{d-1} numbers distributed arbitrarily in a hypercube with 2^d processors. What is the running time of your algorithm?

The first step is to route these numbers so that they occupy one half of the hypercube. This routing step takes $\Theta(\log n)$ time. Next, the maximum of these numbers is computed in $\Theta(\log n)$ time. The total running time is $\Theta(\log n)$.

Another alternative is to use parallel prefix to pack the numbers in the first 2^{d-1} processors and then find their sum using the lower half of the hypercube.

3.25. Consider the partial permutation routing problem on the hypercube in which every processor is the source of at most one packet and the destination of at most one packet. Will Theorem 3.2 hold for this routing problem?

Theorem 3.2 holds for partial permutation routing, and the proof works with no modifications.

3.26. Consider the many-to-many routing problems on the hypercube in which every processor is the source of r packets and the destination of r packets. Suppose we run the greedy algorithm for routing on the hypercube to solve this problem. What will be the maximum queue size?

Theorem 3.2 no longer holds for many-to-many routing. In the proof of Theorem 3.2, $a \leq r2^k - 1$ and $b \leq r2^{d-k} - 1$, and hence the maximum queue size will be $O(r\sqrt{n})$.

3.27. Give an $O(nd)$ time algorithm for the problem of routing in the d-dimensional hypercube if every processor has a packet to be sent to every other processor, where $n = 2^d$. *Hint*: Use randomized routing n times.

Use randomized routing sequentially n times. Each run takes $O(d)$ time for a total of $O(nd)$.

3.28. Give an $O(n)$ time algorithm for the problem in Exercise 3.27.

Use randomized routing in parallel n times. This takes $O(d)$ parallel steps. However, there are queues that will expand the running time. There are $n(n-1)$ paths, and hence each node of the hypercube is included in $\frac{n(n-1)}{n} = n - 1$ paths. This results in a queue of size $O(n)$ at each node. This means the running time will be expanded to $O(n) + O(d) = O(n)$.

3.29. Apply Algorithm HCPARPREFIX for computing parallel prefix on the hypercube on the input sequence $\langle 1, 2, 3, 4, 5, 6, 7, 8 \rangle$. Assume a hypercube with 8 processors.

Similar to the example in Fig. 3.14.

3.30. Give an algorithm to evaluate the polynomial $a_{n-1}x^{n-1} + a_{n-2}x^{n-2} + \cdots + a_1 x + a_0$ at the point x_0 on the d-dimensional hypercube H_d with $n = 2^d$ processors. Assume that each a_i is stored in processor P_i, $0 \leq i \leq n - 1$.

First, use parallel prefix to compute $1, x_0, x_0^2, \ldots, x_0^{n-1}$ in processors $P_0, P_1, \ldots, P_{n-1}$. Next, within each processor, multiply $a_i \times x_0^i$, $0 \leq i \leq n - 1$. Finally, use Algorithm HCSUM in Exercise 3.23 above to find the desired sum. The running time is $\Theta(\log n)$.

3.31. Consider a hypercube with four processors $\{P_0, P_1, P_2, P_3\}$ with initial loads $8, 2, 6, 4$. Perform load balancing on the hypercube so that, at the end, each processor has the same load.

Consider the hypercube with four processors shown in Fig. 3.27(a). The number next to a processor is its initial load. The sum of the initial loads is 20, and so, after balancing, each processor will have 5 units of load. One way to accomplish this is to have processor P_0 send 3 units to processor P_1 and to have processor P_2 send, in parallel, one unit to processor P_3. The time needed for this is 3 units as the

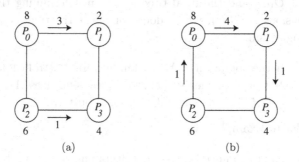

Fig. 3.27.   Exercise 3.31.

transfer from processor P_2 to processor P_3 is overlapped with the
transfer from processor P_0 to processor P_1.

Another possibility is shown in Fig. 3.27(b). In this scheme, processor P_0 sends 4 units to processor P_1. After this transmission is completed, processor P_2 sends one unit to processor P_0 and processor P_1 sends, in parallel, one unit to processor P_3. The total time is 5 units.

3.32. Redo Exercise 3.31 using the algorithm presented in Section 3.13.

Similar to the example described in Section 3.13.

3.33. Consider a hypercube with eight processors $\{P_0, P_1, \ldots, P_7\}$ with initial loads $8, 5, 6, 4, 7, 2, 5, 3$. Perform load balancing on the hypercube using the algorithm described in Section 3.13 so that, at the end, each processor has approximately the same load.

Similar to the example described in Section 3.13.

3.34. Suggest a heuristic to improve the performance of the load balancing algorithm discussed in Section 3.13.

A simple heuristic is to select the next dimension to balance across, as the dimension that maximizes $s_i = \max |L_i - L_j|$ such that P_j is a neighbor of P_i along an unselected dimension. So, first, each processor P_i computes r_i and s_i such that $s_i = \max |L_i - L_j|$, where P_j is a neighbor of P_i, along an unselected dimension. r_i is such that $s_i = |L_i - L_j|$, where j is s_i's neighbor along dimension r_i. Next, the maximum of the s_i's is computed. If this maximum is s_l, then dimension r_l is selected. The time required to select the next dimension is $O(d)$, and the total time spent on determining the order of dimensions is $O(d^2)$, which does not affect the time complexity of the algorithm.

3.35. Illustrate the operation of Algorithm BFODDEVENMERGE for merging on the butterfly to merge the two sorted sequences $A = \langle 1, 4, 6, 9 \rangle$ and $B = \langle 2, 5, 7, 8 \rangle$ on the 3-dimensional butterfly.

Similar to Example 3.4.

3.36. Use the matrix multiplication algorithm on the hypercube discussed in Section 3.16 to compute the product $C = A \times B$ of the two 2×2

matrices A and B shown below. Assume a hypercube with $n = 2^3 = 8$ processors.

$$A = \begin{bmatrix} 1 & 3 \\ 2 & 4 \end{bmatrix} \quad \text{and} \quad B = \begin{bmatrix} 2 & 1 \\ 4 & 3 \end{bmatrix}.$$

Similar to Example 3.6.

3.37. Suggest an algorithm for computing the transitive closure of an adjacency matrix A on the hypercube. What is the running time of the algorithm?

Use an algorithm analogous to the one for the PRAM presented in Section 2.17. Recall that this algorithm computes the transitive closure by squaring the adjacency matrix $\lceil \log n \rceil$ times. Thus, the running time is $O(\log^2 n)$ using $O(n^3)$ processors.

3.38. Suggest an algorithm for computing the shortest paths in a directed graph G represented by its adjacency matrix A on the hypercube. What is the running time of the algorithm?

Use an algorithm analogous to the one for the PRAM presented in Section 2.18. Recall that this algorithm computes the shortest paths by first computing a matrix similar to the transitive closure matrix using repeated squaring of the weight matrix $\lceil \log n \rceil$ times. Hence, the running time is $O(\log^2 n)$ using $O(n^3)$ processors.

3.39. Let $S = \langle x_0, x_1, \ldots, x_{n-1} \rangle$ be a sequence of numbers stored in a hypercube with n processors where x_i is stored in P_i, $0 \leq i < n$, and let y be stored in P_0. Give an algorithm to count the number of elements in S that are larger than y.

First, broadcast y to all processors. Next, each processor P_i sets $z_i = 1$ if $x_i > y$ and $z_i = 0$ if $x_i \leq y$. Finally, find the sum of $z_i, 0 \leq i \leq n - 1$, in all processors, and store the sum, which is the number of 1s, in P_0.

3.40. Following the example shown in Fig. 3.19, show how to compute the prefix sums of the sequence $\langle 1, 2, 3, 4 \rangle$ on the 2-dimensional butterfly.

Similar to Fig. 3.19.

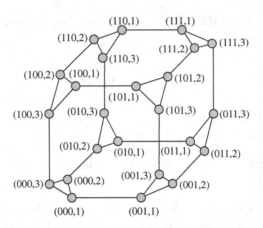

Fig. 3.28.   3-dimensional cube-connected cycles (CCC).

3.41. The d-dimensional cube-connected cycles (CCC) is constructed from the d-dimensional hypercube by replacing each node with a cycle of length d (see Fig. 3.28). The nodes in the cycle corresponding to node x in the hypercube are labeled as $(x, 1), (x, 2), \ldots, (x, d)$. Node (x, i) is connected to node (y, j) if and only if $x = y$ and $|i - j| = 1 \pmod{d}$ or $i = j$ and x and y are connected in the corresponding hypercube. The CCC has $d2^d$ nodes. Derive an algorithm to find the sum of $n = d2^d$ numbers stored in the CCC — one number per processor. The resulting sum should be stored in processor $P_{(0^d, 1)}$.

Let the cycles of the CCC be $C_1, C_2, \ldots, C_{2^d}$, and let t_i be the sum of all numbers in cycle C_i. First, find the sum t_i in each cycle and broadcast it to all processors in the same cycle. This takes $\Theta(d)$ time. Next, find the sum of all totals t_i and store it in $P_{(0^d, 1)}$. The rest, i.e., finding the total of these sums is similar to finding the sum of 2^d numbers in the hypercube (see, for example, Exercise 3.2).

3.42. What are the degree and diameter of the d-dimensional cube-connected cycles described in Exercise 3.41?

Its degree is 3, and its diameter is $\Theta(d) = \Theta(\log n)$.

3.43. What is the bisection width of the d-dimensional cube-connected cycles described in Exercise 3.41?

If we consider a d-dimensional cube-connected cycles with $n = d2^d$ processors and cut it by a line into two halves, the line will cut 2^{d-1} links. Hence, the bisection width of the d-dimensional CCC is $\Theta(n/\log n)$.

3.44. Give an algorithm for computing the prefix sums on the d-dimensional cube-connected cycles described in Exercise 3.41. Your algorithm should run in $O(d) = O(\log n)$ time.

Similar to finding the sum in CCC and finding the prefix sums in the hypercube; see Exercises 3.41 and 3.3.

3.45. Give an embedding function from the d-dimensional hypercube to the d-dimensional cube-connected cycles(CCC) network described in Exercise 3.41. What is the dilation of the embedding?

Map node x in the hypercube to node $(x, 1)$ in the CCC, and map the edge (x, y) in the hypercube to edge $((x, 1), (y, 1))$ (see Fig. 3.29). The dilation of the embedding is $1 + 2\lfloor d/2 \rfloor = \Theta(d)$.

3.46. What is the congestion of the embedding in Exercise 3.45?

Consider Fig. 3.30, which shows a cycle of length d in the d-dimensional cube-connected cycles. It is easy to see that the edge $((00\ldots 0, 1), (00\ldots 0, 2))$ is used by $\lfloor d/2 \rfloor$ paths. Hence, the congestion is $\lfloor d/2 \rfloor = \Theta(d)$.

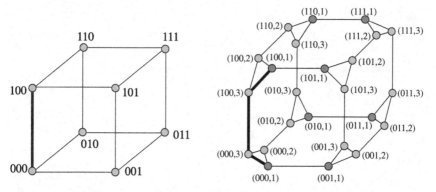

Fig. 3.29. Embedding of d-dimensional hypercube into the d-dimensional cube-connected cycles.

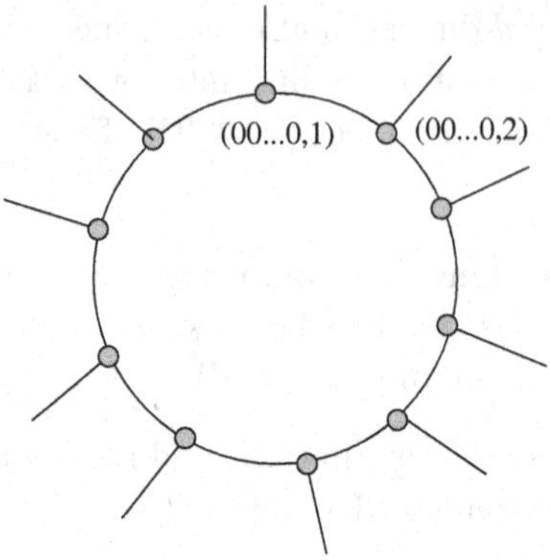

Fig. 3.30.   A cycle in the d-dimensional cube-connected cycles.

3.47. Explain how to simulate a hypercube with 2^d processors on the cube-connected cycles with $d2^d$ processors described in Exercise 3.41.

Any step of the hypercube can be simulated in d steps on the CCC by using one cycle of the CCC to simulate the action of one node of the hypercube.

Chapter 4

The Linear Array and the Mesh

4.1   Introduction

Linear arrays are the simplest example of a fixed-connection network. An example of a linear array is shown in Fig. 4.1(a). It consists of n processors $P_1, P_2, \ldots, P_n$, where each interior processor is connected with bidirectional links to its left neighbor and its right neighbor. The outermost processors P_1 and P_n have just one connection each. If we connect them by a link, we obtain a *ring*, which is a simple extension of the linear array (see Fig. 4.1(b)).

A two-dimensional *mesh* is an extension of the linear array to two dimensions. A mesh of size n consists of n simple processors arranged in a square lattice. To simplify our exposition, it is assumed that $n = 4^k$ for some positive integer k. For all $i, j, 1 \leq i, j \leq \sqrt{n}$, and processor $P_{i,j}$ representing the processor in row i and column j is connected via bidirectional communication links to its four neighbors, processors $P_{i\pm1,j}$ and $P_{i,j\pm1}$ — assuming they exist. (See Fig. 4.1(c)).

A *torus* is simply a mesh with wraparound connections; each row and each column has a wraparound connection. Fig. 4.2 depicts a torus on 16 processors.

159

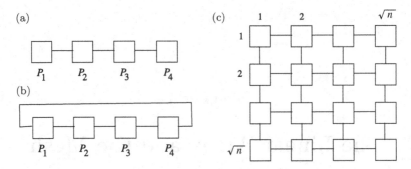

Fig. 4.1.   (a) A linear array. (b) A ring. (c) A mesh.

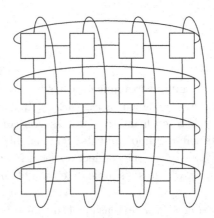

Fig. 4.2.   A torus on 16 processors.

The communication diameter of a mesh of size n is $2(\sqrt{n}-1) = \Theta(\sqrt{n})$, and this can be seen by examining the distance between processors in opposite corners of the mesh. This means if a processor in one corner of the mesh needs data from a processor in another corner of the mesh sometime during the execution of an algorithm, then a lower bound on the running time of the algorithm is $\Omega(\sqrt{n})$.

There is no linear ordering on the set of processors in the mesh. However, there are several two-dimensional orderings, called indexing schemes, like row-major and snakelike shown in Fig. 4.3.

1	2	3	4
5	6	7	8
9	10	11	12
13	14	15	16

(a)

1	2	3	4
8	7	6	5
9	10	11	12
16	15	14	13

(b)

Fig. 4.3.   Mesh indexing schemes. (a) Row-major (b) Snakelike.

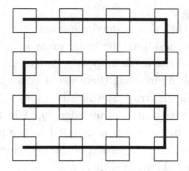

Fig. 4.4.   Embedding a linear array into a mesh.

4.2   Embedding between a Mesh and a Linear Array

We consider the problem of embedding between a mesh and a linear array with the same number of processors. Embedding a linear array into the mesh is obvious; it is illustrated in Fig. 4.4. This mapping has dilation 1, since every edge of the linear array is mapped to one edge of the mesh. The congestion is also 1, since every edge of the mesh is used by exactly one edge of the linear array, as is evident from the figure.

Now, consider inverting the above mapping to obtain the embedding of the mesh into the linear array illustrated in Fig. 4.5. Edge e_1 in the mesh is mapped to the path from s to t in the linear array, which is of length 7.

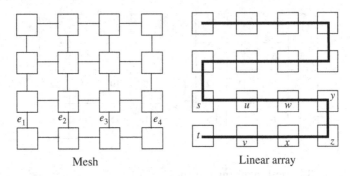

Fig. 4.5.   Embedding a mesh into a linear array.

It is not hard to see that this is maximum, and in general, the dilation of this embedding of the mesh into the linear array is $2\sqrt{n} - 1$. Now, consider the number of edges of the mesh mapped to edge (y, z) in the linear array. It is evident from the figure that there are 4 edges of the mesh mapped to this edge in the linear array. Specifically, e_1, e_2, e_3 and e_4 in the mesh are all mapped to paths that contain edge (y, z) in the linear array. For example, the edge e_2 in the mesh is mapped to the path u, w, y, z, x, v in the linear array. Hence, the congestion of the mapping in Fig. 4.5 is 4. It is not difficult to see that, in general, it is $\sqrt{n}$.

4.3   Broadcasting in the Linear Array and the Mesh

Let L be a linear array of n processors. To broadcast a datum x from P_1 to all other processors, x is sent to $P_2, P_3, \ldots, P_n$ in this order. The number of steps is $n - 1 = \Theta(n)$. If the origin of broadcasting is not P_1, say $P_i(i < n)$, x is sent in both directions in parallel. The number of steps in this case is equal to the maximum of the distances from P_i to P_1 and P_n.

Let M be a mesh of size n. Broadcasting a datum x from $P_{1,1}$ to all other processors can be achieved in two phases. First, x is sent to all processors in row 1. Next, x is sent in parallel from all processors in row 1 along all columns of the mesh. The total number of steps in the two phases is $2(\sqrt{n} - 1) = \Theta(\sqrt{n})$.

If the origin of broadcasting is $P_{i,j}$ (which is different from $P_{1,1}$), then broadcasting of x to all other processors can be achieved in two phases: in phase 1, x is sent to all processors in row i. In phase 2, x is sent in parallel from all processors in row i along all columns in M. The running time is $\Theta(\sqrt{n})$.

4.4 Computing Parallel Prefix on the Mesh

The parallel prefix problem was defined in Section 2.5. In this section, we show how to compute it on the linear array and the mesh. For simplicity, we will assume addition as the binary operation. Let L be a linear array with n processors, where each processor P_i contains item x_i, $1 \le i \le n$. Assume that each processor P_i has register s_i. The algorithm is shown as Algorithm LAPARPREFIX. In this algorithm, s_{i-1} is passed to $P_i, 2 \le i \le n$, where x_i is added to it to produce s_i, as in the sequential algorithm. The algorithm runs in time $\Theta(n)$.

Algorithm 4.1 LAPARPREFIX
Input: $X = \langle x_1, x_2, \ldots, x_n \rangle$, a sequences of n numbers.
Output: $S = \langle s_1, s_2, \ldots, s_n \rangle$, the prefix sums of X.

1. $s_1 \leftarrow x_1$
2. **for** $i \leftarrow 2$ **to** n **do**
3.   Processor P_i computes $s_i \leftarrow s_{i-1} + x_i$.
4. **end for**

Now, we consider computing parallel prefix on the mesh. Let M be a $\sqrt{n} \times \sqrt{n}$ mesh, and assume the row-major indexing scheme. The algorithm is given as Algorithm MESHPARPREFIX. First, the individual prefix sums of all rows are computed using Algorithm LAPARPREFIX. For $1 \le i \le \sqrt{n}$, let the prefix sums of row i be $y_{i,1}, y_{i,2}, \ldots, y_{i,\sqrt{n}}$. Note that these are not the final prefix sums, except for row 1. Next, the prefix sums of column $\sqrt{n}$ are computed, again using Algorithm LAPARPREFIX. These are denoted by $s_{1,\sqrt{n}}, s_{2,\sqrt{n}}, \ldots, s_{\sqrt{n},\sqrt{n}}$, and they are the final prefix sums for column $\sqrt{n}$. Finally, for all processors $P_{i,j}, 2 \le i \le \sqrt{n}, 1 \le j \le \sqrt{n} - 1$, we set $s_{i,j} \leftarrow y_{i,j} + s_{i-1,\sqrt{n}}$. This implies broadcasting $s_{i-1,\sqrt{n}}$ to row i.

Steps 1–3 take $\Theta(\sqrt{n})$ time. Step 4 takes $\Theta(\sqrt{n})$ time too. Steps 5–9 take $\Theta(1)$ time plus the time needed for broadcasting, which is $\Theta(\sqrt{n})$. Hence, the total running time of the algorithm is $\Theta(\sqrt{n})$.

Algorithm 4.2 MESHPARPREFIX
Input: $X = \langle x_{i,j} \mid 1 \le i,j \le \sqrt{n} \rangle$, a sequences of n numbers.
Output: $S = \langle s_{i,j} \mid 1 \le i,j \le \sqrt{n} \rangle$, the prefix sums of X.

1. **for** $i \leftarrow 1$ **to** $\sqrt{n}$ **do in parallel**
2.   Use Algorithm LAPARPREFIX to compute the prefix sums of row i.
       Let these be $y_{i,1}, y_{i,2}, \ldots, y_{i,\sqrt{n}}$.
3. **end for**
4. Use Algorithm LAPARPREFIX to compute the prefix sums
       of column $\sqrt{n}$. Let these be $s_{1,\sqrt{n}}, s_{2,\sqrt{n}}, \ldots, s_{\sqrt{n},\sqrt{n}}$.
5. **for** $i \leftarrow 2$ **to** $\sqrt{n}$ **do in parallel**
6.   **for** $j \leftarrow 1$ **to** $\sqrt{n} - 1$ **do in parallel**
7. $s_{i,j} \leftarrow y_{i,j} + s_{i-1,\sqrt{n}}$
8.   **end for**
9. **end for**

4.5 Odd–Even Transposition Sort

This sorting algorithm is for linear arrays (and rows and columns of meshes). The algorithm is very simple. It alternates between odd steps and even steps. At odd steps, we compare the contents of processors P_1 and P_2, P_3 and P_4, and so on exchanging values if necessary. At even steps, we repeat the same procedure on processors P_2 and P_3, P_4 and P_5, and so on. The algorithm takes n steps to sort its input $\langle x_1, x_2, \ldots, x_n \rangle$, one item x_i per processor P_i, $1 \le i \le n$. Hence its running time is $\Theta(n)$.

Theorem 4.1   Odd–even transposition sort correctly sorts any sequence of numbers.

Proof.   By Lemma 2.1 in Section 2.10, we may assume that the input sequence X consists of 0's and 1's. We prove by induction on $|X|$ that the algorithm sorts the binary sequence X. If $n = 1$ or 2, then the hypothesis is true. So assume it is true for all sequences of size $k, 1 \le k \le n - 1$. Let $X = \langle x_1, x_2, \ldots, x_n \rangle$ stored in processors $P_1, P_2, \ldots, P_n$. Let x_j be the rightmost 1, where $1 \le j \le n$. x_j will start moving rightward in the first or second step of the algorithm. Once it starts moving, it will subsequently move rightward in each step until it reaches the right end — that is, until $x_n = 1$. Now, it remains to sort $X' = \langle x_1, x_2, \ldots, x_{n-1} \rangle$ in processors $P_1, P_2, \ldots, P_{n-1}$. By induction, X' will be sorted by the algorithm. It follows that X will be sorted correctly by the algorithm. $\square$

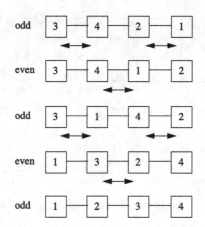

Fig. 4.6. Example of odd–even transposition sort.

Example 4.1 An example of the algorithm is shown in Fig. 4.6. ☐

4.6 Shearsort

This sorting algorithm is for meshes, and it sorts n items in a $\sqrt{n} \times \sqrt{n}$ mesh in snakelike order. It consists of $2 \log \sqrt{n} + 1 = \log n + 1$ phases. The algorithm alternates between odd and even phases. At odd phases, it sorts the rows of the mesh, and at even phases, it sorts its columns. The odd rows are sorted so that smaller numbers move leftward, and the even rows are sorted so that smaller numbers move rightward. The columns are sorted so that smaller numbers move upward. Odd–even transposition sort may be used to sort the rows and columns. In this case, the running time of the algorithm is $\Theta(\sqrt{n} \log n)$. An outline of the algorithm is given as Algorithm SHEARSORT.

Algorithm 4.3 SHEARSORT
Input: A sequence $S = \langle a_1, a_2, \ldots, a_n \rangle$.
Output: The elements in S in sorted order.

1. **for** $i \leftarrow 1$ **to** $\log n + 1$
2.   **if** i is odd **then** sort all rows in snake-like order
3.   **else** sort all columns
4. **end for**

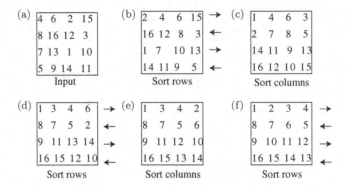

Fig. 4.7. An illustration of Algorithm SHEARSORT.

Example 4.2   An illustration of Algorithm SHEARSORT is given in Fig. 4.7.   □

Theorem 4.2   Algorithm SHEARSORT correctly sorts any sequence of n numbers on a $\sqrt{n} \times \sqrt{n}$ mesh in $2 \log \sqrt{n} + 1$ phases.

Proof.   By Lemma 2.1 in Section 2.10, we may assume that the input consists of 0's and 1's. So, let the input be initially stored in the $\sqrt{n} \times \sqrt{n}$ mesh, one number per processor. A row of the mesh will be called *dirty* if it consists of both 0's and 1's, and *clean* if it consists of only 0's or only 1's. Initially, there may be as many as $\sqrt{n}$ dirty rows. During the execution of the algorithm, there will be rows all 0's followed by dirty rows followed by rows with all 1's. After the algorithm terminates, there will be at most one dirty row. Let an iteration of the algorithm consist of two phases, a row sort phase and a column sort phase. We will show that after each iteration, at least half of the dirty rows become clean. This will imply that after $\log(\sqrt{n})$ iterations there will be at most one dirty row, which can be sorted using an additional sorting phase for a total of $2 \log(\sqrt{n}) + 1 = \log n + 1$ phases. Thus, it remains to show that the number of dirty rows will decrease by a factor of at least 2 in each iteration.

Consider two adjacent rows in an iteration after the phase of row sorting. There are three possibilities according to whether there are more 0's than 1's (Fig. 4.8(a)), more 1's than 0's (Fig. 4.8(b)), or an equal number of 0's and 1's (Fig. 4.8(c)). Now, after sorting the columns of the mesh, each

```
0 ...... 01.... 1      0 ... 01.........1      0 ......01......1
1....10.........0      1........10....0      1......10.......0
```

(a) **more 0s** (b) **more 1s** (c) **equal 0s & 1s**

Fig. 4.8. Dirty rows after rows are sorted.

one of these three cases will contribute at least one clean row. If there are
more 0's than 1's (part (a) of the figure), then after sorting the columns,
there will be at least one more clean row consisting of all 0's. If there are
more 1's than 0's (part (b) of the figure), then after sorting the columns,
there will be at least one more clean row consisting of all 1's. If there are
equal number of 0's and 1's (part (c) of the figure), then after sorting the
columns, there will be two more clean rows one consisting of all 0's and
one consisting of all 1's. Thus the number of dirty rows will decrease by a
factor of at least 2 in each iteration. □

Corollary 4.1 If the number of dirty rows is k, then Algorithm SHEAR-
SORT performs $2 \log k + 1$ phases.

4.7 A Simple $\Theta(\sqrt{n})$ Time Algorithm for Sorting on the Mesh

In this section, we derive a simple $\Theta(\sqrt{n})$ time algorithm for sorting n
numbers on the $\sqrt{n} \times \sqrt{n}$ mesh. It is a divide-and-conquer algorithm, where
the mesh is first partitioned into four submeshes of size $\frac{\sqrt{n}}{2} \times \frac{\sqrt{n}}{2}$ each. The
algorithm first sorts each quadrant recursively in snake-like order. It then
sorts the rows of the entire mesh in snake-like order, and finally performs five
phases of Algorithm SHEARSORT. It is shown as Algorithm MESHSORTREC.

Algorithm 4.4 MESHSORTREC
Input: A sequence $S = \langle a_1, a_2, \ldots, a_n \rangle$.
Output: The elements in S in sorted order.

1. Partition the mesh into four quadrants of size $\frac{\sqrt{n}}{2} \times \frac{\sqrt{n}}{2}$ each.
2. Recursively sort each quadrant in snake-like order.
3. Sort the rows of the entire mesh in snake-like order.
4. Sort the columns top-down.
5. Perform five phases of Algorithm SHEARSORT.

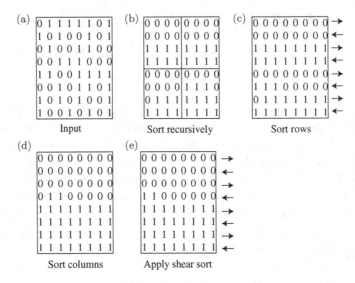

Fig. 4.9.   An illustration of Algorithm MESHSORTREC on input of 0's and 1's.

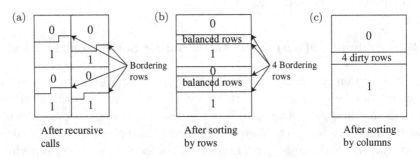

Fig. 4.10.   Proof of Theorem 4.3.

Example 4.3   An illustration of Algorithm MESHSORTREC on input of 0's and 1's is shown in Fig. 4.9.   □

Theorem 4.3   Algorithm MESHSORTREC correctly sorts any sequence of n numbers on a $\sqrt{n} \times \sqrt{n}$ mesh.

Proof.   By the zero-one principle (Lemma 2.1 in Section 2.10), we may consider any input sequence of 0's and 1's. See Fig. 4.10. After the recursive calls, the data in each quadrant is such that all but at most one of the rows are either all 0's or all 1's (see Fig 4.10(a)). A row in the mesh is balanced if the left half consists of all 0's, the right half consists of all 1's, or vice-versa. Thus, in the entire mesh, all, but at most four of the rows are either all 0's, all 1's or balanced. Call these four lines the *borderline* rows.

After sorting all rows, the borderline rows are sorted and both blocks of balanced rows alternate between 1's to the left and 1's to the right (see Fig 4.10(b)).

After sorting all columns, the (at most) four borderline rows will be contiguous (see Fig 4.10(c)), and since there are at most four dirty rows, then by Corollary 4.1, only $2 \log 4 + 1 = 5$ phases of Algorithm SHEARSORT are required to sort the numbers. $\qquad\square$

4.8 Odd–Even Merging and Sorting on the Mesh

In this section, we implement odd–even merging and sorting on a $\sqrt{n} \times \sqrt{n}$ mesh; odd–even merging and sorting on the PRAM were discussed in Section 2.11. Let $A = \langle a_0, a_1, \ldots, a_{n/2-1} \rangle$ and $B = \langle b_0, b_1, \ldots, b_{n/2-1} \rangle$ be two sorted sequences of n distinct numbers, where n is a power of 4. Initially, A and B are input in the first and second $\sqrt{n}/2$ columns of the mesh. The odd–even merging method is outlined in Algorithm MESHOD-DEVENMERGE. k, the number of columns, is input to the algorithm. In the beginning, $k = \sqrt{n}$, which is a power of 2. The algorithm divides the input into $A_{\text{even}}, A_{\text{odd}}, B_{\text{even}}$, and B_{odd}, and each part occupies $k/4$ columns. Next, A_{odd} and B_{odd} are interchanged, and the algorithm recursively merges A_{even} with B_{odd} to produce C, and recursively merges B_{even} with A_{odd} to produce D. C and D are then shuffled into E, which is scanned from left to right (in one parallel step) for pairs that are out of order, which are ordered, if necessary.

Notice that the algorithm is general for any mesh with k columns and $\sqrt{n}$ rows, where k is a power of 2. We express the running time of the algorithm in terms of the number of columns k, $2 \leq k \leq \sqrt{n}$. Step 1 takes $T(2) = \Theta(\sqrt{n})$ time, which is the time needed to merge in a linear array with $2\sqrt{n}$ processors. Steps 2 and 3 take $\Theta(k)$ time, as data has to be routed from left to right and from right to left. Step 4 of interchanging

---

Algorithm 4.5 MESHODDEVENMERGE

Input: Two sorted sequences $A = \langle a_0, a_1, \ldots, a_{n/2-1} \rangle$ and $B = \langle b_0, b_1, \ldots, b_{n/2-1} \rangle$ of $n/2$ elements each sorted in ascending order, where $n = 4^k \geq 4$, number of columns k, $2 \leq k \leq \sqrt{n}$.

Output: The elements in $S = A \cup B$ in sorted order.

1. **if** $k = 2$ **then** merge the two columns using an algorithm for the linear array to produce a sorted snake with two columns and $\sqrt{n}$ rows. Exit.
2. Let $A_{\text{even}} = \langle a_0, a_2, \ldots, a_{n/2-2} \rangle$ and $A_{\text{odd}} = \langle a_1, a_3, \ldots, a_{n/2-1} \rangle$ be the even and odd subsequences of A, respectively. A_{even} and A_{odd} are snakes with $k/4$ columns and $\sqrt{n}$ rows each.
3. Let $B_{\text{even}} = \langle b_0, b_2, \ldots, b_{n/2-2} \rangle$ and $B_{\text{odd}} = \langle b_1, b_3, \ldots, b_{n/2-1} \rangle$ be the even and odd subsequences of B, respectively. B_{even} and B_{odd} are snakes with $k/4$ columns and $\sqrt{n}$ rows each.
4. Interchange A_{odd} with B_{odd}. Thus A_{even} and B_{odd} occupy the first $k/2$ columns, and B_{even} and A_{odd} occupy the next $k/2$ columns.
5. Recursively merge A_{even} and B_{odd} to obtain $C = \langle c_0, c_1, \ldots, c_{n/2-1} \rangle$, a mesh of $k/2$ columns and $\sqrt{n}$ rows.
6. Recursively merge A_{odd} and B_{even} to obtain $D = \langle d_0, d_1, \ldots, d_{n/2-1} \rangle$, a mesh of $k/2$ columns and $\sqrt{n}$ rows.
7. Let E be the shuffle of C and D, that is, $E = \langle c_0, d_0, c_1, d_1, \ldots, c_{n/2-1}, d_{n/2-1} \rangle$.
8. Traverse the pairs (c_i, d_i) in E, $0 \leq i \leq n/2 - 1$, and interchange the elements in each pair if they are out of order to obtain the sorted sequence $S = \langle s_0, s_1, \ldots, s_{n-1} \rangle$ in a mesh with k columns and $\sqrt{n}$ rows.
9. **return** S

---

columns takes $\Theta(k)$ time. Steps 5 and 6 take $T(k/2)$ time. Step 7 of shuffling columns takes $\Theta(k)$ time. Step 8 takes $\Theta(1)$ time. Hence, the running time of the algorithm is governed by the recurrence $T(k) = T(k/2) + \Theta(k)$, whose solution is $T(k) = \Theta(k) + T(2) = \Theta(k) + \Theta(\sqrt{n})$. When $k = \sqrt{n}$, $T(\sqrt{n}) = \Theta(\sqrt{n})$. The proof of correctness is given by Theorem 2.2 in Section 2.11.

Example 4.4 Consider the mesh shown in Fig. 4.11. It consists of four rows and four columns. The first input A is in the first half of the mesh, in the first two columns in a snakelike order. The second input B is in the last two columns in a snakelike order. $A = \langle 3, 5, 6, 9, 11, 13, 14, 16 \rangle$ and $B = \langle 1, 2, 4, 7, 8, 10, 12, 15 \rangle$. First we partition A and B into their even and

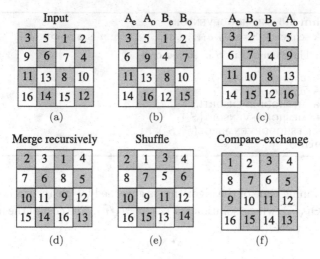

Fig. 4.11. An example of odd–even merging on the mesh.

odd parts. The even parts are shown in shaded squares of Fig. 4.11(a). Thus, $A_{even} = \{3, 6, 11, 14\}$ is in the first column (see part (b) of the figure) and $A_{odd} = \{5, 9, 13, 16\}$ is in the second column. $B_{even} = \{1, 4, 8, 12\}$ is shown in the third column, and $B_{odd} = \{2, 7, 10, 15\}$ is in the last column. These are shown in part (b) of the figure. In part (c) of the figure, A_{odd} is interchanged with B_{odd}. So, the first two columns are merged recursively to produce $C = \langle 2, 3, 6, 7, 10, 11, 14, 15 \rangle$ in snakelike order, and the last two columns are merged recursively to produce $D = \langle 1, 4, 5, 8, 9, 12, 13, 16 \rangle$ in snakelike order. In Fig. 4.11(e), C and D are shuffled to produce $E = \langle 2, 1, 3, 4, 6, 5, 7, 8, 10, 9, 11, 12, 14, 13, 15, 16 \rangle$, which spans the four columns in a snakelike order. The pair $(2, 1)$ is out of order, so 2 and 1 are exchanged. The same applies to the pair $(6, 5)$, etc. The sorted sequence is $S = \langle 1, 2, 3, 4, 5, 6, 7, 8, 9, 10, 11, 12, 13, 14, 15, 16 \rangle$ shown in part (f) of the figure. □

The algorithm for sorting is given as Algorithm MESHODDEVENSORT. It is similar to Algorithm ODDEVENMERGESORT for the PRAM in Section 2.11.

Algorithm 4.6 MESHODDEVENSORT
Input: A sequence $S = \langle a_0, a_1, \ldots, a_{n-1} \rangle$ where n is a power of 4.

Output: The elements in S in sorted order.

1. $S_1 \leftarrow \langle a_0, a_1, \ldots, a_{n/2-1} \rangle$.
2. $S_2 \leftarrow \langle a_{n/2}, a_{n/2+1}, \ldots, a_{n-1} \rangle$.
3. $S_1' \leftarrow$ MESHODDEVENSORT(S_1)
4. $S_2' \leftarrow$ MESHODDEVENSORT(S_2)
5. $S \leftarrow$ MESHODDEVENMERGE(S_1', S_2')
6. **return** S

The running time of the algorithm is governed by the recurrence $T(n) = T(n/2) + \Theta(\sqrt{n})$, whose solution is $T(n) = \Theta(\sqrt{n})$. The cost of the algorithm is $\Theta(\sqrt{n}) \times n = \Theta(n^{1.5})$.

4.9 Routing on the Linear Array and the Mesh

We consider the problem of *permutation routing* on the linear array and the mesh with n processors, in which every processor tries to send to a different destination.

4.9.1 *Routing in the linear array*

Consider the problem of permutation routing in a linear array with n processors. Note that $n - 1$ is a lower bound on the worst case number of steps needed to route a packet at processor P_i to processor P_j, since i and j may be equal to 1 and n, respectively. Consider the following greedy method of routing a packet v from processor P_i to processor P_j. If P_j is to the left of P_i, then move v to the left one step, and if P_j is to the right of P_i, then move v to the right one step. This greedy approach is guaranteed to deliver v to P_j using the least number of steps, which is the distance between P_i and P_j, that is $|i - j|$. Note that no two packets moving in the same direction will contend for the same link. However, two packets may use the same (bidirectional) link if they are moving in opposite directions.

4.9.2 Deterministic routing in the mesh

The greedy algorithm for permutation routing in the $\sqrt{n} \times \sqrt{n}$ mesh is a generalization of that in the linear array. Let v be a packet to be routed from processor $P_{i,j}$ to processor $P_{k,l}$. The algorithm consists of two phases. In the first phase, v is routed along column j towards row k, which is the destination row. In the second phase, v is routed along row k towards its destination processor $P_{k,l}$. In each phase, a row or column is treated like a linear array with $\sqrt{n}$ processors. In the first phase, there is no contention on the links, which implies that all packets will arrive to their destination row in at most $\sqrt{n} - 1$ steps. In the second phase, however, many packets may pile up at an intermediate processor. For example, consider the case in which all processors in column 1 need to send to row $\sqrt{n}/2$. At each single step, processor $P_{\sqrt{n}/2,1}$ receives two packets; one from the top and another from the bottom. This results in half of the incoming packets piling up at this intermediate processor. However, using the right protocol to arbitrate link contention results in an efficient implementation of phase 2. By giving priority to packets that need to go farthest, routing in the second phase can be accomplished in at most $\sqrt{n} - 1$ steps. It follows that using the farthest-first heuristic, all packets can be routed to their destinations in at most $2\sqrt{n} - 2$ steps. To see this, consider the instance in which there is only one queue Q in row i. Let the packets stored in Q be $u_{i,1}, u_{i,2}, \ldots$, where the $u_{i,j}$'s are sorted in decreasing order of the distance from their destinations. Initially, $u_{i,1}$ is allowed to move to its destination without delay. Its destination can be as far as $\sqrt{n}$, which means the distance between Q and the target of $u_{i,1}$ is at most $\sqrt{n} - 1$. In the next step, $u_{i,2}$ is allowed to move to its destination without delay; it follows $u_{i,1}$ and never collides with it. Note in this case that the destination of $u_{i,2}$ can be as far as $\sqrt{n} - 1$ because of the assumption of permutation routing. Hence, it will take $u_{i,2}$ to reach its destination $1 + \sqrt{n} - 2 = \sqrt{n} - 1$ steps. In general, it will take $u_{i,k}$ to reach its destination in at most $k - 1 + \sqrt{n} - k = \sqrt{n} - 1$ steps. The generalization to more than one queue is straightforward.

4.9.3 *Randomized routing on the mesh*

Although, as we have shown, the greedy algorithm is optimal in the sense that it uses the least amount of time, it suffers from large queues being built up at intermediate processors. This makes the greedy algorithm impractical. In this section, we show that using randomization, the maximum queue size can be reduced drastically without increasing the routing time substantially. We show that, using randomization, the routing time is $3\sqrt{n} + o(\sqrt{n})$ using queues of size $O(\log n)$ with high probability. Let v be a packet with source $P_{i,j}$ and destination $P_{k,l}$. The algorithm routes v in three phases:

Phase 1: Route v to a random intermediate processor in column j, say processor $P_{r,j}$.

Phase 2: Send v along the same row r to its destination column l.

Phase 3: Send v to its final destination, i.e., to processor $P_{k,l}$.

In phase 1, assume that edge contention is resolved using the farthest-first protocol. Thus, each packet moves without contention to its randomly chosen row, and thus suffers no delays. Hence, as discussed in Section 4.9.1 for routing in the linear array, phase 1 is completed within $\sqrt{n} - 1$ steps or less.

We will assume that edge contention in phase 2 is resolved by giving priority at a processor to the packet which most recently entered that processor. Thus, once a packet starts moving in a row, it never stops until it reaches its destination column. Consider a packet that starts moving at processor $P_{r,j}$ in phase 2. This packet may be delayed by all packets originating at processors $P_{r,1}, P_{r,2}, \ldots, P_{r,j}$. There are at most $\sqrt{n}$ packets at the end of phase 1 at processor $P_{r,j}$ in column j. Each packet at column j ends up at processor $P_{r,j}$ with probability $\frac{1}{\sqrt{n}}$. For $1 \leq s \leq j$, define the random variable $X_{r,s}$ to be the number of packets at processor $P_{r,s}$ at the start of phase 2. Then, $X_{r,s}$ has the binomial distribution with $\mathbf{E}[X_{r,s}] = \sqrt{n} \times \frac{1}{\sqrt{n}} = 1$ (see Section A.4.3). Let

$$Y_j = \sum_{s=1}^{j} X_{r,s}.$$

That is, Y_j counts the total number of packets at processors $P_{r,1}, P_{r,2}$, ..., $P_{r,j}$ at the start of phase 2. By linearity of expectations (see Section A.4.3),

$$\mu = \mathbf{E}[Y_j] = \mathbf{E}\left[\sum_{s=1}^{j} X_{r,s}\right] = \sum_{s=1}^{j} \mathbf{E}[X_{r,s}] = \sum_{s=1}^{j} 1 = j.$$

(See Section A.4.3). Now, we can apply Chernoff bound in Theorem A.3 to the probability of there being a substantial number of packets delaying a particular packet v at processor $P_{r,j}$. The Chernoff bound is

$$\mathbf{Pr}[Y_j > (1+\delta)\mu] = \mathbf{Pr}\left[\sum_{s=1}^{j} X_{r,s} > (1+\delta)\mu\right] < e^{-\mu\delta^2/4}; \quad (\delta < 2e-1).$$

We compute the probability that v is delayed by $j+\sqrt{4(c+1)j\ln n}$ packets, $c > 0$. So, we require that $(1+\delta)\mu = j+\sqrt{4(c+1)j\ln n}$ or $\delta = \frac{\sqrt{4(c+1)j\ln n}}{j}$. That is,

$$\mathbf{Pr}\left[Y_j > j+\sqrt{4(c+1)j\ln n}\right] < e^{-\left(\sqrt{4(c+1)\ln n}\right)^2/4} = e^{-(c+1)\ln n}$$

$$= n^{-c-1}.$$

Thus, the probability that v is delayed by $j + \sqrt{4(c+1)j\ln n}$ packets is bounded above by n^{-c-1}, $c > 0$. This is a bound for the probability that a given packet is delayed more than $j + \sqrt{4(c+1)j\ln n}$ steps. But we want to get a bound for the probability that no packet gets delayed more than $j + \sqrt{4(c+1)j\ln n}$ steps. For that, it is enough to use Boole's inequality for probabilities as a bound (Eq. (3.1)): There are n packets in total, and the probability that one of these packets is delayed by more than $j + \sqrt{4(c+1)j\ln n}$ steps is bounded above by $n \times n^{-c-1} = n^{-c}, c > 0$. Notice that if a packet at processor $P_{r,j}$ is delayed by $j + \sqrt{4(c+1)j\ln n}$, then it takes $j + \sqrt{4(c+1)j\ln n} + \sqrt{n} - j$ steps for this packet to reach its correct column. This is at most $\sqrt{n} + o(\sqrt{n})$ steps. So we can make the following assertion: With probability at least $1 - \frac{1}{n^c}$ every packet reaches its phase 2 destination in $\sqrt{n} + o(\sqrt{n})$ or fewer steps.

In phase 3, each packet is in its correct column, and there is at most one packet destined for each processor. We will assume that edge contention in phase 3 is resolved using the farthest-first protocol. Hence, this phase is completed within $\sqrt{n} - 1$ steps or less. Thus, the overall running time of the randomized algorithm is $3\sqrt{n} + o(\sqrt{n})$ with probability at least $1 - \frac{1}{n^c}$, $c > 0$.

Now, we bound the queue size in all processors. At the end of phase 1 and during phase 2, the number of packets that can accumulate at any processor is at most $\sqrt{n}$. Recall that the random variable $X_{r,s}$ denotes the number of packets at processor $P_{r,s}$ at the start of phase 2, and that $X_{r,s}$ has the binomial distribution with $\mu = \mathbf{E}[X_{r,s}] = \sqrt{n} \times \frac{1}{\sqrt{n}} = 1$ (see Section A.4.3). Now, we can apply the Chernoff bound in Theorem A.3 to the probability of there being a substantial number of packets at processor $P_{r,s}$ at the end of phase 1 and during phase 2. The Chernoff bound is

$$\mathbf{Pr}\left[X_{r,s} > (1 + \delta)\mu\right] < 2^{-\delta\mu}; \quad (\delta > 2e - 1).$$

We compute the probability that there are more than $1 + (1 + c)\log n$ packets, $c > 0$, at processor $P_{r,s}$, where $\mu = 1$. So, we require that $(1+\delta)\mu = 1 + (1 + c)\log n$, or $\delta = (1 + c)\log n$. That is,

$$\mathbf{Pr}\left[X_{r,s} > 1 + (1 + c)\log n\right] < 2^{-(1+c)\log n}$$
$$= n^{-(1+c)}.$$

Using Boole's inequality (Eq. (3.1)), the probability that there is at least one processor with queue size more than $1 + (1 + c)\log n$ is at most $n \times n^{-(1+c)} = n^{-c}$. It follows that in phases 1 and 2, the queue size is at most $1 + (c + 1)\log n = O(\log n)$ with probability at least $1 - \frac{1}{n^c}$. Since queues can never increase during phase 3, the queue size during this phase is $O(\log n)$.

In summary, the above randomized algorithm runs in time $3\sqrt{n} + o(\sqrt{n})$ steps and uses queues of size $O(\log n)$ with probability at least $1 - O(1/n^c)$, $c > 0$. The running time can be reduced to $2\sqrt{n} + o(\sqrt{n})$ by dividing each column to strips of size $\frac{\sqrt{n}}{\log n}$ and routing each packet in phase 1 to a random location in its own strip. The analysis is similar to the above. Thus, we conclude that there is a randomized algorithm that runs in time

$2\sqrt{n} + o(\sqrt{n})$ steps and uses queues of size $O(\log n)$ with probability at least $1 - O(1/n^c)$, $c > 0$.

4.10 Matrix Multiplication on the Mesh

Consider the problem of matrix multiplication on the mesh: Given two square matrices A and B of order $\sqrt{n} \times \sqrt{n}$, find their product $C = AB$.

4.10.1 *The first algorithm*

In this section, we show how to perform matrix multiplication $C = AB$ of dimensions $\sqrt{n} \times \sqrt{n}$ on a $2\sqrt{n} \times 2\sqrt{n}$ mesh. It is assumed that matrix A is stored in the lower-left quadrant, matrix B is stored in the upper-right quadrant, and the resultant matrix C is to be computed in the lower-right quadrant (see Fig. 4.12 for the case $\sqrt{n} = 4$).

Initially, the values of the $c_{i,j}$'s are set to 0. At time 1, row 1 of matrix A moves one step to the right and column 1 of matrix B moves one step down, and the product of $a_{1,\sqrt{n}} b_{\sqrt{n},1}$ is computed and added to $c_{1,1}$. At time 2, row 1 of matrix A and column 1 of matrix B continue moving in the same directions, and row 2 of matrix A and column 2 of matrix B start moving left to right, and top down, respectively. In general, at time k, the kth row of matrix A and the kth column of matrix B start moving right and

				b_{11}	b_{12}	b_{13}	b_{14}
				b_{21}	b_{22}	b_{23}	b_{24}
				b_{31}	b_{32}	b_{33}	b_{34}
				b_{41}	b_{42}	b_{43}	b_{44}
a_{11}	a_{12}	a_{13}	a_{14}	c_{11}	c_{12}	c_{13}	c_{14}
a_{21}	a_{22}	a_{23}	a_{24}	c_{21}	c_{22}	c_{23}	c_{24}
a_{31}	a_{32}	a_{33}	a_{34}	c_{31}	c_{32}	c_{33}	c_{34}
a_{41}	a_{42}	a_{43}	a_{44}	c_{41}	c_{42}	c_{43}	c_{44}

Fig. 4.12.   Matrix multiplication, the first algorithm.

Table 4.1. Computing $c_{1,1}$ and $c_{1,2}$ by the first matrix multiplication algorithm.

Time	c_{11}	c_{12}
1	$a_{14}b_{41}$	0
2	$a_{14}b_{41} + a_{13}b_{31}$	$a_{14}b_{42}$
3	$a_{14}b_{41} + a_{13}b_{31} + a_{12}b_{21}$	$a_{14}b_{42} + a_{13}b_{32}$
4	$a_{14}b_{41} + a_{13}b_{31} + a_{12}b_{21} + a_{11}b_{11}$	$a_{14}b_{42} + a_{13}b_{32} + a_{12}b_{22}$
5	$a_{14}b_{41} + a_{13}b_{31} + a_{12}b_{21} + a_{11}b_{11}$	$a_{14}b_{42} + a_{13}b_{32} + a_{12}b_{22} + a_{11}b_{12}$

down, respectively. Each processor $P_{i,j}$ upon receiving data from its left and top neighbors, computes the product of these values and adds them to the partial sum $c_{i,j}$. At time $k+1$, each processor sends the values received during time k to its neighboring processors in the direction they are moving. Therefore, at time $\sqrt{n}$, the $\sqrt{n}$th row of matrix A and the $\sqrt{n}$th column of matrix B start moving right and down, respectively, and additional $\sqrt{n} - 1$ steps are needed to reach the processor holding $c_{\sqrt{n},\sqrt{n}}$. Clearly, the running time of the algorithm is $\Theta(\sqrt{n})$.

Example 4.5 Table 4.1 shows the results of the computations of $c_{1,1}$ and $c_{1,2}$ using the first matrix multiplication algorithm. The values of $c_{1,1}$ and $c_{1,2}$ are determined incrementally starting at 0. Note that some of the other computations for the rest of the $c_{i,j}$'s are done concurrently. $\square$

4.10.2   *The second algorithm*

In this section, we show how to compute the matrix product $C = AB$ of dimensions $\sqrt{n} \times \sqrt{n}$ on a mesh of size n, that is, a $\sqrt{n} \times \sqrt{n}$ mesh. Assume that the mesh is a wrap-around mesh (torus), so additions of indices are to be carried out modulo $\sqrt{n}$. Initially, the input matrices are stored in the mesh, where processor $P_{i,j}$ holds the elements $a_{i,j}$ and $b_{i,j}$, and the output elements are to be stored in $c_{i,j}$. The algorithm consists of two phases; the first phase is the shifting phase, and the second phase is the multiplication phase.

In the shifting phase, the $a_{i,j}$'s are shifted to the left, and the $b_{i,j}$'s are shifted upwards as follows. The $a_{1,j}$'s in the first row are shifted to the left by one position, those $a_{2,j}$'s in the second row by two positions, and in

a_{11} b_{11}	a_{12} b_{12}	a_{13} b_{13}	a_{14} b_{14}
a_{21} b_{21}	a_{22} b_{22}	a_{23} b_{23}	a_{24} b_{24}
a_{31} b_{31}	a_{32} b_{32}	a_{33} b_{33}	a_{34} b_{34}
a_{41} b_{41}	a_{42} b_{42}	a_{43} b_{43}	a_{44} b_{44}

(a)

a_{12} b_{21}	a_{13} b_{32}	a_{14} b_{43}	a_{11} b_{14}
a_{23} b_{31}	a_{24} b_{42}	a_{21} b_{13}	a_{22} b_{24}
a_{34} b_{41}	a_{31} b_{12}	a_{32} b_{23}	a_{33} b_{34}
a_{41} b_{11}	a_{42} b_{22}	a_{43} b_{33}	a_{44} b_{44}

(b)

Fig. 4.13. Matrix multiplication, the second algorithm. (a) Initial input. (b) After the shifting phase.

general, the elements $a_{i,j}$ in the ith row are shifted to the left by i positions. The $b_{i,1}$'s in the first column are shifted upwards by one position, those $b_{i,2}$'s in the second column by two positions, and in general, the elements $b_{i,j}$ in the jth column are shifted upwards by j positions. So, the data is rearranged so that processor $P_{i,j}$ holds $a_{i,i+j}$ and $b_{i+j,j}$. Figure 4.13(a) shows the initial input, and Fig. 4.13(b) shows the input after the shifting phase.

In the multiplication phase, $P_{1,1}$ evaluates $c_{1,1}$ by computing the dot product $c_{1,1} = \sum_{k=1}^{\sqrt{n}} a_{1,k} b_{k,1}$ as in the traditional matrix multiplication method. It does this using the following steps (see Fig. 4.13(b)):

(1) Set $c_{1,1} \leftarrow a_{1,2} b_{2,1}$.
(2) Shift the first row to the left and the first column upwards, and set $c_{1,1} \leftarrow c_{1,1} + a_{1,3} b_{3,1}$.

$\vdots$

(3) Shift the first row to the left and the first column upwards, and set $c_{1,1} \leftarrow c_{1,1} + a_{1,\sqrt{n}} b_{\sqrt{n},1}$ (in Fig. 4.13(b), $\sqrt{n} = 4$).
(4) Shift the first row to the left and the first column upwards, and compute the final result $c_{1,1} \leftarrow c_{1,1} + a_{1,1} b_{1,1}$.

The computation of the rest of $c_{i,j}$'s is done in a similar fashion. The algorithm is shown as Algorithm MESHMATRIXMULT. For clarity, the $a_{i,j}$'s and $b_{i,j}$'s will be renamed so that the contents of $P_{i,j}$ after shifting will be

---

Algorithm 4.7 MESHMATRIXMULT
Input: Two $\sqrt{n} \times \sqrt{n}$ matrices A and B.
Output: The product $C = A \times B$.

1. **for** $i \leftarrow 1$ **to** $\sqrt{n}$ **do in parallel**
2.   Shift row i to the left i positions
3. **end for**
4. **for** $j \leftarrow 1$ **to** $\sqrt{n}$ **do in parallel**
5.   Shift column j upwards j positions
6. **end for**
7. **for** $i \leftarrow 1$ **to** $\sqrt{n}$ **do in parallel**
8.   **for** $j \leftarrow 1$ **to** $\sqrt{n}$ **do in parallel**
9. $c_{i,j} \leftarrow a_{i,j}b_{i,j}$
10.   **end for**
11. **end for**
12. **for** $k \leftarrow 1$ **to** $\sqrt{n} - 1$ **do in parallel**
13.   **for** $i \leftarrow 1$ **to** $\sqrt{n}$ **do in parallel**
14.   **for** $j \leftarrow 1$ **to** $\sqrt{n}$ **do in parallel**
15. $a_{i,j} \leftarrow a_{i,j+1}$
16. $b_{i,j} \leftarrow b_{i+1,j}$
17. $c_{i,j} \leftarrow c_{i,j} + a_{i,j}b_{i,j}$
18.   **end for**
19.   **end for**
20. **end for**

---

called $a_{i,j}$ and $b_{i,j}$. Recall that additions of indices are to be carried out modulo $\sqrt{n}$.

Clearly, both the first phase and the second phase take $\Theta(\sqrt{n})$ time, and hence the running time of the entire algorithm is $\Theta(\sqrt{n})$

4.11 Computing the Transitive Closure on the Mesh

Let A be a $\sqrt{n} \times \sqrt{n}$ adjacency matrix of a directed graph G. The *transitive closure* of G is represented as a $\sqrt{n} \times \sqrt{n}$ Boolean matrix A^* in which $A^*(i,j) = 1$ if and only if there is a path in G from i to j, where we assume that the set of vertices is $\{1, 2, \ldots, \sqrt{n}\}$. Computing the transitive closure is critical to a variety of efficient solutions to fundamental graph problems.

Define $A^k(i,j)$ to be 1 if and only if there is a path from i to j that passes by vertices in the set $\{1, 2, \ldots, k\}$, and 0 otherwise. $A^0(i,j) = A(i,j)$

is 1 if and only if there is an edge in G from i to j. Define $a_{i,j}^k = A^k(i,j)$. $A^k(i,j)$ is computed from the recurrence

$$A^k(i,j) = A^{k-1}(i,j) \vee (A^{k-1}(i,k) \wedge A^{k-1}(k,j)); \quad A^0(i,j) = A(i,j).$$
$$(4.1)$$

By Eq. (4.1), we see that

$$A^k(k,k) = A^{k-1}(k,k) \vee (A^{k-1}(k,k) \wedge A^{k-1}(k,k)) = A^{k-1}(k,k), \quad (4.2)$$
$$A^k(k,j) = A^{k-1}(k,j) \vee (A^{k-1}(k,k) \wedge A^{k-1}(k,j)) = A^{k-1}(k,j), \quad (4.3)$$

and

$$A^k(i,k) = A^{k-1}(i,k) \vee (A^{k-1}(i,k) \wedge A^{k-1}(k,k)) = A^{k-1}(i,k). \quad (4.4)$$

The algorithm to be presented makes use of Eqs. (4.1)–(4.4) to compute the transitive closure of A efficiently in parallel. Assume the n processors are numbered $P_{1,1}, P_{1,2}, \ldots, P_{\sqrt{n},\sqrt{n}}$. The algorithm consists of $\sqrt{n}$ phases, where in phase k, the rows of A^k are computed from the rows of A^{k-1} for $1 \leq k \leq \sqrt{n}$. The rows of the matrix $A^0 = A$ are entered from the top of the mesh starting from row 1 one at a time (see Fig. 4.14(a)), and travel in a systolic fashion to the bottom of the mesh, where they exit starting from row 1. We will distinguish between two states of matrix rows. The first state is the "unmarked" state, where all rows are in the unmarked state by default. So, all rows start as unmarked rows once they enter the mesh from the top. The second state is the "marked" state. Matrix row i enters the marked state once it bypasses all marked rows, and stops moving downward when reaching row i of the mesh in step $2i - 1$. It stays as a marked row until all other rows in the matrix pass over it at step $\sqrt{n} + 2i - 1$, where it becomes an unmarked row and starts moving downward again towards the bottom of the mesh.

Consider Fig. 4.14 in which the process is shown using a mesh with four rows. The shaded rectangles are marked rows, while the small white rectangles are unmarked rows. First, row 1 of the input matrix A^0 is entered into row 1 of the mesh (see Fig. 4.14(b)). It immediately becomes a marked row in step 1. The first phase commences next where rows $2, 3, \ldots, \sqrt{n}$, which are unmarked rows, pass over the first marked row (see Figs. 4.14(c)–(e)). Consider the first time unmarked row 2 is moved to the first row of

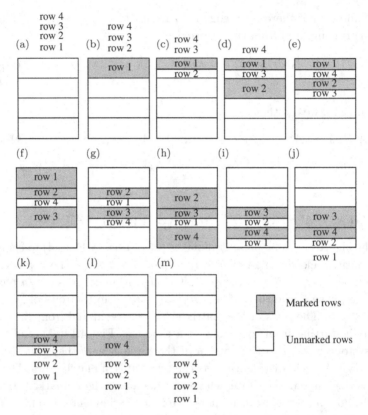

Fig. 4.14.   Computing the transitive closure on the mesh, where $\sqrt{n} = 4$.

the mesh next to the marked row 1 (see Fig. 4.14(c)). First, processor $P_{1,1}$ broadcasts $a_{2,1}^0$ to all other processors in the first row of the mesh. Next, for each $j, 1 \leq j \leq \sqrt{n}$, $a_{2,j}^0$ is updated to $a_{2,j}^1$ using the formula $a_{2,j}^1 = a_{2,j}^0 \vee (a_{2,1}^0 \wedge a_{1,j}^0)$. Next, row 2 of the matrix is moved to row 2 of the mesh and becomes a marked row (Fig. 4.14(d)). Later, when unmarked row i meets marked row 1, processor $P_{1,1}$ broadcasts $a_{i,1}^0$ to all other processors in the first row of the mesh. Next, for each $j, 1 \leq j \leq \sqrt{n}$, $a_{i,j}^0$ is updated to $a_{i,j}^1$ using the formula $a_{i,j}^1 = a_{i,j}^0 \vee (a_{i,1}^0 \wedge a_{1,j}^0)$. As the unmarked rows of A^0 pass over the first marked row, they are thus updated to become the rows of A^1. Once processing row i is complete by marked rows $1, 2, \ldots, i - 1$, it is moved to row i of the mesh and becomes a marked row (see, for example, row 3 in Fig. 4.14(f)).

It should be emphasized, however, that, by Eq. (4.3), the kth row is not processed during the kth phase. This is why, for example, row 1 was not processed in the first phase. In general, the kth phase is accomplished as rows $1, 2, \ldots, k-1$ and $k+1, k+2, \ldots, \sqrt{n}$ pass over the marked row k in some order. By the time an unmarked row reaches the kth marked row in the kth row of the mesh, it has already been updated to be a row of A^{k-1}. (See Figs. 4.14(d)-(h)). As the unmarked ith row passes over the marked kth row, processor $P_{k,k}$ broadcasts $a_{i,k}^{k-1}$ to all processors in the kth row of the mesh. Processor $P_{k,j}$ in this row can update $a_{i,j}^{k-1}$ using the formula $a_{i,j}^{k} = a_{i,j}^{k-1} \vee (a_{i,k}^{k-1} \wedge a_{k,j}^{k-1})$.

Recall that marked row i will be stored in the ith row of the mesh in step $2i-1$, and at step $\sqrt{n}+2i-1$, it becomes an unmarked row and begins moving downward. It will exit the mesh from the bottom at step $2\sqrt{n}+i-1$. The remaining parts of Figs. 4.14 depict the rest of the algorithm. It follows that after a total of $3\sqrt{n}-1$ steps excluding data broadcasting, $A^{*} = A^{\sqrt{n}}$ will have been output from the bottom of the mesh. This implies that the overall running time is $\Theta(\sqrt{n})$ excluding data broadcasting.

Broadcasting of data items can be accomplished efficiently by interleaving it with updating the matrix elements. Figure 4.15 shows how broadcasting at multiple rows can be interleaved with row computations. In Fig. 4.15(a), broadcasting of $a_{4,k}^{k}$ in a 4×4 mesh is shown for $0 \leq k \leq 3$. Note that broadcasting many elements can take place concurrently in the same row. For example, broadcasting of $a_{3,1}^{0}$ may be in progress in row 1 while $a_{4,1}^{0}$ is moving to the right.

In Fig. 4.16, the overall data flow for the construction of transitive closure is shown without the details of synchronization; delays are required in

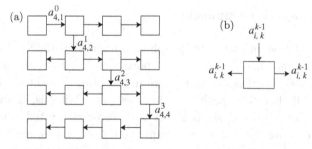

Fig. 4.15. Interleaving broadcasting with updating elements of the transitive closure in a 4×4 mesh.

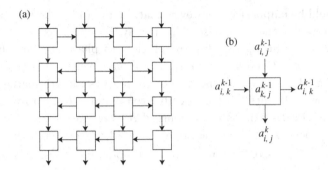

Fig. 4.16.   Data flow in computing the transitive closure in a 4×4 mesh.

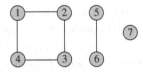

Fig. 4.17.   An undirected graph with three connected components.

some data transmissions. As shown in Fig. 4.16(b), each processor computes $a_{i,j}^k$ using the formula $a_{i,j}^k = a_{i,j}^{k-1} \vee (a_{i,k}^{k-1} \wedge a_{k,j}^{k-1})$. Thus, the construction of the transitive closure is not performed row by row; each element of the matrix moves downward independently.

The foregoing description implies that the overall running time of the construction of transitive closure on a $\sqrt{n} \times \sqrt{n}$ mesh, including broadcasting, is $\Theta(\sqrt{n})$.

4.12   Connected Components

Let $G = (V, E)$ be an undirected graph with adjacency matrix A and transitive closure matrix $A^* = \{a_{i,j}\}$. A^* partitions V into *connected components*, where two vertices a_i and a_j are in the same connected component if and only if there is a path in G between them, that is, if and only if $a_{i,j}^* = 1$. Figure 4.17 shows a graph with three connected components. Thus, to compute the connected components of G, we compute the transitive closure A^*. For example, the connected components in Fig. 4.17 are $\{1, 2, 3, 4\}, \{5, 6\}, \{7\}$.

4.13 Shortest Paths

Let $G = (V, E)$ be a weighted directed graph on n vertices with no loops, in which each edge (i, j) has a weight $w[i, j]$. If there is no edge from vertex i to vertex j, then $w[i, j] = \infty$. For simplicity, we will assume that $V = \{1, 2, \ldots, \sqrt{n}\}$. We assume that G does not have negative weight cycles, that is, cycles whose total weight is negative. The problem is to find the *distance* from each vertex to all other vertices, where the distance from vertex i to vertex j is the length of a shortest path from i to j. Let i and j be two different vertices in V. Define $A^k(i, j)$ to be the shortest distance from i to j that passes by vertices in the set $\{1, 2, \ldots, k\}$, and $A^0(i, j) = w(i, j)$. $A^k(i, j)$ is computed from the recurrence

$$A^k(i, j) = \min\{A^{k-1}(i, j), A^{k-1}(i, k) + A^{k-1}(k, j)\}; \quad A^0(i, j) = A(i, j).$$
$$(4.5)$$

By Eq. (4.5), we see that

$$A^k(k, j) = \min\{A^{k-1}(k, j), A^{k-1}(k, k) + A^{k-1}(k, j)\} = A^{k-1}(k, j), \quad (4.6)$$

and

$$A^k(i, k) = \min\{A^{k-1}(i, k), A^{k-1}(i, k) + A^{k-1}(k, k)\} = A^{k-1}(i, k). \quad (4.7)$$

Notice the resemblance between Eqs. 4.1–4.4 and Eqs. 4.5–4.7. Hence, the algorithm for transitive closure on the $\sqrt{n} \times \sqrt{n}$ mesh discussed in Section 4.11 can be used with simple modifications. Specifically, $\vee$ and $\wedge$ in Eqs. 4.1–4.4 and the rest of the algorithm for transitive closure are replaced by min and +. It follows that computing all shortest paths can be effected in $\Theta(\sqrt{n})$ time on a $\sqrt{n} \times \sqrt{n}$ mesh, which is optimal.

4.14 Computing the Convex Hull of a Set of Points on the Mesh

Let $S = \{p_1, p_2, \ldots, p_n\}$ be a set of n points in the plane stored in a $\sqrt{n} \times \sqrt{n}$ mesh one point per processor, where n is a power of 4. For definitions related to the convex hull, refer to Section 2.20; In this section, we present two algorithms for computing the convex hull of S, $CH(S)$, on the $\sqrt{n} \times \sqrt{n}$ mesh; the first runs in time $O(\sqrt{n}\log n)$ and the other in time $\Theta(\sqrt{n})$.

4.14.1 *The first algorithm*

The first algorithm is almost a straightforward implementation of the PRAM algorithm presented in Section 2.20, and given in Algorithm PAR-CONVEXHULL. The algorithm consists of repeated applications of the steps given in Observations 2.2 and 2.3.

As a preprocessing step, the points in S are first sorted in ascending order of their x-coordinates in $\Theta(\sqrt{n})$ time. So, assume that $x(p_1) \leq x(p_2) \leq \ldots \leq x(p_n)$, where $x(p_i)$ denotes the x-coordinate of point p_i. We will assume for simplicity that no three points of S are collinear, and no two points have the same x-coordinate. Next, the set of points S is divided into four parts $S_1 = \{p_1, p_2, \ldots, p_{n/4}\}$, $S_2 = \{p_{n/4+1}, p_{n/4+2}, \ldots, p_{n/2}\}$, $S_3 = \{p_{n/2+1}, p_{n/2+2}, \ldots, p_{3n/4}\}$ and $S_4 = \{p_{3n/4+1}, p_{3n/4+2}, \ldots, p_n\}$, and arranged in the mesh as shown in Fig. 4.18(b). Now, we recursively determine the four convex hulls of the four parts $CH(S_1)$, $CH(S_2)$, $CH(S_3)$ and $CH(S_4)$. Figure 4.18(c) shows the four convex hulls of the points in part (a) of the figure.

From $CH(S_1)$ and $CH(S_2)$, we identify $CH(S_1 \cup S_2)$, and denote the set of vertices representing $S_1 \cup S_2$ as P. From $CH(S_3)$ and $CH(S_4)$, we identify $CH(S_3 \cup S_4)$, and denote the set of vertices representing $S_3 \cup S_4$ as Q. From $CH(P)$ and $CH(Q)$, we identify $CH(P \cup Q)$, which is the desired convex hull $CH(S)$. In what follows, we turn our attention to computing the upper hull of P, $UH(P)$. Computing the lower hull of P, $LH(P)$, and hence $CH(P)$ can be determined in a similar fashion and in parallel with $UH(P)$. Finally, finding $CH(Q)$, and hence $CH(S)$ can be achieved by a similar means.

The steps for finding $UH(P)$ and hence $LH(P)$ are similar to those described in Section 2.20. In each iteration of the binary search, vertex x_i of $UH(S_1)$ is broadcast to the processors holding the vertices of $UH(S_2)$ and one of those processors succeeds in finding its tangent line $\overline{x_i v_i}$ with $UH(S_2)$. Clearly, this takes $\Theta(\sqrt{n})$ time on the $\frac{\sqrt{n}}{2} \times \frac{\sqrt{n}}{2}$ mesh. Since there are $O(\log n)$ iterations in the binary search for finding the upper common tangent, the overall running time for finding this tangent is $O(\sqrt{n}\log n)$. Recall that the computation of $LH(P)$ is done in parallel with that of

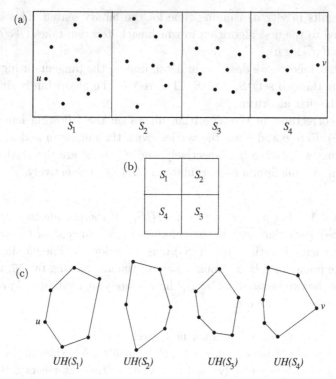

Fig. 4.18.   (a) The set of points S. (b) Arrangement of the subsets on the mesh. (c) Convex hulls of S_1, S_2, S_3 and S_4.

$UH(P)$. Clearly, the remaining work of finding $UH(P)$ and then $CH(P)$ takes $\Theta(\sqrt{n})$ time. Hence the overall running time for finding $CH(P)$ from $CH(S_1)$ ad $CH(S_2)$ is $O(\sqrt{n}\log n)$. It should be noted that finding $CH(P)$ and $CH(Q)$ are done concurrently, and it remains to find $CH(S)$, which asymptotically takes the same running time. It follows that the running time of the algorithm obeys the recurrence $T(n) = T(n/4) + O(\sqrt{n}\log n) = O(\sqrt{n}\log n)$.

4.14.2   The second algorithm

The algorithm to be presented is similar to the first algorithm. However, the main difference is in the binary search and how it is conducted. In this algorithm, the number of elements considered in iteration i is $O(\sqrt{n/2^i})$, which results in $\Theta(\sqrt{n})$ running time for the binary search. This is to be contrasted to the first algorithm in which each iteration takes $O(\sqrt{n})$ for a total of $O(\sqrt{n}\log n)$.

In what follows, we describe in detail finding the tangents using binary search for the two sets S_1 and S_2. The rest of the algorithm is similar to that of the first algorithm.

The correctness of the algorithm hinges on the following lemma (see Fig. 4.19). Here v and u are the vertices with the minimum and maximum x-coordinates in $CH(S_1)$, respectively, and v' and u' are the vertices with minimum and maximum x-coordinate in $CH(S_2)$, respectively.

Lemma 4.1   Let w be a vertex of $CH(S_1)$. If there is another vertex w' of $CH(S_2)$ such that $\overline{ww'}$ is the common upper tangent of $CH(S_1)$ and $CH(S_2)$, then all vertices in $CH(S_2)$ must lie below the line passing by $\overline{xw}$ and some points in $CH(S_2)$ must lie above the line passing by $\overline{wy}$, where x and y are the two vertices in $CH(S_1)$ immediately succeeding and preceding w in counterclockwise order.

Proof.   The tangent line must lie entirely within the wedge defined by $\overline{xw}$ and $\overline{wy}$. If $\overline{xw}$ is not above all points in $CH(S_2)$, then any line that passes by w and lies entirely inside the wedge either intersects $CH(S_2)$ at more than one point or lies below the line $\overline{v'u'}$. On the other hand, if $\overline{wy}$ is above $CH(S_2)$, then this wedge does not contain a point from $CH(S_2)$. In both cases, there does not exist a common upper tangent $\overline{ww'}$ of $CH(S_1)$ and $CH(S_2)$. $\square$

Lemma 4.1 suggests the following method for identifying the vertex w. We perform binary search on the set of vertices of $CH(S_1)$. Initially, w is assigned the hull vertex in $CH(S_1)$ that is half the way between u and v in counterclockwise order. Next, in each iteration, we do one of the following according to the result of the test implied by Lemma 4.1 (see Fig. 4.19).

(a) If all vertices in $CH(S_2)$ lie below the line passing by $\overline{xw}$ and some points in $CH(S_2)$ lie above the line passing by $\overline{wy}$, then w, x and y have been identified.

(b) If $\overline{xw}$ is not above $CH(S_2)$, then assign the vertex x to u and recompute w as the middle between u and v in counterclockwise order.

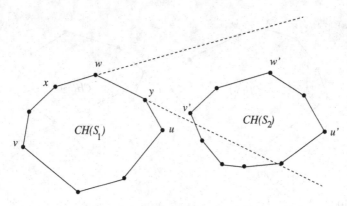

Fig. 4.19. Proof of Lemma 4.1

(c) If (a) above is not satisfied and $\overline{xw}$ is above $CH(S_2)$, then assign vertex y to v and recompute w as the middle between u and v in counterclockwise order.

Example 4.6   Consider Fig. 4.20 in which the steps of binary search are shown. In Fig. 4.20(a), the two convex hulls are shown. w is set half the way between v and u, in counterclockwise order. The extension of the line $\overline{xw}$ crosses $CH(S_2)$ at more than one point. Hence, the vertex x is assigned to u. w is recomputed as half the way between u and v and x and y are relocated as shown in Fig. 4.20(b). y is assigned to the vertex before w in counterclockwise order, which happens to be u. Next, since the extensions of both $\overline{xw}$ and $\overline{wy}$ are above $CH(S_2)$, v is set equal to y in Fig. 4.20(c). Then, w, x and y are recomputed as shown in Fig. 4.20(c). In this part of the figure, $u = v = w$, and the test in (a) above is satisfied, so the search is halted, and w is declared as one end of the tangent line.   □

If we perform binary search naturally, each iteration takes $\Theta(\sqrt{n})$ for a total of $\Theta(\sqrt{n}\log n)$. Hence, an approach is needed to reduce the running time. We will succeed if we can reduce the running time of the ith iteration of binary search to $\Theta(\sqrt{n/2^i})$. Luckily, this can be done by eliminating half of the vertices in $CH(S_1)$ and $CH(S_2)$ from future consideration by binary search. Thus, after the end of each iteration of the binary search, the remaining vertices in $CH(S_1)$ and $CH(S_2)$ are compressed using parallel prefix. Hence, in the ith iteration, the binary search is performed on $\Theta(n/2^i)$ vertices, which means that the ith iteration takes $\Theta(\sqrt{n/2^i})$ time, including the time required for broadcasting and data compression. This implies that

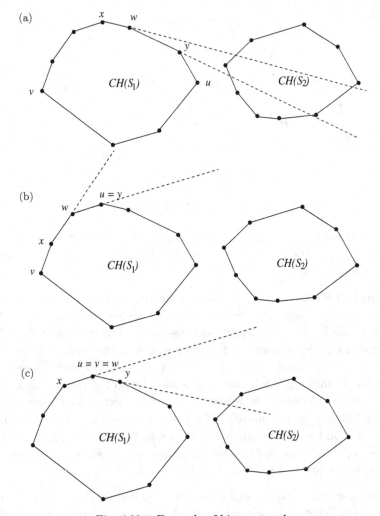

Fig. 4.20. Example of binary search.

the total running time for the binary search is $\sum_{i=0}^{O(\log n)} \Theta(\sqrt{n/2^i})$, which is $\Theta(\sqrt{n})$.

Note that in each iteration, w, x and y are broadcast to the processors holding hull vertices in $CH(S_2)$ above the line $\overline{u'v'}$. Then, the equations of the two lines $\overline{xw}$ and $\overline{wy}$ are computed. The results of the tests given in (a)–(c) above are sent to the vertices of $CH(S_1)$ above the line $\overline{vu}$.

Similar computations of all the above are performed to identify $w', \overline{w'x'}, \overline{y'w'}$ for $CH(S_2)$. It is important that identifying w and w' be done simultaneously, and so is data compression for the remaining data of $CH(S_1)$ and $CH(S_2)$. This is to ensure that half the number of hull vertices after compression in $CH(S_1)$ between v and u and in $CH(S_2)$ between v' and u' are eliminated from further inspection in subsequent iterations of the two binary searches.

Let $P = S_1 \cup S_2$ and $Q = S_3 \cup S_4$. Now, we construct $CH(P) = CH(S_1) \cup CH(S_2)$ by connecting w and w' and z and z' by two edges, where $\overline{zz'}$ is the lower tangent. Also, the vertices inside the quadrilateral defined by w, w', z and z' are removed. At the same time, we construct $CH(Q) = CH(S_3) \cup CH(S_4)$, and finally CH(S)= $CH(P) \cup CH(Q)$. Note that the computations of $CH(P)$ and $CH(Q)$ are done concurrently. The above discussion implies that the overall running time of the algorithm obeys the recurrence $T(n) = T(n/4) + \Theta(\sqrt{n}) = \Theta(\sqrt{n})$.

4.15 Labeling Connected Components

In this section, we consider the problem of labeling figures, i.e., connected black components, of a digitized black picture on a white background. The components are represented as n contiguous 0–1 pixel values stored on a $\sqrt{n} \times \sqrt{n}$ mesh, where n is a power of 4. Two black pixels are neighbors if and only if they are adjacent horizontally, vertically or diagonally. Two black pixels are connected if they are in the same connected component. Every processor that contains a black pixel uses its snake-like index as the initial label of its pixel. When a labeling algorithm terminates, every processor that contain a black pixel will store the minimum label in the component that it belongs to. Figure 4.21 depicts an example in which part (a) is the initial input, and part (b) is the final assignment of labels to connected components.

4.15.1 *The propagation algorithm*

The first algorithm is a simple *propagation* algorithm. In this algorithm, every processor that contains a black pixel (black processor) defines its initial label as its snake-like index. During each subsequent iteration of the algorithm, every black processor sends its current component label to its (at most) eight black neighbors. Every black processors then compares its

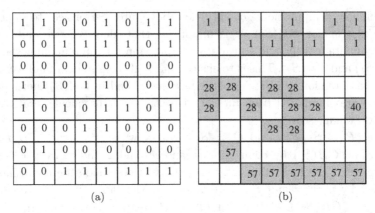

Fig. 4.21.   Labeling connected components.

label with the (at most) eight labels just received, and keeps the minimum of these labels as its component label. This process is repeated for each black processor until all neighboring black processors have the same label.

Let d be the maximum internal distance between any processor P containing a black pixel and the processor P' containing the pixel of minimum label in its component, where the distance is measured in terms of the number of black pixels between P and P'. Then, the maximum number of iterations of the algorithm is d. For instance, in Fig. 4.22, $d = 4$. It is easy to see that d can be as large as $\Theta(n)$ as shown in the instance in Fig. 4.23. Hence, the running time of the propagation algorithm is $O(n)$.

Example 4.7   An example of the propagation algorithm is shown in Fig. 4.22. The number of steps is 4.   □

4.15.2   *The recursive algorithm*

The large cost of the propagation algorithm calls for another alternative that labels the components in $o(n)$ time. One possibility is an algorithm that uses divide-and-conquer to label the figures in time $O(\sqrt{n})$ regardless of the number or shape of the figures. In this algorithm, the pixels are partitioned into four equal quadrants, where the components in each quadrant are labeled independently. After the recursive calls, the only components that may have an incorrect label are those that have a pixel on the border

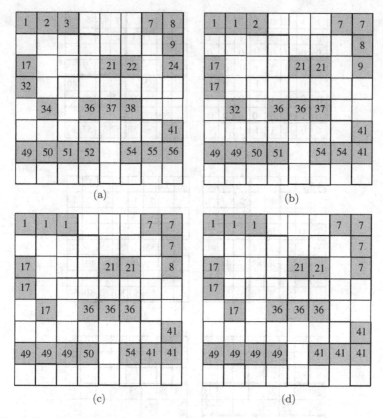

Fig. 4.22. Labeling connected components using the propagation method.

Fig. 4.23. Worst case instance of the propagation method.

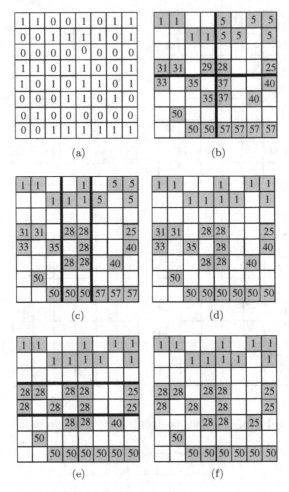

Fig. 4.24. The recursive algorithm for labeling connected components.

between the quadrants. An example is shown in Fig. 4.24. Part (b) of the figure is the result of the recursive calls on the instance shown in part (a).

Next, we merge components that cross the quadrant boundaries. This will be accomplished in two phases. In the first phase, we update the labels of pixels in components that cross the vertical boundary. In the second phase, we update the labels of pixels in components that cross the horizontal boundary.

First, we describe how to merge components around the vertical boundary. The first step is to apply the propagation algorithm on pixels inside the vertical strip consisting of the two middle columns. This will take $O(\sqrt{n})$ time since the number of pixels is $2\sqrt{n}$.

For clarity, we will now use the two-dimensional numbering of processors. Assume that there are two registers associated with every processor in the vertical strip: $\alpha_{i,j}$ and $\beta_{i,j}$, $1 \leq i \leq \sqrt{n}$, $\frac{\sqrt{n}}{2} \leq j \leq \frac{\sqrt{n}}{2}+1$. $\alpha_{i,j}$ will hold the label of the pixel in processor $P_{i,j}$ just after the recursive calls, and $\beta_{i,j}$ will hold the label of the pixel in processor $P_{i,j}$ just after the propagation process in the vertical boundary (for white pixels, $\alpha_{i,j} = \beta_{i,j} = 0$ shown as blank in the figure). Figure 4.24(c) depicts the two columns associated with Fig. 4.24(b) after applying the propagation algorithm on their pixels. For instance, as shown in these two figures, $\alpha_{1,5} = 5$ and $\beta_{1,5} = 1$.

We copy the α and β values in column $\frac{\sqrt{n}}{2}$ to all columns all the way to the left of the mesh, and the α and β values in column $\frac{\sqrt{n}}{2}+1$ to all columns all the way to the right. In other words, for each row i, we copy $\alpha_{i,\sqrt{n}/2}$ and $\beta_{i,\sqrt{n}/2}$ all the way to the left, and copy $\alpha_{i,\sqrt{n}/2+1}$ and $\beta_{i,\sqrt{n}/2+1}$ all the way to the right. (See Exercise 4.39 for the α and β values corresponding to Fig. 4.24(c)). Then, we pipeline all $(\alpha_{i,j}, \beta_{i,j})$ pairs vertically through every pixel. Each time a new pair arrives, we test its α value with the label of the current processor. If they are equal, we set the value of the pixel label equal to the β value of the pair. Thus, every processor will inspect $\sqrt{n}$ pairs, and will process them in $O(\sqrt{n})$ time. Since this is done in parallel among all columns, the total time for all columns is $O(\sqrt{n})$. Figure 4.24(d) shows the labels after the (vertical) updates.

The second phase is symmetrical to the first phase, in which we process the horizontal strip consisting of the two middle horizontal rows. Assume in this phase that there are two registers associated with every processor in the horizontal strip: $\alpha_{i,j}$ and $\beta_{i,j}$, $1 \leq j \leq \sqrt{n}$, $\frac{\sqrt{n}}{2} \leq i \leq \frac{\sqrt{n}}{2}+1$, where the β values are as defined in phase 1, and the α values are the pixel values after the vertical update discussed above. We copy the α and β values in row $\frac{\sqrt{n}}{2}+1$ to all rows all the way to the bottom. Note that we do not need to copy row $\frac{\sqrt{n}}{2}$ to the top half of the mesh, since all labels in the upper half of the mesh are smaller than the labels in the lower half. Figure 4.24(e) depicts the two horizontal rows associated with Fig. 4.24(b) after applying the propagation algorithm on their pixels. Figure 4.24(f) shows the final labels. As in the first phase, the second phase will take

$O(\sqrt{n})$ time. It follows that the overall time taken by the algorithm is given by the recurrence $T(n) = T(n/4) + \Theta(\sqrt{n}) = \Theta(\sqrt{n})$.

4.16   Columnsort

The $r \times s$ two-dimensional mesh is a generalization of the square mesh. It has r rows and s columns. Columnsort is a sorting algorithm designed especially for the $r \times s$ mesh in which $r \geq 2(s-1)^2$. The algorithm is shown as Algorithm COLUMNSORT. It is a generalization of Algorithm ODDEVEN-MERGE for odd–even merging. Assume an $r \times s$ mesh, where $r \geq 2(s-1)^2$, $n = rs$ and $s \mid r$, where n is the number of elements to be sorted. The algorithm sorts into column-major order, so after completion of the algorithm, the (i,j)th entry, $0 \leq i \leq r-1$, $0 \leq j \leq s-1$, will contain the kth item, where $k = i + jr$.

There are eight steps in the algorithm. In Steps 1, 3, 5 and 7, the elements within each column are sorted. In Step 2, the elements are permuted by performing a row-column transformation that corresponds to a transpose of the matrix that defines the mesh, as shown in Fig. 4.25. Step 4 is the reverse of Step 2, as shown in the same figure.

Step 6 of the algorithm consists of a shift of the elements by $\lfloor r/2 \rfloor$ positions, as shown in Fig. 4.26, and Step 8 is the reverse of Step 6.

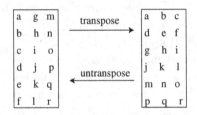

Fig. 4.25.   Transpose and untranspose operations.

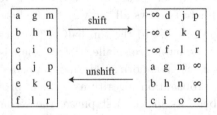

Fig. 4.26.   Shift and unshift operations.

Algorithm 4.8 COLUMNSORT
Input: $X = \langle x_0, x_1, \ldots, x_{n-1} \rangle$, a sequences of n numbers, where $n = rs$.
Output: X sorted in ascending order.

1. Sort each column.
2. Perform a row-column transposition.
3. Sort each column.
4. Perform the inverse transformation of Step 2.
5. Sort each column.
6. Shift the entries by $\lfloor r/2 \rfloor$ positions.
7. Sort each column.
8. Perform the inverse of Step 6.

As will be shown in Lemmas 4.2 and 4.3 below, after Step 4, every element will be within $(s-1)^2$ of its correct sorted position. In the special case where $r = n/2$ and $s = 2$, the algorithm reduces to Algorithm ODDEVENMERGE. In Algorithm ODDEVENMERGE, the input sequence is divided into two subsequences of $n/2$ elements each. These two subsequences are sorted as done in Step 1 of the algorithm. Then, the odd-index numbers in each subsequence are combined to form a new subsequence, as are the even-index numbers. This corresponds to the transpose operation in Step 2 of Algorithm COLUMNSORT. Next, each subsequence is sorted, as is done in Step 3 of Algorithm COLUMNSORT. In Algorithm ODDEVENMERGE, this is done by calling the algorithm recursively. After sorting, the subsequences are shuffled together, as is done in Step 4 of Algorithm COLUMNSORT. At this point, every number is within $(s-1)^2 = 1$ of its correct sorted position, so each number is compared and possibly exchanged with its neighbor, which completes the sorting. In Step 5 of Algorithm COLUMNSORT, all but the top and bottom numbers in each column are compared to their neighbors by sorting the columns. Steps 6–8 ensure that comparisons are made between numbers at the bottom of one column and the top of the next column.

Example 4.8   An illustration of the algorithm is shown in Fig. 4.27. The input is shown in Fig. 4.27(a). Notice that, for simplicity, we have chosen $r = 6$ and $s = 3$ even though it does not satisfy the constraint $r \geq 2(s-1)^2$. The results of applying Steps 1–8 are shown in Figs. 4.27(b)–(i).   □

An equivalent sorting method is given by Algorithm COLUMNSORT2. Here, the shift operation has been replaced by sorting the columns in

(a)

6	15	12
14	4	7
10	1	13
3	16	9
17	8	2
5	11	0

Input

(b)

3	1	0
5	4	2
6	8	7
10	11	9
14	15	12
17	16	13

Step 1

(c)

3	5	6
10	14	17
1	4	8
11	15	16
0	2	7
9	12	13

Step 2

(d)

0	2	6
1	4	7
3	5	8
9	12	13
10	14	16
11	15	17

Step 3

(e)

0	3	10
2	5	14
6	8	16
1	9	11
4	12	15
7	13	17

Step 4

(f)

0	3	10
1	5	11
2	8	14
4	9	15
6	12	16
7	13	17

Step 5

(g)

-∞	4	9	15
-∞	6	12	16
-∞	7	13	17
0	3	10	∞
1	5	11	∞
2	8	14	∞

Step 6

(h)

-∞	3	9	15
-∞	4	10	16
-∞	5	11	17
0	6	12	∞
1	7	13	∞
2	8	14	∞

Step 7

(i)

0	6	12
1	7	13
2	8	14
3	9	15
4	10	16
5	11	17

Step 8

Fig. 4.27.   Illustration of Algorithm COLUMNSORT.

alternating order in Step 5, and applying two steps of Odd-Even transposition sort to each row in Step 6.

Algorithm 4.9 COLUMNSORT2

Input: $X = \langle x_0, x_1, \ldots, x_{n-1} \rangle$, a sequences of n numbers, where $n = rs$.

Output: X sorted in ascending order.

1. Sort each column.
2. Perform a row-column transposition.
3. Sort each column.
4. Perform the inverse transformation of Step 2.
5. Sort each column in alternating order.
6. Apply two steps of Odd-Even transposition sort to each row.
7. Sort each column.

Example 4.9   An illustration of Algorithm COLUMNSORT2 is shown in Fig. 4.28. The input is shown in Fig. 4.28(a). The results of applying Steps 1–7 are shown in Figs. 4.28(b)–(h).   □

We now prove the correctness of Algorithm COLUMNSORT. Recall that rank(x, S) is the number of elements less than x in S.

(a)		
7	9	12
4	16	1
18	5	14
2	17	8
15	11	6
10	3	13

Input

(b)		
2	3	1
4	5	6
7	9	8
10	11	12
15	16	13
18	17	14

Step 1

(c)		
2	4	7
10	15	18
3	5	9
11	16	17
1	6	8
12	13	14

Step 2

(d)		
1	4	7
2	5	8
3	6	9
10	13	14
11	15	17
12	16	18

Step 3

(e)		
1	3	11
4	6	15
7	9	17
2	10	12
5	13	16
8	14	18

Step 4

(f)		
1	14	11
2	13	12
4	10	15
5	9	16
7	6	17
8	3	18

Step 5

(g)		
1	11	14
2	12	13
4	10	15
5	9	16
6	7	17
3	8	18

Step 6

(h)		
1	7	13
2	8	14
3	9	15
4	10	16
5	11	17
6	12	18

Step 7

Fig. 4.28. Illustration of Algorithm COLUMNSORT2.

Lemma 4.2 Let S be a sequence of rs elements to be sorted by Algorithm COLUMNSORT in an $r \times s$ mesh, and let x be any element in S that is in position (i, j) of the mesh after Step 3 of the algorithm. Then, rank(x, S) is at least $is + js - (s - 1)^2$.

Proof. From the position of x after Step 3, we know that x is greater than or equal to at least $i + 1$ elements in the jth column of the mesh after Step 2. Let α_k denote the number of these $i + 1$ elements that originally come from column k of the mesh, i.e., before Step 2 transposed the elements. By definition,

$$i + 1 = \sum_{k=0}^{s-1} \alpha_k. \tag{4.8}$$

Since only the jth and every sth element thereafter of the sorted kth column after Step 1 appear in the jth column after Step 2, this means that x is greater than or equal to at least $(\alpha_k - 1)s + j + 1$ elements in the kth column of the mesh after Step 1. Hence, the true rank of x is at least

$$\sum_{k=0}^{s-1} [(\alpha_k - 1)s + j + 1] - 1. \tag{4.9}$$

Substituting $i + 1$ for $\sum_{k=0}^{s-1} \alpha_k$ in (4.9) and simplifying, we find that the true rank of x is at least

$$is + js - (s - 1)^2.$$

□

Example 4.10　We illustrate the proof of Lemma 4.2. Let $x = 12$ in Fig. 4.27. As is evident from Fig. 4.27(d), $i = 3$ and $j = 1$ (Recall that indices start from 0). After Step 3 (Fig. 4.27(d)), there are $i + 1 = 4$ elements on or above the (i, j)th entry. These elements are $\{2, 4, 5, 12\}$. Thus, $\alpha_0 = \alpha_1 = 1$ and $\alpha_2 = 2$. The true rank of x is at least $is + js - (s - 1)^2 = 3 \times 3 + 1 \times 3 - 4 = 8$.

□

Lemma 4.3　Let S be a sequence of rs elements to be sorted by Algorithm COLUMNSORT in an $r \times s$ mesh, and let x be any element in S that is in position (i, j) of the mesh after Step 3 of the algorithm. Then, $\text{rank}(x, S)$ is at most $is + js$.

Proof.　We use an argument similar to that in Lemma 4.2. From the position of x after Step 3, we know that x is less than or equal to at least $r - i$ elements in the jth column of the mesh after Step 2. Let β_k denote the number of these $r - i$ elements that originally come from column k of the mesh, i.e., before Step 2 transposed the elements. By definition,

$$r - i = \sum_{k=0}^{s-1} \beta_k. \tag{4.10}$$

Since only the jth and every sth element thereafter of the sorted kth column after Step 1 appear in the jth column after Step 2, this means that x is less than or equal to at least $(\beta_k - 1)s + s - j$ elements in the kth column of the mesh after Step 1. Hence, the number of elements greater than or equal to x is at least

$$\sum_{k=0}^{s-1} [(\beta_k - 1)s + s - j]. \tag{4.11}$$

Substituting $r - i$ for $\sum_{k=0}^{s-1} \beta_k$ in (4.11) and simplifying, we find that the number of elements greater than or equal to x is at least

$$(r - i)s - js = rs - is - js.$$

Hence, the true rank of x is at most

$$rs - (rs - is - js) = is + js.$$

$\square$

Example 4.11 We illustrate the proof of Lemma 4.3. Let $x = 5$ in Fig. 4.27. As is evident from Fig. 4.27(d), $i = 2$ and $j = 1$ (Recall that indices start from 0). After Step 3 (Fig. 4.27(d)), there are $r - i = 6 - 2 = 4$ elements on or below the (i, j)th entry. These elements are $\{5, 12, 14, 15\}$. Thus, $\beta_0 = 2, \beta_1 = \beta_2 = 1$. The true rank of x is at most $is + js = 2 \times 3 + 1 \times 3 = 9$. $\square$

Theorem 4.4 Let S be a sequence of rs elements to be sorted by Algorithm COLUMNSORT in an $r \times s$ mesh, and let x be any element in S that is in position (i, j) of the mesh after Step 3 of the algorithm. Then, the position of x after Step 4 is within $(s - 1)^2$ from its correct position.

Proof. Consider an element x that is in position (i, j) of the mesh after Step 3. Clearly, x is sent to a position in Step 4 that corresponds to a rank of

$$is + j \tag{4.12}$$

in the sorted list. (Recall our convention that the smallest number has rank zero). By Lemma 4.2, $\text{rank}(x, S)$ is at least $is + js - (s - 1)^2$. Hence, subtracting this quantity from (4.12), the position of x after Step 4 is at most

$$(is + j) - (is + js - (s - 1)^2) = (s - 1)^2 - j(s - 1) \le (s - 1)^2$$

beyond its correct position. By Lemma 4.3, $\text{rank}(x, S)$ is at most $is + js$. Hence, subtracting (4.12) from this quantity, the position of x after Step 4 is at most

$$(is + js) - (is + j) = j(s - 1) \leq (s - 1)^2$$

short of its correct sorted position. Thus, we have established that every element is within $(s-1)^2$ of its correct position after Step 4 of the algorithm.

□

Theorem 4.5   Algorithm COLUMNSORT correctly sorts an arbitrary sequence of rs elements in an $r \times s$ mesh with $r \geq 2(s-1)^2$.

Proof.   By Theorem 4.4, we only need to show that Steps 5–8 will be sufficient to finish the sorting. For simplicity, we assume that every number is within $\lfloor r/2 \rfloor$ of its correct sorted position. Since $r \geq 2(s-1)^2$, we are always guaranteed that this condition is met after completion of Step 4. After Step 5, every number that belongs in the top half of column j is in the top half of column j or the bottom half of column $j-1$, and every number that belongs in the bottom half of column j is in the bottom half of column j or the top half of column $j+1$. Otherwise, some number would be more than $\lfloor r/2 \rfloor$ away from its correct position. Hence, Steps 6–8 complete the sorting.   □

4.17   3-dimensional Mesh

A 3-dimensional mesh of sides $m = n^{1/3}$ can be viewed as a connection of m successive levels of 2-D meshes of size $m \times m$. It has $n = m^3$ processors and $3m^3 - 3m^2$ links. Two processors are connected by a two-way link if and only if they differ in precisely one coordinate and if the absolute value of the difference in that coordinate is 1 (see Fig. 4.29). In this figure, $m = 4$ and $n = 64$.

In 3-D mesh, the degree of each node is between 3 and 6, so meshes are not regular. Of course, the degree of a corner vertex is less than the degree of an internal vertex. The diameter is $3(m-1) = \Theta(n^{1/3})$.

4.17.1   *Sorting on 3-dimensional meshes*

Consider the problem of sorting $n = m^3$ numbers on a 3-dimensional mesh with n processors in lexicographic zyx-order. In a zyx-ordering, elements

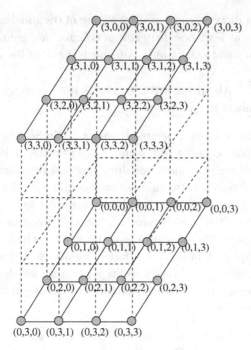

Fig. 4.29.   A 3-dimensional mesh.

of processors in the plane with coordinate $z = 0$ come first, followed by those with $z = 1$, and so on. The xy-planes are sorted in yx-order, that is, in columnwise order. The following algorithm needs just five steps, where each step sorts numbers within 2-D meshes. These steps are outlined in Algorithm THREEDMESHSORT.

Algorithm 4.10 THREEDMESHSORT

Input: $n = m^3$ elements stored in a 3-D mesh.

Output: The elements sorted in ascending zyx-order.

1. Sort all xz-planes in zx-order.
2. Sort all yz-planes in zy-order.
3. Sort all xy-planes in yx-order. Reverse the order on every other plane.
4. Perform one Odd-Even and one even-odd transposition within all columns in parallel.
5. Sort all xy-planes in yx-order.

Recall that a dirty row is a row consisting of 0's and 1's. A dirty plane is one containing at least one dirty row or column. A z-column is a column of processors parallel to the z-axis. A 0-row is a row of 0's and no 1's.

Theorem 4.6   Algorithm THREEDMESHSORT correctly sorts a given sequence of numbers in zyx-order.

Proof.   By the zero-one principle (Lemma 2.1 in Section 2.10), we may consider any input sequence of 0's and 1's. After Step 1 is completed, in every xz-plane, there is at most one dirty row and therefore the difference in the number of zeroes between any two z-columns in the same xz-plane is at most one. Hence, any two yz-planes can differ in at most m 0's. It follows that after Step 2 is completed, the difference in the number of 0-rows between any two yz-planes is at most one, which means that all dirty rows can span at most two adjacent xy-planes. If there is only one dirty xy-plane, we can go directly to Step 5 and we are done. If there are two dirty xy-planes, Steps 3 and 4 eliminate at least one of them and Step 5 completes the sorting.   □

Example 4.12   Figure 4.30 illustrates the algorithm on a sequence of 0's and 1's shown in part (a). First, the xz-planes are sorted in Fig. 4.30 (b). Next, the yz-planes are sorted in Fig. 4.30 (c). In this part of the figure, both the middle and top xy-planes are dirty, and so Steps 3 and 4 are needed, as shown in parts (d) and (e) of the figure. Finally, Fig. 4.30(f) shows the result after Step 5 is executed, in which the input is sorted. Note that there is only one dirty plane, the middle xy-plane.   □

Example 4.13   Figure 4.31 illustrates the algorithm on a sequence of integers shown in part (a). First, the xz-planes are sorted in Fig. 4.31 (b). Next, the yz-planes are sorted in Fig. 4.31 (c). The xy-planes are then

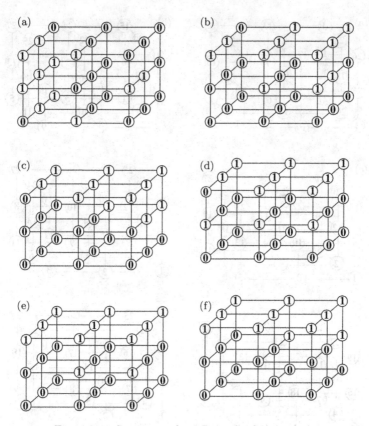

Fig. 4.30. Sorting in the 3-D mesh of 0's and 1's

sorted in reverse order according to Step 3 of the algorithm as shown in part (d) of the figure. Next, two iterations of odd–even sort are executed, and the result is shown in Fig. 4.31(e). Finally, Fig. 4.31(f) shows the result after Step 5 is executed, in which the input is sorted. □

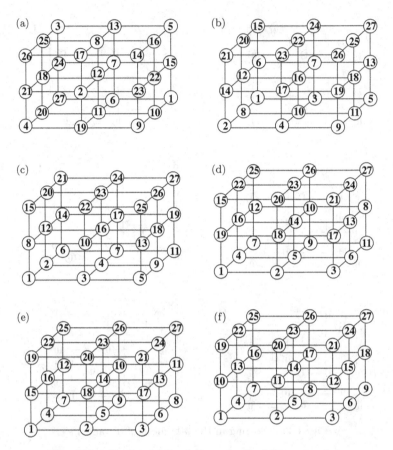

Fig. 4.31.   Sorting in the 3-D mesh of arbitrary numbers

4.18   Bibliographic Notes

There are a number of books that cover parallel algorithms on the mesh. These include Akl [4], Akl [5], Akl [6], Cosnard and Trystram [29], Grama, Gupta, Karypis and Kumar [39], Horowitz, Sahni and Rajasekaran [43], Leighton [57], Miller and Boxer [66], and Miller and Stout [67]. A survey of parallel sorting and selection algorithms can be found in Rajasekaran [75]. Parallel algorithms for many problems including problems in computational geometry on the mesh can be found in Miller and Stout [67], and Leighton [57]. The randomized algorithm for packet routing is due to

Valiant and Brebner[101]. For deterministic algorithms on routing, see Leighton, Makedon and Tollis [58], and Nassimi [71]. Shearsort was presented independently by Sado and Igarashi[79] and Scherson, Sen and Shamir [81]. The odd–even mergesort on the mesh can be found in Thompson and Kung [92]. The algorithm for transitive closure is due to Christopher [24]. The algorithm presented is a modified version of the algorithm presented in Leighton [57]. Columnsort algorithm is from Leighton [56]. For more references on parallel algorithms on the mesh interconnection network, see for instance Miller and Stout [67].

4.19   Exercises

4.1. What are the expansion and load of the embedding of the linear array into the mesh shown in Fig. 4.4 (page 161)? How about the embedding of the mesh into the linear array shown in Fig. 4.5?

4.2. Explain how to broadcast an item x in an arbitrary processor to all other processors in the ring with n processors.

4.3. Describe an algorithm to find the sum of all elements $\{x_1, x_2, \ldots, x_n\}$ stored in a $\sqrt{n} \times \sqrt{n}$ mesh and store the sum in all processors. How many steps are required by the algorithm?

4.4. One method to smooth a picture is as follows. Let p be the pixel in the middle of a square of a 3×3 square of pixels. Replace the value of p by the average of all the 3×3 pixels. Suggest a computation model to solve this problem, and show how to solve it.

4.5. What is the bisection width of the $\sqrt{n} \times \sqrt{n}$ mesh? Assume $\sqrt{n}$ is even.

4.6. Give a lower bound on the problems of sorting and routing on the mesh.

4.7. What is the bisection width of the $\sqrt{n} \times \sqrt{n}$ torus? Assume $\sqrt{n}$ is even (see Fig. 4.2).

4.8. Give a recursive algorithm to find the maximum of n numbers stored in a $\sqrt{n} \times \sqrt{n}$ mesh. Analyze its running time.

4.9. Give a recursive algorithm to find the prefix sums of n numbers $x_1, x_2, \ldots, x_n$ stored in a $\sqrt{n} \times \sqrt{n}$ mesh. Analyze its running time.

4.10. Illustrate your solution to Exercise 4.9 on the input $\langle 1, 2, 3, \ldots, 16 \rangle$.

4.11. The transpose of a matrix A, denoted by A^T, is the matrix whose columns are the rows of A. That is, if

$$A = \begin{bmatrix} a_{1,1} & a_{1,2} & \cdots & a_{1,n} \\ a_{2,1} & a_{2,2} & \cdots & a_{2,n} \\ \vdots & \vdots & \vdots & \vdots \\ a_{n,1} & a_{n,2} & \cdots & a_{n,n} \end{bmatrix}$$

then

$$A^T = \begin{bmatrix} a_{1,1} & a_{2,1} & \cdots & a_{n,1} \\ a_{1,2} & a_{2,2} & \cdots & a_{n,2} \\ \vdots & \vdots & \vdots & \vdots \\ a_{1,n} & a_{2,n} & \cdots & a_{n,n} \end{bmatrix}$$

Given the matrix A stored one element per processor in an $n \times n$ mesh, show how to compute A^T. What is the number of steps in your algorithm?

4.12. Apply the algorithm for odd–even transposition sort on the input $\langle 3, 7, 5, 2 \rangle$. Assume a linear array with four processors.

4.13. Consider Algorithm MERGE-SPLIT, which is a generalization of odd–even transposition sort for the case $p < n$. Let S be a sequence of numbers to be sorted, and assume that each of the p processors in the linear array holds a subsequence of S of length n/p. In Algorithm MERGE-SPLIT, the comparison-exchange operations of odd–even transposition sort are replaced with merge-split operations on subsequences. Let S_i denote the subsequence held by processor P_i. In Step 1, each P_i sorts S_i using a sequential algorithm. In Step 2 each odd-numbered processor P_i merges the two subsequences S_i and S_{i+1}, into a sorted sequence S_i'. It retains the first half of S_i'

and assigns to its neighbor P_{i+1} the second half. Step 3 is identical to 2 except that it is performed by all even-numbered processors. Steps 2 and 3 are repeated alternately. After $\lceil p/2 \rceil$ iterations, no further exchange of elements can take place between two processors, where an iteration consists of Steps 2 and 3. Analyze the running time of this algorithm.

4.14. Do Exercise 4.13 for the case $p = \log n$. Is the algorithm optimal?

4.15. Consider the problem of permutation routing on the mesh with n processors, in which every processor tries to send to a different destination. Outline a sorting-based algorithm to route every packet to its destination. Compare your algorithm with the greedy algorithm.

4.16. Modify your algorithm in Exercise 4.15 so that it works for the more general one-to-one routing problem, in which not every processor is the source of a packet. Note here that no processors P_i and P_j send to the same destination.

4.17. Illustrate the operation of the odd–even merging algorithm on the input:

$$A = \langle 1, 9, 8, 17, 3, 11, 14, 12 \rangle \quad \text{and} \quad B = \langle 2, 5, 15, 7, 13, 9, 16, 10 \rangle.$$

Assume a mesh of 16 processors.

4.18. Show how to compute the prefix sums on the mesh for the snakelike indexing scheme.

4.19. In a window broadcast, we start with data in the top left $w \times w$ submesh of a $\sqrt{n} \times \sqrt{n}$ mesh, where $w \mid \sqrt{n}$, that is, w divides $\sqrt{n}$. Following the window broadcast operation, the initial $w \times w$ window tiles the entire mesh. Outline an algorithm to implement this operation. What is the running time of your algorithm?

4.20. Give an algorithm to evaluate the polynomial $a_{n-1}x^{n-1} + a_{n-2}x^{n-2} + \cdots + a_1 x + a_0$ at the point x_0 on the $\sqrt{n} \times \sqrt{n}$ mesh. Assume that each a_i is stored in processor P_i, $0 \le i \le n - 1$ (the processors are indexed as $P_0, P_1, \ldots, P_{n-1}$). What is the running time of your algorithm?

4.21. Consider the following method for sorting on the mesh. The method alternately sorts all rows from left to right and all columns from top to bottom. Will this method always work in sorting any input? Assume an unlimited amount of time.

4.22. Consider sorting the rows and then the columns of a $2 \times n$ mesh M. Does this leave the rows in sorted order?

4.23. This is a generalization of Exercise 4.22. Consider sorting the rows and then the columns of a general $n \times n$ mesh. Does this leave the rows in sorted order?

4.24. Let $A = \langle a_1, a_2, \ldots, a_n \rangle$ be a sequence of elements stored in the processors of a $\sqrt{n} \times \sqrt{n}$ mesh, one element per processor, and let x be a given element. Design an algorithm for the search problem in the mesh: If $a_i = x$ for some i, $1 \le i \le n$, then return i, else return 0. Analyze its running time.

4.25. How many steps are required by the matrix multiplication algorithm on the mesh of Section 4.10.1?

4.26. Show the results of the computations of $c_{1,3}$ and $c_{1,4}$ in the matrix multiplication algorithm on the mesh of Section 4.10.1.

4.27. Give an algorithm for the $\sqrt{n} \times \sqrt{n}$ mesh to determine whether a given graph G is cyclic or acyclic. What is the running time of your algorithm?

4.28. Let G be a connected undirected and unweighted graph on n vertices. A breadth-first spanning tree for G is a spanning tree that can be obtained by performing breadth-first traversal on G starting at some vertex, say r. Equivalently, a breadth-first spanning tree of G is a tree in which every path from the root to any vertex is of shortest length, where the distance is measured in terms of number of edges. Present an efficient algorithm to find such a tree for the $\sqrt{n} \times \sqrt{n}$ mesh. What is the running time of your algorithm?

4.29. Suggest another algorithm for computing the transitive closure of a matrix A different from the one given in Section 4.11. What is the running time of the algorithm?

4.30. Suggest another algorithm for computing the shortest paths in a directed graph G different from the one given in Section 4.13. What is the running time of the algorithm?

4.31. Illustrate the operation of Algorithm COLUMNSORT discussed in Section 4.16 on the input

$$17, 1, 18, 12, 8, 10, 11, 2, 4, 14, 5, 6, 9, 13, 15, 16, 7, 3,$$

where $n = 18$. Assume an $r \times s$ mesh, where $r = 6$ and $s = 3$.

4.32. Illustrate the operation of Algorithm COLUMNSORT2 discussed in Section 4.16 on the input

$$8, 10, 11, 2, 4, 14, 5, 6, 17, 1, 18, 12, 9, 13, 15, 16, 7, 3,$$

where $n = 18$. Assume an $r \times s$ mesh, where $r = 6$ and $s = 3$.

4.33. Explain why Algorithm COLUMNSORT does not work on square meshes.

4.34. This exercise is similar to Exercise 2.12. Consider Algorithm COLUMNSORT discussed in Section 4.16. If we let $s = 2$, then the algorithm reduces to Algorithm ODDEVENMERGE in Section 2.11 for odd–even merging with the even part of A merged with the even part of B and the odd part A merged with the odd part of B. Let A and B be the first and second columns after Step 1, respectively. Let C and D be the first and second columns after Step 3, respectively. Let E be the whole list after Step 5. Assume the elements in $A \cup B$ are distinct. Given a sequence X and an element x, recall that $\text{rank}(x, X)$ is the number of elements in X less than x. Express $\text{rank}(x, C)$ and $\text{rank}(x, D)$ in terms of $\text{rank}(x, A)$ and $\text{rank}(x, B)$.

4.35. This exercise is similar to Exercise 2.13. Use the result of Exercise 4.34 to show that for $c \in C$, either c is in its correct position in E or to the right of it.

4.36. This exercise is similar to Exercise 2.14. Use the result of Exercise 4.34 to show that for $d \in D$, either d is in its correct position in E or to the left of it.

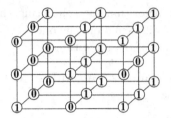

Fig. 4.32.   Exercise 4.37.

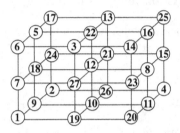

Fig. 4.33.   Exercise 4.38.

4.37. Illustrate the operation of the algorithm for sorting on a 3-dimensional mesh/sorting on 3-dimensional meshes on the input shown in Fig. 4.32.

4.38. Illustrate the operation of the algorithm for sorting on a 3-dimensional mesh/sorting on 3-dimensional meshes on the input shown in Fig. 4.33.

4.39. Compute the values of α and β corresponding to Fig. 4.24(c).

4.20   Solutions

4.1. What are the expansion and load of the embedding of the linear array into the mesh shown in Fig. 4.4? How about the embedding of the mesh into the linear array shown in Fig. 4.5?

In both embeddings, the expansion is 1. The load is also 1 in both embeddings, as precisely one node is mapped to each image node.

4.2. Explain how to broadcast an item x in an arbitrary processor to all other processors in the ring with n processors.

One copy of x moves $n/2$ steps to the left, and another copy moves $n/2$ steps to the right.

4.3. Describe an algorithm to find the sum of all elements $\{x_1, x_2, \ldots, x_n\}$ stored in a $\sqrt{n} \times \sqrt{n}$ mesh and store the sum in all processors. How many steps are required by the algorithm?

Find the sum of all numbers and store it in processor P_1. Next, broadcast the sum to all other processors. The number of steps is $(2\sqrt{n} - 2) + (2\sqrt{n} - 2) = 4\sqrt{n} - 4$. See Exercise 8.5 for a more efficient implementation.

4.4. One method to smooth a picture is as follows. Let p be the pixel in the middle of a square of a 3×3 square of pixels. Replace the value of p by the average of all the 3×3 pixels. Suggest a computation model to solve this problem, and show how to solve it.

The mesh is the natural model to solve this problem. Do smoothing for all squares in parallel.

4.5. What is the bisection width of the $\sqrt{n} \times \sqrt{n}$ mesh? Assume $\sqrt{n}$ is even.

If we consider a mesh of size n, and cut it by a line through the center, the line will cut $\sqrt{n}$ links. Hence, the bisection width of the mesh is $\sqrt{n}$.

4.6. Give a lower bound on the problems of sorting and routing on the mesh.

Since all n data items may have to cross from one side of the mesh to the other, at least $\lceil n/\sqrt{n} \rceil = \Omega(\sqrt{n})$ time is required just to get data across the middle of the mesh (see Exercise 4.5). That is, the lower bound is $\Theta(\sqrt{n})$

4.7. What is the bisection width of the $\sqrt{n} \times \sqrt{n}$ torus? Assume $\sqrt{n}$ is even (see Fig. 4.2).

If we consider a torus of size n, and cut it by a line through the center, the line will cut $2\sqrt{n}$ links. Hence, the bisection width of the torus is $2\sqrt{n}$.

4.8. Give a recursive algorithm to find the maximum of n numbers stored in a $\sqrt{n} \times \sqrt{n}$ mesh. Analyze its running time.

Assume the processors are numbered as $P_1, P_2, \ldots, P_n$, and that n is a power of 4. Partition the mesh into four submeshes of the same size, that is, of size $\frac{\sqrt{n}}{2} \times \frac{\sqrt{n}}{2}$ each. Recursively find the maximum in each quadrant, and store the result in the processor near the center of the mesh. Finally, find the maximum of the four computed maxima, and route it to processor P_1. The running time is governed by the recurrence $T(n) = T(n/4) + \Theta(\sqrt{n})$, whose solution is $T(n) = \Theta(\sqrt{n})$.

4.9. Give a recursive algorithm to find the prefix sums of n numbers $x_1, x_2, \ldots, x_n$ stored in a $\sqrt{n} \times \sqrt{n}$ mesh. Analyze its running time.

Assume that n is a power of 4. For convenience, assume also the proximity indexing scheme shown in Fig. 6.7. First, partition the mesh into four submeshes of the same size, that is, of size $\frac{\sqrt{n}}{2} \times \frac{\sqrt{n}}{2}$ each. Recursively find the prefix sum in each quadrant, and store the final prefix sum y_j in the processor closest to the center of the mesh. This takes $\Theta(\sqrt{n})$ time since it requires sending the final sums to the appropriate processors near the center. At this point, $y_1 = x_1 + x_2 + \cdots + x_{n/4}$, $y_2 = x_{n/4+1} + x_{n/4+2} + \cdots + x_{n/2}$, $y_3 = x_{n/2+1} + x_{n/2+2} + \cdots + x_{3n/4}$, and $y_4 = x_{3n/4+1} + x_{3n/4+2} + \cdots + x_n$. Next, find the prefix sums of y_1, y_2, y_3, y_4 and store them in registers z_1, z_2, z_3, z_4. Now, rotate the values stored in registers z_j; that is, for $j = 1, 2, 3$, set $z_{j+1} \leftarrow z_j$, and set $z_1 \leftarrow 0$. Note that finding the prefix sums of y_1, y_2, y_3, y_4 and rotating the z_j's take constant time. Finally, for $j = 1, 2, 3, 4$, broadcast z_j to all processors in quadrant j, and add z_j to all prefix sums computed earlier in quadrant j. This broadcasting step takes $\Theta(\sqrt{n})$ time. It follows that the running time of the algorithm is governed by the recurrence $T(n) = T(n/4) + \Theta(\sqrt{n})$, whose solution is $T(n) = \Theta(\sqrt{n})$. A summary of the algorithm is shown as Algorithm MESHPREFIXSUMREC.

4.10. Illustrate your solution to Exercise 4.9 on the input $\langle 1, 2, 3, \ldots, 16 \rangle$.

The algorithm in the solution of Exercise 4.9 is illustrated in Figs. 4.34 and 4.35. The input is shown in Fig. 4.34(a). The prefix sums of the four partitions are shown in Fig. 4.34(b). Part (c) of the figure shows the four final prefix sums — that is, the totals of

---

Algorithm 4.11 MESHPREFIXSUMREC

Input: n numbers $x_1, x_2, \ldots, x_n$ stored in a mesh of size n, one element per processor.

Output: The prefix sums $s_1, s_2, \ldots, s_n$.

1. if $n = 1$ then set $s_1 \leftarrow x_1$ and exit
2. Partition the mesh into four submeshes of size $\frac{\sqrt{n}}{2} \times \frac{\sqrt{n}}{2}$ each. Recursively find the prefix sum in each quadrant, and store the final prefix sum in the processor closest to the center of the mesh in register y_j, $j = 1, 2, 3, 4$.
3. Find the prefix sums of y_1, y_2, y_3, y_4 and store them in z_1, z_2, z_3, z_4.
4. Rotate the values stored in z_j: for $j = 1, 2, 3$: set $z_{j+1} \leftarrow z_j$, and set $z_1 \leftarrow 0$.
5. For $j = 1, 2, 3, 4$, broadcast z_j to all processors in quadrant j.
6. Every processor P_i in the mesh sets $s_i \leftarrow s_i + z_j$.

---

all elements in each quadrant. These are the contents of registers y_j, $j = 1, 2, 3, 4$. The prefix sums of these four values is computed in part (d). Next, these prefix sums are rotated in part (e), and y_1 is set to 0. Now, these entries are broadcast in all four quadrants as shown in part (f). Finally, Fig. 4.35 shows the final prefixes after summing the entries in part (f) with those in part (b) of Fig. 4.34.

4.11. The transpose of a matrix A, denoted by A^T, is the matrix whose columns are the rows of A. That is, if

$$A = \begin{bmatrix} a_{1,1} & a_{1,2} & \cdots & a_{1,n} \\ a_{2,1} & a_{2,2} & \cdots & a_{2,n} \\ \vdots & \vdots & \vdots & \vdots \\ a_{n,1} & a_{n,2} & \cdots & a_{n,n} \end{bmatrix}$$

then

$$A^T = \begin{bmatrix} a_{1,1} & a_{2,1} & \cdots & a_{n,1} \\ a_{1,2} & a_{2,2} & \cdots & a_{n,2} \\ \vdots & \vdots & \vdots & \vdots \\ a_{1,n} & a_{2,n} & \cdots & a_{n,n} \end{bmatrix}$$

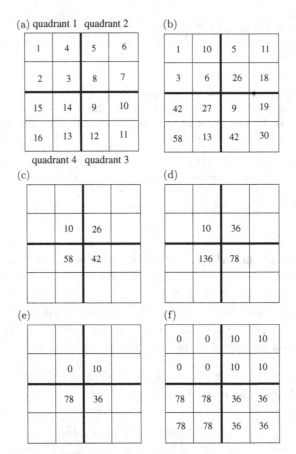

Fig. 4.34. Example of Algorithm MESHPREFIXSUMREC for finding the prefix sums on the mesh recursively (Exercise 4.10).

1	10	15	21
3	6	36	28
120	105	45	55
136	91	78	66

Fig. 4.35. Solution to Exercise 4.10 *continued*.

Given the matrix A stored one element per processor in an $n \times n$ mesh, show how to compute A^T. What is the number of steps in your algorithm?

This is a special case of the routing problem. Assume the processors are numbered as $P_{1,1}, P_{1,2}, \ldots, P_{n,n}$. The elements in the diagonal will not change; only elements below the diagonal and elements above the diagonal will change. The elements of A will move in parallel. An element below the diagonal stored in processor $P_{i,j}$ moves rightward until it reaches the diagonal where it switches direction and moves upward until it reaches processor $P_{j,i}$. An element above the diagonal stored in processor $P_{k,l}$ moves downward until it reaches the diagonal where it switches direction and moves leftward until it reaches processor $P_{l,k}$. The number of steps is $2n - 2$ since element $a_{1,n}$ in processor $P_{1,n}$ requires this number of moves.

4.12. Apply the algorithm for odd–even transposition sort on the input $\langle 3, 7, 5, 2 \rangle$. Assume a linear array with four processors.

Similar to Example 4.1.

4.13. Consider Algorithm MERGE-SPLIT, which is a generalization of odd–even transposition sort for the case $p < n$. Let S be a sequence of numbers to be sorted, and assume that each of the p processors in the linear array holds a subsequence of S of length n/p. In Algorithm MERGE-SPLIT, the comparison-exchange operations of odd–even transposition sort are replaced with merge-split operations on subsequences. Let S_i denote the subsequence held by processor P_i. In Step 1, each P_i sorts S_i using a sequential algorithm. In Step 2 each odd-numbered processor P_i merges the two subsequences S_i and S_{i+1}, into a sorted sequence S_i'. It retains the first half of S_i' and assigns to its neighbor P_{i+1} the second half. Step 3 is identical to 2 except that it is performed by all even-numbered processors. Steps 2 and 3 are repeated alternately. After $\lceil p/2 \rceil$ iterations, no further exchange of elements can take place between two processors, where an iteration consists of Steps 2 and 3. Analyze the running time of this algorithm.

There are p phases, where an iteration consists of two phases. The first phase, the sorting step, takes $O(\frac{n}{p} \log \frac{n}{p})$ time. The merge-split phases after that take $O(\frac{n}{p})$ time each for a total of $O(n)$ time. Hence, the running time is $O(\max\{\frac{n}{p}\log\frac{n}{p}, n\})$.

4.14. Do Exercise 4.13 for the case $p = \log n$. Is the algorithm optimal?

If $p = \log n$, then the running time is $\Theta(n)$, which is optimal.

4.15. Consider the problem of permutation routing on the mesh with n processors, in which every processor tries to send to a different destination. Outline a sorting-based algorithm to route every packet to its destination. Compare your algorithm with the greedy algorithm.

Sort the packets into column-major order according to the column destination of each packet. It can be shown that this algorithm uses queues of size 1, since there is never any contention for edges. If we use a $\Theta(\sqrt{n})$ sorting algorithm, the running time will be $\Theta(\sqrt{n})$. However, the running time is more than the greedy algorithm by a constant factor.

4.16. Modify your algorithm in Exercise 4.15 so that it works for the more general one-to-one routing problem, in which not every processor is the source of a packet. Note here that no processors P_i and P_j send to the same destination.

First, sort the packets into column-major order according to the column destination of each packet. Then, route each packet to its correct column, and then on to its correct destination. It can be shown that this algorithm uses queues of size 1, since there is never any contention for edges. If we use a $\Theta(\sqrt{n})$ sorting algorithm, the running time will be $\Theta(\sqrt{n})$. However, the running time is more than the greedy algorithm by a constant factor.

4.17. Illustrate the operation of the odd–even merging algorithm on the input:

$$A = \langle 1, 9, 8, 17, 3, 11, 14, 12 \rangle \quad \text{and} \quad B = \langle 2, 5, 15, 7, 13, 9, 16, 10 \rangle.$$

Assume a mesh of 16 processors.

Similar to Example 4.4.

4.18. Show how to compute the prefix sums on the mesh for the snakelike indexing scheme.

Similar to that for the row-major indexing scheme discussed in Section 4.4.

4.19. In a window broadcast, we start with data in the top left $w \times w$ submesh of a $\sqrt{n} \times \sqrt{n}$ mesh, where $w \mid \sqrt{n}$, that is w divides $\sqrt{n}$. Following the window broadcast operation, the initial $w \times w$ window tiles the entire mesh. Outline an algorithm to implement this operation. What is the running time of your algorithm?

The data in the initial window simply moves to the bottom and to the right. The algorithm takes $2(\sqrt{n} - w)$ steps.

4.20. Give an algorithm to evaluate the polynomial $a_{n-1}x^{n-1} + a_{n-2}x^{n-2} + \cdots + a_1 x + a_0$ at the point x_0 on the $\sqrt{n} \times \sqrt{n}$ mesh. Assume that each a_i is stored in processor P_i, $0 \le i \le n - 1$ (the processors are indexed as $P_0, P_1, \ldots, P_{n-1}$). What is the running time of your algorithm?

Compute the sequence $1, x_0, x_0^2, \ldots, x_0^{n-1}$ using parallel prefix. Each x_0^j is stored in P_j, $0 \le j \le n-1$. Next, compute the products $a_j \times x_0^j$, $0 \le j \le n - 1$. Finally, compute the sum $a_0 + a_1 x_0 + a_2 x_0^2 + \cdots + a_{n-1}x_0^{n-1}$. The total running time is $\Theta(\sqrt{n})$.

4.21. Consider the following method for sorting on the mesh. The method alternately sorts all rows from left to right and all columns from top to bottom. Will this method always work in sorting any input? Assume an unlimited amount of time.

The method will not work in sorting any input. We will succeed in showing this, if we can exhibit an example in which the method does not terminate, or terminates before sorting the input. We will choose

the latter. Let $\mathbf{M} = \begin{vmatrix} x_{1,1} & x_{1,2} \\ x_{2,1} & x_{2,2} \end{vmatrix}$

where $x_{1,1} = 3, x_{1,2} = 2, x_{2,1} = 1$ and $x_{2,2} = 4$. After sorting by rows and then by columns, M becomes:

$$\mathbf{M_h} = \begin{vmatrix} 2 & 3 \\ 1 & 4 \end{vmatrix} \qquad\qquad \mathbf{M_v} = \begin{vmatrix} 1 & 3 \\ 2 & 4 \end{vmatrix}.$$

Clearly, M_v is sorted by rows and by columns, but the input is not sorted. So, the method terminated without sorting the input.

4.22. Consider sorting the rows and then the columns of a $2 \times n$ mesh M. Does this leave the rows in sorted order?

Call a column C_j of the mesh "good" if sorting that column leaves the rows sorted. We prove by induction on the number of columns that all columns are good, and hence sorting the mesh by columns leaves the rows sorted. If all columns are unsorted, then there is nothing to prove, as exchanging the two rows leaves them sorted. So, assume without loss of generality that column $C_1 = \langle x_{1,1}, x_{2,1} \rangle$ is sorted, that is, $x_{1,1} < x_{2,1}$. Hence, column C_1 is good by assumption. Assume for the induction hypothesis that column C_{k-1} is good, $1 < k < n$. We show that column C_k is also good. We have the following situation:

$$M = \begin{vmatrix} x_{1,1} & \cdots & x_{1,k-1} & x_{1,k} & \cdots \\ x_{2,1} & \cdots & x_{2,k-1} & x_{2,k} & \cdots \end{vmatrix}.$$

By induction, $x_{1,k-1} < x_{2,k-1} < x_{2,k}$. If $x_{1,k} > x_{2,k}$, then we have the following situation after sorting column C_k:

$$M = \begin{vmatrix} x_{1,1} & \cdots & x_{1,k-1} & x_{2,k} & \cdots \\ x_{2,1} & \cdots & x_{2,k-1} & x_{1,k} & \cdots \end{vmatrix}.$$

In this case, we have $x_{1,k-1} < x_{2,k-1} < x_{2,k} < x_{1,k}$, whence $x_{1,k-1} < x_{2,k}$ and $x_{2,k-1} < x_{1,k}$. Thus, column C_k is good, and, by induction, all columns are good. It follows that if all columns are sorted, then the rows will remain sorted.

4.23. This is a generalization of Exercise 4.22. Consider sorting the rows and then the columns of a general $n \times n$ mesh. Does this leave the rows in sorted order?

Call a column C_j of the mesh "good" if sorting that column leaves the rows sorted. We prove by induction on the number of columns that all columns are good, and hence sorting the mesh by columns leaves the rows sorted. Let the first column be $C_1 = \langle x_{1,1}, x_{2,1}, \ldots, x_{n,1} \rangle$ and let C_1 after sorting be $C_1' = \langle x_{1,1}', x_{2,1}', \ldots, x_{n,1}' \rangle$. Thus, we have $x_{j,1}' \leq x_{j,1}$ for $1 \leq j \leq n$. Since row i is sorted, and since $x_{i,1}' \leq x_{i,1}$, we have $x_{i,1}' \leq x_{i,2}$. Therefore, we may assume without loss of generality that column C_1 is sorted. Hence, column C_1 is good by assumption. Assume for the induction hypothesis that column C_{k-1} is good, $1 < k < n$. We show that column C_k is also good. We have the following situation:

$$M = \begin{vmatrix} & \vdots & \vdots & \\ \cdots & x_{i,k-1} & x_{i,k} & \cdots \\ & \vdots & \vdots & \\ \cdots & x_{j,k-1} & x_{j,k} & \cdots \\ & \vdots & \vdots & \end{vmatrix},$$

We show that sorting column k leaves the rows sorted. We will use selection sort algorithm to sort column k. Recall that this algorithm sorts by interchanging the elements to be sorted if they are out of order. Let $x_{i,k}$ and $x_{j,k}$, where $i < j$, be the next two numbers in column k to be interchanged because $x_{i,k} > x_{j,k}$. We have the following situation for columns $k - 1$ and k after the interchange of $x_{i,k}$ and $x_{j,k}$:

$$M = \begin{vmatrix} & \vdots & \vdots & \\ \cdots & x_{i,k-1} & x_{j,k} & \cdots \\ & \vdots & \vdots & \\ \cdots & x_{j,k-1} & x_{i,k} & \cdots \\ & \vdots & \vdots & \end{vmatrix},$$

where $x_{i,k-1} < x_{i,k}$ and $x_{j,k-1} < x_{j,k}$. By Exercise 4.22, exchanging $x_{i,k}$ and $x_{j,k}$ will leave the two rows i and j sorted. Now, the procedure is repeated for each pair $x_{i',k}$ and $x_{j',k}$ that are out of order until column k is sorted. Thus, column C_k is good, and, by induction, all columns are good. It follows that if all columns are sorted, then the rows will remain sorted.

4.24. Let $A = \langle a_1, a_2, \ldots, a_n \rangle$ be a sequence of elements stored in the processors of a $\sqrt{n} \times \sqrt{n}$ mesh, one element per processor, and let x be a given element. Design an algorithm for the search problem in the mesh: If $a_i = x$ for some i, $1 \le i \le n$, then return i, else return 0. Analyze its running time.

Assume the processors are numbered $P_1, P_2, \ldots, P_n$. First, initialize the search index $k \leftarrow 0$, which is stored in P_1. Next broadcast x to all processors in $\Theta(\sqrt{n})$ time. Each processor P_j now compares a_j with x. If $a_j = x$, then processor P_j sends j to P_1 in $\Theta(\sqrt{n})$ time, which sets $k \leftarrow j$. Note that we have assumed here that the a_j's are distinct. The total running time is $\Theta(\sqrt{n})$.

4.25. How many steps are required by the matrix multiplication algorithm on the mesh of Section 4.10.1?

The $\sqrt{n}$th row (and column) will start moving in the $\sqrt{n}$th step, and it needs $\sqrt{n} - 1$ steps to arrive at the processor holding $c_{\sqrt{n}, \sqrt{n}}$. Hence, the total number of steps is $2\sqrt{n} - 1$.

4.26. Show the results of the computations of $c_{1,3}$ and $c_{1,4}$ in the matrix multiplication algorithm on the mesh of Section 4.10.1.

Similar to Table 4.1 in Example 4.5.

4.27. Give an algorithm for the $\sqrt{n} \times \sqrt{n}$ mesh to determine whether a given graph G is cyclic or acyclic. What is the running time of your algorithm?

Let A be the adjacency matrix of G. Find A^*, the transitive closure of A. G is cyclic if and only if there is a 1 in the diagonal of A^*. The running time is $\Theta(\sqrt{n})$.

4.28. Let G be a connected undirected and unweighted graph on n vertices. A breadth-first spanning tree for G is a spanning tree that can be obtained by performing breadth-first traversal on G starting at some vertex, say r. Equivalently, a breadth-first spanning tree of G is a tree in which every path from the root to any vertex is of shortest length, where the distance is measured in terms of number of edges. Present an efficient algorithm to find such a tree for the $\sqrt{n} \times \sqrt{n}$ mesh. What is the running time of your algorithm?

Define the weight matrix w by: $w[i, j] = 1$ if there is an edge between i and j, and $w[i, j] = \infty$ if there is no such edge. Use the shortest paths algorithm to find the distance $d[r, j]$ from r to every other vertex j. Then, $d[r, j]$ is the level of vertex j. For all vertices in $V(G) - \{r\}$, select an edge that connects a vertex at level l to a vertex at level

$l - 1$. The resulting tree is a breadth-first spanning tree for G. The running time is $\Theta(\sqrt{n})$.

4.29. Suggest another algorithm for computing the transitive closure of a matrix A different from the one given in Section 4.11. What is the running time of the algorithm?

Use an algorithm analogous to the one for the PRAM presented in Section 2.17. Recall that this algorithm computes the transitive closure by squaring the adjacency matrix $\lceil \log n \rceil$ times. Thus, the running time is $\Theta(\sqrt{n} \log n)$.

4.30. Suggest another algorithm for computing the shortest paths in a directed graph G different from the one given in Section 4.13. What is the running time of the algorithm?

Use an algorithm analogous to the one for the PRAM presented in Section 2.18. The running time is $\Theta(\sqrt{n} \log n)$.

4.31. Illustrate the operation of Algorithm COLUMNSORT discussed in Section 4.16 on the input

$$17, 1, 18, 12, 8, 10, 11, 2, 4, 14, 5, 6, 9, 13, 15, 16, 7, 3,$$

where $n = 18$. Assume an $r \times s$ mesh, where $r = 6$ and $s = 3$.

Similar to Example 4.8.

4.32. Illustrate the operation of Algorithm COLUMNSORT2 discussed in Section 4.16 on the input

$$8, 10, 11, 2, 4, 14, 5, 6, 17, 1, 18, 12, 9, 13, 15, 16, 7, 3,$$

where $n = 18$. Assume an $r \times s$ mesh, where $r = 6$ and $s = 3$.

Similar to Example 4.9.

4.33. Explain why Algorithm COLUMNSORT does not work on square meshes.

Note that after Step 4, every number will be within $(s - 1)^2$ of its correct sorted position. Thus, if we let $r = s = \sqrt{n}$, every number will be within $(\sqrt{n} - 1)^2 = \Theta(n)$ of its correct sorted position, which means that nothing is gained by applying the algorithm on a square mesh.

4.34. This exercise is similar to Exercise 2.12. Consider Algorithm COLUMNSORT discussed in Section 4.16. If we let $s = 2$, then the algorithm reduces to Algorithm ODDEVENMERGE in Section 2.11 for odd–even merging with the even part of A merged with the even part of B and the odd part A merged with the odd part of B. Let A and B be the first and second columns after Step 1, respectively. Let C and D be the first and second columns after Step 3, respectively. Let E be the whole list after Step 5. Assume the elements in $A \cup B$ are distinct. Given a sequence X and an element x, recall that $\text{rank}(x, X)$ is the number of elements in X less than x. Express $\text{rank}(x, C)$ and $\text{rank}(x, D)$ in terms of $\text{rank}(x, A)$ and $\text{rank}(x, B)$.

Let $x \in A \cup B$. Then,

$$\text{rank}(x, C) = \left\lceil \frac{\text{rank}(x, A)}{2} \right\rceil + \left\lceil \frac{\text{rank}(x, B)}{2} \right\rceil,$$

and

$$\text{rank}(x, D) = \left\lfloor \frac{\text{rank}(x, A)}{2} \right\rfloor + \left\lfloor \frac{\text{rank}(x, B)}{2} \right\rfloor.$$

4.35. This exercise is similar to Exercise 2.13. Use the result of Exercise 4.34 to show that for $c \in C$, either c is in its correct position in E or to the right of it.

For $x \in X$, let $\text{pos}(x, X)$ be the position of x in the sequence X, where $\text{pos}(x, X) \geq 0$. Thus, if X is sorted, then $\text{pos}(x, X) = \text{rank}(x, X)$. For $c \in C$, let $r_1 = \text{rank}(c, A)$ and $r_2 = \text{rank}(c, B)$, and $r_c = r_1 + r_2$. Either $c \in A$ or $c \in B$. If $c \in A$, then r_1 is even since $\text{pos}(c, A)$ is even, and it follows that the position of c in E is

$$\begin{aligned}
\text{pos}(c, E) &= 2\, \text{rank}(c, C) \\
&= 2\left\lceil \tfrac{r_1}{2} \right\rceil + 2\left\lceil \tfrac{r_2}{2} \right\rceil \\
&\leq r_1 + (r_2 + 1), \quad \text{since } r_1 \text{ is even} \\
&= r_c + 1.
\end{aligned}$$

Since $r_c = r_1 + r_2 \leq 2\left\lceil \tfrac{r_1}{2} \right\rceil + 2\left\lceil \tfrac{r_2}{2} \right\rceil = \text{pos}(c, E)$, we have

$$r_c \leq \text{pos}(c, E) \leq r_c + 1. \tag{4.13}$$

Thus, either $\text{pos}(c, E) = r_c$ or $\text{pos}(c, E) = r_c + 1$. That is, either c is in its correct position in E or to the right of it.

On the other hand, if $c \in B$, then r_2 is even since $\text{pos}(c, B)$ is even, and we get the same inequalities.

4.36. This exercise is similar to Exercise 2.14. Use the result of Exercise 4.34 to show that for $d \in D$, either d is in its correct position in E or to the left of it.

For $x \in X$, let $\text{pos}(x, X)$ be the position of x in the sequence X, where $\text{pos}(x, X) \geq 0$. Thus, if X is sorted, then $\text{pos}(x, X) = \text{rank}(x, X)$. For $d \in D$, let $r_3 = \text{rank}(d, A), r_4 = \text{rank}(d, B)$ and $r_d = r_3 + r_4$. If $d \in A$ then r_3 is odd since $\text{pos}(d, A)$ is odd. It follows that if $d \in A$, then the position of d in E is

$$\begin{aligned}
\text{pos}(d, E) &= 2 \,\text{rank}(d, D) + 1 \\
&= 2 \lfloor \tfrac{r_3}{2} \rfloor + 2 \lfloor \tfrac{r_4}{2} \rfloor + 1 \\
&\leq (r_3 - 1) + (r_4) + 1, \text{ since } r_3 \text{ is odd} \\
&= r_d.
\end{aligned}$$

Since $r_d - 1 = (r_3 - 1) + (r_4) \leq 2 \lfloor \tfrac{r_3}{2} \rfloor + 2 \lfloor \tfrac{r_4}{2} \rfloor + 1 = \text{pos}(d, E)$, we have

$$r_d - 1 \leq \text{pos}(d, E) \leq r_d. \tag{4.14}$$

Thus, either $\text{pos}(d, E) = r_d$ or $\text{pos}(d, E) = r_d - 1$. That is, either d is in its correct position in E or to the left of it.

If $d \in B$, then r_4 is odd, and we get the same inequalities.

4.37. Illustrate the operation of the algorithm for sorting on a 3-dimensional mesh/sorting on 3-dimensional meshes on the input shown in Fig. 4.36.

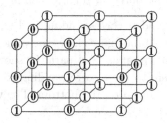

Fig. 4.36. Exercise 4.37.

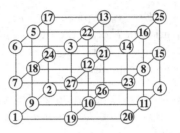

Fig. 4.37.   Exercise 4.38.

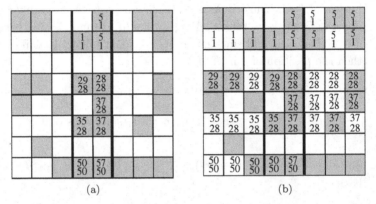

Fig. 4.38.   The values of α and β corresponding to Fig. 4.24(c)(Exercise 4.39).

Similar to Example 4.12.

4.38. Illustrate the operation of the algorithm for sorting on 3-dimensional mesh on the input shown in Fig. 4.37.

Similar to Example 4.13.

4.39. Compute the values of α and β corresponding to Fig. 4.24(c).

The values of α and β corresponding to Fig. 4.24(c) are shown in Fig. 4.38. Part (a) of the figure shows the values of α and β computed in the middle two columns, and part (b) shows the α and β values after copying them to their corresponding rows. In this figure, α is shown on the top and β on the bottom. The values with $\alpha = \beta = 0$ are not shown.

Chapter 5

Fast Fourier Transform

5.1   Introduction

The Fourier transform has a wide range of applications in science and engineering. We will describe a version of Fourier transform called *discrete Fourier transform*(DFT), and present a fast method for computing the DFT, called the *fast Fourier transform*(FFT).

Let r and θ be the polar coordinates of the point (x, y) corresponding to the complex number $z = x + iy$, where $i = \sqrt{-1}$. Since $x = r\cos\theta$ and $y = r\sin\theta$, z can be written in polar form as $z = r(\cos\theta + i\sin\theta)$. Using Euler's formula $e^{i\theta} = \cos\theta + i\sin\theta$, z can also be written as $z = re^{i\theta}$.

For $n \geq 2$, the n distinct roots of the equation $x^n - 1 = 0$ are called the n roots of unity. Define the complex number

$$\omega = e^{i2\pi/n} = \cos\tfrac{2\pi}{n} + i\sin\tfrac{2\pi}{n}.$$

ω is called a *primitive* nth root of unity, which means $\omega^n = 1$ and $\omega^j \neq 1$ for $0 < j < n$. If $\omega^n = 1$, then $(\omega^j)^n = (\omega^n)^j = 1$. Hence, the remaining complex roots of unity are the powers of ω. That is, $1 = \omega^0, \omega, \omega^2, \ldots, \omega^{n-1}$ constitute the n *distinct roots of unity*, where

$$\omega^k = e^{i2\pi k/n} = \cos\tfrac{2\pi k}{n} + i\sin\tfrac{2\pi k}{n}.$$

Pictorially, these roots are distributed in the complex plane evenly around the circumference of the unit circle. Figure 5.1 illustrates the n roots of unity for $n = 2, 4, 8$, which are powers of 2. As shown in the figure,

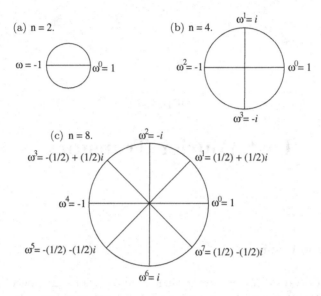

Fig. 5.1.   The n roots of unity for $n = 2, 4, 8$.

the pairs ω^j and $\omega^{j+n/2}$ are symmetrically located with respect to the origin. Algebraically, we have $\omega^{j+n/2} = -\omega^j$ (Property 5.2), and in particular, $\omega^{n/2} = -1$.

Let $\mathbf{a}$ be the column vector $[a_0, a_1, \ldots, a_{n-1}]^T$, where n is a power of 2. Let F_n be the Vandermonde matrix

$$
\begin{pmatrix}
1 & 1 & 1 & \cdots & 1 \\
1 & \omega & \omega^2 & \cdots & \omega^{n-1} \\
1 & \omega^2 & \omega^4 & \cdots & \omega^{2n-2} \\
\vdots & \vdots & \vdots & \vdots & \vdots \\
1 & \omega^{n-2} & \omega^{2(n-2)} & \cdots & \omega^{(n-1)(n-2)} \\
1 & \omega^{n-1} & \omega^{2(n-1)} & \cdots & \omega^{(n-1)^2}
\end{pmatrix}
$$

Then, the product $\mathbf{b} = F_n \mathbf{a}$ is called the *Discrete Fourier Transform* (DFT) of $\mathbf{a}$.

Thus, computing the DFT $\mathbf{b}$ of a vector $\mathbf{a}$ is equivalent to evaluating the polynomial $P(x) = a_0 + a_1 x + \ldots + a_{n-1} x^{n-1}$ at the points $1, \omega, \omega^2, \ldots, \omega^{n-1}$.

It is easy to see that the DFT of a vector $\mathbf{a}$ can be computed in $\Theta(n^2)$ sequential time and $\Theta(\log n)$ parallel time using $n^2/\log n$ processors on the PRAM. We now show that it can be computed in optimal $\Theta(n \log n)$ sequential time and $\Theta(\log n)$ parallel time using n processors on the PRAM. The efficiency of the algorithm is based on the following properties of the n roots of unity.

Property 5.1 For even n, if ω is an nth root of unity, then ω^2 is an $(n/2)$th root of unity.

Property 5.2 For even n, $\omega^{k+n/2} = -\omega^k$.

For $0 \leq i < n/2$, b_i can be expressed as

$$
\begin{aligned}
b_i &= \sum_{j=0}^{n-1} (\omega^i)^j a_j \\
&= (\omega^i)^0 a_0 + (\omega^i)^1 a_1 + \cdots + (\omega^i)^{n-1} a_{n-1} \\
&= (\omega^i)^0 a_0 + (\omega^i)^2 a_2 + \cdots + (\omega^i)^{n-2} a_{n-2} \\
&\quad + (\omega^i)^1 a_1 + (\omega^i)^3 a_3 + \cdots + (\omega^i)^{n-1} a_{n-1} \\
&= \sum_{j=0}^{(n/2)-1} (\omega^i)^{2j} a_{2j} + \sum_{j=0}^{(n/2)-1} (\omega^i)^{2j+1} a_{2j+1} \\
&= \sum_{j=0}^{(n/2)-1} (\omega^{2i})^j a_{2j} + \omega^i \sum_{j=0}^{(n/2)-1} (\omega^{2i})^j a_{2j+1}.
\end{aligned} \tag{5.1}
$$

Since

$$
(\omega^{i+(n/2)})^k = \begin{cases} \omega^{ki} & \text{if } k \text{ is even} \\ -\omega^{ki} & \text{if } k \text{ is odd}, \end{cases}
$$

we have

$$
b_{i+(n/2)} = \sum_{j=0}^{(n/2)-1} (\omega^{2i})^j a_{2j} - \omega^i \sum_{j=0}^{(n/2)-1} (\omega^{2i})^j a_{2j+1}. \tag{5.2}
$$

By Eqs. (5.1) and (5.2), $F_n \mathbf{a}$ is computed recursively from $F_{(n/2)} \mathbf{a}_e$ and $F_{(n/2)} \mathbf{a}_o$, where $\mathbf{a}_e$ and $\mathbf{a}_o$ are, respectively, the even and odd parts of $\mathbf{a}$.

Let

$$\mathbf{c} = F_{(n/2)} \begin{pmatrix} a_0 \\ a_2 \\ a_4 \\ \vdots \\ a_{n-2} \end{pmatrix} \quad \text{and} \quad \mathbf{d} = F_{(n/2)} \begin{pmatrix} a_1 \\ a_3 \\ a_5 \\ \vdots \\ a_{n-1} \end{pmatrix}$$

Then, for $0 \le i < n/2$, Eqs. (5.1) and (5.2) can be rewritten as

$$b_i = c_i + \omega^i d_i, \tag{5.3}$$

and

$$b_{i+n/2} = c_i - \omega^i d_i. \tag{5.4}$$

On the PRAM, this gives rise to the recurrence $T(n) = T(n/2) + \Theta(1)$, which solves for $T(n) = \Theta(\log n)$. The number of processors needed is $\Theta(n)$.

Example 5.1   Let $\mathbf{a} = [1, 2, 3, 4]^T$. In this example, we compute $F_4\mathbf{a}$, where

$$F_4 = \begin{pmatrix} 1 & 1 & 1 & 1 \\ 1 & i & -1 & -i \\ 1 & -1 & 1 & -1 \\ 1 & -i & -1 & i \end{pmatrix}.$$

Since $F_2 = \begin{pmatrix} 1 & 1 \\ 1 & -1 \end{pmatrix}$, $\mathbf{c} = \begin{pmatrix} 1 & 1 \\ 1 & -1 \end{pmatrix}\begin{pmatrix} 1 \\ 3 \end{pmatrix} = \begin{pmatrix} 4 \\ -2 \end{pmatrix}$, and $\mathbf{d} = \begin{pmatrix} 1 & 1 \\ 1 & -1 \end{pmatrix}\begin{pmatrix} 2 \\ 4 \end{pmatrix} = \begin{pmatrix} 6 \\ -2 \end{pmatrix}$. By Eq. (5.3), $b_0 = c_0 + i^0 d_0 = 10$, and $b_1 = c_1 + i^1 d_1 = -2 - 2i$, since $\omega = i$. By Eq. (5.4), $b_2 = c_0 - i^0 d_0 = -2$, and $b_3 = c_1 - i^1 d_1 = -2 + 2i$. Hence,

$$\mathbf{b} = F_4\mathbf{a} = \begin{pmatrix} 10 \\ -2 - 2i \\ -2 \\ -2 + 2i \end{pmatrix},$$

as can be verified by direct multiplication.   □

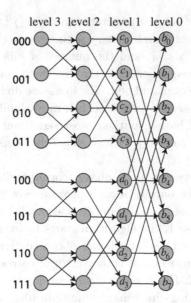

level 3   level 2   level 1   level 0

Fig. 5.2.   Implementation of FFT on the butterfly for $n = 8$.

5.2   Implementation on the Butterfly

By Eqs. 5.3 and 5.4, the implementation of the Fourier transform on the d-dimensional butterfly, where $n = 2^d$, is straightforward. These two equations are implemented naturally on the butterfly as shown in Fig. 5.2 for $n = 8$. The b_i's are computed recursively in level 0, and c_i's and d_i's are computed recursively in level 1, and so on. As an example in the figure, b_3 is computed as $b_3 = c_3 + \omega^3 d_3$ and b_6 is computed as $b_6 = c_2 - \omega^2 d_2$.

Each parallel step is carried out by one level of the butterfly. Hence, the number of parallel steps can be expressed by the recurrence $T(n) = T(n/2) + 1$, whence the number of steps is equal to $d = \log n$.

5.3   Iterative FFT on the Butterfly

Unfolding recursion in the FFT algorithm discussed above results in a simple iterative procedure for computing $F_n\mathbf{a}$ on the d-dimensional butterfly, where $n = 2^d$. The algorithm proceeds in the reverse order, from level d to level 0, where the processors in level d contain the input.

If $\mathbf{a} = [a_1, a_2, \ldots, a_n]^T$, then a_j is stored in node (j^R, d), where j^R is the number whose representation in binary is the reverse of the representation of j. For example, if $j = 1$, and the number of bits is 3, then $j^R = 4$. The reason for this renumbering is that in the recursive algorithm, the items are divided into even and odd. The items are divided into two halves; those even in the upper half have 0 as their most significant bit, and those odd in the lower half have 1 as their most significant bit. Appending 0's and 1's is repeated recursively with repeated divisions into even and odd halves.

The algorithm proceeds in d phases corresponding to levels $d - 1$, $d - 2, \ldots, 0$, where the output of each phase except the last is the input to the next. Each phase is carried out in one parallel step, for a total of d parallel steps. In phase 1, the algorithm starts by evaluating the contents of the processors at level $d - 1$. Each pair of consecutive processors perform the multiplication $F_2 \mathbf{u}$, where $\mathbf{u}$ is the vector of corresponding pair of values entered at level d. $F_2 \mathbf{u}$ is not computed using the recursive algorithm discussed above, or using direct matrix multiplication; it is computed using Eqs. (5.3) and (5.4). There are $n/2$ computations of the products $F_2 \mathbf{u}$. Next, in phase 2, each group of four consecutive processors in level $d - 2$ perform the multiplication $F_4 \mathbf{v}$ using Eqs. (5.3) and (5.4), where $\mathbf{v}$ is the vector of corresponding four elements computed in phase 1 while processing level $d - 1$. There are $n/4$ computations of the products $F_4 \mathbf{v}$. This process of doubling the group size in each phase and computing the Fourier transforms using Eqs. (5.3) and (5.4) is repeated in the following phases, phases $3, 4, \ldots, d$, until the final product $F_n \mathbf{a}$ is computed. In general, in phase j, $n/2^j$ computations of $F_{2^j} \mathbf{w}$ in level $d - j$ are carried out using Eqs. (5.3) and (5.4).

Example 5.2   (See Fig. 5.3). As in Example 5.1, let $\mathbf{a} = [1, 2, 3, 4]^T$. We compute $F_4 \mathbf{a}$. The input is entered into level $d = 2$, where a_j is stored in node (j^R, d), as explained above. In phase 1 of the algorithm, the contents of the processors at level $d - 1 = 1$ are evaluated. Each pair of consecutive processors perform the multiplication $F_2 \mathbf{u}$ using Eqs. 5.3 and 5.4, where $\mathbf{u}$ is the vector of corresponding pair of values entered at level 2. For example, the contents of node $(0, 1)$ are computed as $c_0 + (-1)^0 d_0 = 1 + (-1)^0 3 = 4$ (here $\omega = -1$). Similarly, the contents of node $(1, 1)$ are computed as

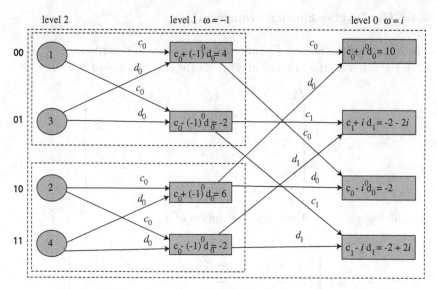

Fig. 5.3. Iterative FFT on the butterfly.

$c_0 - (-1)^0 d_0 = 1 - (-1)^0 3 = -2$. Hence, $F_2 \mathbf{u} = \begin{pmatrix} 1 & 1 \\ 1 & -1 \end{pmatrix} \begin{pmatrix} 1 \\ 3 \end{pmatrix} = \begin{pmatrix} 4 \\ -2 \end{pmatrix}$.
Likewise, in the lower half of level 1, $\begin{pmatrix} 1 & 1 \\ 1 & -1 \end{pmatrix} \begin{pmatrix} 2 \\ 4 \end{pmatrix} = \begin{pmatrix} 6 \\ -2 \end{pmatrix}$. Next, in
phase 2, the group of four consecutive processors in level 0 perform the
multiplication $F_4 \mathbf{v}$ using Eqs. 5.3 and 5.4, where $\mathbf{v} = [4, -2, 6, -2]^T$ is the
vector of corresponding four elements computed in phase 1. For example,
the contents of node $(0,0)$ are computed as $c_0 + i^0 d_0 = 4 + i^0 6 = 10$
(here $\omega = i$). Similarly, the contents of node $(1,0)$ are computed as
$c_1 + i d_1 = -2 + i(-2) = -2 - 2i$. Likewise, the contents of nodes $(2,0)$
and $(3,0)$ are computed as -2 and $-2 + 2i$, respectively. Hence,

$$F_4 \mathbf{a} = F_4 \mathbf{v} = \begin{pmatrix} 1 & 1 & 1 & 1 \\ 1 & i & -1 & -i \\ 1 & -1 & 1 & -1 \\ 1 & -i & -1 & i \end{pmatrix} \begin{pmatrix} 4 \\ -2 \\ 6 \\ -2 \end{pmatrix} = \begin{pmatrix} 10 \\ -2 - 2i \\ -2 \\ -2 + 2i \end{pmatrix}.$$

This conforms with the result obtained in Example 5.1. □

5.4   The Inverse Fourier Transform

The inverse of the matrix F_n turns out to be easy to describe:
for $1 \le k < n$, the kth row of nF_n^{-1} is the $n - k$th row of F_n:

$$F_n^{-1} = \frac{1}{n} \begin{pmatrix} 1 & 1 & 1 & \cdots & 1 \\ 1 & \omega^{n-1} & \omega^{2(n-1)} & \cdots & \omega^{(n-1)^2} \\ 1 & \omega^{n-2} & \omega^{2(n-2)} & \cdots & \omega^{(n-1)(n-2)} \\ \vdots & \vdots & \vdots & \vdots & \vdots \\ 1 & \omega^2 & \omega^4 & \cdots & \omega^{2n-1} \\ 1 & \omega & \omega^2 & \cdots & \omega^{n-1} \end{pmatrix}$$

Simplifying yields another easy description of F_n^{-1}:

$$F_n^{-1} = \frac{1}{n} \begin{pmatrix} 1 & 1 & 1 & \cdots & 1 \\ 1 & \omega^{-1} & \omega^{-2} & \cdots & \omega^{-(n-1)} \\ 1 & \omega^{-2} & \omega^{-4} & \cdots & \omega^{-2(n-1)} \\ \vdots & \vdots & \vdots & \vdots & \vdots \\ 1 & \omega^{-(n-2)} & \omega^{-2(n-2)} & \cdots & \omega^{-(n-2)(n-1)} \\ 1 & \omega^{-(n-1)} & \omega^{-2(n-1)} & \cdots & \omega^{-(n-1)^2} \end{pmatrix}$$

That is,

$$(F_n^{-1})_{ij} = \frac{\omega^{-ij}}{n}.$$

So, the inverse of F_n is $1/n$ times the Fourier transform matrix of a different primitive root of unity, namely ω^{-1}.

To show that it is indeed the inverse of F_n, we need the following property.

Property 5.3   Since

$$\sum_{j=0}^{n-1} \omega^j = \frac{\omega^n - 1}{\omega - 1} = \frac{1 - 1}{\omega - 1} = 0,$$

we have

$$\sum_{j=0}^{n-1} \omega^{ij} = \begin{cases} 0 & \text{if } i \not\equiv 0 \pmod{n} \\ n & \text{if } i \equiv 0 \pmod{n}. \end{cases}$$

By Property 5.3, we have

$$(F_n \times F_n^{-1})_{ij} = \frac{1}{n} \sum_{k=0}^{n-1} \omega^{ik} \omega^{-kj}$$

$$= \frac{1}{n} \sum_{k=0}^{n-1} \omega^{k(i-j)}$$

$$= 1 \text{ if } i = j \text{ and } 0 \text{ otherwise.}$$

Example 5.3

Since $F_4 = \begin{pmatrix} 1 & 1 & 1 & 1 \\ 1 & i & -1 & -i \\ 1 & -1 & 1 & -1 \\ 1 & -i & -1 & i \end{pmatrix}$, $F_4^{-1} = \frac{1}{4} \begin{pmatrix} 1 & 1 & 1 & 1 \\ 1 & -i & -1 & i \\ 1 & -1 & 1 & -1 \\ 1 & i & -1 & -i \end{pmatrix}$

as can be easily verified. □

Clearly, the algorithm for the inverse Fourier transform is the same as the algorithm for FFT described above.

5.5 Product of Polynomials

Let $f(x)$ be a polynomial of degree $n - 1$, that is,

$$f(x) = a_0 + a_1 x + \cdots + a_{n-1} x^{n-1}.$$

A *point-value* representation of $f(x)$ is a sequence of n (point, value) pairs

$$\langle (x_0, f(x_0)), (x_1, f(x_1)), \ldots, (x_{n-1}, f(x_{n-1})) \rangle$$

such that the x_j's are distinct. The process of computing the coefficients of $f(x)$ from its point-value representation is called *interpolation*. For example, the pairs $\langle (0, 1), (2, 3) \rangle$ is a representation of the polynomial $f(x) = x + 1$, whose coefficients can be obtained by interpolating this sequence of (point, value) pairs.

Let $f(x)$ and $g(x)$ be two polynomials of degree $n - 1$, where

$$f(x) = \sum_{j=0}^{n-1} a_j x^j \quad \text{and} \quad g(x) = \sum_{j=0}^{n-1} b_j x^j,$$

where n is a power of 2. The product polynomial $h(x)$ is given by

$$h(x) = f(x)g(x) = \sum_{j=0}^{2n-1} c_j x^j,$$

where $c_{2n-1} = 0$.

Recall that if $\mathbf{a}$ is a vector of n coefficients of the polynomial $f(x)$, then $F_n \mathbf{a}$ denotes the vector consisting of the values of $f(x)$ evaluated at the n roots of unity. Likewise, $F_n \mathbf{b}$ denotes the vector consisting of the values of $g(x)$ evaluated at the n roots of unity. That is,

$$\begin{pmatrix} f(\omega^0) \\ f(\omega^1) \\ \vdots \\ f(\omega^{n-1}) \end{pmatrix} = F_n \begin{pmatrix} a_0 \\ a_1 \\ \vdots \\ a_{n-1} \end{pmatrix} \quad \text{and} \quad \begin{pmatrix} g(\omega^0) \\ g(\omega^1) \\ \vdots \\ g(\omega^{n-1}) \end{pmatrix} = F_n \begin{pmatrix} b_0 \\ b_1 \\ \vdots \\ b_{n-1} \end{pmatrix}.$$

By inverting F_n, we can perform the process of interpolation, which in the above functions obtains the a_i's from the vector of $f(\omega_i)$'s, and the b_i's from the vector of $g(\omega_i)$'s. That is,

$$\begin{pmatrix} a_0 \\ a_1 \\ \vdots \\ a_{n-1} \end{pmatrix} = F_n^{-1} \begin{pmatrix} f(\omega^0) \\ f(\omega^1) \\ \vdots \\ f(\omega^{n-1}) \end{pmatrix} \quad \text{and} \quad \begin{pmatrix} b_0 \\ b_1 \\ \vdots \\ b_{n-1} \end{pmatrix} = F_n^{-1} \begin{pmatrix} g(\omega^0) \\ g(\omega^1) \\ \vdots \\ g(\omega^{n-1}) \end{pmatrix}.$$

The componentwise product of vectors $F_n \mathbf{a}$ and $F_n \mathbf{b}$ is

$$\begin{pmatrix} f(\omega^0)g(\omega^0) \\ f(\omega^1)g(\omega^1) \\ \vdots \\ f(\omega^{n-1})g(\omega^{n-1}) \end{pmatrix},$$

where $f(\omega^i)g(\omega^i) = h(\omega^i)$, $0 \le i \le n - 1$. By taking the inverse Fourier transform of the componentwise product of vectors $F_n \mathbf{a}$ and $F_n \mathbf{b}$, we can obtain $h(x)$ in its coefficient form. There is a little difficulty, however. Given a polynomial $p(x)$ of degree m in its (point, value) pairs, it is well-known that $m + 1$ points are needed in order to reconstruct $p(x)$ in its coefficient form. The componentwise product of $F_n \mathbf{a}$ and $F_n \mathbf{b}$ provides the values of $h(x)$ at only n points, but $h(x)$ is of degree $2n - 2$. Hence, we extend $f(x)$ and $g(x)$ to degree $2n - 1$ by adding zeros for the terms with degree n through $2n - 1$. Thus, define $\mathbf{a}' = [a_0, a_1, a_2, \ldots, a_{n-1}, 0, 0, \ldots, 0]^T$, and $\mathbf{b}' = [b_0, b_1, b_2, \ldots, b_{n-1}, 0, 0, \ldots, 0]^T$. We compute the coefficients of $h(x)$ as

$$
\begin{pmatrix} c_0 \\ c_1 \\ \vdots \\ c_{2n-1} \end{pmatrix} = F_{2n}^{-1} \begin{pmatrix} f(\omega^0)g(\omega^0) \\ f(\omega^1)g(\omega^1) \\ \vdots \\ f(\omega^{2n-1})g(\omega^{2n-1}) \end{pmatrix}.
$$

Note here that ω is the $2n$th primitive root of unity. In summary, to construct the product $h(x) = f(x)g(x)$, we do the following steps:

(1) Compute $\mathbf{c_1} = F_{2n}\mathbf{a}'$, and $\mathbf{c_2} = F_{2n}\mathbf{b}'$.
(2) Perform the componentwise product $\mathbf{d} = \mathbf{c_1} \odot \mathbf{c_2}$.
(3) Interpolate by computing the inverse Fourier transform $\mathbf{c} = F_{2n}^{-1}\mathbf{d}$.
(4) Output $\mathbf{c} = [c_0, c_1, c_2, \ldots, c_{2n-1}]^T$.

Steps 1 and 3 take $\Theta(\log n)$ parallel time on the d-dimensional butterfly using $\Theta(n \log n)$ operations. Step 2 takes $\Theta(1)$ parallel time. Hence, the algorithm for computing the product of two polynomials requires $\Theta(n \log n)$ operations, and runs in $\Theta(\log n)$ parallel time on the $\log n$-dimensional butterfly. This is much more efficient than the $\Theta(n^2)$ direct multiplication algorithm.

Example 5.4 Let $f(x) = 1 + 2x$ and $g(x) = 1 + 3x$. We will compute the product $h(x) = f(x)g(x)$ using the fast Fourier transform. Write $f(x) = \mathbf{a}x$, where $\mathbf{a} = [1, 2]$, and $\mathbf{x} = [1, x]^T$, and $g(x) = \mathbf{b}x$, where $\mathbf{b} = [1, 3]$. Let $\mathbf{a}' = [1, 2, 0, 0]^T$ and $\mathbf{b}' = [1, 3, 0, 0]^T$. Then,

$$
\mathbf{c_1} = F_4\mathbf{a}' = \begin{pmatrix} 1 & 1 & 1 & 1 \\ 1 & i & -1 & -i \\ 1 & -1 & 1 & -1 \\ 1 & -i & -1 & i \end{pmatrix} \begin{pmatrix} 1 \\ 2 \\ 0 \\ 0 \end{pmatrix} = \begin{pmatrix} 3 \\ 1 + 2i \\ -1 \\ 1 - 2i \end{pmatrix}.
$$

Similarly,

$$\mathbf{c_2} = F_4 \mathbf{b'} = \begin{pmatrix} 1 & 1 & 1 & 1 \\ 1 & i & -1 & -i \\ 1 & -1 & 1 & -1 \\ 1 & -i & -1 & i \end{pmatrix} \begin{pmatrix} 1 \\ 3 \\ 0 \\ 0 \end{pmatrix} = \begin{pmatrix} 4 \\ 1+3i \\ -2 \\ 1-3i \end{pmatrix}.$$

Now, we compute $\mathbf{c_1} \odot \mathbf{c_2}$, which is the componentwise multiplication of $\mathbf{c_1}$ and $\mathbf{c_2}$.

$$\mathbf{c_1} \odot \mathbf{c_2} = \begin{pmatrix} 3 \\ 1+2i \\ -1 \\ 1-2i \end{pmatrix} \odot \begin{pmatrix} 4 \\ 1+3i \\ -2 \\ 1-3i \end{pmatrix} = \begin{pmatrix} 12 \\ -5+5i \\ 2 \\ -5-5i \end{pmatrix}.$$

Next, we interpolate.

$$\mathbf{c} = F_4^{-1}(\mathbf{c_1} \odot \mathbf{c_2})$$

$$= \frac{1}{4} \begin{pmatrix} 1 & 1 & 1 & 1 \\ 1 & -i & -1 & i \\ 1 & -1 & 1 & -1 \\ 1 & i & -1 & -i \end{pmatrix} \begin{pmatrix} 12 \\ -5+5i \\ 2 \\ -5-5i \end{pmatrix} = \frac{1}{4} \begin{pmatrix} 4 \\ 20 \\ 24 \\ 0 \end{pmatrix} = \begin{pmatrix} 1 \\ 5 \\ 6 \\ 0 \end{pmatrix}.$$

Hence, $h(x) = 1 + 5x + 6x^2$, as can be verified by direct multiplication. □

Computing the product of more than two polynomials can be found in the exercises (see Exercises 5.5, 5.6 and 5.7).

5.6 Computing the Convolution of Two Vectors

Given two vectors

$$\mathbf{a} = a_0, a_1, \ldots, a_{n-1} \quad \text{and} \quad \mathbf{b} = b_0, b_1, \ldots, b_{m-1},$$

the *convolution* of $\mathbf{a}$ and $\mathbf{b}$, denoted by $\mathbf{a} \otimes \mathbf{b}$, is defined as the vector $\mathbf{c} = [c_0, c_1, \ldots, c_{m+n-1}]^T$, such that

$$c_i = \sum_{j=0}^{i} a_j b_{i-j},$$

where $a_j = 0$ for $j > n - 1$, and $b_j = 0$ for $j > m - 1$. Convolution is closely related to polynomial multiplication. So, if

$$f(x) = \sum_{j=0}^{n-1} a_j x^j \quad \text{and} \quad g(x) = \sum_{j=0}^{m-1} b_j x^j,$$

then the kth term in $f(x)g(x)$ is the kth element in the vector $\mathbf{a} \otimes \mathbf{b}$. Thus, to find the convolution of $\mathbf{a}$ and $\mathbf{b}$, use the DFT algorithm to compute the product $f(x)g(x)$, and extract the coefficients of the resulting multiplication. When $n = m$, the running time on the PRAM or the butterfly is $\Theta(\log n)$ using $O(n)$ processors.

Example 5.5 Let $\mathbf{a} = [1, 2]^T$ and $\mathbf{b} = [1, 3]^T$. Then,

$$f(x)g(x) = (a_0 b_0) + (a_0 b_1 + a_1 b_0)x + (a_0 b_2 + a_1 b_1 + a_2 b_0)x^2 = 1 + 5x + 6x^2.$$

Note that $a_2 = b_2 = 0$. It follows that $c_0 = a_0 b_0 = 1$, $c_1 = a_0 b_1 + a_1 b_0 = 5$, and $c_2 = a_0 b_2 + a_1 b_1 + a_2 b_0 = 6$. $\qquad\square$

5.7 The Product of a Toeplitz Matrix and a Vectors

A Toeplitz matrix T is defined as an $n \times n$ matrix in which $T[i, j] = T[i - 1, j - 1]$ for $2 \leq i, j \leq n$. Equivalently, the elements in each diagonal are equal. The entries of T will be indexed as shown below

$$\begin{pmatrix} t_{n-1} & t_{n-2} & \cdots & t_2 & t_1 & t_0 \\ t_n & t_{n-1} & t_{n-2} & \cdots & t_2 & t_1 \\ t_{n+1} & t_n & t_{n-1} & t_{n-2} & \cdots & t_2 \\ \vdots & \vdots & \vdots & \vdots & \cdots & \vdots \\ t_{2n-3} & t_{2n-4} & \cdots & t_n & t_{n-1} & t_{n-2} \\ t_{2n-2} & t_{2n-3} & \cdots & t_{n+1} & t_n & t_{n-1} \end{pmatrix}$$

A Toeplitz matrix can conveniently be represented by the vector $\mathbf{t}$ of $2n - 1$ entries appearing in the first row and first column. That is, $\mathbf{t} = [t_0, t_1, \ldots, t_{2n-2}]^T$.

Example 5.6   Let

$$T = \begin{pmatrix} 4 & 3 & 2 & 1 \\ 5 & 4 & 3 & 2 \\ 6 & 5 & 4 & 3 \\ 7 & 6 & 5 & 4 \end{pmatrix}$$

Then, T is defined by the vector $\mathbf{t} = [1, 2, 3, 4, 5, 6, 7]^T$.   □

Let $\mathbf{a} = [a_0, a_1, \ldots, a_{n-1}]^T$ be a vector of n elements, and let T be a Toeplitz matrix. We are interested in computing the product $\mathbf{b} = T\mathbf{a}$. Using direct matrix by vector multiplication, the kth entry in $\mathbf{b}$ is given by

$$b_k = \sum_{j=0}^{n-1} a_j t_{n+k-j-1}. \tag{5.5}$$

Now, consider computing the convolution $\mathbf{c}$ of $\mathbf{a}$ and $\mathbf{t}$ given by

$$c_i = \sum_{j=0}^{i} a_j t_{i-j},$$

Substituting $n + k - 1$ for i yields

$$c_{n+k-1} = \sum_{j=0}^{n+k-1} a_j t_{n+k-j-1}$$

$$= \sum_{j=0}^{n-1} a_j t_{n+k-j-1}, \tag{5.6}$$

since $a_j = 0$ for $j > n - 1$. Comparing the right hand sides of Eq. (5.5) with Eq. (5.6), we see that they are identical. Hence, $b_k = c_{n+k-1}$.

Following this, to compute the product $T\mathbf{a}$, we compute $a \otimes t$ and set $b_k = c_{n+k-1}$. This takes $\Theta(\log n)$ time using $O(n)$ processors on the PRAM and butterfly.

Example 5.7   Consider computing he product $T\mathbf{a}$, where

$$T = \begin{pmatrix} 4 & 3 & 2 & 1 \\ 5 & 4 & 3 & 2 \\ 6 & 5 & 4 & 3 \\ 7 & 6 & 5 & 4 \end{pmatrix} \quad \text{and} \quad \mathbf{a} = \begin{pmatrix} 1 \\ 2 \\ 3 \\ 4 \end{pmatrix}.$$

First, the vector $\mathbf{t}$ is determined to be $[1,2,3,4,5,6,7]^T$. Computing the convolution $a \otimes t$ yields the vector $\mathbf{c}$, which is equal to $[1,4,10,20,30,40, 50,52,45,28]^T$. Hence, $b_0 = c_{4+0-1} = c_3 = 20$, $b_1 = c_{4+1-1} = c_4 = 30$, $b_2 = c_{4+2-1} = c_5 = 40$, and $b_3 = c_{4+3-1} = c_6 = 50$. That is, $Ta = [20,30,40,50]^T$, as can be verified by direct multiplication. $\qquad\square$

5.8 Using Modular Arithmetic

In many applications, the aim is always to perform error-free computations of the fast Fourier transform. It turns out that this can be achieved by performing the FFT computations in modulo arithmetic. Let m be a positive integer. The set Z_m^* is the set of positive integers relatively prime to m. For example, $Z_9^* = \{1,2,4,5,7,8\}$. It is a group under multiplication modulo m. An element α is a primitive root of unity for a group if it generates such a multiplicative group. For instance, $\alpha = 2$ generates all elements of the multiplicative group Z_9^* under the operation of multiplication modulo 9. That is, $2^0 = 1, 2^1 = 2, 2^2 = 4, 2^3 = 8, 2^4 = 7, 2^5 = 5$, where all powers are computed modulo 9. There are no primitive roots for $Z_8^* = \{1,3,5,7\}$.

Let $n = 2^j, \alpha = 2^k, l = n/2$ and $m = \alpha^l + 1 = 2^{kl} + 1$. Then, α is a primitive root of unity over the set of integers modulo m. It is not hard to see that the fast Fourier transform works correctly by replacing ω by α. Figure 5.4 illustrates the n roots of unity for $n = 8$ (mod 17) generated by the primitive root 2. As shown in the figure, the pairs α^j and $\alpha^{j+n/2}$ are symmetrically located with respect to the origin. Algebraically, we have $\alpha^{j+n/2} = -\alpha^j$ (Property 5.2), and in particular, $\alpha^{n/2} = -1$. In this section,

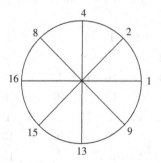

Fig. 5.4.   The 8 roots of unity mod 17 generated by the primitive root 2.

all arithmetic will be done modulo m; we will simply write $x + y$ to mean $x + y \pmod{m}$.

Using α as a primitive root of unity, the transformation matrix F_n looks like:

$$
\begin{pmatrix}
1 & 1 & 1 & \cdots & 1 \\
1 & \alpha & \alpha^2 & \cdots & \alpha^{n-1} \\
1 & \alpha^2 & \alpha^4 & \cdots & \alpha^{2n-2} \\
\vdots & \vdots & \vdots & \vdots & \vdots \\
1 & \alpha^{n-2} & \alpha^{2(n-2)} & \cdots & \alpha^{(n-1)(n-2)} \\
1 & \alpha^{n-1} & \alpha^{2(n-1)} & \cdots & \alpha^{(n-1)^2}
\end{pmatrix}
$$

whose inverse is

$$
F_n^{-1} = n^{-1}
\begin{pmatrix}
1 & 1 & 1 & \cdots & 1 \\
1 & \alpha^{-1} & \alpha^{-2} & \cdots & \alpha^{-(n-1)} \\
1 & \alpha^{-2} & \alpha^{-4} & \cdots & \alpha^{-2(n-1)} \\
\vdots & \vdots & \vdots & \vdots & \vdots \\
1 & \alpha^{-(n-2)} & \alpha^{-2(n-2)} & \cdots & \alpha^{-(n-2)(n-1)} \\
1 & \alpha^{-(n-1)} & \alpha^{-2(n-1)} & \cdots & \alpha^{-(n-1)^2}
\end{pmatrix}
$$

It is clear that F_n and F_n^{-1} are obtained from the usual FFT matrices by substituting α for ω.

Example 5.8 Let $n = 8, \alpha = 2$ and $m = 17$. Then,

$$
F_8 =
\begin{pmatrix}
1 & 1 & 1 & 1 & 1 & 1 & 1 & 1 \\
1 & 2 & 4 & 8 & 16 & 15 & 13 & 9 \\
1 & 4 & 16 & 13 & 1 & 4 & 16 & 13 \\
1 & 8 & 13 & 2 & 16 & 9 & 4 & 15 \\
1 & 16 & 1 & 16 & 1 & 16 & 1 & 16 \\
1 & 15 & 4 & 9 & 16 & 2 & 13 & 8 \\
1 & 13 & 16 & 4 & 1 & 13 & 16 & 4 \\
1 & 9 & 13 & 15 & 16 & 8 & 4 & 2
\end{pmatrix},
$$

and

$$
F_8^{-1} = \begin{pmatrix}
15 & 15 & 15 & 15 & 15 & 15 & 15 & 15 \\
15 & 16 & 8 & 4 & 2 & 1 & 9 & 13 \\
15 & 8 & 2 & 9 & 15 & 8 & 2 & 9 \\
15 & 4 & 9 & 16 & 2 & 13 & 8 & 1 \\
15 & 2 & 15 & 2 & 15 & 2 & 15 & 2 \\
15 & 1 & 8 & 13 & 2 & 16 & 9 & 4 \\
15 & 9 & 2 & 8 & 15 & 9 & 2 & 8 \\
15 & 13 & 9 & 1 & 2 & 4 & 8 & 16
\end{pmatrix},
$$

The second row of F_8 contains the powers of $\alpha = 2$, the third contains the powers of $\alpha^2 = 4$, and so on. On the other hand, the second row of F_8^{-1} contains the powers of $\alpha^{-1} = 2^{-1} = 9$ multiplied by $8^{-1} = 15 = -2$. For example, the second entry in the second row is $\alpha^{-1}8^{-1} = 9 \times (-2) = -18 = -1 = 16$. The third row contains the powers of $\alpha^{-2} = 2^{-2} = 13$ multiplied by $8^{-1} = 15 = -2$, and so on. □

Example 5.9 Let $f(x) = 1 + 2x$ and $g(x) = 1 + 3x$. We will compute the product $h(x) = f(x)g(x)$ using FFT modulo 17. Let $n = 4, \alpha = 4$ and $m = 17$. Then,

$$
F_4 = \begin{pmatrix}
1 & 1 & 1 & 1 \\
1 & 4 & 16 & 13 \\
1 & 16 & 1 & 16 \\
1 & 13 & 16 & 4
\end{pmatrix}
\quad \text{and} \quad
F_4^{-1} = \begin{pmatrix}
13 & 13 & 13 & 13 \\
13 & 16 & 4 & 1 \\
13 & 4 & 13 & 4 \\
13 & 1 & 4 & 16
\end{pmatrix}.
$$

Write $f(x) = \mathbf{ax}$, where $\mathbf{a} = [1, 2]$, and $\mathbf{x} = [1, x]^T$, and $g(x) = \mathbf{bx}$, where $\mathbf{b} = [1, 3]$. Let $\mathbf{a}' = [1, 2, 0, 0]^T$ and $\mathbf{b}' = [1, 3, 0, 0]^T$. Then,

$$
\mathbf{c_1} = F_4\mathbf{a}' = \begin{pmatrix}
1 & 1 & 1 & 1 \\
1 & 4 & 16 & 13 \\
1 & 16 & 1 & 16 \\
1 & 13 & 16 & 4
\end{pmatrix}
\begin{pmatrix}
1 \\ 2 \\ 0 \\ 0
\end{pmatrix}
=
\begin{pmatrix}
3 \\ 9 \\ 16 \\ 10
\end{pmatrix}.
$$

Similarly,

$$
\mathbf{c_2} = F_4\mathbf{b}' = \begin{pmatrix}
1 & 1 & 1 & 1 \\
1 & 4 & 16 & 13 \\
1 & 16 & 1 & 16 \\
1 & 13 & 16 & 4
\end{pmatrix}
\begin{pmatrix}
1 \\ 3 \\ 0 \\ 0
\end{pmatrix}
=
\begin{pmatrix}
4 \\ 13 \\ 15 \\ 6
\end{pmatrix}.
$$

Now, we compute $\mathbf{c_1} \odot \mathbf{c_2}$, which is the componentwise multiplication of $\mathbf{c_1}$ and $\mathbf{c_2}$.

$$\mathbf{c_1} \odot \mathbf{c_2} = \begin{pmatrix} 3 \\ 9 \\ 16 \\ 10 \end{pmatrix} \odot \begin{pmatrix} 4 \\ 13 \\ 15 \\ 6 \end{pmatrix} = \begin{pmatrix} 12 \\ 15 \\ 2 \\ 9 \end{pmatrix}.$$

Next, we interpolate.

$$\mathbf{c} = F_4^{-1}(\mathbf{c_1} \odot \mathbf{c_2}) = \begin{pmatrix} 13 & 13 & 13 & 13 \\ 13 & 16 & 4 & 1 \\ 13 & 4 & 13 & 4 \\ 13 & 1 & 4 & 16 \end{pmatrix} \begin{pmatrix} 12 \\ 15 \\ 2 \\ 9 \end{pmatrix} = \begin{pmatrix} 1 \\ 5 \\ 6 \\ 0 \end{pmatrix}.$$

Hence, $h(x) = 1 + 5x + 6x^2$, as can be verified by direct multiplication. $\square$

5.9 Bibliographic Notes

The fast Fourier transform is created by Cooley and Tukey [27]. See also Kronsjo [48] and Winograd [98]. Blahut [16] and McClellan [64] cover many fast Fourier transform algorithms for computing DFT and convolution. See, for example, Borodin and Moenck [17] and Fiduccia [36] for algorithms for polynomial evaluation and interpolation using the fast Fourier transform. For a good introduction to fast Fourier transform using modular arithmetic, see Lakshmivarahan and Dhall [52].

5.10 Exercises

5.1. Prove Property 5.1: For even n, if ω is an nth root of unity, then ω^2 is an $(n/2)$th root of unity.

5.2. Prove Property 5.2: For even n, $\omega^{k+n/2} = -\omega^k$.

5.3. Show that if ω is a primitive nth root of unity, then ω^{-1} is also a primitive nth root of unity.

5.4. Let $f(x) = 2 + x$ and $g(x) = 3 + 2x$. Compute the product $h(x) = f(x)g(x)$ using fast Fourier transform.

5.5. Let $f_1(x), f_2(x)$ and $f_3(x)$ be three polynomials of degree $n - 1$ each. Apply DFT to find their multiplication $f_1(x)f_2(x)f_3(x)$ on the PRAM with $O(n)$ processors. What is the running time of your algorithm?

5.6. Generalize Exercise 5.5 to $k \geq 2$ polynomials of degree $n - 1$ each. Your algorithm should run in time $O(\log kn)$ on the PRAM. How many processors are needed?

5.7. Let $f_1(x) = 1 + 2x, f_2(x) = 1 + 3x$ and $f_3(x) = 1 + x$. Apply Exercise 5.6 to compute the product $g(x) = f_1(x)f_2(x)f_3(x)$ using fast Fourier transform.

5.8. Give an efficient algorithm to compute $(1 + x)^n$. What is the running time of your algorithm? How many processors are required by your algorithm?

5.9. Carry out the DFT algorithm to find the convolution of the two vectors $[2, 3]^T$ and $[4, 1]^T$.

5.10. Is the sum of two Toeplitz matrices Toeplitz? Prove your answer.

5.11. Is the product of two Toeplitz matrices Toeplitz? Prove your answer.

5.12. How quickly can you multiply two Toeplitz matrices A and B? Explain.

5.13. Let $n = 4, \alpha = 2$ and $m = 5$ in the specification of FFT in modular arithmetic. Compute F_4 and F_4^{-1}.

5.14. Use your answer to Exercise 5.13 to find the product $f(x)g(x)$, where $f(x) = 2 + x$ and $g(x) = 3 + 2x$ in modular arithmetic.

5.15. Evaluate $f(x) = (1 + x + x^2)^2$ in modular arithmetic. You may use F_8 and F_8^{-1} in Example 5.8. Note that $\alpha = 2$ and $m = 17$.

5.16. Let $\mathbf{a} = [2, 1]^T$ and $\mathbf{b} = [4, 3]^T$. Use your answer to Exercise 5.13 to find the convolution of $\mathbf{a}$ and $\mathbf{b}$ in modular arithmetic.

5.17. Is it possible to have $n = 6, \alpha = 2$ and $m = 9$ in the specification of FFT in modular arithmetic? Explain.

5.18. What are the primitive roots of unity of $Z_5^* = \{1, 2, 3, 4\}$?

5.19. How many primitive roots (generators) are there for Z_m^*?

5.11 Solutions

5.1. Prove Property 5.1: For even n, if ω is an nth root of unity, then ω^2 is an $(n/2)$th root of unity.

$(\omega^2)^k = (\omega^k)^2$. That is, the powers of ω^2 are

$$\omega^2, \omega^4, \ldots, \omega^{2(n/2-1)}, \omega^{2(n/2)}.$$

Moreover, $(\omega^2)^{n/2} = \omega^n = 1$, and $(\omega^2)^j = \omega^{2j} \neq 1$ for $0 < j < n/2$.

5.2. Prove Property 5.2: For even n, $\omega^{k+n/2} = -\omega^k$.

$$\omega^{k+n/2} = \omega^k \times \omega^{n/2} = \omega^k \times (-1) = -\omega^k.$$

5.3. Show that if ω is a primitive nth root of unity, then ω^{-1} is also a primitive nth root of unity.

The n powers of ω^{-1} are $\omega^{-1}, (\omega^{-1})^2, (\omega^{-1})^3, \ldots, (\omega^{-1})^n$, or $\omega^{-1}, \omega^{-2}, \omega^{-3}, \ldots, \omega^{-n}$. Multiplying by ω^n yields the sequence $\omega^{n-1}, \omega^{n-2}, \omega^{n-3}, \ldots, \omega^0$. These are precisely the n powers of ω. It follows that ω^{-1} is a primitive nth roots of unity.

5.4. Let $f(x) = 2 + x$ and $g(x) = 3 + 2x$. Compute the product $h(x) = f(x)g(x)$ using fast Fourier transform.

Similar to Example 5.4.

5.5. Let $f_1(x), f_2(x)$ and $f_3(x)$ be three polynomials of degree $n - 1$ each. Apply DFT to find their multiplication $f_1(x)f_2(x)f_3(x)$ on the PRAM with $O(n)$ processors. What is the running time of your algorithm?

First, note that the degree of the product is $3n - 3$. Let m be the least power of 2 greater than or equal to $3n - 2$. Let a_1, a_2 and a_3 be the vectors of coefficients of $f_1(x), f_2(x)$ and $f_3(x)$, respectively. The steps for the construction of the product $g(x) = f_1(x)f_2(x)f_3(x)$ are shown in Algorithm POLYNOMIALMULTIP1. Steps 1 and 3 take

---

Algorithm 5.1 POLYNOMIALMULTIP1
Input: Three polynomials $f_1(x), f_2(x)$ and $f_3(x)$.
Output: The product $g(x) = f_1(x)f_2(x)f_3(x)$.

1. Compute $\mathbf{d_1} = F_m \mathbf{a'_1}$, $\mathbf{d_2} = F_m \mathbf{a'_2}$, and $\mathbf{d_3} = F_m \mathbf{a'_3}$, where $\mathbf{a'_1}, \mathbf{a'_2}$ and $\mathbf{a'_3}$ are $\mathbf{a_1}, \mathbf{a_2}$ and $\mathbf{a_3}$ padded with 0s to length m.
2. Perform the componentwise product $\mathbf{c} = \mathbf{d_1} \odot \mathbf{d_2} \odot \mathbf{d_3}$.
3. Interpolate by computing the inverse Fourier transform $\mathbf{e} = F_m^{-1}\mathbf{c}$.
4. Output $\mathbf{e} = [e_0, e_1, e_2, \ldots, e_{m-1}]^T$; $\mathbf{e}$ is the vector of coefficients of the product $g(x)$.

$\Theta(\log n)$ parallel time on the PRAM using $O(n)$ processors. Step 2 takes $\Theta(1)$ parallel time. Hence, the algorithm for computing the product of three polynomials runs in $\Theta(\log n)$ parallel time on the PRAM with $O(n)$ processors.

5.6. Generalize Exercise 5.5 to $k \geq 2$ polynomials of degree $n - 1$ each. Your algorithm should run in time $O(\log kn)$ on the PRAM. How many processors are needed?

First, note that the degree of the product is $kn - k$. Let m be the least power of 2 greater than or equal to $kn - k + 1$. Let $\mathbf{a_1}, \mathbf{a_2}, \ldots, \mathbf{a_k}$ be the vectors of the coefficients of the k polynomials. The idea is to evaluate the polynomials at m points, multiply them componentwise, and then interpolate by applying the inverse DFT. The steps for the construction of the product $g(x) = f_1(x)f_2(x) \ldots f_k(x)$ are shown in Algorithm POLYNOMIALMULTIP2. Steps 1 and 3 take

---

Algorithm 5.2 POLYNOMIALMULTIP2
Input: $k \geq 2$ polynomials $f_1(x), f_2(x), \ldots, f_k(x)$ of degree $n - 1$.
Output: The product $g(x) = f_1(x)f_2(x) \ldots f_k(x)$.

1. Compute $\mathbf{d_1} = F_m \mathbf{a'_1}$, $\mathbf{d_2} = F_m \mathbf{a'_2}$, $\ldots$, $\mathbf{d_k} = F_m \mathbf{a'_k}$, where $\mathbf{a'_1}, \mathbf{a'_2}, \ldots, \mathbf{a'_k}$ are $\mathbf{a_1}, \mathbf{a_2}, \ldots, \mathbf{a_k}$ padded with 0s to length m.
2. Perform the componentwise product $\mathbf{c} = \mathbf{d_1} \odot \mathbf{d_2} \odot \ldots \odot \mathbf{d_k}$.
3. Interpolate by computing the inverse Fourier transform $\mathbf{e} = F_m^{-1}\mathbf{c}$.
4. Output $\mathbf{e} = [e_0, e_1, e_2, \ldots, e_{m-1}]^T$; $\mathbf{e}$ is the vector of coefficients of the product $g(x)$.

$O(\log kn)$ parallel time on the PRAM using $O(kn)$ processors, since there are $O(kn)$ coefficients in $\mathbf{c}$. Computing the componentwise product in Step 2 can be done recursively in $\Theta(\log n)$ time using $O(kn)$ processors. It follows that the running time of the algorithm is $O(\log n + \log kn) = O(\log kn)$ on the PRAM with $O(kn)$ processors.

5.7. Let $f_1(x) = 1 + 2x$, $f_2(x) = 1 + 3x$ and $f_3(x) = 1 + x$. Apply Exercise 5.6 to compute the product $g(x) = f_1(x)f_2(x)f_3(x)$ using fast Fourier transform.

Write $f_1(x) = \mathbf{a_1}\mathbf{x}$, $f_2(x) = \mathbf{a_2}\mathbf{x}$ and $f_3(x) = \mathbf{a_3}\mathbf{x}$, where $\mathbf{a_1} = [1, 2]$, $\mathbf{a_2} = [1, 3]$, $\mathbf{a_3} = [1, 1]$ and $\mathbf{x} = [1, x]^T$. Let $\mathbf{a_1'} = [1, 2, 0, 0]^T$, $\mathbf{a_2'} = [1, 3, 0, 0]^T$ and $\mathbf{a_3'} = [1, 1, 0, 0]^T$. Then,

$$
\mathbf{c_1} = F_4\mathbf{a_1'} = \begin{bmatrix} 1 & 1 & 1 & 1 \\ 1 & i & -1 & -i \\ 1 & -1 & 1 & -1 \\ 1 & -i & -1 & i \end{bmatrix} \begin{bmatrix} 1 \\ 2 \\ 0 \\ 0 \end{bmatrix} = \begin{bmatrix} 3 \\ 1 + 2i \\ -1 \\ 1 - 2i \end{bmatrix}.
$$

Similarly,

$$
\mathbf{c_2} = F_4\mathbf{a_2'} = \begin{bmatrix} 1 & 1 & 1 & 1 \\ 1 & i & -1 & -i \\ 1 & -1 & 1 & -1 \\ 1 & -i & -1 & i \end{bmatrix} \begin{bmatrix} 1 \\ 3 \\ 0 \\ 0 \end{bmatrix} = \begin{bmatrix} 4 \\ 1 + 3i \\ -2 \\ 1 - 3i \end{bmatrix},
$$

and

$$
\mathbf{c_3} = F_4\mathbf{a_3'} = \begin{bmatrix} 1 & 1 & 1 & 1 \\ 1 & i & -1 & -i \\ 1 & -1 & 1 & -1 \\ 1 & -i & -1 & i \end{bmatrix} \begin{bmatrix} 1 \\ 1 \\ 0 \\ 0 \end{bmatrix} = \begin{bmatrix} 2 \\ 1 + i \\ 0 \\ 1 - i \end{bmatrix}.
$$

Now, we compute $\mathbf{c} = \mathbf{c_1} \odot \mathbf{c_2} \odot \mathbf{c_3}$, which is the componentwise multiplication of $\mathbf{c_1}$, $\mathbf{c_2}$ and $\mathbf{c_3}$.

$$
\mathbf{c} = \begin{bmatrix} 3 \\ 1 + 2i \\ -1 \\ 1 - 2i \end{bmatrix} \odot \begin{bmatrix} 4 \\ 1 + 3i \\ -2 \\ 1 - 3i \end{bmatrix} \odot \begin{bmatrix} 2 \\ 1 + i \\ 0 \\ 1 - i \end{bmatrix} = \begin{bmatrix} 24 \\ -10 \\ 0 \\ -10 \end{bmatrix}.
$$

Finally, we interpolate:

$$\mathbf{e} = F_4^{-1}\mathbf{c} = \frac{1}{4}\begin{bmatrix} 1 & 1 & 1 & 1 \\ 1 & -i & -1 & i \\ 1 & -1 & 1 & -1 \\ 1 & i & -1 & -i \end{bmatrix}\begin{bmatrix} 24 \\ -10 \\ 0 \\ -10 \end{bmatrix} = \frac{1}{4}\begin{bmatrix} 4 \\ 24 \\ 44 \\ 24 \end{bmatrix} = \begin{bmatrix} 1 \\ 6 \\ 11 \\ 6 \end{bmatrix}.$$

Hence, $g(x) = 1 + 6x + 11x^2 + 6x^3$, and we can verify this by direct multiplication.

5.8. Give an efficient algorithm to compute $(1+x)^n$. What is the running time of your algorithm? How many processors are required by your algorithm?

We use the fast Fourier transform. This is similar to Exercise 5.6 with k replaced by n, and n replaced by 2. The highest degree in the product is n, so let m be the least power of 2 greater than or equal to $n+1$. Let $\mathbf{a} = [1, 1, 0, 0 \ldots, 0]$ ($m-2$ 0s). Compute the componentwise product $\mathbf{c} = \mathbf{a} \odot \mathbf{a} \odot \ldots, \odot \mathbf{a}$ (n times). This is equal to $[a_0^n + a_1^n + \ldots + a_{m-1}^n]^T$. These powers can be computed in $\Theta(\log n)$ time by assigning each number to one processor, which raises that number to the nth power in sequential $\Theta(\log n)$ time. Thus, this step can be done in parallel in $\Theta(\log n)$ time. Finally, apply the inverse DFT on $\mathbf{c}$ to obtain the final result. Since there are $O(n)$ coefficients in $\mathbf{c}$, applying the inverse DFT requires $\Theta(\log n)$ time. It follows that the running time of the algorithm is $\Theta(\log n)$ on the PRAM using $O(n)$ processors.

5.9. Carry out the DFT algorithm to find the convolution of the two vectors $[2, 3]^T$ and $[4, 1]^T$.

Similar to Example 5.5.

5.10. Is the sum of two Toeplitz matrices Toeplitz? Prove your answer.

Yes. Let $A + B = C$, where A and B are Toeplitz. Then, $c_{i,j} = a_{i,j} + b_{i,j} = a_{i-1,j-1} + b_{i-1,j-1} = c_{i-1,j-1}$. It follows that C is Toeplitz.

5.11. Is the product of two Toeplitz matrices Toeplitz? Prove your answer.

No. Let

$$A = \begin{pmatrix} 1 & 1 & 1 \\ 0 & 1 & 1 \\ 1 & 0 & 1 \end{pmatrix}.$$

Then,

$$A^2 = \begin{pmatrix} 2 & 2 & 3 \\ 1 & 1 & 2 \\ 2 & 1 & 2 \end{pmatrix},$$

which is not Toeplitz.

5.12. How quickly can you multiply two Toeplitz matrices A and B? Explain.

Treat B as a sequence of vectors, and apply the convolution method individually to multiply A by each vector. This results in time complexity $n \times \Theta(\log n) = \Theta(n \log n)$ parallel time using $O(n)$ processors. If the number of processors is $O(n^2)$, then the running time reduces to $\Theta(\log n)$, as all matrix by vector multiplications can be carried out in parallel using the convolution method.

5.13. Let $n = 4, \alpha = 2$ and $m = 5$ in the specification of FFT in modular arithmetic. Compute F_4 and F_4^{-1}.

$$F_4 = \begin{pmatrix} 1 & 1 & 1 & 1 \\ 1 & 2 & 4 & 3 \\ 1 & 4 & 1 & 4 \\ 1 & 3 & 4 & 2 \end{pmatrix} \quad \text{and} \quad F_4^{-1} = \begin{pmatrix} 4 & 4 & 4 & 4 \\ 4 & 2 & 1 & 3 \\ 4 & 1 & 4 & 1 \\ 4 & 3 & 1 & 2 \end{pmatrix}.$$

5.14. Use your answer to Exercise 5.13 to find the product $f(x)g(x)$, where $f(x) = 2 + x$ and $g(x) = 3 + 2x$ in modular arithmetic.

Similar to Example 5.9.

5.15. Evaluate $f(x) = (1 + x + x^2)^2$ in modular arithmetic. You may use F_8 and F_8^{-1} in Example 5.8. Note that $\alpha = 2$ and $m = 17$.

Similar to Example 5.9.

5.16. Let $\mathbf{a} = [2, 1]^T$ and $\mathbf{b} = [4, 3]^T$. Use your answer to Exercise 5.13 to find the convolution of $\mathbf{a}$ and $\mathbf{b}$ in modular arithmetic.

Similar to Example 5.5

5.17. Is it possible to have $n = 6, \alpha = 2$ and $m = 9$ in the specification of FFT in modular arithmetic? Explain.

No, it is impossible since 6 is not invertible modulo 9; 6 and 9 are not relatively prime. 6^{-1} is needed to compute the inverse.

5.18. What are the primitive roots of unity of $Z_5^* = \{1, 2, 3, 4\}$?

There are two of them: 2 and 3.

5.19. How many primitive roots (generators) are there for Z_m^*?

If there is one generator, then there are $\phi(\phi(m))$ generators, where $\phi(k)$ is the number of elements less than k and relatively prime to k. For example, for $m = 5$, there are $\phi(\phi(5)) = \phi(4) = 2$ generators. Note that these generators generate all elements in the group.

Chapter 6

Tree-based Networks

6.1 The Tree Network

A *tree* of size $n = 2^h$ is an interconnection network constructed from a complete binary tree with n processors in the base level $P_1, P_2, \ldots, P_n$, and a total of $2n - 1 = 2^{h+1} - 1$ processors. Here $h = \log n$ is the height of the tree. Each tree has $h + 1$ levels: $0, 1, \ldots, h$. The leaf nodes at level h are connected by two-way communication links to their parents only, and the root is connected to its two children. Every other processor is connected by two-way communication links to its parent and its two children. Therefore, the tree has degree 3. See Fig. 6.1 for an eight-leaf tree.

The communication diameter of a tree of size n is only $\Theta(\log n)$, which is very low compared to a linear array of the same size. This is true since any two processors in the tree can communicate in $O(\log n)$ time. However, it may require as much as $2 \log n = \Omega(\log n)$ time for communication that requires an exchange of information between two arbitrary processors. This makes the tree ideal for computing problems like semigroup operations, e.g., summation and finding the maximum, which require $O(\log n)$ time. However, for problems that demand extensive data movement such as sorting and routing data in the base, $\Omega(n)$ time may be required, since only $\Theta(1)$ wires cross the middle of the tree, which means that the bisection width of the tree is $\Theta(1)$ — and that is very low. For instance, it may be required to move data from the $n/2$ left processors to the $n/2$ right processors, which requires $\Omega(n)$ time, since the root serves as a bottleneck.

253

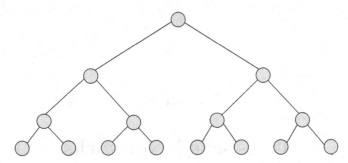

Fig. 6.1.   A tree of size 8.

An algorithm that runs on the tree is called *normal tree algorithm* if no two processors at different levels are active at the same time. That is, at any given time, only processors in the same level are participating in the computation. A single step of a normal tree algorithm can be simulated in one step of the hypercube, given the embedding shown in Fig. 3.12.

6.1.1   *Semigroup operations*

Due to its low communication diameter, the tree is ideal for semigroup operations, e.g., addition and finding the maximum. These operations can be performed in $\Theta(\log n)$ time as follows. Assume that n pieces of data are distributed one per base processor. Then, in order to compute a semigroup operation ∘ over this set of data, it can be applied to disjoint pairs of partial results in parallel as data moves up the tree level by level. After $\Theta(\log n)$ steps, the final result will be known to the root processor. Naturally, if all processors need to know the final result, it can be broadcast from the root to all other processors in $\Theta(\log n)$ time. This means a cost of $\Theta(n \log n)$ on a tree with n base processors, which is a factor of $\Theta(\log n)$ from optimal. Thus, the tree provides a major benefit over the linear array and the mesh in terms of combining information.

6.1.2   *Sorting by minimum extraction*

Assume that a tree with n leaves is available for sorting the sequence $\langle x_1, x_2, \ldots, x_n \rangle$ of distinct integers. The n integers are initially loaded into the leaf processors. Now, each internal processor determines the smaller of the two integers held by its children and routes it to its parent. After $\log n + 1$ steps, the minimum element exits the machine from the root, and is placed in a memory buffer for storing the output. If the process is continued, the next element in increasing order is obtained at every other step. Thus, as mentioned above, the first element requires $\log n + 1$ steps to exit the root. Each one of the remaining $n - 1$ elements requires two steps to be produced. It follows that a constant multiple of $2n + \log n - 1$ time units are needed to produce the sorted sequence. Hence, the running time is $\Theta(n)$, and since there are $2n - 1$ processors, the cost is $\Theta(n^2)$.

6.1.3 *Sorting by partitioning*

Assume that a tree with $k = \log n$ leaves is available for sorting a sequence of $n = 2^k$ numbers. Each processor at level j, $0 \le j \le \log k$, can store $n/2^j$ elements and can execute a median finding and sorting algorithm. The n numbers are initially loaded into the root processor. First, the root finds the median and splits the sequence into two halves, where the half with numbers less than or equal to the median is passed to its left child, and the other half with numbers greater than the median is passed to its right child. Upon receiving its half, each child finds the median of its subsequence and passes those elements less than or equal to the median to its left child and passes those elements larger than the median to its right child. This process of finding the median, partitioning and passing elements continues until the leaf nodes are reached. Finally, each leaf node sorts its $n/\log n$ elements and places them in the output buffer. The algorithm is shown as Algorithm TREESORT

The running time of the algorithm is computed as follows. Finding the median and splitting the sequence at level j takes $\Theta(n/2^j)$. The sorting step takes $\Theta((n/\log n)\log(n/\log n)) = \Theta(n)$ time. The time needed to find the median and output the sequences at level j is $\Theta(n/2^j)$. Hence, the overall running time of the algorithm is expressed as

$$\Theta(n) + \sum_{j=0}^{k} \Theta(n/2^j) = \Theta(n) + \Theta(n) = \Theta(n).$$

The total cost of the algorithm is $\log n \times \Theta(n) = \Theta(n \log n)$, which is optimal.

Algorithm 6.1 TREESORT

Input: A sequence of n numbers, where $n = 2^k$.

Output: The input sorted in ascending order.

1. **for** $j \leftarrow 0$ **to** $\log k - 1$
2. 　　**for** all processors P at level j
3. 　　　　Processor P finds the median m and routes all elements $\leq m$ to the left child and all elements $> m$ to the right child.
4. 　　**end for**
5. **for** all leaf processors P
6. 　　Processor P sorts the currently held elements and places them in the output buffer.
7. **end for**

6.1.4　*Selection*

Recall the problem of selection discussed in Section 2.14: Given a sequence $A = \langle a_1, a_2, \ldots, a_n \rangle$ of n elements and a positive integer k, $1 \leq k \leq n$, find the kth smallest element in A. In this section we consider the problem of finding the k'th smallest element in a sequence of n elements stored at the leaves of an n-leaf tree of height h, where $n = 2^h$ and $h = 2^m$. A straightforward solution would be to sort A and return the kth smallest element. However, sorting on the tree is expensive, and takes a lot of time. The easiest selection problem is $k = 1$, which amounts to finding the minimum in $\Theta(\log n)$ time. We observe that if we adopt a modification of the sorting method of minimum extraction outlined above, then the kth smallest element can be found in $\Theta(\log n + k)$ time, which in the worst case is $\Theta(n)$, e.g., finding the median.

We will simplify discussion by assuming that all the elements are distinct. The algorithm is given as Algorithm TREESELECT (see Fig. 6.2). Initially, each item is "active", and may later become "inactive" when it is known that it cannot be the answer.

Steps 3 to 13 are repeated until the kth smallest element is found. In each iteration, $\sqrt{n}$ recursive calls are executed on $\sqrt{n}$ elements each to find the median of each group. Thus, there are $\sqrt{n}$ parallel simultaneous calls plus one call to find the median of medians *med*. Let $T(n)$ denote the total running time. Then, these calls take $2T(\sqrt{n})$. In each iteration, at least $1/4$ of the elements will be deactivated, and hence the number of iterations is at most $\log_{4/3} n = ch$, where $c = 1/\log(4/3)$ (see Section 2.14

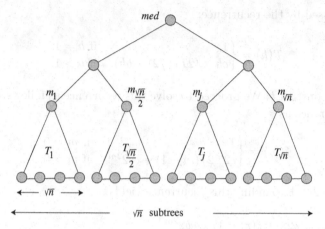

Fig. 6.2.   Illustration of Algorithm TREESELECT.

Algorithm 6.2 TREESELECT

Input: A sequence of n numbers, where $n = 2^h$ and an integer k, $1 \leq k \leq n$.

Output: The kth smallest element in the sequence.

1. **if** $n \leq 2$ **then** return the answer.
2. **else repeat** Steps 3 to 13
3. Each processor at level $\log n/2$ computes the median of the active items beneath it. It stores this median as its value.
4. The root computes recursively the median of medians of the items found in the previous step, call this *med*.
5. The root transmits *med* to all processors in the base.
6. Each base processor sends up a 1 if its item is less than or equal to *med*. These 1's are summed on their way up to the root. Let s be the sum of these 1's.
7. **if** $k = s$ **then** **return** *med*
8. **else if** $k < s$ **then**
9.   Deactivate all items in the base $\geq$ *med*
10. **else**
11.   Deactivate all items in the base $\leq$ *med*
12.   Set $k \leftarrow k - s$
13. **end if**

---

and Exercise 2.17). Broadcasting and summing the 1's takes $O(\log n)$. To see how much time the algorithm takes, it is easiest to work with the height of the tree (i.e., $h = \log n$) instead of its width. The running time can therefore be expressed by the recurrence:

$$T(h) = \begin{cases} 1 & \text{if } h = 1 \\ ch \times (2T(h/2) + bh) & \text{if } h > 1, \end{cases}$$

for some constant b. We proceed to solve this recurrence as follows. Rewrite the recurrence as

$$f(m) = \begin{cases} 1 & \text{if } m = 0 \\ c2^m 2f(m-1) + cb2^{2m} & \text{if } m > 0, \end{cases}$$

since $h = 2^m$. Expanding this recurrence yields

$$f(m) = c2^{m+1}f(m-1) + cb2^{2m}$$
$$\vdots$$
$$= c^5 2^{5m-5} f(m-5) + cb2^{2m}$$
$$\times \left(c^4 2^{4m-10} + c^3 b 2^{3m-6} + c^2 b 2^{2m-3} + cb2^{m-1} + 1\right)$$
$$\vdots$$
$$= c^j 2^{jm-j(j-3)/2} f(m-j) + cb2^{2m}\left(c^j 2^{jm-j(j+1)/2}\right.$$
$$\left. + \cdots + c^4 2^{4m-10} + c^3 2^{3m-6} + c^2 2^{2m-3} + c2^{m-1} + 1\right)$$
$$\vdots$$
$$= c^m 2^{m^2-m(m-3)/2} f(0) + cb2^{2m}\left(c^{m-1} 2^{(m-1)m-(m-1)(m)/2}\right.$$
$$\left. + \cdots + c^4 2^{4m-10} + c^3 2^{3m-6} + c^2 2^{2m-3} + c2^{m-1} + 1\right)$$
$$= c^m 2^{m(m+3)/2} + cb2^{2m} \sum_{j=0}^{m-1} c^j 2^{jm-j(j+1)/2}$$
$$\leq c^m h^{(m+3)/2} + cb2^{2m} \times m \times c^{m-1} 2^{(m-1)m-((m-1)(m)/2)}$$
$$= c^m h^{(m+3)/2} + b2^{2m} \times m \times c^m 2^{m(m-1)/2}$$
$$= c^m h^{(m+3)/2} + b \times m \times c^m 2^{m(m+3)/2}$$
$$= c^m h^{(m+3)/2} + bmc^m h^{(m+3)/2}$$
$$= O(mc^m h^{(m+3)/2})$$
$$= O(\log\log n \; c^{\log\log n} (\log n)^{(\log\log n+3)/2}).$$

Hence, $T(n) = o(n^\epsilon)$ for any $\epsilon > 0$.

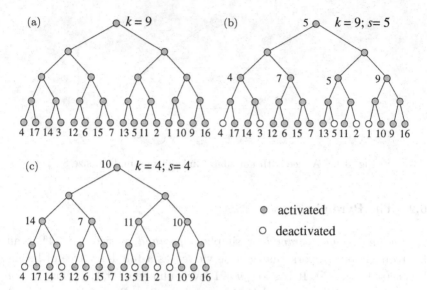

Fig. 6.3. Example 6.1 for the selection algorithm on the tree.

Example 6.1   Figure 6.3 illustrates the operation of Algorithm TREESE-LECT. In this example, we use the algorithm to find the 9th smallest element of the 16 items: 4, 17, 14, 3, 12, 6, 15, 7,13, 5, 11, 2, 1, 10, 9, 16. Fig. 6.3(a) shows the initial input, which is entered at the leaves. In part (b) of the figure, $\sqrt{n} = 4$ calls are executed in parallel, and then one call with the medians resulting from these 4 calls as the input. This results in 5 being the median of medians. After broadcasting 5, processors with elements 1, 2, 3, 4 and 5 send a 1 each to the root for a total of $s = 5$, which is shown in Fig. 6.3(b). The deactivated processors are shown as white. More 5 calls are executed in Fig. 6.3(c), after which the 9th smallest element, 10, is found.   □

6.1.5   *The one-dimensional pyramid*

A *one-dimensional pyramid*, or simply a 1-*pyramid*, of size n is an interconnection network obtained from the tree of processors with n leaves by adding two-way communication links between adjacent processors at the same level. Thus, it forms a linear array at each level. See Fig. 6.4 for an eight-leaf 1-pyramid. Like the tree, communication diameter of a 1-pyramid of size n is only $\Theta(\log n)$.

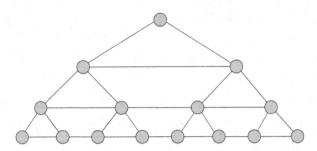

Fig. 6.4.   A tree with horizontal links (1-pyramid) of size 8.

6.2   The Pyramid

A *two-dimensional pyramid* or simply a *pyramid* of size $n = 4^d$ is an interconnection network that can be viewed as a full 4-ary tree of height $\log_4 n$ (see Fig. 6.5). It has $\log_4 n + 1$ levels numbered $0, 1, \ldots, \log_4 n$. For simplicity, we will assume that the base is at level 0, and the root is at level $\log_4 n$. The base consists of n processors arranged in the form of a $\sqrt{n} \times \sqrt{n}$ mesh of processors. In general, level k consists of a mesh of $n/4^k$ processors. In particular, level $\log_4 n$ consists of one processor referred to as the *apex*. A pyramid of size n has a total of $(4n-1)/3$ processors. Each processor at level k is connected via bidirectional communication links to its nine neighbors (if they exist): four siblings at level k, four children at level $k - 1$ and a parent at level $k + 1$.

The pyramid can be projected into a regular pattern in the plane, which makes it ideal for VLSI implementation and provides the possibility of constructing pyramids with thousands or millions of processors (see Fig. 6.6). A pyramid may be regarded as a combination of a mesh and a tree machine architecture.

One advantage of the pyramid over the mesh is that the communication diameter of the pyramid of size n is only $\Theta(\log n)$. This is true since any two processors in the pyramid can communicate through the apex in $O(\log n)$ time. However, it may require $\Omega(\log n)$ time for communication that require exchange of information between two arbitrary processors. This makes the pyramid suitable for problems like semigroup operations, e.g., summation and finding the maximum, which require $O(\log n)$ time. However, for problems that demand extensive data movement such as sorting and routing all data in the base, $\Omega(\sqrt{n})$ time is required (Exercise 6.8).

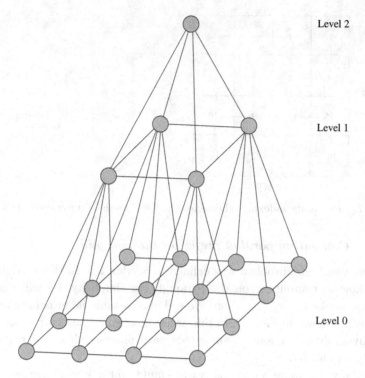

Level 2

Level 1

Level 0

Fig. 6.5.   A pyramid of size 16.

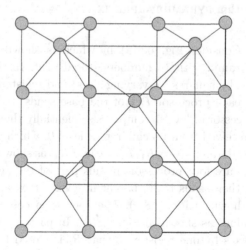

Fig. 6.6.   A pyramid of size 16.

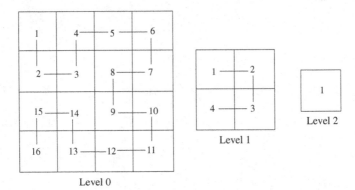

Fig. 6.7.　Proximity indexing scheme for the three levels of a pyramid of size 16.

6.2.1　*Computing parallel prefix on the pyramid*

The parallel prefix problem was defined in Section 2.5. In this section, we show how to compute it on the pyramid. For simplicity, we will assume addition as the binary operation. We will also assume the proximity indexing scheme shown in Fig. 6.7. In this ordering scheme, consecutive elements are physically contiguous. Assume that each processor has four registers: R_1, R_2, R_3 and R_4.

Initially, the items $x_1, x_2, \ldots, x_n$ are input to the $n = 4^d$ processors at level 0. The algorithm consists of two passes: Bottom-up and top-down. It is given as Algorithm PYRAMIDPARPREFIX.

Example 6.2 Consider Fig. 6.8(a) in which is shown the base of a 2-dimensional pyramid with 16 numbers stored in it. In this figure, processors are shown by squares (of varying sizes) and registers are shown by circles. Initially, each processor $P_{0,j}$ of the base sends its value x_j to its parent. Each processor of level 1 computes sequentially the four prefixes of the four values received from its children in level 0, which are then stored orderly in its four data registers R_1, R_2, R_3 and R_4, as shown in Fig. 6.8(b). Notice that there are four processors in this part of the figure. Each processor of level 1 then sends to its parent in level 2 (the apex) the fourth prefixes R_4, as shown in Fig. 6.8(c). The apex then computes the prefix sums of these values as shown in Fig. 6.8(d). In part (e) of the figure, it shifts these prefixes by one register so that R_i is stored in register R_{i+1}, $1 \leq i \leq 3$, and puts 0 in R_1. It then copies the contents of the four registers

---

Algorithm 6.3 PYRAMIDPARPREFIX
Input: $X = \langle x_1, x_2, \ldots, x_n \rangle$, a sequences of n numbers, where $n = 4^d$ stored at the base of the pyramid.
Output: $S = \langle s_1, s_2, \ldots, s_n \rangle$, the prefix sums of X.

(a) Bottom-up phase.

   (1) Each processor $P_{0,j}$ of the base sends its value x_j to its parent.
   (2) **for** $k = 1, 2, \ldots, \log_4 n$ **do**
      Each processor $P_{k,j}$ of level k computes sequentially the four prefixes of the four values received from its children, which are then stored orderly in the four data registers R_1, R_2, R_3 and R_4, then sends to its parent the fourth prefix R_4. As $k = \log_4 n$, the apex contains in its four registers the four prefixes $s_{n/4}, s_{n/2}, s_{3n/4}, s_n$.

(b) Top-down phase.

   (1) The apex moves the contents of register R_i into register R_{i+1}, $1 \le i \le 3$, and puts 0 into R_1. Then, it sends these values orderly to its four children (i.e., R_1 goes to the first child, R_2 to the second, etc.)
   (2) **for** $k = \log_4 n - 1, \ldots, 1$ **do**
      Each processor $P_{k,j}$ adds sequentially the value received from its parent to the values stored in its four data registers. Then, each processor $P_{k,j}$ moves the contents of its register R_i, $1 \le i \le 3$ into its register R_{i+1}, and moves the contents of its register R_4 into the register R_1 of processor $P_{k,j+1}$ (if it exists, processor $P_{k,1}$ puts 0 into its register R_1). Finally, $P_{k,j}$ sends the values stored in R_1, R_2, R_3 and R_4 orderly to its four children.
   (3) Each processor $P_{0,j}$ at the base adds the value received from the parent to its x_j value. Now, each processor $P_{0,j}$ at the base contains the partial sum s_j.

---

into the four processors in level 1, as shown in Fig. 6.8(f). Each processor $P_{1,j}$ then adds sequentially the value received from its parent to the values stored in its four data registers, as shown in Fig. 6.8(g). Then, each processor $P_{1,j}$ in level 1 moves the contents of its register R_i, $1 \le i \le 3$, into its register R_{i+1}, and moves the contents of its register R_4 into the register R_1 of processor $P_{1,j+1}$ (if it exists, processor $P_{1,1}$ puts 0 into its register R_1). This is shown in Fig. 6.8(h). Next, $P_{1,j}$ sends the values stored in R_1, R_2, R_3 and R_4 orderly to its four children in level 0. Finally, each processor $P_{0,j}$ at the base adds the value received from its parent to its x_j value. Now, each processor $P_{0,j}$ at the base contains the partial sum s_j. This is shown in Fig. 6.8(i). $\qquad\square$

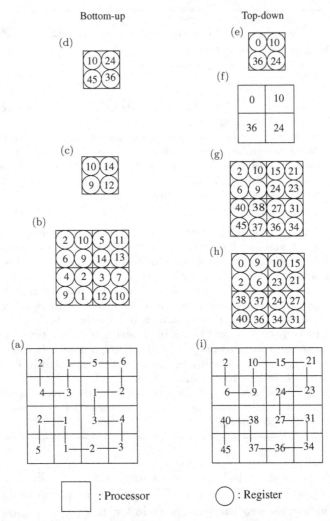

Fig. 6.8. Example of computing parallel prefix on the pyramid.

6.3 Mesh of Trees

A *mesh of trees* of size n, where we assume for simplicity that n is a perfect square, is an interconnection network constructed from a $\sqrt{n} \times \sqrt{n}$ mesh, in which the processors of every row and column are the leaves of a complete

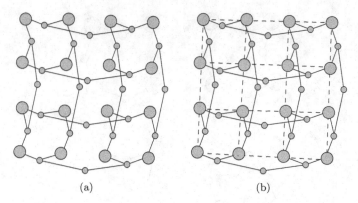

Fig. 6.9. A mesh of trees of size 16. (a) Regular. (b) With base connections.

binary tree. The base consists of n processors arranged in the form of a $\sqrt{n} \times \sqrt{n}$ mesh. The base processors are either disjoint or have connections as in the regular mesh (see Fig. 6.9(a) and (b)). The mesh of trees of size n has $3n - 2\sqrt{n}$ processors. Each row or column has $\sqrt{n}$ processors at level $\log \sqrt{n}$. All row trees are disjoint, and all column trees are disjoint. Every row tree has exactly one leaf processor in common with every column tree. In each tree, the leaf and the root has degree 2, and every other processor has degree 3. Like the pyramid, the communication diameter of the mesh of trees of size n is only $\Theta(\log n)$, which is very low compared to a mesh of the same size. This is true since any two processors in the mesh of trees can communicate in $O(\log n)$ time. However, it may require as much as $4 \log \sqrt{n} = \Omega(\log n)$ time for communication that requires exchanging of information between two arbitrary processors. This makes the mesh of trees suitable for problems like semigroup operations, e.g., summation and finding the maximum, which require $O(\log n)$ time. However, for problems that demand extensive data movement such as sorting and routing all data in the base, $\Omega(\sqrt{n})$ time may be required, since only $\sqrt{n}$ wires cross the middle of the mesh of trees.

The processor connections in the base may be added, but this does not improve the computing power of the mesh of trees; it is only useful in applications like image processing where direct connections between the base processors is desirable. The mesh of trees has a recursive structure. If we remove all the $2\sqrt{n}$ roots and their incident edges, we will be left with four copies of the $\frac{\sqrt{n}}{2} \times \frac{\sqrt{n}}{2}$ mesh of trees. For instance, Fig. 6.10 shows the

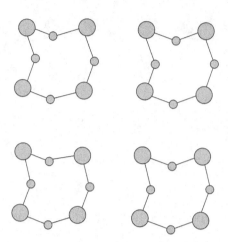

Fig. 6.10.   Recursive structure of the mesh of trees.

four copies of the 2×2 mesh of trees resulting from removing the roots and their incident edges in Fig. 6.9 (a). Henceforth, the processors of the base will be numbered as $P_{i,j}, 1 \leq i, j \leq \sqrt{n}$.

The trees in the mesh of trees simplify many computations that can be completed in $\Theta(\log n)$ time. For instance, to broadcast a datum x from $P_{1,1}$ to all other processors in the base, first x is broadcast to the first row tree (the topmost tree). From the leaves of this tree, $\sqrt{n}$ copies are passed to all column trees, where x is passed to the leaves of those column trees. The semigroup operations like summation and finding the maximum are straightforward. For instance, to find the sum of n numbers stored in the base, $\sqrt{n}$ row sums are first found by row trees and stored in the first column, followed by summing those totals in the first column tree and storing the final sum in $P_{1,1}$.

6.3.1   *Sorting on the mesh of trees*

The bisection width of the mesh of trees has a lower bound of $\Omega(\sqrt{n})$, which means that it is not suitable for sorting data of size in the order of $\Omega(n)$ efficiently, since $\Omega(\sqrt{n})$ of the data might have to move from one side of the base to the opposite side. However, for a smaller amount of data, it may be possible to sort more efficiently. Consider, for instance, sorting $\sqrt{n}$ numbers $a_1, a_2, \ldots, a_{\sqrt{n}}$ stored in processors $P_{1,1}, P_{1,2}, \ldots, P_{1,\sqrt{n}}$ in the base — that is, in the first row. We compute the rank of each element $r(a_i)$, which is the number of items less than a_i, and store a_i in processor number $r(a_i) + 1$ in the first row. For simplicity, assume that all items are distinct. First, for $1 \leq j \leq \sqrt{n}$, we use the column trees to broadcast a_j in column j, after which processor $P_{i,j}$ will store a copy of a_j, $1 \leq i \leq \sqrt{n}$. Next, for $1 \leq i \leq \sqrt{n}$, we broadcast a_i from processor $P_{i,i}$ in row i to all processors in row i. Now, every processor $P_{i,j}$ in the base contains the pair (a_i, a_j). Row i will now be responsible for finding $r(a_i)$, the rank of a_i; it achieves this by counting the elements a_j smaller than a_i. Specifically, if $a_j < a_i$, then we store 1 in $P_{i,j}$, else we store 0 in $P_{i,j}$, and so finding the rank amounts to counting the number of 1's, and storing the sum in all processors $P_{i,j}$ in row i. The sum can easily be found using a row tree, which is then broadcast from the root to its leaves. Finally, a column broadcast is used within every column to broadcast a_i from processor $P_{i,r(a_i)+1}$ to processor $P_{1,r(a_i)+1}$ (recall that all processors in row i contain a_i). It is easy to see that computing the rank and broadcasting a_i to its final destination takes $\Theta(\log n)$ time. It follows that the overall time taken by the algorithm is $\Theta(\log n)$, which is optimal since the diameter is $\Theta(\log n)$. The cost is $\Theta(n \log n)$, which is not optimal in view of the $\Theta(\sqrt{n} \log n)$ time sequential algorithm. An outline of the above description is given as Algorithm MOTSORT.

Algorithm 6.4 MOTSORT
Input: $\sqrt{n}$ numbers $a_1, a_2, \ldots, a_{\sqrt{n}}$ stored in processors $P_{1,1}, P_{1,2}, \ldots, P_{1,\sqrt{n}}$ in the base.
Output: Sort the numbers and store them in $P_{1,1}, P_{1,2}, \ldots, P_{1,\sqrt{n}}$.

1. **for** $j \leftarrow 1$ **to** $\sqrt{n}$ **do in parallel**
2.   Use column tree j to broadcast a_j to processors $P_{i,j}$, $1 \leq i \leq \sqrt{n}$.
3. **end for**
4. **for** $i \leftarrow 1$ **to** $\sqrt{n}$ **do in parallel**
5.   broadcast a_i from processor $P_{i,i}$ in row i to all processors in row i.
6. **end for**
7. **for** $i \leftarrow 1$ **to** $\sqrt{n}$ **do in parallel**
8.   **for** $j \leftarrow 1$ **to** $\sqrt{n}$ **do in parallel**
9.   **if** $a_j < a_i$, **then** store 1 in $P_{i,j}$, **else** store 0 in $P_{i,j}$.
10.   **end for**
11.   Compute the sum of 1's in row i and store it in all processors $P_{i,j}$ of row i.
12.   Perform column broadcasts to broadcast a_i from processor $P_{i,r(a_i)+1}$ to processor $P_{1,r(a_i)+1}$.
13. **end for**

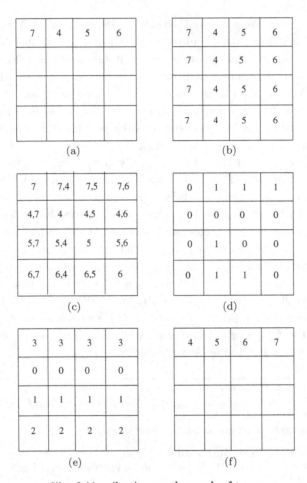

Fig. 6.11.   Sorting on the mesh of trees.

Example 6.3   Consider Fig. 6.11(a), in which the numbers $7, 4, 5, 6$ are to be sorted in a mesh of trees of size 16; only the base is shown in the figure. First, for $1 \leq j \leq 4$, we use the column trees to broadcast a_j in column j as shown in Fig. 6.11(b), after which processor $P_{i,j}$ will store a copy of a_j, $1 \leq i \leq 4$. Next, for $1 \leq i \leq 4$, we broadcast a_i from processor $P_{i,i}$ in row i to all processors in row i. Now, every processor $P_{i,j}$ in the base contains the pair (a_i, a_j) (see Fig. 6.11(c)). Next, we compute the rank of a_i by counting the number of elements a_j smaller than a_i. Specifically, if

$a_j < a_i$, then we store 1 in $P_{i,j}$, else we store 0 in $P_{i,j}$ (see Fig. 6.11(d)). Now, finding the rank amounts to counting the number of 1's, and storing the sum in all processors $P_{i,j}$ in row i. The sum can easily be found using a row tree, which is then broadcast from the root to its leaves, as shown in Fig. 6.11(e). Finally, a column broadcast is used within every column to broadcast a_i from processor $P_{i,r(a_i)+1}$ to processor $P_{1,r(a_i)+1}$, as shown in Fig. 6.11(f). □

6.3.2 *Routing in the mesh of trees*

The bisection width of the mesh of trees has a lower bound of $\Omega(\sqrt{n})$, which means that, as in the case of sorting, it is not suitable for routing data of size in the order of $\Omega(n)$, since $\Omega(\sqrt{n})$ of the data might have to move from one side of the base to the opposite side. However, for a smaller amount of data, it may be possible to route data more efficiently. Consider, for instance, routing $\sqrt{n}$ packets $v_1, v_2, \ldots, v_{\sqrt{n}}$ stored in processors $P_{1,1}, P_{1,2}, \ldots, P_{1,\sqrt{n}}$ in the base, that is, in the first row to destination processors $P_{\sqrt{n}, \delta(v_1)}, P_{\sqrt{n}, \delta(v_2)}, \ldots, P_{\sqrt{n}, \delta(v_{\sqrt{n}})}$. First, for $1 \leq j \leq \sqrt{n}$, we use the column trees to send v_j to processor $P_{j,j}$. Next, for $1 \leq j \leq \sqrt{n}$, we use the row trees to send v_j to processor $P_{j,\delta(v_j)}$. Finally, for $1 \leq j \leq \sqrt{n}$, we use the column trees to send v_j to processor $P_{\sqrt{n}, \delta(v_j)}$. Each of these steps of data movements takes $\Theta(\log n)$ time. It follows that the overall time taken by the algorithm is $\Theta(\log n)$. An outline of the above description is given as Algorithm MOTROUTE.

Algorithm 6.5 MOTROUTE

Input: $\sqrt{n}$ packets $v_1, v_2, \ldots, v_{\sqrt{n}}$ stored in processors $P_{1,1}, P_{1,2}, \ldots, P_{1,\sqrt{n}}$ in the base, and destinations $\delta(v_1), \delta(v_2), \ldots, \delta(v_{\sqrt{n}})$.

Output: Route the packets to destination processors
$$P_{\sqrt{n}, \delta(v_1)}, P_{\sqrt{n}, \delta(v_2)}, \ldots, P_{\sqrt{n}, \delta(v_{\sqrt{n}})}.$$

1. **for** $j \leftarrow 2$ **to** $\sqrt{n}$ **do in parallel**
2.   Use column tree j to send v_j to processor $P_{j,j}$.
3. **end for**
4. **for** $j \leftarrow 1$ **to** $\sqrt{n}$ **do in parallel**
5.   Use row tree j to send v_j to processor $P_{j,\delta(v_j)}$.
6. **end for**
7. **for** $j \leftarrow 1$ **to** $\sqrt{n}$ **do in parallel**
8.   Use column tree $\delta(v_j)$ to send v_j to processor $P_{\sqrt{n}, \delta(v_j)}$.
9. **end for**

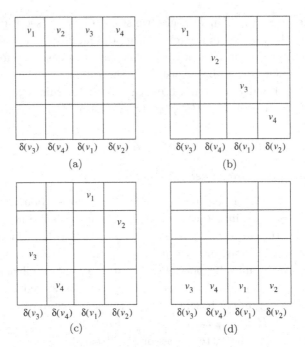

Fig. 6.12.   Routing on the mesh of trees.

Example 6.4   Figure 6.12(a) shows an example in which the packets v_1, v_2, v_3, v_4, initially in processors $P_{1,1}, P_{1,2}, P_{1,3}, P_{1,4}$ are to be routed in a mesh of trees of size 16 to processors $P_{4,3}, P_{4,4}, P_{4,1}, P_{4,2}$ in this order. Only the base is shown in the figure. First, for $1 \le j \le 4$, we use the column trees to send v_j to processor $P_{j,j}$ as shown in Fig. 6.12(b). Next, for $1 \le j \le 4$, we use the row trees to send v_j to processor $P_{j,\delta(v_j)}$ as shown in Fig. 6.12(c). Finally, for $1 \le j \le 4$, we use the column trees to send v_j to processor $P_{4,\delta(v_j)}$ as shown in Fig. 6.12(d). $\qquad \square$

6.4   Computing Parallel Prefix on the Mesh of Trees

The parallel prefix problem was defined in Section 2.5. In this section, we show how to compute it on the mesh of trees assuming addition as the binary operation. So, given a sequence of n numbers $\langle x_{i,j} \mid 1 \le i, j \le \sqrt{n} \rangle$ stored in the base processors, we consider the problem of finding their prefix sums $\langle s_{i,j} \mid 1 \leq i, j \leq \sqrt{n} \rangle$ on the mesh of trees. For simplicity, we will assume without loss of generality that the mesh of trees has mesh connections. We will also assume the row major ordering scheme. We will use Algorithm BFPARPREFIX used for binary trees in Section 3.14 to compute parallel prefix on the butterfly. We assume there are n registers $y_{i,j}$ associated with the n processors of the base. Also, we assume there are $\sqrt{n}$ registers z_i associated with processor $P_{1,\sqrt{n}}, P_{2,\sqrt{n}}, \ldots, P_{\sqrt{n},\sqrt{n}}$, and $n - 2\sqrt{n} + 1$ registers $l_{i,j}$ associated with processor $P_{i,j}$, $2 \leq i \leq \sqrt{n}$, $1 \leq j \leq \sqrt{n} - 1$. First, the prefix sums of all rows are computed individually in parallel using Algorithm BFPARPREFIX for binary trees. This takes $\Theta(\log n)$ time. For $1 \leq i \leq \sqrt{n}$, let the prefix sums of row i be $y_{i,1}, y_{i,2}, \ldots, y_{i,\sqrt{n}}$. Note that these are not the final prefix sums, except for row 1. Next, the prefix sums of column $\sqrt{n}$ are computed, again using Algorithm BFPARPREFIX. These are denoted by $s_{1,\sqrt{n}}, s_{2,\sqrt{n}}, \ldots, s_{\sqrt{n},\sqrt{n}}$, and they are the final prefix sums for column $\sqrt{n}$. This also takes $\Theta(\log n)$ time. Next, for all processors $P_{i,\sqrt{n}}$, we set $z_i \leftarrow s_{i,\sqrt{n}}$, $1 \leq i \leq \sqrt{n}$. This is followed by setting $z_i \leftarrow z_{i-1}$, $2 \leq i \leq \sqrt{n}$ (recall that there are mesh connections). Now, for rows i, $2 \leq i \leq \sqrt{n}$, we broadcast z_i to row tree i, after which z_i is copied to all leaves of row tree i and stored in register $l_{i,j}$, $1 \leq j \leq \sqrt{n} - 1$. Finally, for $2 \leq i \leq \sqrt{n}$, $1 \leq j \leq \sqrt{n} - 1$ we execute the assignment $s_{i,j} \leftarrow y_{i,j} + l_{i,j}$.

Algorithm 6.6 MOTPARPREFIX

Input: $X = \langle x_{i,j} \mid 1 \leq i, j \leq \sqrt{n} \rangle$, a sequences of n numbers.

Output: $S = \langle s_{i,j} \mid 1 \leq i, j \leq \sqrt{n} \rangle$, the prefix sums of X.

1. **for** $i \leftarrow 1$ **to** $\sqrt{n}$ **do in parallel**
2.   Use Algorithm BFPARPREFIX to compute the prefix sums of row i. Let these be $y_{i,1}, y_{i,2}, \ldots, y_{i,\sqrt{n}}$.
3. **end for**
4. Use Algorithm BFPARPREFIX to compute the prefix sums of column $\sqrt{n}$. Let these be $s_{1,\sqrt{n}}, s_{2,\sqrt{n}}, \ldots, s_{\sqrt{n},\sqrt{n}}$.
5. **for** all processors $P_{i,\sqrt{n}}$, set $z_i \leftarrow s_{i,\sqrt{n}}$, $1 \leq i \leq \sqrt{n}$.
6. **for** $i \leftarrow 2$ **to** $\sqrt{n}$ **do in parallel** $z_i \leftarrow z_{i-1}$
7. Broadcast z_i to row tree i, $2 \leq i \leq \sqrt{n}$, and store z_i in the register $l_{i,j}$ of every leaf.
8. **for** $i \leftarrow 2$ **to** $\sqrt{n}$ **do in parallel**
9.   **for** $j \leftarrow 1$ **to** $\sqrt{n} - 1$ **do in parallel**
10. $s_{i,j} \leftarrow y_{i,j} + l_{i,j}$
11.   **end for**
12. **end for**

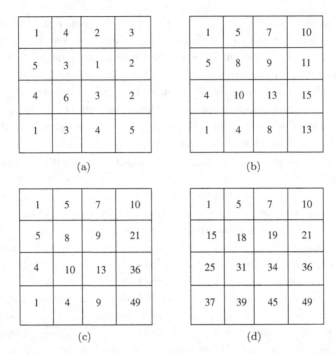

Fig. 6.13.   Illustration of the operation of Algorithm MOTPARPREFIX.

Broadcasting takes $\Theta(\log n)$ time, and the parallel assignments take constant time. It follows that the running time of the algorithm is $\Theta(\log n)$. An outline of the above description is given as Algorithm MOTPARPREFIX.

Example 6.5   Figure 6.13 shows an illustration of the operation of Algorithm MOTPARPREFIX. The input is given in Fig. 6.13(a). Fig. 6.13(b) shows the prefixes of all rows individually. In part (c), the prefix sums of column $\sqrt{n}$ are computed, and in part (d) the final prefix sums are shown.   □

6.5   Comparison Between the Mesh of Trees and the Pyramid

At first glance, the structure of the mesh of trees appears to be similar to that of the pyramid. They are both constructed from the combination of trees and the mesh. Moreover, both have $\Theta(n)$ processors, $\Theta\sqrt{n}$ bisection width and $\Theta(\log n)$ diameter. The difference between the two is that in the case of the pyramid, the apex is a bottleneck, while in the case of the mesh of trees, there is no such bottleneck. So, one might expect that the mesh of trees is more powerful than the pyramid. In fact, due to its $\Theta\sqrt{n}$ bisection width, this is not the case in problems that require extensive data movement. It is only in the case of some problems with moderate amounts of data movement — that the mesh of trees can solve faster than the pyramid.

6.6 Bibliographic Notes

There are a number of books that cover parallel algorithms on the tree, pyramid and mesh of trees. These include Akl [4], Akl [5], Akl [6], Leighton [57], and Miller and Stout [67]. The algorithm for selection on the tree machine is from Stout [89]. The pyramid has long been proposed for performing high-speed low-level image processing computations. See, for instance, Cantoni and Levialdi [19], and Rosenfeld [78]. Parallel prefix computation on the pyramid computer is from Cinque and Bongiovanni [25]. Detailed parallel algorithms for many problems on the pyramid can be found in Miller and Stout [67]. The mesh of trees was proposed independently by several authors; see, for instance, Leighton [55]. Parallel algorithms for many problems on the mesh of trees can be found in Leighton [57]. For more references on parallel algorithms on the tree, pyramid and mesh of trees interconnection networks, see, for instance, Leighton [57], and Miller and Stout [67].

6.7 Exercises

6.1. Design an algorithm to find the sum of n numbers on a tree network with n leaf processors. The input numbers are stored at the leaves, and the output is to be stored in the root processor. What is the time complexity of your algorithm?

6.2. Design an algorithm to find the maximum of n numbers on a tree-connected computer with $O(\log n)$ processors. The input numbers are stored at the leaves, and the output is to be stored in the root processor. What is the time complexity of your algorithm?

6.3. Give a recursive algorithm for finding the maximum in the tree machine.

6.4. Illustrate the operation of Algorithm TREESELECT to find the 13th smallest element of the 16 items: 7, 10, 15, 13, 2, 9, 5, 12, 3, 8, 11, 4, 6, 14, 17, 16 on the tree machine with 16 processors.

6.5. (a) What is the bisection width of the 1-dimensional pyramid?
     (b) Give a lower bound on the problems of sorting and routing on the 1-dimensional pyramid.

6.6. What is the diameter of the 2-dimensional pyramid?

6.7. Use Algorithm PYRAMIDPARPREFIX to compute the prefix sums of the 16 numbers: 2, 1, 1, 3, 2, 1, 2, 4, 3, 5, 1, 4, 2, 1, 3, 1 stored in the base of a 2-dimensional pyramid.

6.8. (a) Compute the bisection width of the 2-dimensional pyramid.
     (b) Give a lower bound on the problems of sorting and routing on the 2-dimensional pyramid.

6.9. Assume that a digitized black/white picture is initially stored one pixel per processor in the base of the pyramid. Give an algorithm to find the area of the picture, that is, the total number of black pixels in the picture, on the pyramid machine.

6.10. Give an algorithm to determine whether there are more black pixels than white pixels in a digitized picture consisting of n pixels stored in the base of the pyramid of size n (refer to Exercise 6.9).

6.11. Give an algorithm to determine the sum of n numbers stored in the base of the pyramid.

6.12. Explain how to compute parallel prefix of n numbers on the pyramid of size $O(n/\log n)$ processors. What is the cost of your algorithm?

6.13. Assess the pyramid machine in terms of sorting and routing.

6.14. What is the diameter of the mesh of trees?

6.15. Give an algorithm for finding the sum of n numbers on the mesh of trees of size n. The numbers are initially loaded into the mesh of trees, one element per processor, and their sum is to be stored in the topleft processor.

6.16. (a) Compute the bisection width of the mesh of trees.

(b) Give a lower bound on the problems of sorting and routing n items on the mesh of trees of size n.

6.17. Use Algorithm MOTSORT to sort the 4 numbers: 2, 1, 3, 5 on the mesh of trees of size 16.

6.18. Give an assessment of the mesh of trees in terms of sorting and routing.

6.19. Use Algorithm MOTROUTE to route the numbers $5, 3, 2, 4$, initially stored in processors $P_{1,1}, P_{1,2}, P_{1,3}, P_{1,4}$ in a mesh of trees of size 16 to processors $P_{4,2}, P_{4,3}, P_{4,1}, P_{4,4}$ in this order.

6.20. Let A be an algorithm that runs on the pyramid of size n in time $t(n)$. What will be the running time of A when simulated on the mesh of trees of the same size? Explain.

6.21. Generalize Exercise 6.20 to any network. That is, what will be the running time of A when simulated on a network of the same size?

6.8 Solutions

6.1. Design an algorithm to find the sum of n numbers on a tree network with n leaf processors. The input numbers are stored at the leaves, and the output is to be stored in the root processor. What is the time complexity of your algorithm?

Similar to finding the sum on the PRAM using the tree method. The time complexity is $\Theta(\log n)$.

6.2. Design an algorithm to find the maximum of n numbers on a tree-connected computer with $O(\log n)$ processors. The input numbers are stored at the leaves, and the output is to be stored in the root processor. What is the time complexity of your algorithm?

Assign $O(n/\log n)$ elements to each leaf processor. Initially, each leaf processor finds the maximum of its assigned elements. The rest is as in Exercise 6.1. The running time is $O(n/\log n + \log\log n) = O(n/\log n)$.

6.3. Give a recursive algorithm for finding the maximum in the tree machine.

Recursively find the two individual maxima in the two subtrees of the root, and compute their maximum.

6.4. Illustrate the operation of Algorithm TREESELECT to find the 13th smallest element of the 16 items: 7, 10, 15, 13, 2, 9, 5, 12, 3, 8, 11, 4, 6, 14, 17, 16 on the tree machine with 16 processors.

Similar to Example 6.1.

6.5. (a) What is the bisection width of the 1-dimensional pyramid?
(b) Give a lower bound on the problems of sorting and routing on the 1-dimensional pyramid.

(a) If we consider a 1-dimensional pyramid of size n, and cut it by a line slightly off-center, the line will cut $\log n + 1$ links. Hence, the bisection width of the 1-dimensional pyramid is $\log n + 1$.

(b) Since all n data items at the leaves of the 1-dimensional pyramid may have to cross from one side to the other, at least $\lceil n/(\log n + 1)\rceil = \Omega(n/\log n)$ time is required just to get data across the middle of the 1-dimensional pyramid (see Exercise 6.5(a)). Hence, the lower bound is $\Omega(n/\log n)$.

6.6. What is the diameter of the 2-dimensional pyramid?

The diameter of the 2-dimensional pyramid is $2\log_4 n$.

6.7. Use Algorithm PYRAMIDPARPREFIX to compute the prefix sums of the 16 numbers: 2, 1, 1, 3, 2, 1, 2, 4, 3, 5, 1, 4, 2, 1, 3, 1 stored in the base of a 2-dimensional pyramid.

Similar to Example 6.2.

6.8. (a) Compute the bisection width of the 2-dimensional pyramid.

(b) Give a lower bound on the problems of sorting and routing on the 2-dimensional pyramid.

(a) Consider the number of links crossing the middle of the pyramid of size n. In the base of the pyramid, there are $\sqrt{n}$ links crossing the middle of the pyramid, in the next level, there are $\sqrt{n}/2$ such links, and so forth. Thus, the total number of links that cross the middle of the pyramid is

$$\sum_{j=0}^{\log_4 n - 1} \frac{\sqrt{n}}{2^j} = 2\sqrt{n} - 2.$$

Hence, the bisection width of the 2-dimensional pyramid is $2\sqrt{n} - 2 = \Theta(\sqrt{n})$.

(b) Since all n data items in the base of the pyramid may have to cross from one side of the base mesh to the other, at least $\lceil n/(2\sqrt{n} - 2) \rceil = \Omega(\sqrt{n})$ time is required just to get data across the middle of the pyramid (see Exercise 6.8 (a)). That is, the lower bound is $\Omega(\sqrt{n})$.

6.9. Assume that a digitized black/white picture is initially stored one pixel per processor in the base of the pyramid. Give an algorithm to find the area of the picture, that is, the total number of black pixels in the picture, on the pyramid machine.

The area of the picture can be determined as follows: In stage 1 of the algorithm, every processor in level 1 obtains the values of the pixels stored in its four children in the base processors, computes the number of black pixels, and sends the count to its parent. In general, at stage $j, 1 \leq j \leq \log_4 n$, of the algorithm, every processor P at level j obtains the values of the pixels stored in its four children at level $j - 1$, and computes the total number of black pixels in the subpyramid under P. Finally, at the final stage, the apex obtains the values of the pixels stored in its four children at level $\log_4 n - 1$, and computes the total number of black pixels in the pyramid. The total number of stages is $\log_4 n$, and each stage takes $\Theta(1)$ time for a total of $\Theta(\log n)$.

6.10. Give an algorithm to determine whether there are more black pixels than white pixels in a digitized picture consisting of n pixels stored in the base of the pyramid of size n (refer to Exercise 6.9).

Similar to the bit counting problem in Exercise 6.9.

6.11. Give an algorithm to determine the sum of n numbers stored in the base of the pyramid.

Similar to the bit counting problem in Exercise 6.9.

6.12. Explain how to compute parallel prefix of n numbers on the pyramid of size $O(n/\log n)$ processors. What is the cost of your algorithm?

Assign $O(\log n)$ elements to each leaf processor in the base. First, find the prefix sums in each group in the base sequentially in $O(\log n)$ time. Next, apply the prefix sums algorithm for the pyramid on the final sums of all groups in time $O(\log(n/\log n)) = O(\log n)$. Finally, update the prefix sums in all groups in the base sequentially in $O(\log n)$ time. The running time is $O(\log n)$.

6.13. Assess the pyramid machine in terms of sorting and routing.

By Exercise 6.8(b), it takes $\Omega(\sqrt{n})$ time to sort n numbers on the pyramid. This shows that the pyramid is a poor choice for problems that require intensive data movements such as sorting, routing and some problems in computational geometry.

6.14. What is the diameter of the mesh of trees?

The diameter of the mesh of trees is the smallest distance between two processors in opposite corners, which is $4\lfloor \log n \rfloor$.

6.15. Give an algorithm for finding the sum of n numbers on the mesh of trees of size n. The numbers are initially loaded into the mesh of trees — one element per processor, and their sum is to be stored in the topleft processor.

First, each row tree finds the sum of the elements stored at its leaves and stores the sum in its root in $\Theta(\log n)$ time. Next, the sums in all these roots are routed to the leaves of the leftmost column tree in $\Theta(\log n)$ time. Finally, the elements at the leaves of this column tree are summed and their sum is routed to the topleft processor in $\Theta(\log n)$ time. The total running time is $\Theta(\log n)$.

6.16. (a) Compute the bisection width of the mesh of trees.

(b) Give a lower bound on the problems of sorting and routing n items on the mesh of trees of size n.

(a) The number of links crossing the middle of the mesh of trees of size n (without the base connections) is $\sqrt{n}$. Thus, the bisection width of the mesh of trees is $\sqrt{n} = \Theta(\sqrt{n})$.

(b) Since all n data items in the base of the mesh of trees may have to cross from one side of the base mesh to the other, at least $\lceil n/\sqrt{n} \rceil = \Omega(\sqrt{n})$ time is required just to get data across the middle of the mesh of trees (see Exercise 6.16 (a)). That is, the lower bound is $\Theta(\sqrt{n})$.

6.17. Use Algorithm MOTSORT to sort the 4 numbers: 2, 1, 3, 5 on the mesh of trees of size 16.

Similar to Example 6.3.

6.18. Give an assessment of the mesh of trees in terms of sorting and routing.

By Exercise 6.16(b), it takes $\Omega(\sqrt{n})$ time to sort or route n numbers on the mesh of trees. It follows that the mesh of trees is not a good choice for problems that require intensive data movements such as sorting, routing and some problems in computational geometry. However, unlike the pyramid, the mesh of trees is capable of sorting a restricted amount of data in certain configurations in $\Theta(\log n)$ time (see Section 6.3.1).

6.19. Use Algorithm MOTROUTE to route the numbers $5, 3, 2, 4$, initially stored in processors $P_{1,1}, P_{1,2}, P_{1,3}, P_{1,4}$ in a mesh of trees of size 16 to processors $P_{4,2}, P_{4,3}, P_{4,1}, P_{4,4}$ in this order.

Similar to Example 6.4.

6.20. Let A be an algorithm that runs on the pyramid of size n in time $t(n)$. What will be the running time of A when simulated on the mesh of trees of the same size? Explain.

There will be a slow-down by a factor of $O(\log n)$ — that is, the running time will be $O(t(n) \log n)$. To see this, let P_i and P_j be two adjacent processors on the pyramid machine, and suppose they are mapped to processors P_k and P_l on the mesh of trees. The transfer of data between processors P_i and P_j on the pyramid, which takes constant time, is simulated in $O(\log n)$ time between processors P_k and P_l on the mesh of trees.

6.21. Generalize Exercise 6.20 to any network. That is, what will be the running time of A when simulated on a network of the same size?

The mesh of trees with n processors can simulate any network of the same size with a slow-down factor of $O(\log n)$. The justification is the same as that of Exercise 6.20.

Chapter 7

The Star Network

7.1 Introduction

An efficient interconnection topology usually possesses the following properties: small diameter, low degree, high connectivity, regularity, node symmetry, and a simple routing algorithm. The small diameter shortens the message routing delay while the low degree of nodes is necessary to limit the number of input-output ports to some acceptable value. Regular graphs with the property of node symmetry play the most important role in network design, due to the simplicity of designing routing algorithms. One of the most efficient interconnection networks has been the well-known binary hypercube; it has been used to design various commercial multiprocessor machines and it has been extensively studied. Another regular interconnection network was proposed as an attractive alternative to the hypercube, called the *star*. The star, also called *d-star*, is node and edge symmetric, and strongly hierarchical as is the case with the hypercube. Let d be a positive integer. The d-dimensional star, denoted by S_d, is defined as follows. Consider the $n = d!$ permutations with d symbols, typically 1 to d. $d!$ processors are defined, one per permutation, such that two processors are connected by a bidirectional link if and only if their corresponding permutations differ only in the leftmost and any other position. That is, there is a connection between processor P_α and processor P_β if and only if β can be obtained from α by interchanging the first and the jth symbols of α, $2 \leq j \leq d$ (see Fig. 7.1). For example, consider the case when $d = 3$.

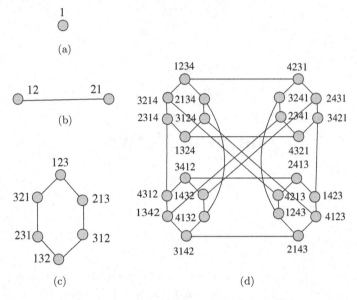

Fig. 7.1.   *d*-dimensional star interconnection network; $d = 1, 2, 3, 4$.

In this case, there are six processors: $P_{123}, P_{132}, P_{213}, P_{231}, P_{312}$ and P_{321}. Figure 7.1(c) shows the connections between these processors.

The *d*-dimensional star can also be defined by recursive construction, where it is constructed from d copies of $(d - 1)$-stars, denoted by $S_{d-1}(1), S_{d-1}(2), \ldots, S_{d-1}(d)$, as follows. Here, the vertices of $S_{d-1}(i)$ are labeled by the $(d - 1)$-permutations of the symbols $1, 2, \ldots, d$ except i. We add the symbol i at the end of each label of $S_{d-1}(i)$. For example, the four S_3's in Fig. 7.1(d) are constructed from the S_3 in Fig. 7.1(c) by appending the digit $i, 1 \leq i \leq 4$. Two vertices in two different substars are connected if and only if one permutation can be obtained from the other by exchanging the first and last symbols. For instance, in Fig. 7.1(d), processor 1234 is connected to processor 4231.

The *d*-dimensional star S_d compares with the hypercube favorably in several aspects. Its diameter is $\lfloor 3(d - 1)/2 \rfloor = \Theta(d)$, and its degree is $d - 1 = \Theta(d)$, which are sublogarithmic in term of the number of processors (Notice that $d < \log(d!) = \Theta(d \log d)$). Like the hypercube, the star graph is vertex-symmetric in the sense that any two vertices are similar, that is, the graph looks the same when viewed from any vertex. Each edge connects an odd permutation with an even permutation, and so S_n is bipartite, and contains no C_4 (the cycle on 4 vertices).

7.2   Ranking of the Processors

For some problems, e.g., the problem of sorting, it is imperative to impose a linear order on the processors. Let P_α and P_β be two processors of S_d, where $\alpha = a_1 a_2 \ldots a_d$ and $\beta = b_1 b_2 \ldots b_d$. The ordering $\prec$ on the processors is defined as follows: $P_\alpha \prec P_\beta$ (or $\alpha \prec \beta$) if there exists an $i, 1 \le i \le d$, such that $a_j = b_j$ for $j > i$ and $a_i > b_i$. For example, $2314 \prec 3214$. To see this, let $i = 2$; then $a_3 a_4 = b_3 b_4$ and $a_2 > b_2$. The *rank* of a processor P_β, denoted by $r(P_\beta)$ is defined as the number of processors P_α such that $P_\alpha \prec P_\beta$ plus one. Table 7.1 shows the ranks of the processors of the 4-dimensional star.

Figure 7.2 shows the star in Fig. 7.1(d) redrawn with processors' ranks.

The labels in Table 7.1 and their corresponding ranks can be generalized for any dimension d as follows. We describe the procedure for generating

Table 7.1.   The ranks of processors of the 4-dimensional star.

label	r	label	r	label	r	label	r	label	r	label	r
1234	1	2134	2	1324	3	3124	4	2314	5	3214	6
1243	7	2143	8	1423	9	4123	10	2413	11	4213	12
1342	13	3142	14	1432	15	4132	16	3412	17	4312	18
2341	19	3241	20	2431	21	4231	22	3421	23	4321	24

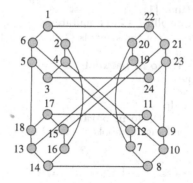

Fig. 7.2.   4-dimensional star interconnection network with processors' ranks.

the labels in connections with the example 4-dimensional star. There are four steps to follow:

(1) Generate the 4! permutations of $\{1, 2, 3, 4\}$.

1234, 1243, 1324, 1342, 1423, 1432, 2134, 2143, 2314, 2341, 2413, 2431,
3124, 3142, 3214, 3241, 3412, 3421, 4123, 4132, 4213, 42314312, 4321.

(2) Revere their order.

4321, 4312, 4231, 4213, 4132, 4123, 3421, 3412, 3241, 3214, 3142, 3124,
2431, 2413, 2341, 2314, 2143, 2134, 1432, 1423, 1342, 1324, 1243, 1234.

(3) Reverse every item in the list.

1234, 2134, 1324, 3124, 2314, 3214, 1243, 2143, 1423, 4123, 2413, 4213,
1342, 3142, 1432, 4132, 3412, 4312, 2341, 3241, 2431, 4231, 3421, 4321.

(4) Partition the list of 24 items into four sublists of six elements each corresponding to the four substars.

$1234 \prec 2134 \prec 1324 \prec 3124 \prec 2314 \prec 3214 \prec$
$1243 \prec 2143 \prec 1423 \prec 4123 \prec 2413 \prec 4213 \prec$
$1342 \prec 3142 \prec 1432 \prec 4132 \prec 3412 \prec 4312 \prec$
$2341 \prec 3241 \prec 2431 \prec 4231 \prec 3421 \prec 4321.$

Obtaining this set of labels can be achieved in parallel using the routine given in Algorithm STARLABELS.

Algorithm 7.1 STARLABELS(d)
Input: An integer $d \geq 1$

Output: Generate the labels of star S_d.

1. If $d = 1$ **then return** $\{1\}$.
2. Recursively generate all $(d - 1)$-permutations
   $A = \alpha_1, \alpha_2, \ldots, \alpha_{(d-1)!}$ of the symbols $\{1, 2, \ldots, d - 1\}$:
   $A \leftarrow$ STARLABELS$(d - 1)$.
3. **for** $j \leftarrow 1$ to $(d - 1)!$ **do in parallel**
4. $\beta_{0,j} \leftarrow$ Append d to α_j
5. **end for**
6. **for** $i \leftarrow 1$ to $d - 1$, **do**
7.   **for** $j \leftarrow 1$ to $(d - 1)!$ **do in parallel**
8. $\beta_{i,j} \leftarrow$ Interchange symbols $d - i$ and $d - i + 1$ in $\beta_{i-1,j}$
9.   **end for**
10. **end for**
11. **return** $\{\beta_{i,j} \mid 0 \leq i \leq d - 1, 1 \leq j \leq (d - 1)!\}$

Assume that the labels are arranged into the rectangular table

$$\{\beta_{i,j} \mid 0 \le i \le d-1, 1 \le j \le (d-1)!\}$$

of dimensions $d \times (d-1)!$ such that the entries in row i are the labels for substar $S_{d-1}(d-i)$, $0 \le i \le d-1$. We now show how to fill out this table by showing how to obtain each row of the table from its predecessor. The first step is to recursively generate all $(d-1)$-permutations $A = \alpha_1, \alpha_2, \ldots, \alpha_{(d-1)!}$ of the symbols $\{1, 2, \ldots, d-1\}$. Append the symbol d to each α_j to form the first row of the table. This is done in Steps 3 to 5. Next, interchange the symbols d and $d-1$ in each $\beta_{0,j}$ to form the second row of the table. Thus, the symbol $d-1$ is the last symbol in every label of the second row. This is followed by the row that consists of labels in which $d-1$ and $d-2$ are exchanged, which will make the symbol $d-2$ the last symbol in every label of the third row. This procedure continues until the last row is computed, in which 2 and 1 are exchanged. Thus, the symbol 1 is the last symbol in every label of the last row. This procedure for processing all the remaining $d-1$ rows is done in Steps 6 to 10.

The ranks are computed simply as increasing from left to right and from top to bottom. In fact, the rank of processor $P_{i,j}$ is given by the formula $r(P_{i,j}) = i \times (d-1)! + j$. This guarantees that those ranks in the same row are localized to one substar.

The running time of Algorithm STARLABELS(d) is given by the recurrence $T(d) = T(d-1) + \Theta(d)$, which leads to a running time of $T(n) = \Theta(d^2)$.

7.3 Routing between Substars

Let $S_{d-1}(a)$ and $S_{d-1}(b)$ be two different substars of a star S_d, and suppose we want to transfer data from $S_{d-1}(a)$ to $S_{d-1}(b)$ such that data from two source processors go to different destination processors. That is, no two sources send to the same destination. There are two types of routes as shown in Fig. 7.3: Direct and indirect. In a direct route, there is a direct link between the source and destination, as shown in part (a) of the figure. The other type, shown in part (b) of the figure, is the indirect route, which

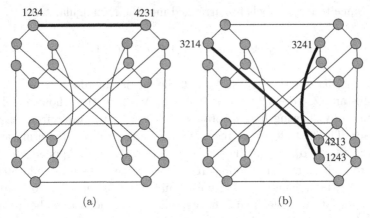

Fig. 7.3.   Routes between two substars: (a) Direct. (b) Indirect.

consists of a path from the source to the destination. Specifically, there is a path of three links connecting the source to the destination.

The method of routing between the two substars is accomplished by Algorithm STARROUTE. In the algorithm, both α and β consist of $d-2$ symbols. Clearly, the running time of the algorithm is $\Theta(1)$.

Algorithm 7.2 STARROUTE(a,b)
Input: Two integers a and b, $1 \leq a < b \leq d$.
Output: Send data from $S_{d-1}(a)$ to $S_{d-1}(b)$.

1. There are $(d-2)!$ processors P_u with label $u = b\alpha a$. These processors send their data immediately in one step from P_u in $S_{d-1}(a)$ to P_v in $S_{d-1}(b)$, where $v = a\alpha b$.
2. The remaining $(d-1)! - (d-2)!$ processors P_w in $S_{d-1}(a)$ with $w = c\alpha a$, $c \neq a, b$, send their data from $S_{d-1}(a)$ to P_x in $S_{d-1}(b)$, where $x = c\beta b$ in three substeps:

   (a) First, data is sent from processors P_w in $S_{d-1}(a)$ to processors P_y in $S_{d-1}(c)$, where $y = a\alpha c$.
   (b) Next, processors P_y send the data they received to P_z in the same substar $S_{d-1}(c)$, where $z = b\beta c$.
   (c) Finally, processors P_z send the data they received to P_x in $S_{d-1}(b)$, where $x = c\beta b$, as stated above.

Example 7.1   Suppose we want to carry on data transfers from $S_3(4)$ to $S_3(1)$ in Fig. 7.1(d). The following steps will take place.

(1) $1234 \to 4231$,
(2) $1324 \to 4321$,
(3) $3214 \to 4213 \to 1243 \to 3241$,
(4) $2314 \to 4312 \to 1342 \to 2341$,
(5) $2134 \to 4132 \to 1432 \to 2431$, and
(6) $3124 \to 4123 \to 1423 \to 3421$.   □

7.4   Computing Parallel Prefix on the Star

In this section, assume that the $d!$ processors are numbered by their ranks, that is by the integers 1 to $d!$. It is important that every processor P_α knows its label α as well as its rank $r(P_\alpha)$. This can be done in $\Theta(d^2)$ time (Exercise 7.1). For convenience, we will assume addition as the binary operation. Let a sequence of elements $\langle a_1, a_2, \ldots, a_{d!} \rangle$ be given, stored in the processors of S_d, one element per processor. Thus a_i is initially stored in P_i, where the index i is the rank of the processor, as explained above. The problem is to find the prefix sums of $\langle a_1, a_2, \ldots, a_{d!} \rangle$, which are $a_1, a_1 + a_2, a_1 + a_2 + a_3, \ldots, a_1 + a_2 + \cdots + a_{d!}$. For simplicity, we will assume that d is a power of 2; otherwise, it would only make the presentation complex (see Example 7.2).

We divide the d substars into groups. Initially, there are d groups, each containing only one substar and the algorithm is applied recursively to that substar. Next, there are $d/2$ groups: $\{S_{d-1}(1), S_{d-1}(2)\}$, $\{S_{d-1}(3), S_{d-1}(4)\}, \ldots, \{S_{d-1}(d-1), S_{d-1}(d)\}$. In the next iteration, there are $d/4$ groups: $\{S_{d-1}(1), S_{d-1}(2), S_{d-1}(3), S_{d-1}(4)\}, \ldots, \{S_{d-1}(d-3), S_{d-1}(d-2), S_{d-1}(d-1), S_{d-1}(d)\}$, and so on. Suppose that we have computed the prefix sums for two groups of substars as follows. Group 1: $S_{d-1}(i), S_{d-1}(i+1), \ldots, S_{d-1}(i+s)$, and Group 2: $S_{d-1}(i+s+1), S_{d-1}(i+s+2), \ldots, S_{d-1}(i+2s+1)$. Here, $s = 1, 2, 4, \ldots$. There are two variables associated with each processor, x and y, for storing the partial prefix sum so far and the total sum of values in the group to which it belongs, respectively. Let the total sum in Group 1 be y_1 and the total sum in

Group 2 be y_2. We first use Algorithm STARROUTE in Section 7.3 to send y_1 to every processor in Group 2 and y_2 to every processor in Group 1. The prefix sums of processors in Group 1, the x_1's, remain the same, while the prefix sum x_2 in a processor in Group 2 becomes $x_2 + y_1$. The total sum for all processors in both groups becomes $y_1 + y_2$. It is important to note that all of these steps require $\Theta(1)$ time. Now, combining Group 1 and Group 2 forms a single group. The steps just described are then used to merge the new group with another group formed in the same way. This continues until all the prefix sums have been computed.

The above procedure induces a binary tree for the computation of the prefix sums (see Fig. 7.4 for example). When the recursion terminates, each processor in the group holds the variables x and y required at the beginning of the merging phase. The groups are now merged in pairs, as described in the previous paragraph.

The merging process is performed as follows. We first merge $d/2$ consecutive pairs of substars to yield $d/2$ groups of size 2. Next, we merge $d/4$ pairs of consecutive 2-substar groups to yield $d/4$ groups of size 4. Continuing this way, in the jth iteration, we merge $d/2^j$ pairs of groups of size 2^{j-1} to yield $d/2^j$ groups of size 2^j. Algorithm STARPARPREFIX implements this idea. The algorithm maintains the variable s which is the size of groups

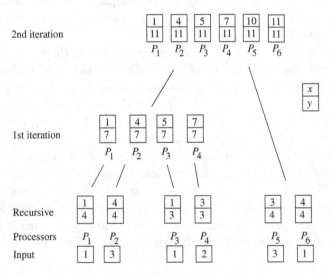

Fig. 7.4.   Illustration of computing the prefix sums on the star.

Algorithm 7.3 STARPARPREFIX

Input: A sequence of $d!$ values $\langle a_1, a_2, \ldots, a_{d!} \rangle$ stored in $d!$ processors $P_1, P_2, \ldots, P_{d!}$, where d is a power of 2.

Output: The prefix sums of the sequence.

1. Recursively find the prefix sums in all $(d-1)$-substars in parallel. Store the prefix sums of a $(d-1)$-substar in the x registers, and the totals in the y registers of all its processors.
2. $t \leftarrow 1$
3. **while** $t \leq d/2$
4. $s \leftarrow t; \quad t \leftarrow 2s; \quad i \leftarrow 0; \quad v \leftarrow d/t$
5.   **for** $k \leftarrow 0$ **to** $v - 1$ **do in parallel**
6. $i \leftarrow kt$
7.   **for** $j \leftarrow i + 1$ **to** $i + s$ **do in parallel**
8. $S_{d-1}(j)$ sends to $S_{d-1}(j + s)$ its y_1 register, and $S_{d-1}(j + s)$ sends to $S_{d-1}(j)$ its y_2 register using Algorithm STARROUTE in Section 7.3
9.   Each processor in $S_{d-1}(j)$ adds y_2 to its y_1 register.
10.   Each processor in $S_{d-1}(j + s)$ adds y_1 to its x_1 and y_1 registers.
11.   **end for**
12.   **end for**
13. **end while**

---

to be merged as discussed above. Initially, s is set to 1, and is doubled in each iteration of the **while** loop. $i + 1$, $i + s$ and $i + t$, where $t = 2s$, define the boundaries of the two groups to be merged. The **while** loop is executed $\log(d/2) = \Theta(\log d)$ times. Step 8 takes $\Theta(1)$ time (see Section 7.3). Hence, the above description of the algorithm leads to a running time of $T(d) = T(d-1) + \Theta(\log d) = \Theta(d \log d)$.

Example 7.2 Let $d = 3$, so the number of processors is $n = d! = 6$. Note here that d is not a power of 2. Figure 7.4 shows an illustration of the flow of Algorithm STARPARPREFIX. There are 6 processors numbered $P_1, P_2, \ldots, P_6$. The input is shown in the bottom: $1, 3, 1, 2, 3, 1$. The results of the initial recursive calls are shown in the lowest level of the tree. For example, the prefix sums computed recursively in processors P_1 and P_2 are 1 and 4, shown in the top box, and the sum of values is shown as 4 in the bottom box. In the next level, processors P_1, P_2 are merged with processors P_3, P_4, and the prefix sums are shown as $1, 4, 5, 7$ and the total is 7. There is no other group to merge with processors P_5, P_6, so they are passed to the next iteration. In the last iteration, the group of processors P_1, P_2, P_3, P_4 are merged with the group of processors P_5, P_6. The resulting prefix sums are $1, 4, 5, 7, 10, 11$ and the total sum is 11.   □

7.5   Computing the Maximum

In this section, we show how to compute the maximum of $d!$ numbers stored one per processor of a d-dimensional star. The algorithm to be presented is a modification of the algorithm for computing parallel prefix, as discussed in Section 7.4. In fact, the following algorithm is a simplification of it. Instead of discussing the differences between the two algorithms, we will present the maximum finding algorithm for completeness. Assume that the $d!$ processors are numbered by the integers 0 to $d! - 1$. Let a sequence of elements $\langle a_0, a_1, \ldots, a_{d!-1} \rangle$ be given, stored in the processors of S_d, one element per processor. Thus a_i is initially stored in P_i, where the index i is the rank of the processor minus 1, as described in Section 7.2. For simplicity, we will assume that d is a power of 2; otherwise, it would only make the presentation complex (see Example 7.3).

We divide the d substars into groups. Initially, there are d groups, each containing only one substar and the algorithm is applied recursively to that substar. Next, there are $d/2$ groups: $\{S_{d-1}(1), S_{d-1}(2)\}, \{S_{d-1}(3), S_{d-1}(4)\}, \ldots, \{S_{d-1}(d - 1), S_{d-1}(d)\}$. In the next iteration, there are $d/4$ groups: $\{S_{d-1}(1), S_{d-1}(2), S_{d-1}(3), S_{d-1}(4)\}, \ldots, \{S_{d-1}(d - 3), S_{d-1}(d - 2), S_{d-1}(d - 1), S_{d-1}(d)\}$, and so on. Suppose that we have computed the maximum for two groups of substars as follows. Group 1: $S_{d-1}(i), S_{d-1}(i + 1), \ldots, S_{d-1}(i + s)$, and Group 2: $S_{d-1}(i + s + 1), S_{d-1}(i + s + 2), \ldots, S_{d-1}(i + 2s + 1)$, where $s = 1, 2, 4, \ldots$. Suppose also that each processor holds the variable x for storing the maximum so far in the group to which it belongs. Let the maximum in Group 1 be x_1 and the maximum in Group 2 be x_2. We first use Algorithm STARROUTE to send x_1 to every processor in Group 2 and x_2 to every processor in Group 1. Then, the maximums in processors in Group 1 and in processors in Group 2 become $\max\{x_1, x_2\}$. All of these steps require $\Theta(1)$ time since routing takes $\Theta(1)$ time, as described in Section 7.3. Group 1 and Group 2 now form a single group. The steps just described are then used to merge the new group with another group formed in the same way. This continues until the maximum has been computed.

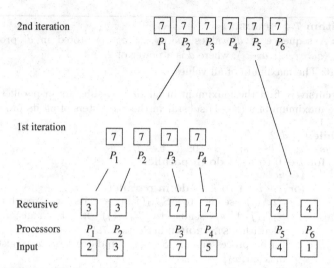

Fig. 7.5.   Illustration of computing the maximum on the star.

The above procedure induces a binary tree for the computation of the maximum (see Fig. 7.5 for example). When the recursion terminates, each processor in the group holds the variable x required at the beginning of the merging phase for holding the maximum. The groups are now merged in pairs, as described in the previous paragraph. The merging process is performed as follows. We first merge $d/2$ consecutive pairs of substars to yield $d/2$ groups of size 2. Next, we merge $d/4$ pairs of consecutive 2-substar groups to yield $d/4$ groups of size 4. Continuing this way, in the jth iteration, we merge $d/2^j$ pairs of groups of size 2^{j-1} to yield $d/2^j$ groups of size 2^j. Algorithm STARMAX implements this idea. The algorithm maintains the variable s which is the size of the groups to be merged as discussed above. Initially, s is set to 1, and is doubled in each iteration of the **while** loop. $i+1$, $i+s$ and $i+t$, where $t = 2s$ define the boundaries of the two groups to be merged. The **while** loop is executed $\log(d/2) = \Theta(\log d)$ times. Step 8 takes $\Theta(1)$ time (see Section 7.3). Hence, the above description of the algorithm leads to a running time of $T(d) = T(d-1) + \Theta(\log d) = \Theta(d \log d)$.

Example 7.3   Let $d = 3$, so the number of processors is $n = d! = 6$. Note here that d is not a power of 2. Figure 7.5 shows an illustration of the flow of Algorithm STARMAX. There are 6 processors numbered $P_1, P_2, \ldots, P_6$. The input is shown in the bottom: $2, 3, 7, 5, 4, 1$. The results of the initial

---

Algorithm 7.4 STARMAX

Input: A sequence of $d!$ values $\langle a_0, a_1, \ldots, a_{d!-1} \rangle$ stored in $d!$ processors $\langle a_0, a_1, \ldots, a_{d!-1} \rangle$, where d is a power of 2.

Output: The maximum of all values.

1. Recursively find the maximum in all $(d-1)$-substars in parallel. Store the maximum of a $(d-1)$-substar in the x registers of all its processors.
2. $t \leftarrow 1$
3. **while** $t \leq d/2$
4. $s \leftarrow t$; $t \leftarrow 2s$; $i \leftarrow 0$; $v \leftarrow d/t$
5.   **for** $k \leftarrow 0$ **to** $v - 1$ **do in parallel**
6. $i \leftarrow kt$
7.   **for** $j \leftarrow i + 1$ **to** $i + s$ **do in parallel**
8. $S_{d-1}(j)$ sends to $S_{d-1}(j + s)$ its x_1 register, and $S_{d-1}(j + s)$ sends to $S_{d-1}(j)$ its x_2 register using Algorithm STARROUTE in Section 7.3
9.   Each processor in $S_{d-1}(j)$ updates its x register to $\max\{x_1, x_2\}$.
10.   Each processor in $S_{d-1}(j + s)$ updates its x register to $\max\{x_1, x_2\}$.
11.   **end for**
12.   **end for**
13. **end while**

---

recursive calls is shown in the lowest level of the tree. For example, the maximum computed in processors P_1 and P_2 is 3, and it is stored in both processors. In the next level, processors P_1, P_2 are merged with processors P_3, P_4, and the maximum is shown as 7, again stored in all four processors. There is no other group to merge with processors P_5, P_6, so they are passed to the next iteration. In the last iteration, the group of processors P_1, P_2, P_3, P_4 are merged with the group of processors P_5, P_6. The resulting maximum is 7, stored in all processors.   □

7.6 Neighborhood Broadcasting and Recursive Doubling

Assume that the source processor P_x, where $x = a\beta c$, wants to send a message in its substar $S_{d-1}(c)$ to the $d - 2$ processors

$$b\beta c, \quad \text{for all } b \neq a, c.$$

The technique of *recursive doubling* is used to generate the labels of processors in substar $S_{d-1}(c)$ reachable from the source processor P_x efficiently.

It is important to note that the generated labels have distinct starting symbols, that is, no two labels have the same starting symbol. Initially, the source processor is the only one with the message. In one step, it sends the message through a direct link to one of its neighbors. Now two processors have the message and they in turn send the message to two other processors in such a way that the source sends its message to another neighbor in one step and the neighbor which has received the message in the previous step sends the message to one of its neighbors in one step. The number of processors with the message is now four (the source processor and the other three processors) and these four processors send the message to four more processors in the same substar in the same fashion. The algorithm continues until all $d - 2$ processors receive the message.

One possible implementation is given in Algorithm STARRECDUB. Given the source processor $\alpha = a_1 a_2 a_3 \ldots a_d$, the algorithm simply selects the middle symbol and exchanges it with the first symbol to obtain the label β. It then transmits the message to the processor with the newly generated label, and repeats the same procedure recursively on the left half of α and the right half of β in parallel. The initial call of the algorithm is STARRECDUB$(\alpha, 1, d)$, where α is the source label. The number of labels generated by the algorithm is $d - 1$, that is, $d - 2$ plus the source processor label. Recall that the generated labels have distinct starting symbols. This procedure of repetitive doubling leads to a running time of $T(d) = T(d/2) + \Theta(1) = \Theta(\log d)$.

Algorithm 7.5 STARRECDUB

Input: A processor label $\alpha = a_1, a_2, \ldots, a_d$, and two integers l and h, $1 \leq l \leq h \leq d$.

Output: $d - 1$ processor labels $\beta_j = b_1 b_2 \ldots, b_d$, where $b_d = a_d$, with the property that the first symbol b_1 is different in all labels β_j.

1. **if** $h > l$ **then**
2. $m \leftarrow \lfloor (l + h)/2 \rfloor$
3. $\beta \leftarrow$ swap a_1 and a_m in α.
4.   Output β
5.   **do in parallel**
6.   Recursively call STARRECDUB(α, l, m)
7.   Recursively call STARRECDUB$(\beta, m + 1, h)$
8.   **end**
9. **end if**

Example 7.4   Consider applying the algorithm on the label 1234. STARRECDUB(1234, 1, 4) results in 3 labels: **2**134, **1**234 and **3**124. Applying the algorithm on the label 12345, STARRECDUB(12345, 1, 5) results in 4 labels: **3**2145, **2**1345, **1**2345 and **4**2135. Observe that the generated labels have distinct starting symbols. If we choose $\alpha = $ 5234161011987, the call STARRECDUB(5234161011987, 1, 11) results in 10 labels: **6**234151011987, **3**254161011987, **2**534161011987, **5**234161011987, **1**254361011987,   **4**253161011987,   **9**234151011687,   **1**123415106987, **1**023415611987, **8**234151011697.   □

Example 7.5   The algorithm can be applied on general labels, not just those composed of digits. If we choose $\alpha = $ abcdefghk, the call STARRECDUB(abcdefghk, 1, 9) results in 8 labels: ebcdafghk, cbadefghk, bacdefghk, abcdefghk, dbacefghk, gbcdafehk, fbcdaeghk, hbcdafegk.   □

7.7   Broadcasting in the Star

In this section, we discuss broadcasting in the d-dimensional star S_d. In the description that follows, note that u, v, x, y and β are permutations, so they don't have repeated symbols. Further, if one of them is combined with other symbols, e.g., a, b and c, then it is assumed that they do not contain these symbols, and these symbols themselves are different. We assume that there is a message to be broadcast from processor P_x, where $x = a\beta b$, $1 \leq a, b \leq d$, in substar $S_{d-1}(b)$ to all other processors in the star S_d. The action of broadcasting can be accomplished in the following three steps.

(1) Use the algorithm for neighborhood broadcasting discussed in Section 7.6 to broadcast the message to the $d - 2$ processors

$$c\beta b, \quad \text{for all } c \neq a, b$$

in the substar $S_{d-1}(b)$ containing the source processor.

(2) In this step, each of the $d - 1$ processors P_u, where $u = c\beta b$, $c \neq b$, in substar $S_{d-1}(b)$, sends the message it received in Step 1 to processor P_v, where $v = b\beta c$ in substar $S_{d-1}(c)$.

(3) Finally, all processors P_y, where $y = b\beta c$, in substars $S_{d-1}(c)$, $c \in \{1, 2, \ldots, d\} - \{b\}$, recursively broadcast the message in substars $S_{d-1}(c)$. The source processor P_x, where $x = a\beta b$, recursively broadcasts the message in $S_{d-1}(b)$.

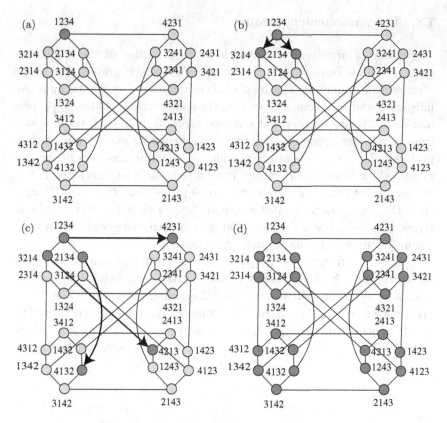

Fig. 7.6. Example of broadcasting in the star.

The above procedure leads to the following recurrence for the running time: $T(d) = T(d-1) + \Theta(\log d)$, whose solution is $\Theta(d \log d) = \Theta(\log d!)$.

Example 7.6 The algorithm for broadcasting in the star is illustrated in Fig. 7.6. Initially, processor 1234 in the star S_4 holds the message to be broadcast. By Step 1 and Example 7.4, the message is propagated to processors 2134 and 3214, as shown in Fig. 7.6 (b), in which the processors that hold the message are shown as dark nodes, and the message transmissions are shown by thick lines. After Step 2 of the algorithm, the message is transmitted to processors 4231, 4132 and 4213, as shown in Fig. 7.6 (c) by the dark nodes. Finally, as shown in Fig. 7.6 (d), the message is broadcast recursively in all substars. □

7.8   The Arrangement Graph

The family of *arrangement graphs* is a generalization of the star graph
topology. It is a family of graphs that contains the star graphs. The (d, k)-
arrangement graph, denoted by $A_{d,k}$, is characterized by the two positive
integers d and k, where $1 \le k < d$. Its nodes consist of the $\frac{d!}{(d-k)!}$ permutations (arrangements) of d symbols, typically $1, 2, \ldots, d$, taken k at a
time. The edges connect nodes that are different in exactly one of their
positions. The arrangement graph addresses a major drawback of the star
graph, which is scalability; to go from dimension d to dimension $d + 1$,
the number of processors in the star graph grows from $d!$ to $(d + 1)!$. Further, the arrangement graphs are more flexible than the star graphs in
terms of choosing the main design parameters such as degree and diameter.
Figure 7.7 shows different arrangement graphs.

The (d, k)-arrangement graph has $d!/(d - k)!$ nodes, and is regular
of degree $k(d - k)$. Its diameter is $\lfloor 3k/2 \rfloor$. As in the hypercube and the
star, it is vertex-transitive, and has a hierarchical structure. The $(d, 1)$-
arrangement graph $A_{d,1}$ is K_d, the complete graph on d vertices. The
$(d, d - 1)$-arrangement graph $A_{d,d-1}$ is isomorphic to the usual star graph.
In Fig. 7.7, $A_{3,2}$ is C_6, the cycle on 6 vertices; it is also S_3, the star graph

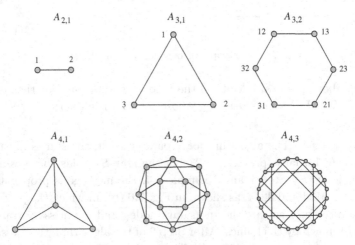

Fig. 7.7.   Arrangement graphs.

on 6 vertices, and $A_{4,3}$ is S_4, the star graph on 24 vertices; it is the same as the graph shown in Fig. 7.1(d).

7.9   The (d, k)-Star Graph

A major practical difficulty with the d-star is the restriction on the number of nodes: $d!$ for a d-star . The set of values of $d!$ is spread widely over the set of integers; so, one may be faced with the choice of either too few or too many available nodes. To relax the restriction of the number of nodes $d!$ in the d-star, the class of generalized star graphs, called arrangement graphs, was discovered. The arrangement graph was discussed in the previous section. When designing an interconnection network based on the arrangement graph, we can make a more suitable choice for the number of nodes by tuning the two parameters d and k. Nevertheless, the degree of the resulting network, which is $k(d - k)$, may be very high. This is a very significant factor from the architectural point of view since the relatively high node degree results in additional difficulty in interconnection and extra complexity in processor design.

As an alternative to overcome the difficulties mentioned above for the star graph and the arrangement graph, another generalization of the star graph, called the (d, k)-*star*, was proposed. As in the arrangement graph, the (d, k)-star graph, denoted by $S_{d,k}$, consists of the $\frac{d!}{(d-k)!}$ permutations (arrangements) of d symbols, typically $1, 2, \ldots, d$, taken k at a time. It is regular of degree $d - 1$, number of nodes $d!/(d - k)!$, and diameter $2k - 1$ for $k < \lfloor d/2 \rfloor$ and $k + \lfloor (d - 1)/2 \rfloor$ for $k \geq \lfloor d/2 \rfloor + 1$. The (d, k)-star preserves many attractive properties of the d-star graph such as node symmetry, low degree, small diameter, hierarchical structure, maximal fault tolerance, and simple shortest routing. In addition, the $(d, d - 1)$-star is isomorphic to the d-star, and hence, all these properties can be derived for the d-star graph as it is a special case of the (d, k)-star graph. A $(4, 2)$-dimensional and a $(5, 2)$-dimensional star connection network are each shown in Fig 7.8. It is important to note that $S_{d,k}$ can be formed by interconnecting d $S_{d-1,k-1}$'s. Fig 7.8(a) shows that $S_{4,2}$ can be viewed as an interconnection of four $S_{3,1}$'s through 2-edges (see next paragraph), and Fig 7.8(b) shows that $S_{5,2}$ can be viewed as an interconnection of five $S_{4,1}$'s through 2-edges. In fact,

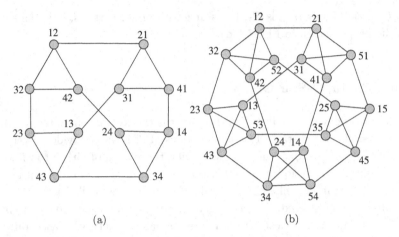

Fig. 7.8.   (4, 2)-dimensional and (5, 2)-dimensional star connection networks.

like the d-star graph S_d, $S_{d,k}$ can be decomposed into $S_{d-1,k-1}$'s along
any dimension $i, 2 \leq i \leq k$. That is, an $S_{d,k}$ can be decomposed into d
node-disjoint $S_{d-1,k-1}$'s different ways by fixing the symbol in any position
$i, 2 \leq i \leq k$. This decomposition can be carried out recursively on each
$S_{d-1,k-1}$ to obtain smaller subgraphs.

Let d and k be two integers satisfying: $1 \leq k \leq d-1$. For simplicity, let
$\langle d \rangle = \{1, 2, \ldots, d\}$ and $\langle k \rangle = \{1, 2, \ldots, k\}$. A (d, k)-star graph is specified
by two integers d and k, where $1 \leq k \leq d-1$. The node set of $S_{d,k}$ is denoted
by $\{a_1 a_2 \ldots a_k \mid a_i \in \langle d \rangle$ and $a_i \neq a_j$ for $i \neq j\}$. The adjacency is defined as
follows: $a_1 a_2 \ldots a_i \ldots a_k$ is adjacent to (1) $a_i a_2 \ldots a_1 \ldots a_k$ through an edge
of dimension i, where $2 \leq i \leq k$ (interchange a_1 with a_i), and (2) $x a_2 \ldots a_k$
through dimension 1, where $x \in \langle d \rangle - \{a_i \mid 1 \leq i \leq k\}$. The edges of type
(1) are referred to as i-edges (e.g., 2-edges and 3-edges), and the edges of
type (2) are referred to as 1-edges. Note that the degree of each node is
$d-1$; each node is connected with $(d-k)$ 1-edges, and an i-edge for each
$i, 2 \leq i \leq k$. Let u be a node, and v a neighbor of u. v is called a 1-neighbor
of u if they are connected by a 1-edge, and it is called an i-neighbor of u if
they are connected by an i-edge.

Example 7.7   Consider the graph shown in Fig 7.9(a) (it is the same as
the graph shown in Fig. 7.8(a)). $\langle d \rangle = \{1, 2, 3, 4\}$. The edge $(21, 31)$ is a
1-edge since 31 is obtained from 21 by replacing 2 in 21 with $3 \in \langle d \rangle - \{2, 1\}$.
On the other hand, the edge $(21, 12)$ is a 2-edge since 12 is obtained from

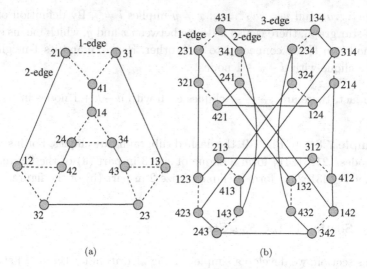

Fig. 7.9. $(4,2)$ and $(4,3)$-dimensional star connection networks.

21 by swapping a_1 and a_2. Hence, 31 is a 1-neighbor of 21 and 12 is a 2-neighbor of 21.

Now, consider Fig 7.9(b). $\langle d \rangle = \{1, 2, 3, 4\}$. The edge $(431, 231)$ is a 1-edge since 231 is obtained from 431 by replacing 4 in 431 with $2 \in \langle d \rangle - \{4, 3, 1\}$. On the other hand, the edge $(431, 341)$ is a 2-edge since 341 is obtained from 431 by swapping a_1 and a_2, and the edge $(431, 134)$ is a 3-edge since 134 is obtained from 431 by swapping a_1 and a_3. Hence, 231 is a 1-neighbor of 431, 341 is a 2-neighbor of 431 and 134 is a 3-neighbor of 431. All dashed lines in the figure are 1-edges. □

In $S_{d,k}$, given an arbitrary node u, there exists a cycle between u and all u's 1-neighbors (Exercise 7.14). In $S_{d,k}$, given two nodes which are not connected by a 1-edge, then cycles formed with these two nodes with their 1-neighbors are disjoint from each other. It can be shown that $S_{d,k}$ can be decomposed into $\frac{d!}{(d-k+1)!}$ vertex-disjoint cycles of length $d - k + 1$.

Theorem 7.1 In $S_{d,k}$, for any node v, v and all its 1–neighbors form a clique K_{d-k+1} of size $d - k + 1$.

Proof. Given any node $v = a_1 a_2 \ldots a_k$ and its 1-neighbor set, which is denoted by U, we need to prove that any two nodes in U are connected with each other by an edge. Suppose x and y are two nodes in U. Let

$x = ia_2 \ldots a_k$ and $y = ja_2 \ldots a_k$, $x \neq y$ implies $i \neq j$. By definition of the (d, k)-star graph, there is also a 1-edge between x and y, which means every two nodes in U are connected to each other. Hence, v and its 1-neighbors form a clique with $d - k + 1$ nodes.   □

In fact, there are $\frac{d!}{(d-k+1)!}$ cliques each with $d - k + 1$ nodes in $S_{d,k}$.

Example 7.8   In Fig. 7.9, the dashed subgraphs are cliques. For instance, the nodes $\{21, 31, 41\}$ form a clique of size 3 in part (a) of the figure, and the nodes $\{431, 231\}$ form a clique of size 2 in part (b) of the figure.   □

7.10   Sorting in the $S_{d,k}$ Star

In this section, we develop a simple sorting algorithm for the (d, k)-star by embedding a 2-dimensional mesh into $S_{d,k}$. For convenience, we will refer to a processor and its label interchangeably. In this embedding, the vertices of $S_{d,k}$ are arranged into a 2-dimensional $d \times \frac{(d-1)!}{(d-k)!}$ mesh in row-major order. The nodes are labeled as described in Section 7.2; we repeat this description for $S_{4,2}$. There are four steps to follow:

(1) Generate the 12 2-permutations of $\{1, 2, 3, 4\}$.
    12, 13, 14, 21, 23, 24, 31, 32, 34, 41, 42, 43
(2) Revere their order.
    43, 42, 41, 34, 32, 31, 24, 23, 21, 14, 13, 12.
(3) Reverse every item in the list.
    34, 24, 14, 43, 23, 13, 42, 32, 12, 41, 31, 21.
(4) Partition the list of 12 items into four sublists of three elements each corresponding to the four substars.
    $34 \prec 24 \prec 14 \rightarrow S_{4,2}(4)$
    $43 \prec 23 \prec 13 \rightarrow S_{4,2}(3)$
    $42 \prec 32 \prec 12 \rightarrow S_{4,2}(2)$
    $41 \prec 31 \prec 21 \rightarrow S_{4,2}(1)$

This ordering suggests the embedding shown in Fig. 7.10. It is important to note that in this embedding each column consists of processors with the same rank in their respective substar. For instance, processors 24, 23, 32 and 31 have rank 2 in their substars.

34	24	14
43	23	13
42	32	12
41	31	21

Fig. 7.10. Example of embedding a mesh into a $(4, 2)$-dimensional star.

Now, we apply Algorithm SHEARSORT of Section 4.6, which sorts the rows and columns alternately $\log d$ times. This is described in Algorithm STARDKSORT.

Algorithm 7.6 STARDKSORT
Input: A sequence of $n = \frac{d!}{(d-k)!}$ elements $\langle a_1, a_2, \ldots, a_n \rangle$ stored in (d, k)-star $S_{d,k}$.
Output: The sequence sorted in snakelike order.

1. If $k = 1$ **then** sort the elements in $S_{d-k+1,1} = K_{d-k+1}$ using a straightforward method.
2. **for** $i \leftarrow 1$ **to** $\log d$ **do**
3.   **for** $j \leftarrow 1$ **to** d **do in parallel**
4.   Recursively sort $S_{d-1,k-1}(j)$ in forward direction if j is odd and in reverse direction if j is even.
5.   Sort the columns in upward direction.
6.   **end for**
7. **end for**

In Step 1, the star reduces to a clique $S_{d-k+1,1}$, which can be sorted using a sorting algorithm for the PRAM in time $O(\log(d - k + 1))$ since all processors are connected. The inner loop from Step 3 to Step 6, which constitutes one of the $\log d$ phases of the algorithm, alternates between sorting the rows and sorting the columns. In sorting the rows, the elements in $S_{d-1,k-1}(j), 1 \leq j \leq d$, are sorted recursively in parallel, where sorting is in the forward direction for odd j and in the reverse direction for even j.

In algorithm SHEARSORT, each column sorting is done in $O(d)$ time. Since each edge of the mesh is mapped to a path of length $O(d)$, each step of the mesh is simulated by $O(d)$ steps of the star. It follows that the running time of each iteration of the algorithm is given by the recurrence

$$t(d,k) = t(d-1,k-1) + O(d)O(d); \quad t(d-k+1,1) = O(\log(d-k+1)),$$

whose solution is

$$t(d,k) = O(d^2) + O((d-1)^2) + \cdots + O((d-k+1)^2) + O(\log(d-k+1))$$
$$= O(kd^2),$$

since the depth of recursion is $\min\{d,k\} = k$. Thus, the overall running time in all $\log d$ iterations of the algorithm is $T(d,k) = O(kd^2 \log d)$.

Unraveling recursion leads to a recursion tree similar to that for the $(4,3)$-star shown in Fig. 7.11.

As shown in the figure, sorting a $(4,3)$-star induces four sorting instances of $(3,2)$-stars, which in turn induce 12 sorting instances of $(2,1)$-stars, i.e., cliques. These cliques of size 2 are shown in Fig. 7.9 as dashed edges. In general, sorting a (d,k)-star induces d sorting instances of $(d-1,k-1)$-stars, which in turn induces $(d-1)$ sorting instances of $(d-2,k-2)$-stars and so on. This continues until the base of recursion is reached, in which $\frac{d!}{(d-k+1)!}$ instances of $(d-k+1,1)$-stars, i.e., cliques, are generated. Thus the problem of sorting reduces to sorting columns of stars of decreasing sizes. Since each step, e.g., element comparison, requires $O(d)$ low-level routing steps, each column sorting takes $O(d^2)$ time (as explained above).

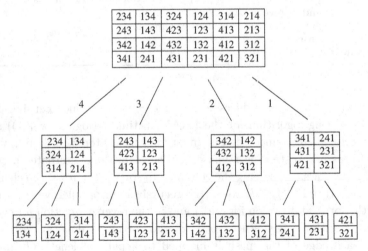

Fig. 7.11. Recursion tree for sorting on the (d,k)-star.

This leads to a running time of

$$O(d^2) + O((d-1)^2) + \cdots + O((d-k)^2) + O(\log(d-k+1)) = O(kd^2)$$

for each iteration, for an overall running time of $O(kd^2 \log d)$, which matches the above derivation. Exercise 7.18 shows how to improve the running time to $O(kd \log d)$.

7.11 Bibliographic Notes

The star network was proposed by Akers, Harel and Krishnamurthy as an alternative to the hypercube [1]. A good introduction to the star network can be found in the book by Akl [5]. For more on the star graphs and the more general Cayley graphs, see for example, Akers and Krishnamurthy [2]. See also Dietzfelbinger, Madhavapeddy and Sudborough [34]. Algorithms for optimal broadcasting in the star graph can be found in Mendia and Sarkar [65], and Sheu, Wu and Chen [85]. Arrangement graphs were introduced by Day and Tripathy [32] as a generalization of the star graphs. For routing, broadcasting, prefix sums, and sorting algorithms on the arrangement graph, see Li and Qiu [59]. The (n, k)-star graph was proposed by Chiang and Chen as a generalized star graph [23]. Topological properties of the (n, k)-star graph can be found in Chiang [22] and He [42]. Many algorithms for the star graph (see, e.g., Akl, Qiu and Stojmenovic [9]) may adapt to the (n, k)-star graph with slight modifications. For more references on the star network, see Akl [5].

7.12 Exercises

7.1. Given a permutation $\pi = k_1 k_2 \ldots k_d$, show how to compute its rank efficiently.

7.2. Analyze the sequential running time of Algorithm STARLABELS.

7.3. Analyze the parallel running time of Algorithm STARLABELS using the star graph as a model. That is, given a star graph of processors, how long does it take for the processors to know their ranks?

7.4. Show the steps for data transfers from $S_3(2)$ to $S_3(3)$ in the star S_4 such that no two sources send to the same destination (see Fig. 7.3).

7.5. Illustrate the operation of Algorithm STARPARPREFIX for computing parallel prefix on the star described in Section 7.4 to find the prefix sums of $2, 1, 3, 1, 4, 2$. Assume a 3-dimensional star with 6 processors.

7.6. Illustrate the operation of Algorithm STARMAX for computing the maximum on the star described in Section 7.5 to find the maximum of $3, 5, 8, 1, 5, 2$. Assume a 3-dimensional star with 6 processors.

7.7. Apply Algorithm STARRECDUB in Section 7.6 on the label 21435.

7.8. Show that any neighborhood broadcasting algorithm on a network with degree d must require $\Omega(\log d)$.

7.9. Illustrate the operation of the algorithm for broadcasting in the star discussed in Section 7.7 to broadcast a datum initially stored in processor 2134 of the star S_4.

7.10. Show that any broadcasting algorithm on a graph with n nodes must require time $\Omega(\log n)$.

7.11. Show that the arrangement graph $A_{4,2}$ can be partitioned into cliques of size 3, i.e., triangles.

7.12. Generalize the result of Exercise 7.11 for the arrangement graph $A_{d,k}$. That is, show that the arrangement graph $A_{d,k}$ can be partitioned into cliques of size $d - k + 1$.

7.13. Show that the (d, k)-star $S_{d,1}$ is a clique K_d.

7.14. In $S_{d,k}$, given an arbitrary node u, show that there exists a cycle between u and all u's 1-neighbors.

7.15. Explain how to find simple disjoint paths (linear arrays) of length d in the (d, k)-star.

7.16. Apply Exercise 7.15 on the embedding of $S_{4,3}$ shown in Fig. 7.11 to obtain 6 disjoint paths (linear arrays) of length 4.

7.17. Prove the correctness of your solution to Exercise 7.15.

7.18. Use the result of Exercise 7.15 to improve the running time of the sorting algorithm presented in Section 7.10.

7.19. A *dominating set* S in a graph $G = (V, E)$ is a subset of V such that every element $x \in V$ is in S or adjacent to an element y in S. Explain how to find a dominating set of minimum size in the (d, k)-star.

7.20. Apply Exercise 7.19 on the embedding of $S_{4,3}$ shown in Fig. 7.11 to obtain 4 dominating sets of minimum size.

7.21. Prove your answer to Exercise 7.19.

7.13 Solutions

7.1. Given a permutation $\pi = k_1 k_2 \ldots k_d$, show how to compute its rank efficiently.

Let permutation $\pi = k_1 k_2 \ldots k_d$ be given. Then, its rank $r(\pi)$ is given by

$$r(\pi) = 1 + \sum_{i=2}^{d} \left(|k_i - i - \sum_{l=i+1}^{d} t_l| \right) \times (i-1)!,$$

where $t_i = 1$ if $k_i > k_l$, and 0 otherwise. This is shown in pseudocode in Algorithm COMPSTARRANK. Its running time is computed as follows. Steps 5 and 7 are executed $\Theta(d)$ times each. Hence, the total running time is $\Theta(d^2)$.

7.2. Analyze the sequential running time of Algorithm STARLABELS.

Each table entry takes constant time to produce. This implies a running time of $\Theta(d!)$. So, it is linear in the number of processors.

Algorithm 7.7 COMPSTARRANK(S_d)
Input: d-dimensional star S_d
Output: Generate the ranks of S_d.

1. **for** $j \leftarrow 1$ **to** $d!$ **do in parallel**
2. $r \leftarrow 1$
3.   Let permutation $\pi_j = k_1 k_2 \ldots k_d$
4. $t \leftarrow 1$
5.   **for** $i \leftarrow 2$ **to** d **do**
6. $s \leftarrow k_i - i$
7.   **for** $l \leftarrow i + 1$ **to** d **do**
8.   **if** $k_i > k_l$ **then** $s \leftarrow s - 1$
9.   **end for**
10. $t \leftarrow t \times (i - 1)$
11. $r \leftarrow r + \mid s \mid \times t$
12.   **end for**
13. **end for**

7.3. Analyze the parallel running time of Algorithm STARLABELS using the star graph as a model. That is, given a star graph of processors, how long does it take for the processors to know their ranks?

All columns of the table can be evaluated in parallel. Each column can be evaluated sequentially in time $\Theta(d)$. This implies the running time recurrence $T(d) = T(d-1) + \Theta(d)$, whose solution is $T(d) = \Theta(d^2)$.

7.4. Show the steps for data transfers from $S_3(2)$ to $S_3(3)$ in the star S_4 such that no two sources send to the same destination (see Fig. 7.3). Similar to Example 7.1.

7.5. Illustrate the operation of Algorithm STARPARPREFIX for computing parallel prefix on the star described in Section 7.4 to find the prefix sums of $2, 1, 3, 1, 4, 2$. Assume a 3-dimensional star with 6 processors. Similar to Example 7.2.

7.6. Illustrate the operation of Algorithm STARMAX for computing the maximum on the star described in Section 7.5 to find the maximum of $3, 5, 8, 1, 5, 2$. Assume a 3-dimensional star with 6 processors. Similar to Example 7.3.

7.7. Apply Algorithm STARRECDUB in Section 7.6 on the label 21435. Similar to Example 7.4.

7.8. Show that any neighborhood broadcasting algorithm on a network with degree d must require $\Omega(\log d)$.

At each time unit, one processor with the messages can only send to one of its neighbors, so after every step, the number of neighbors which have received the information can at most double. The maximum number of neighbors of a node is d, so the least time to solve the neighborhood broadcasting problem must be $\Omega(\log d)$.

7.9. Illustrate the operation of the algorithm for broadcasting in the star discussed in Section 7.7 to broadcast a datum initially stored in processor 2134 of the star S_4.

Similar to Example 7.6.

7.10. Show that any broadcasting algorithm on a graph with n nodes must require time $\Omega(\log n)$.

Note that after each time unit the number of processors that have received the information being broadcast can at most double.

7.11. Show that the arrangement graph $A_{4,2}$ can be partitioned into cliques of size 3, i.e., triangles.

$A_{4,2}$ can be partitioned into $\dfrac{|V(A_{4,2})|}{3} = 4$ triangles in two ways as shown in Fig. 7.12.

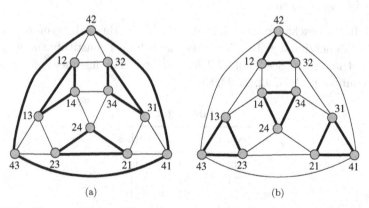

(a)   (b)

Fig. 7.12. Two partitions of the arrangement graph $A_{4,2}$ into four triangles (dark edges).

7.12. Generalize the result of Exercise 7.11 for the arrangement graph $A_{d,k}$. That is, show that the arrangement graph $A_{d,k}$ can be partitioned into cliques of size $d - k + 1$.

Let $I_d = \{1, 2, \ldots, d\}$, and for a fixed i, $1 \le i \le k$, let

$$V_i = \{a_1 \ldots a_{i-1} b_i a_{i+1} \ldots a_k \mid b_i \in I_d - \{a_1, \ldots, a_{i-1}, a_{i+1}, \ldots a_k\}.$$

Then, $|V_i| = d - k + 1$. There are $|P_{k-1}^d|$ such V_i's, where P_{k-1}^d is the number of permutations of d items taken k at a time. It is easy to see that the subgraph induced by V_i is a complete graph K_{d-k+1}. In particular, $K_{d-k+1} = K_d$ if $k = 1$, and $K_{d-k+1} = K_2$ if $k = d - 1$.

7.13. Show that the (d, k)-star $S_{d,1}$ is a clique K_d.

By Theorem 7.1 (All edges are 1-edges).

7.14. In $S_{d,k}$, given an arbitrary node u, show that there exists a cycle between u and all u's 1-neighbors.

Since $S_{d,k}$ is node-symmetric, we may assume without loss of generality that $u = 123 \ldots k$. Then, u is connected by a 1-edge to $(k+1)23 \ldots k$, which in turn is connected to $(k+2)23 \ldots k$, and so on. Hence, $123 \ldots k, (k+1)23 \ldots k, (k+2)23 \ldots k, \ldots, d23 \ldots k, 123 \ldots k$ is a cycle in $S_{d,k}$.

7.15. Explain how to find simple disjoint paths (linear arrays) of length d in the (d, k)-star.

If we exchange the 1st symbol with the kth symbol in the 2-dimensional embedding, then the columns constitute simple paths of length d. See Table 7.2 for example. For instance, one possible simple path is, $42, 32, 23, 13$.

Table 7.2.

path 1	path 2	path 3
43	42	41
34	32	31
24	23	21
14	13	12

Table 7.3.

path 1	path 2	path 3	path 4	path 5	path 6
432	431	423	421	413	412
342	341	324	321	314	312
243	241	234	231	214	213
143	142	134	132	124	123

7.16. Apply Exercise 7.15 on the embedding of $S_{4,3}$ shown in Fig. 7.11 to obtain 6 disjoint paths (linear arrays) of length 4.

From the first column of Table 7.3, we obtain the path $432, 342, 243, 143$. The other paths can be found similarly.

7.17. Prove the correctness of your solution to Exercise 7.15.

Any column of the two dimensional embedding looks like the following

$\alpha_1 d$
$\alpha_2(d-1)$
$\alpha_3(d-2)$
$\vdots$
$\alpha_{d-1}2$
$\alpha_d 1.$

If we swap the first and kth symbol, we obtain

$d\beta_1$
$(d-1)\beta_2$
$(d-2)\beta_3$
$\vdots$
$2\beta_{d-1}$
$1\beta_d.$

Now, exchanging d in $d\beta_1$ with (d-1) yields $(d-1)\beta_2$, exchanging $(d-1)$ in $d\beta_2$ with $(d-2)$ yields $(d-2)\beta_3$, and so on. Thus, $d\beta_1$, $(d-1)\beta_2, \ldots, 2\beta_{d-1}, 1\beta_d$ is a simple path of length $d-1$. In other words, it represents d processors forming a linear array.

7.18. Use the result of Exercise 7.15 to improve the running time of the sorting algorithm presented in Section 7.10.

Do the following steps.
  (1) Preprocessing step: Before the algorithm starts, copy the contents of every processor $a\alpha b$ to processor $b\alpha a$.
  (2) Sort as in Algorithm STARDKSORT.
  (3) Postprocessing step: After the sorting algorithm halts, copy back the contents of every processor $b\alpha a$ to processor $a\alpha b$.

Both the preprocessing and postprocessing steps take $\Theta(1)$ time. It follows that performing the above procedure will reduce the time complexity to $O(kd \log d)$, that is, it will be faster by a factor of $O(d)$, as the algorithm will work on columns of adjacent elements.

7.19. A *dominating set* S in a graph $G = (V, E)$ is a subset of V such that every element $x \in V$ is in S or adjacent to an element y in S. Explain how to find a dominating set of minimum size in the (d, k)-star.

If we exchange the 1st symbol with the kth symbol in the 2-dimensional embedding as in the previous exercises, then the rows constitute dominating sets of minimum size. See Table 7.2. For example, one possible dominating set of minimum size is, $43, 42, 41$.

7.20. Apply Exercise 7.19 on the embedding of $S_{4,3}$ shown in Fig. 7.11 to obtain 4 dominating sets of minimum size.

From the first row of Table 7.3, we obtain the dominating set $432, 431, 423, 421, 413, 412$. The other dominating sets can be found similarly.

7.21. Prove your answer to Exercise 7.19.

First, note that all elements in the same row start with the same symbol. This means that they form an independent set, that is, no one is connected to the other. Next, each row of elements of the form

$a\alpha_1, a\alpha_2, \ldots, a\alpha_{(d-1)!}$ consists of all permutations of the symbols in $\{1, 2, \ldots, d\} - \{a\}$ prefixed with the symbol a. Hence, if β is any permutation that does not start with a, then it must be a neighbor of one of these $(d-1)!$ permutations. This implies that this dominating set is of minimum size.

Chapter 8

Optical Transpose Interconnection System (OTIS)

8.1 Introduction

When communication distances exceed a few millimeters, optical interconnects provide speed and power advantages over electronic interconnects. Therefore, in the construction of very large multiprocessor machines, it is prudent to interconnect physically close processors using electronic interconnects and to use optical interconnects for pairs of processors that are distant. This led to the introduction of *optical transpose interconnection system* (OTIS). Specifically, in OTIS, there are n^2 processors organized into n groups of n processors each. The intergroup interconnects are optical, while the intragroup interconnects are electronic. It can be shown that when the number of groups equals the number of processors, the bandwidth and power efficiency are maximized, and system area and volume are minimized. Each processor is indexed by the pair (g, p), $0 \leq g, p < n$, where g is the group index, i.e., the group the processor is in, and p is the processor index within each group. Processor p in group g is connected to processor g in group p, $0 \leq p, g < n$. Every group can be realized as one of the well-studied interconnection networks, e.g., mesh, hypercube, butterfly, mesh of trees, and so forth. This results in OTIS-Mesh, OTIS-Hypercube, OTIS-butterfly, and so on.

Optical links have much larger bandwidth than electronic links do, and transfer times including latency are different on optical and electronic links. Therefore, we will occasionally count communication along optical and electronic interconnects separately. However, we use the simplifying assumption that any constant amount of data can be communicated over an optical link during an optical communication step, while only a unit amount of data can be communicated over an electronic communication step.

8.2   The OTIS-Mesh

The OTIS-Mesh consists of n groups of n processors each, where each group of processors forms a $\sqrt{n} \times \sqrt{n}$ mesh. Processor p in mesh (group) g is connected to processor g in mesh (group) p, $0 \leq g, p < n$. Figure 8.1 shows an OTIS-Mesh with 4 meshes of 4 processors each for a total of 16 processors. In this figure, the optical links are shown in thick lines. As shown in the figure, processor $(00, 01)$ is connected to processor $(01, 00)$, processor $(01, 10)$ is connected to processor $(10, 01)$, and so forth. Figure 8.2 shows an OTIS-Mesh with 9 meshes of 9 processors each for a total of 81 processors.

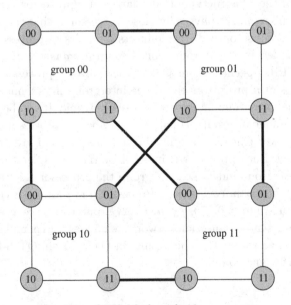

Fig. 8.1.   OTIS-Mesh with 16 processors.

8.2.1 *Data movements in the OTIS-Mesh*

Consider embedding a $\sqrt{n} \times \sqrt{n} \times \sqrt{n} \times \sqrt{n}$ 4-dimensional mesh on the OTIS-Mesh. Corresponding to this embedding, the processors in the OTIS-Mesh can be labeled by the quadruple (i, j, k, l), where $0 \leq i, j, k, l \leq \sqrt{n} - 1$. Here, the group number is $i\sqrt{n} + j$ and the processor number in each group is $k\sqrt{n} + l$. Each move in the 4-D mesh can be simulated by at most three moves in the OTIS-Mesh as follows. The 4-D mesh moves $(i, j, k \pm 1, l)$ and $(i, j, k, l \pm 1)$ take one electronic move each, since they are local to the group. The 4-D mesh move $(i \pm 1, j, k, l)$ can be simulated by one electronic move

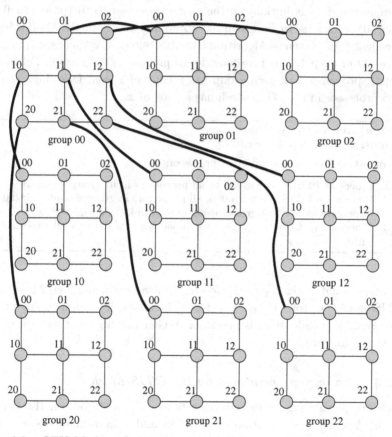

Fig. 8.2. OTIS-Mesh with 81 processors (only some of the optical links are shown).

and two optical moves as follows

$$(i,j,k,l) \xrightarrow{o} (k,l,i,j) \xrightarrow{e} (k,l,i+1,j) \xrightarrow{o} (i+1,j,k,l),$$

where $\xrightarrow{e}$ is an electronic move and $\xrightarrow{o}$ is an optical move. In some data movements, we will use the letters u, v, x and y to refer to the four dimensions of the 4-D mesh as well as its embedding on the OTIS-Mesh. Thus, each move along the x and y dimensions takes one step, and each move along the u and v dimensions takes three steps.

8.2.2 *Broadcasting in the OTIS-Mesh*

Assume the data is initially in the single processor $(0,0)$ (processor 0 in group 0), and it is to be broadcast to all processors in the OTIS-Mesh. The algorithm, shown as Algorithm OTISMESHBROADCAST, consists of three steps. After Step 1, x is broadcast to all processors in group 0. Following Step 2, processor 0 of each group has a copy of x, and following Step 3, each processor in the OTIS-Mesh has a copy of x.

Algorithm 8.1 OTISMESHBROADCAST
Input: x stored in processor $(0,0)$.

Output: Broadcast x to all other processors.

1. Processor $(0,0)$ broadcasts x to all processors in its group, group 0.
2. Perform an OTIS move. That is, all processors in group 0 send their data to processors in other groups using optical links (see Fig. 8.2).
3. Processor $(g,0)$ in every group g broadcasts its data to all processors within its group.

Steps 1 and 3 take $2(\sqrt{n}-1)$ electronic moves each, and Step 2 takes one OTIS move. The total is $4\sqrt{n}-3$ steps. The above discussion assumes that the origin of broadcasting is processor 0. Generalizing to other processors is straightforward.

8.2.3 *Semigroup operations on the OTIS-Mesh*

Consider performing semigroup operations, e.g., addition, on the OTIS-Mesh. Assume the operation of addition and that n numbers are distributed one per processor. The 2-tuple index (g,p) of a processor may be transformed into a scalar $i = gn + p$ with $0 \le i < n^2$. Let x_i be the data stored in processor i, $0 \leq i < n^2$. Notice that the sum is to be stored in all processors of the OTIS-Mesh. The algorithm, shown as Algorithm OTISMESHSUM, consists of three steps. After Step 1, the sum of all values in every group is computed and stored in all processors of that group. Following Step 2, for all groups g, $0 \leq g \leq n - 1$, processor (p, g) contains the sum of all elements in group p, and following Step 3, each processor in the OTIS-Mesh has a copy of the desired sum $x_0 + x_1 + \cdots + x_{n-1}$.

Algorithm 8.2 OTISMESHSUM

Input: x_i stored in processor i, $0 \leq i < n^2$.

Output: The sum of values x_i stored in all processors.

1. Each group performs the sum of its local data.
2. Perform an OTIS move. That is, for all groups g and all processors p, (g, p) sends the local sum in its group computed in Step 1 to processor (p, g) using optical links.
3. Each group computes the total of its local sums computed in Step 1.

Steps 1 and 3 take $4(\sqrt{n} - 1)$ electronic moves each (Exercise 4.3), and Step 2 takes one OTIS move. The total is $8(\sqrt{n} - 1)$ electronic moves and one OTIS move.

Example 8.1 Consider running Algorithm OTISMESHSUM for finding the sum on the OTIS-Mesh with 16 processors (see Fig. 8.1). The contents of the processors will be represented by a set of four sets, each representing a group of processors. Suppose that initially the contents of the processors are

$$\{\{1, 2, 1, 3\}, \{2, 4, 1, 3\}, \{1, 3, 2, 4\}, \{2, 4, 1, 2\}\}.$$

Following the first step, computing the local sums, we obtain

$$\{\{7, 7, 7, 7\}, \{10, 10, 10, 10\}, \{10, 10, 10, 10\}, \{9, 9, 9, 9\}\}.$$

After performing the OTIS move in Step 2, the contents become

$$\{\{7, 10, 10, 9\}, \{7, 10, 10, 9\}, \{7, 10, 10, 9\}, \{7, 10, 10, 9\}\}.$$

Finally, after performing the addition in Step 3, we obtain

$$\{\{36, 36, 36, 36\}, \{36, 36, 36, 36\}, \{36, 36, 36, 36\}, \{36, 36, 36, 36\}\},$$

which is the desired sum. Note that all processors contain the final sum.   □

8.2.4 *Parallel prefix in OTIS-Mesh*

The parallel prefix problem for the mesh was discussed in Section 4.4. In this section, we show how to compute it on the OTIS-Mesh. For simplicity, we will assume addition as the binary operation. The 2-tuple index (g, p) of a processor may be transformed into a scalar $i = gn + p$ with $0 \leq i < n^2$. Let x_i be the data stored in processor i. It is required to compute the prefix sums $x_0, x_0 + x_1, x_0 + x_1 + x_2, \ldots, x_0 + x_1 + \cdots + x_{n-1}$. The algorithm is shown as Algorithm OTISMESHPARPREFIX. It consists of six phases. (Recall that processor p in group g is denoted by (g, p)). In Phase 1 of the algorithm, each group computes its local prefix sums. After Phase 2, the partial sum computed in processor $(g, n - 1)$ is copied to processor $(n - 1, g)$ for all $g, 0 \leq g \leq n - 1$. As a result, group $n - 1$ will hold the partial sums stored in all processors $(g, n - 1)$. Let these sums be $s_0, s_1, \ldots, s_{n-1}$. Phase 3 computes the modified partial sums in group $n - 1$:

$$t_p = \sum_{j=0}^{p-1} s_j, \quad 0 \leq p \leq n - 1.$$

These valves are then copied to processors $(g, n - 1)$ in Phase 4 for all $g, 0 \leq g \leq n - 1$. The data in processor $(g, n - 1)$ is then broadcast to all processors in group g for all $g, 0 \leq g \leq n - 1$. Finally, in Phase 6, each processor (g, p) in the OTIS-Mesh adds the local prefix sum computed in Phase 1 and the modified prefix sum t_g it received in Phase 5.

The analysis of the algorithm is straightforward. Phases 1 and 3 take $\Theta(\sqrt{n})$ steps each. Broadcasting in Phase 5 costs $\Theta(\sqrt{n})$ time and addition in Phase 6 takes $\Theta(1)$ time. Phases 2 and 4 take one OTIS move each. It follows that the running time is $\Theta(\sqrt{n})$.

Example 8.2   Consider finding the prefix sums in the OTIS-Mesh with 16 processors (see Fig. 8.1). The contents of the processors will be represented by a set of four sets, each representing a group of processors. Initially, the contents of the processors are

$$\{\{1, 2, 1, 3\}, \{2, 4, 1, 3\}, \{1, 3, 2, 4\}, \{2, 4, 1, 2\}\}.$$

Algorithm 8.3 OTISMESHPARPREFIX

Input: x_i stored in processor i, $0 \leq i < n^2$.

Output: Compute the prefix sums of the x_i's.

1. Perform a local prefix sum within each group as discussed in Section 4.4.
2. Perform an OTIS move of the prefix sums computed in Phase 1 for all processors $(g, n-1)$. That is, for all groups g, copy the contents of processor $(g, n-1)$ to processor $(n-1, g)$ in group $n-1$. Call these sums $s_0, s_1, \ldots, s_{n-1}$.
3. Group $n-1$ computes a modified prefix sum of the values s_j received in Phase 2. In this modification, processor $(n-1, p)$ computes $t_p = \sum_{j=0}^{p-1} s_j$, $0 \leq p \leq n-1$.
4. Perform an OTIS move of the modified prefix sums computed in Phase 3. That is, for all groups g, copy t_g that is computed in the previous phase to processor $(g, n-1)$ in group g.
5. Each group g performs a local broadcast of the modified prefix sum t_g received by its processor $(g, n-1)$.
6. Each processor (g, p) in the OTIS-Mesh adds the local prefix sum computed in Phase 1 and the modified prefix sum t_g it received in Phase 5.

After computing the local prefix sums in Phase 1, we obtain

$$\{\{1, 3, 4, 7\}, \{2, 6, 7, 10\}, \{1, 4, 6, 10\}, \{2, 6, 7, 9\}\}.$$

The contents after Phase 2 change as follows

$$\{\{1, 3, 4, 7\}, \{2, 6, 7, 10\}, \{1, 4, 6, 10\}, \{(2, 7), (6, 10), (7, 10), (9, 9)\}\}.$$

Here, the fourth group consists of pairs of values; the first value in each group-processor pair $(3, p)$ is the local prefix sum computed earlier and the second is the prefix sum s_p of group p received in Phase 2. So, in group 3, $s_0 = 7, s_1 = 10, s_2 = 10$ and $s_3 = 9$. Following Phase 3, the contents become

$$\{\{1, 3, 4, 7\}, \{2, 6, 7, 10\}, \{1, 4, 6, 10\}, \{(2, 0), (6, 7), (7, 17), (9, 27)\}\}.$$

Here, $0, 7, 17, 27$ are the modified prefix sums t_p of $7, 10, 10, 9$ stored in group 3. Following Phase 4, the contents of the processors become

$$\{\{1, 3, 4, (7, 0)\}, \{2, 6, 7, (10, 7)\}, \{1, 4, 6, (10, 17)\}, \{(2, 0), (6, 7), (7, 17), (9, 27)\}\},$$

that is, the contents of group 3 are copied to processors $(g, 3)$ in all groups g. After broadcasting in Phase 5, the contents are represented by the pairs

$$\{\{(1, 0), (3, 0), (4, 0), (7, 0)\}, \{(2, 7), (6, 7), (7, 7), (10, 7)\},$$

$$\{(1,17),(4,17),(6,17),(10,17)\},\{(2,27),(6,27),(7,27),(9,27)\}\}.$$

Finally, after addition in Phase 6, the contents in all processors become

$$\{\{1,3,4,7\},\{9,13,14,17\},\{18,21,23,27\},\{29,33,34,36\}\},$$

which are the desired prefix sums, as can be seen by inspection. □

8.2.5 *Shift operations on the OTIS-Mesh*

In this operation, data in all groups is shifted to the right (or left) along one of its coordinates by k positions, where $-\sqrt{n} < k < \sqrt{n}$. For example, data is shifted from (u,v,x,y) to $(u+k,v,x,y)$ along coordinate u, or shifted from (u,v,x,y) to $(u,v,x+k,y)$ along coordinate x. Here, we have assumed that the processors are labeled by the quadruple (u,v,x,y). Shifting along coordinates x and y is straightforward, as it is a standard mesh operation. Hence, we will concentrate on shifting along coordinates u and v. Algorithm OTISMESHSHIFT describes how to shift along coordinate u or along coordinate v. In Step 1, for all groups $g, 0 \le g \le n-1$, processor (g,p) copies its element to processor (p,g), and following Step 2, the elements in each group are shifted. Shifting is performed along x coordinate if the original shifting is by u, and is done along y coordinate if the original shifting is by v. Finally, after Step 3, for all groups $g, 0 \le g \le n-1$, processor (g,p) copies its element to processor (p,g).

Steps 1 and 3 take one OTIS move each, and Step 2 takes k electronic moves.

Algorithm 8.4 OTISMESHSHIFT
Input: n^2 elements stored in OTIS-Mesh and an integer k, $-\sqrt{n} < k < \sqrt{n}$.
Output: The elements are shifted to the right or the bottom by k positions along the u or v coordinates.

1. Perform an OTIS move. That is, for all groups g and all processors p, (g,p) sends its element to processor (p,g) using optical links.
2. Each group shifts its local data along coordinate x or y row-wise or column-wise.
3. Perform an OTIS move as in Step 1.

Example 8.3 Consider running Algorithm OTISMESHSHIFT for shifting the elements in the OTIS-Mesh with 16 processors one element to the right along the u-coordinate (see Fig. 8.1). The contents of the processors will be represented by a set of four sets, each representing a group of processors. Suppose that initially the contents of the processors are

$$\{\{1,2,3,4\}, \{5,6,7,8\}, \{9,10,11,12\}, \{13,14,15,16\}\}.$$

It is important to note that each set of four numbers constitutes a 2×2 mesh. Following Step 1, we obtain

$$\{\{1,5,9,13\}, \{2,6,10,14\}, \{3,7,11,15\}, \{4,8,12,16\}\}.$$

After Step 2, the contents of the processors become

$$\{\{0,1,0,9\}, \{0,2,0,10\}, \{0,3,0,11\}, \{0,4,0,12\}\}.$$

Finally, following Step 3, we obtain

$$\{\{0,0,0,0\}, \{1,2,3,4\}, \{0,0,0,0\}, \{9,10,11,12\}\},$$

which is the desired result. □

Example 8.4   Consider running Algorithm OTISMESHSHIFT — for shifting the elements in the OTIS-Mesh with 16 processors — one element to the right along the v-coordinate (see Fig. 8.1). Suppose that initially the contents of the processors are

$$\{\{1,2,3,4\}, \{5,6,7,8\}, \{9,10,11,12\}, \{13,14,15,16\}\}.$$

Following Step 1, we obtain

$$\{\{1,5,9,13\}, \{2,6,10,14\}, \{3,7,11,15\}, \{4,8,12,16\}\}.$$

After Step 2, the contents of the processors become

$$\{\{0,0,1,5\}, \{0,0,2,6\}, \{0,0,3,7\}, \{0,0,4,8\}\}.$$

Finally, following Step 3, we obtain

$$\{\{0,0,0,0\}, \{0,0,0,0\}, \{1,2,3,4\}, \{5,6,7,8\}\},$$

which is the desired result. □

8.2.6   *Permutation routing in OTIS-Mesh*

We consider the problem of *permutation routing* in the OTIS-Mesh with n^2 processors, in which every processor tries to send to a different destination. We will denote a processor $P_{k,l}$ in group (i, j) by the quadruple (i, j, k, l).

8.2.6.1   *Deterministic routing in the OTIS-Mesh*

The greedy algorithm for permutation routing in the OTIS-Mesh is a generalization of the greedy algorithm for the 2-dimensional mesh discussed in Section 4.9.2. Let π be a packet to be routed from processor (u, v, x, y) to processor (u', v', x', y'). The greedy algorithm consists of the following phases.

Phase 1: Route π from processor (u, v, x, y) to processor (u, v, u', v') as detailed in Section 4.9.2.

Phase 2: Send π from processor (u, v, u', v') to processor (u', v', u, v) using one optical move.

Phase 3: Route π from processor (u', v', u, v) to processor (u', v', x', y') as detailed in Section 4.9.2.

Phases 1 and 3 take at most $2\sqrt{n} - 2$ steps each, and Phase 2 takes one step for a total of at most $4\sqrt{n} - 3$ steps. However, many packets may pile up at intermediate processors. Moreover, many packets may pile up at processor (u, v, u', v') after Phase 1; in the worst case all processors from group (u, v) may want to send to all processors in group (u', v'). In this case, $\Theta(n)$ packets may accumulate at processor (u, v, u', v') after Phase 1. This implies that the delay, and hence the total number of steps, is $O(n)$.

8.2.6.2   *Randomized routing in the OTIS-Mesh*

As pointed out in the previous section, the greedy algorithm may result in large queue sizes and hence large delays. This renders the greedy algorithm impractical. To circumvent this difficulty, we use randomization. One possibility is to use the randomized algorithm of Section 4.9.3 twice for both phases 1 and 3 of the greedy algorithm of the previous section. However, this will not prevent the accumulation of packets at intermediate processors, which may result from many packets sent from one particular group to another group. Hence, we use randomization to first send the packets to random locations within the OTIS-Mesh. The proposed randomized algorithm consists of the following four phases. Recall that the source packet is π at (u, v, x, y) and is destined to (u', v', x', y').

Phase 1: Route π to a random processor (u'', v'', x'', y''). It first chooses u'' randomly and moves to (u'', v, x, y). It then chooses v'' randomly and moves to (u'', v'', x, y), then chooses x'' randomly and moves to (u'', v'', x'', y) and finally chooses y'' randomly and moves to (u'', v'', x'', y''). Traversing in the u, v dimensions can be converted to traversals in the x, y dimensions as follows. First, π moves from the source processor (u, v, x, y) to processor (u, v, u'', v) along the x-dimension, then moves along the transpose connection to (u'', v, u, v), and finally in the (u'', v) group to (u'', v, x, y). Similarly, it then moves from (u'', v, x, y) to (u'', v'', x, y). Next, it moves in group (u'', v'') to (u'', v'', x'', y'') first on the x-dimension and then on the y-dimension. It can be shown using an analysis similar to that in Section 4.9.3 that this takes at most $4\sqrt{n} + o(\sqrt{n})$ steps using queues of size $O(\log n)$ with high probability.

Phase 2: Route π from processor (u'', v'', x'', y'') to processor (u'', v'', u', v'). This can be done by traveling first along the x-dimension and then along the y-dimension. It can be shown that the delay is $o(\sqrt{n})$. Since the distance traveled is at most $\sqrt{n}$, routing along the x-dimension takes at most $\sqrt{n} + o(\sqrt{n})$ with high probability. Similarly, routing along the y-direction takes at most $\sqrt{n} + o(\sqrt{n})$. Hence, this data movement, which is local to group (u'', v''), takes at most $2\sqrt{n} + o(\sqrt{n})$ steps with high probability.

Phase 3: Send π from processor (u'', v'', u', v') to processor (u', v', u'', v'') using one optical move.

Phase 4: Route π from processor (u', v', u'', v'') to the destination processor (u', v', x', y'). It does this by traveling first along the x-dimension and then along the y-dimension. As in Phase 2, this involves routing local to group (u', v'), and it takes at most $2\sqrt{n} + o(\sqrt{n})$ steps with high probability.

In all phases, the farthest-destination-first priority scheme is employed. The total number of steps is $8\sqrt{n} + o(\sqrt{n})$ using queues of size $O(\log n)$ with high probability.

8.2.7 *Sorting on OTIS-Mesh*

Sorting on the OTIS-Mesh can be achieved by simulating an algorithm for sorting on the 4-dimensional mesh. It is not difficult to extend the algorithm for sorting on the 3-dimensional mesh described in Section 4.17.1 so that it runs on the 4-dimensional mesh using $O(\sqrt{n})$ steps. The algorithm for the 3-dimensional mesh can be generalized to 4-dimensions by replacing planes by 3-dimensional meshes with side length $\sqrt{n}$. Sorting in planes becomes sorting in 3-dimensional meshes as described in Section 4.17.1. The result is an algorithm that runs in $O(\sqrt{n})$ steps. (See the Bibliographic notes for more discussion of sorting on the 4-dimensional mesh and the OTIS-Mesh).

8.3 The OTIS-Hypercube

The OTIS-Hypercube consists of $n = 2^d$ groups of n processors each for a total of n^2 processors, where each group of processors forms a conventional hypercube with $n = 2^d$. Processor p in hypercube (group) g is connected to processor g in hypercube (group) p, $0 \leq g, p < n$. Figure 8.3 shows an OTIS-Hypercube with 8 hypercubes of 8 processors each for a total of 64 processors. The thick lines represent optical links and the thin lines represent connections within the hypercubes. The number below each group is its number. For clarity, only some of the optical connections are shown in the figure.

As shown in the figure, processor $(000, 010)$ is connected to processor $(010, 000)$, processor $(101, 111)$ is connected to processor $(111, 101)$, and so forth. Each processor in the OTIS-Hypercube has degree $d + 1$; there are d connections to other processors in its group as well as one optical link. The diameter of the OTIS-Hypercube is $2d + 1$; the shortest distance between processors $(0, 0)$ and $(n - 1, n - 1)$ is $2d + 1$ (Exercise 8.10).

8.3.1 *Simulation of an n^2-processor hypercube*

An n^2-processor OTIS-Hypercube can simulate a regular n^2-processor hypercube. A processor (g, p) of the OTIS-Hypercube can be represented by the $2d$ bits

$$g_{d-1}g_{d-2}\cdots, g_0 p_{d-1}p_{d-2}\cdots p_0,$$

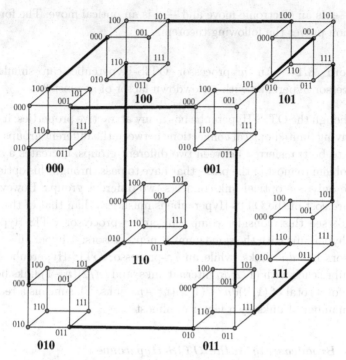

Fig. 8.3. OTIS-Hypercube with 64 processors. Only some of the optical links are shown.

where $g_{d-1}g_{d-2}\ldots g_0$ is the group address and $p_{d-1}p_{d-2}\ldots p_0$ is the local processor address. A hypercube move moves data from processor with label q to processor $q^{(k)}$, where $q^{(k)}$ is obtained from the binary representation of q by complementing the kth bit. When k is in the lower half, the move is done in the hypercube by a local intragroup hypercube move. When k is in the upper half, the move is done in the group using the following steps.

$$(g_{d-1}g_{d-2}\cdots, g_0 p_{d-1}p_{d-2}\cdots p_0)$$

$$\xrightarrow{o} (p_{d-1}p_{d-2}\cdots, p_0 g_{d-1}g_{d-2}\cdots g_j \cdots g_0)$$

$$\xrightarrow{e} (p_{d-1}p_{d-2}\cdots, p_0 g_{d-1}g_{d-2}\cdots \overline{g_j} \cdots g_0)$$

$$\xrightarrow{o} (g_{d-1}g_{d-2}\cdots \overline{g_j} \cdots g_0 p_{d-1}p_{d-2}\cdots, p_0),$$

Here, $\xrightarrow{e}$ is an electronic move and $\xrightarrow{o}$ is an optical move. The foregoing discussion proves the following theorem.

Theorem 8.1   An n^2-processor OTIS-Hypercube can simulate an n^2-processor hypercube with a slowdown factor of at most 3.

Although the OTIS-Hypercube has many attractive properties, it suffers from having limited optical connections between the different groups. When data is to be transferred between two different groups, it creates a congestion problem to most of the paths that have to pass through this optical link because only one optical link connects two different groups. However, the hardware cost of the OTIS-Hypercube is mush less than that of the hypercube. To see this, consider comparing an n^2-processor OTIS-Hypercube with a hypercube with the same number of processors. A hypercube with n^2 processors has dn^2 links, while an n^2-processor OTIS-Hypercube has n^2 hypercubes each with $(1/2)dn$ internal links, and $(n/2)(n-1)$ links between groups for a total of $(1/2)dn^2 + (1/2)(n^2 - n)$ links. This means a reduction in the number of links by a factor of almost 2.

8.3.2   *Broadcasting in the OTIS-Hypercube*

The algorithm for broadcasting in the OTIS-Hypercube is similar to that for the OTIS-Mesh discussed in Section 8.2.2, and outlined in Algorithm OTISMESHBROADCAST. Steps 1 and 3 of Algorithm OTISMESHBROADCAST when adapted for the OTIS-Hypercube take $\log n$ electronic moves each, and Step 2 takes one OTIS move. The total is $2 \log n + 1$ steps.

8.3.3   *Semigroup operations on the OTIS-Hypercube*

The algorithm for semigroup operations in the OTIS-Hypercube is similar to that for the OTIS-Mesh discussed in Section 8.2.3, and the algorithm for addition is similar to Algorithm OTISMESHSUM. Steps 1 and 3 of Algorithm OTISMESHSUM — when adapted for the OTIS-Hypercube — take $\log n$ electronic moves each, and Step 2 takes one OTIS move. The total is $2 \log n$ electronic moves and one OTIS move.

Alternatively, we may use the technique of reduction as outlined in Algorithm OTISHCADDITION. In this algorithm, the data in each group g is first added, and the sum is stored in processor $(g, 0)$. The contents of all processors $(g, 0)$ are then transferred to group 0 using one optical move.

Finally, group 0 computes the sum of the contents in all its processors and stores the result in processor $(0,0)$. Notice that the sum is stored in processor $(0,0)$ only. The analysis of the algorithm is similar to that of the previous algorithm, that is, the running time is $2 \log n$ electronic moves and one optical move.

Algorithm 8.5 OTISHCADDITION

Input: x_i stored in processor i, $0 \leq i < n^2$.

Output: The sum of values x_i in all processors.

1. Each group g performs addition of its local data and stores the sum in processor $(g, 0)$ of group 0.
2. Each group g moves the content of its processor $(g, 0)$ to processor $(0, g)$.
3. Group 0 performs addition of the sums computed in Step 1 and stores the total in processor $(0, 0)$.

Example 8.5 Consider running Algorithm OTISHCADDITION for finding the sum on the OTIS-Hypercube with 16 processors (see Fig. 8.1). The contents of the processors will be represented by a set of four sets, each representing a group of processors. Suppose that initially the contents of the processors are

$$\{\{1, 2, 1, 3\}, \{2, 4, 1, 3\}, \{1, 3, 2, 4\}, \{2, 4, 1, 2\}\}.$$

Following the first step, computing the local sums, we obtain

$$\{\{7, x, x, x\}, \{10, x, x, x\}, \{10, x, x, x\}, \{9, x, x, x\}\},$$

where x stands for anything. After performing the OTIS move in Step 3, the contents become

$$\{\{7, 10, 10, 9\}, \{10, x, x, x\}, \{10, x, x, x\}, \{9, x, x, x\}\},$$

Finally, after performing the addition in Step 3, we obtain

$$\{\{36, x, x, x\}, \{10, x, x, x\}, \{10, x, x, x\}, \{9, x, x, x\}\}, \qquad \square$$

8.3.4   *Sorting and routing in the OTIS-Hypercube*

Theorem 8.1 can be employed to simulate sorting and routing on the OTIS-Hypercube. For sorting, Algorithm SAMPLESORT discussed in Section 3.10 for the hypercube can be used. The running time will be $\Theta\left(\frac{n}{p} \log \frac{n}{p}\right)$, where

p is the number of processors and n is the number of elements. Here, we have assumed that the number of processors is less than the number of elements.

Alternatively, Algorithm BFODDEVENMERGESORT for odd–even sorting on the butterfly network discussed in Section 3.9 can also be used, since it is a normal butterfly algorithm (see definition of normal butterfly algorithm in Section 3.2). The running time will be $\Theta(\log^2 n)$.

The problem of routing in the OTIS-Hypercube can be solved by simulating the randomized algorithm for routing in the hypercube discussed in Section 3.6.2. When adapting this algorithm on an n^2-hypercube, its running time becomes at most $8 \times 2d = 16d$ steps with high probability. Hence, by Theorem 8.1, the running time on the OTIS-Hypercube will be at most $3 \times 16d = 48d = \Theta(\log n)$ steps with high probability.

8.4 Other OTIS Networks

8.4.1 The OTIS-Star

The OTIS-Star consists of $n = d!$ groups of n processors each, where each group of processors forms a d-dimensional star. Processor p in star (group) g is connected to processor g in star (group) p, $0 \le g, p < n$. Figure 8.4 shows an OTIS-Star with 6 stars of 6 processors each for a total of 36 processors. As shown in the figure, processor $(123, 213)$ is connected to processor $(213, 123)$, processor $(123, 132)$ is connected to processor $(132, 123)$, and so forth. The diameter of the OTIS-Star is $2\lfloor 3(d-1)/2 \rfloor + 1 = \Theta(d)$, and its degree is d, which are sublogarithmic in terms of the number of processors (Notice that $d < \log(d!)^2 = \Theta(d \log d)$).

8.4.2 The OTIS-MOT

The OTIS-MOT consists of n groups of n processors each, where each group of processors forms a mesh of trees. In this construction, it is more convenient to use a slightly different model of mesh of trees than the one described in Section 6.3; see Fig. 8.5 for an example. In this figure, each node is labeled with the row and column numbers. Here, the processors in each row are connected to form a binary tree, and the processors in each column are connected to form a binary tree. The roots of these binary trees are the processors in the leftmost column and topmost row. The total

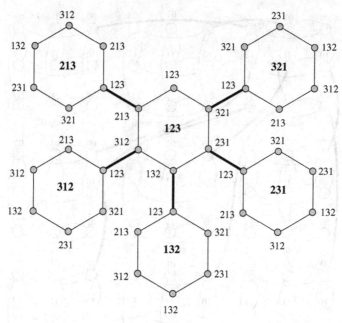

Fig. 8.4. OTIS-Star with 36 processors (only some of the optical links are shown).

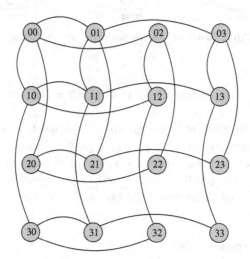

Fig. 8.5.   Mesh of trees with 16 processors.

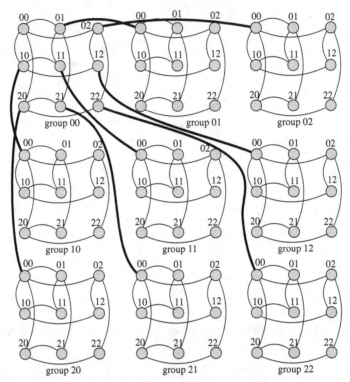

Fig. 8.6. OTIS-MOT with 81 processors (only some of the optical links are shown).

number of processors in this model is n, which is the same as that of the $\sqrt{n} \times \sqrt{n}$ mesh.

Processor p in mesh of trees (group) g is connected to processor g in mesh of trees (group) p, $0 \leq g, p < n$. Figure 8.6 shows an OTIS-MOT with 9 groups of 9 processors each for a total of 81 processors. As shown in the figure, processor $(00, 01)$ is connected to processor $(01, 00)$, processor $(00, 22)$ is connected to processor $(22, 00)$, and so forth.

8.5 Bibliographic Notes

Optical transpose interconnection system (OTIS) technologies have been proposed and investigated in Marsden, Marchand, Harvey and Esener [63],

Szymanski [90] and Szymanski and Hinton [91]. Topological properties of OTIS networks were studied in Day and Al-Ayyoub [31]. A number of algorithms have been developed for the OTIS networks such as Akhgari, Ziaie and Ghodsi [3], Gupta, Singh and Bhati [41], Gupta and Sarkar [40], Lucas and Jana [60], Najaf-abadi and Sarbazi-azad [70], Osterloh [73], Rajasekaran and Sahni [76], Wang and Sahni ([95], [96], [97]) and Zane, Marchand, Pahuri and Esener [103]. Algorithms for basic operations on the OTIS-mesh can be found in Wang and Sahni [95]. The randomized routing algorithm for the OTIS-mesh in Section 8.2.6.2 is a modification of an algorithm presented in Rajasekaran and Sahni [76]. An $O(\sqrt{n})$ time algorithm for sorting can be obtained by simulating an algorithm with similar complexity for the 4-dimensional mesh as suggested in Section 8.2.7. Another possibility is to use Kunde's sorting algorithm for the 4-dimensional mesh in Kunde [47]. The sorting algorithm presented in this paper is for the more general r-dimensional meshes, $r \geq 3$. There are some complex algorithms for sorting on the OTIS-mesh. The deterministic algorithm in Wang and Sahni [95] for the OTIS-mesh runs in $O(\sqrt{n})$ steps, and the randomized algorithm in Rajasekaran and Sahni [76] runs in time $O(\sqrt{n})$ with high probability. Algorithms for the OTIS-hypercube have been developed in Sahni and Wang [80] and Wang and Sahni [94]. A comparative evaluation of adaptive and deterministic routing in the OTIS-hypercubes appears in Najaf-abadi and Sarbazi-azad [69]. Theorem 8.1 can be found in Zane, Marchand, Pahuri and Esener [103]. The OTIS-Star was studied by Awwad [13], Al-Sadi, Awwad, and AlBdaiwi [10] and Awwad and Al-Sadi [14]. Sorting and routing on OTIS-Mesh of trees can be found in Lucas and Jana [60] and Lucas and Jana [61]. Algorithms for OTIS-Hyper Hexa-Cell can be found in Gupta and Sarkar [40] and Gupta, Singh and Bhati [41] (For definitions of the hyper hexa-cell and the OTIS-Hyper Hexa-Cell, see also Mahafzah, Hamad, Ahmad and Abu-Kabeer [62]).

8.6 Exercises

8.1. Suppose we want to move data from processor p_1 in group g_1 to processor p_2 in group g_2. One possibility is to use the sequence of moves:

$$(g_1, p_1) \xrightarrow{e^*} (g_1, g_2) \xrightarrow{o} (g_2, g_1) \xrightarrow{e^*} (g_2, p_2),$$

where $\xrightarrow{\;o\;}$ is an optical move and $\xrightarrow{\;e^*\;}$ stands for a sequence of zero or more electronic moves. Suggest another sequence of moves.

8.2. Is Algorithm OTISMESHBROADCAST discussed in Section 8.2.2 for broadcasting in the OTIS-Mesh optimal? Justify your answer.

8.3. In a window broadcast, we start with data in the top left $w \times w$ submesh of a single group g, where $w \mid \sqrt{n}$, that is w divides $\sqrt{n}$. Following the window broadcast operation, the initial $w \times w$ window tiles the entire OTIS-Mesh. (See Exercise 4.19). Outline an algorithm to implement this operation. What is the running time of your algorithm?

8.4. Apply the addition algorithm for the OTIS-Mesh discussed in Section 8.2.3 on the input

$$\{\{1,3,2,4\},\{2,1,5,1\},\{2,4,5,1\},\{2,1,3,2\}\}.$$

8.5. Explain how to implement Step 1 in Algorithm OTISMESHSUM of Section 8.2.3 efficiently.

8.6. Apply the parallel prefix algorithm for the OTIS-Mesh discussed in Section 8.2.4 on the input

$$\{\{2,4,2,1\},\{1,3,1,4\},\{5,2,1,3\},\{2,3,5,1\}\}.$$

8.7. Illustrate the operation of Algorithm OTISMESHSHIFT in Section 8.2.5 given the processor contents

$$\{\{3,8,1,14\},\{2,13,5,11\},\{9,7,10,6\},\{4,15,12,8\}\}.$$

Assume an OTIS-Mesh with 16 processors, and the elements are to be shifted along the u-coordinate.

8.8. Repeat Exercise 8.7 with shifting the elements along the v-coordinate instead.

8.9. Modify the algorithm for randomized routing in the OTIS-Mesh discussed in Section 8.2.6.2 so that it runs in time $4\sqrt{n} + o(\sqrt{n})$.

8.10. Verify that the diameter of the OTIS-Hypercube is $2d + 1$.

8.11. Analyze the running time of the algorithm in Section 8.3.2 for broadcasting in the OTIS-Hypercube by simulating an n^2-hypercube.

8.12. Analyze the running time of the algorithm in Section 8.3.3 for addition in the OTIS-Hypercube by simulating an n^2-hypercube.

8.13. Suppose that each of the n groups in an OTIS-Hypercube has a datum in an arbitrary processor. Give an algorithm to collect these n data items in a specified group k so that group k will have one item per processor.

8.14. Illustrate your solution to Exercise 8.13 given the processor contents

$$\{\{x, x, 1, x\}, \{2, x, x, x\}, \{x, x, x, 3\}, \{x, x, 4, x\}\},$$

which are to be sent to group 2. Assume an OTIS-Hypercube with four groups. Here, x stands for anything, and the contents of the processors are represented by a set of four sets, each representing a group of processors.

8.15. Suppose that group k in an OTIS-Hypercube has n data items located one per processor. Give an algorithm to replicate these items in each of the n groups.

8.16. Illustrate your solution to Exercise 8.15 for replicating the numbers $\{1, 7, 3, 4\}$ in group 2 in an OTIS-Hypercube with four groups.

8.17. Outline a deterministic algorithm for routing on the OTIS-Hypercube.

8.18. Discuss the drawbacks of the deterministic algorithm for routing in the OTIS-Hypercube in Exercise 8.17.

8.19. Outline an algorithm for broadcasting a datum in processor (g, p) in the OTIS-Star.

8.20. What is the degree of OTIS-MOT?

8.21. What is the diameter of OTIS-MOT with n^2 processors? Assume the mesh of trees depicted in Fig. 8.5.

8.22. Give two nodes in the OTIS-MOT shown in Fig. 8.6 that realize the diameter derived in the solution to Exercise 8.21

8.7 Solutions

8.1. Suppose we want to move data from processor p_1 in group g_1 to processor p_2 in group g_2. One possibility is to use the sequence of moves:

$$(g_1, p_1) \xrightarrow{e^*} (g_1, g_2) \xrightarrow{o} (g_2, g_1) \xrightarrow{e^*} (g_2, p_2),$$

where $\xrightarrow{o}$ is an optical move and $\xrightarrow{e^*}$ stands for a sequence of zero or more electronic moves. Suggest another sequence of moves.

One possibility is the sequence:

$$(g_1, p_1) \xrightarrow{e^*} (g_1, p_2) \xrightarrow{o} (p_2, g_1) \xrightarrow{e^*} (p_2, g_2) \xrightarrow{o} (g_2, p_2).$$

8.2. Is Algorithm OTISMESHBROADCAST discussed in Section 8.2.2 for broadcasting in the OTIS-Mesh optimal? Justify your answer.

Algorithm OTISMESHBROADCAST for broadcasting in the OTIS-Mesh is optimal since the diameter of the OTIS-Mesh is $4\sqrt{n} - 3$; the distance between processor $(0,0)$ and processor $(n-1, n-1)$ is $4\sqrt{n} - 3$.

8.3. In a window broadcast, we start with data in the top left $w \times w$ submesh of a single group g, where $w \mid \sqrt{n}$, that is w divides $\sqrt{n}$. Following the window broadcast operation, the initial $w \times w$ window tiles the entire OTIS-Mesh. (See Exercise 4.19). Outline an algorithm to implement this operation. What is the running time of your algorithm?

The algorithm is shown as Algorithm OTISMESHWINBROADCAST. Following Step 1, the initial window properly tiles the group g. In Step 2, data $d(g, p)$ from processor (g, p) is moved to (p, g), $0 \leq p < n$. In Step 3, $d(g, p)$ is broadcast to all processors (p, k), $0 \leq p, k < n$. Finally, in Step 4, $d(g, p)$ is moved to (k, p), $0 \leq k, p < n$. By Exercise 4.19, Step 1 takes $2(\sqrt{n} - w)$ electronic moves. Steps 2 and 4 take one OTIS move each. Step 3 takes $2(\sqrt{n} - 1)$ electronic moves. The total is $4\sqrt{n} - 2w - 2$ electronic and two OTIS moves.

Algorithm 8.6 OTISMESHWINBROADCAST

1. Do a window broadcast within the initial group g as outlined in the solution of Exercise 4.19.
2. Perform an OTIS move. That is, all processors in group g send their data to processors in other groups using optical links.
3. Perform data broadcast from processor g of each group to all processors of that group.
4. Perform an OTIS move.

8.4. Apply the addition algorithm for the OTIS-Mesh discussed in Section 8.2.3 on the input

$$\{\{1,3,2,4\}, \{2,1,5,1\}, \{2,4,5,1\}, \{2,1,3,2\}\}.$$

Similar to Example 8.1.

8.5. Explain how to implement Step 1 in Algorithm OTISMESHSUM of Section 8.2.3 efficiently.

If we compute the sum in processor $(0,0)$, it will take $4(\sqrt{n}-1)$; $2(\sqrt{n}-1)$ for transferring the elements to processor $(0,0)$ and $2(\sqrt{n}-1)$ for broadcasting the sum. So, we compute the sum in the middle processor instead. In this case, the number of steps will be $2\sqrt{n}$; $\sqrt{n}$ for transferring the elements to the middle processor and $\sqrt{n}$ for broadcasting the sum.

8.6. Apply the parallel prefix algorithm for the OTIS-Mesh discussed in Section 8.2.4 on the input

$$\{\{2,4,2,1\}, \{1,3,1,4\}, \{5,2,1,3\}, \{2,3,5,1\}\}.$$

Similar to Example 8.2.

8.7. Illustrate the operation of Algorithm OTISMESHSHIFT in Section 8.2.5 given the processor contents

$$\{\{3,8,1,14\}, \{2,13,5,11\}, \{9,7,10,6\}, \{4,15,12,8\}\}.$$

Assume an OTIS-Mesh with 16 processors, and the elements are to be shifted along the u-coordinate.

Similar to Example 8.3.

8.8. Repeat Exercise 8.7 with shifting the elements along the v-coordinate instead.

Similar to Example 8.4.

8.9. Modify the algorithm for randomized routing in the OTIS-Mesh discussed in Section 8.2.6.2 so that it runs in time $4\sqrt{n} + o(\sqrt{n})$.

One possibility is the following modification to Phase 1. Partition the OTIS-Mesh into slices, i.e., 4-D submeshes, of size

$$\frac{\sqrt{n}}{q} \times \frac{\sqrt{n}}{q} \times \frac{\sqrt{n}}{q} \times \frac{\sqrt{n}}{q}$$

each, $1 \le q \le \sqrt{n}$. In the first phase, a packet traverses to a random processor (u'', v'', x'', y'') in its own slice of origin. The rest of the algorithm is as in Section 8.2.6.2. The maximum distance traveled in the first phase becomes $\le 4\sqrt{n}/q$. Thus, the time needed for Phase 1 is $4\sqrt{n}/q + o(\sqrt{n})$, and the total time of the algorithm becomes at most $4\sqrt{n} + 4\sqrt{n}/q + o(\sqrt{n})$. Choose a suitable q such as $q = \log n$ so that the total time of the algorithm becomes at most $4\sqrt{n} + o(\sqrt{n})$.

8.10. Verify that the diameter of the OTIS-Hypercube is $2d + 1$.

To go from $(0, 0)$ to $(n - 1, n - 1)$, follow the path:

$$(0,0) \xrightarrow{e} (0, n - 1) \xrightarrow{o} (n - 1, 0) \xrightarrow{e} (n - 1, n - 1),$$

where $\xrightarrow{o}$ is an optical move and $\xrightarrow{e}$ stands for electronic moves. The total number of steps is $d + 1 + d = 2d + 1$.

8.11. Analyze the running time of the algorithm in Section 8.3.2 for broadcasting in the OTIS-Hypercube by simulating an n^2-hypercube.

Since the cost of broadcasting in an n^2 hypercube is $\log n^2 = 2 \log n$ steps, by Theorem 8.1, direct simulation of an n^2 hypercube costs at most $3 \times 2\log n = 6 \log n$ steps (electronic and optical).

8.12. Analyze the running time of the algorithm in Section 8.3.3 for addition in the OTIS-Hypercube by simulating an n^2-hypercube.

Since the cost of addition in an n^2 hypercube is $\log n^2 = 2 \log n$ steps, by Theorem 8.1, direct simulation of an n^2 hypercube costs at most $3 \times 2\log n = 6 \log n$ steps (electronic and optical).

8.13. Suppose that each of the n groups in an OTIS-Hypercube has a datum in an arbitrary processor. Give an algorithm to collect these n data items in a specified group k so that group k will have one item per processor.

See Algorithm OTISHCPROBLEM1. Step 1 takes no more than $\log n$ electronic moves, and Step 2 takes one optical move. (See Exercise 8.14).

Algorithm 8.7 OTISHCPROBLEM1

1. For $0 \leq g \leq n-1$, group g sends its datum to processor k in that group.
2. For $0 \leq g \leq n-1$, the datum from processor k of group g is sent to processor g of group k using one optical move.

8.14. Illustrate your solution to Exercise 8.13 given the processor contents

$$\{\{x,x,1,x\},\{2,x,x,x\},\{x,x,x,3\},\{x,x,4,x\}\},$$

which are to be sent to group 2. Assume an OTIS-Hypercube with four groups. Here, x stands for anything, and the contents of the processors are represented by a set of four sets, each representing a group of processors.

Initially, the contents of the processors are

$$\{\{x,x,1,x\},\{2,x,x,x\},\{x,x,x,3\},\{x,x,4,x\}\}.$$

In the first step, group g, $0 \leq g \leq 3$, sends its datum to processor 2 in that group. Following this step, we obtain

$$\{\{x,x,1,x\},\{x,x,2,x\},\{x,x,3,x\},\{x,x,4,x\}\},$$

Finally, the datum from processor 2 of group g, $0 \leq g \leq 3$, is sent to processor g of group 2. After this final step, we obtain

$$\{\{x,x,x,x\},\{x,x,x,x\},\{1,2,3,4\},\{x,x,x,x\}\}.$$

8.15. Suppose that group k in an OTIS-Hypercube has n data items located one per processor. Give an algorithm to replicate these items in each of the n groups.

See Algorithm OTISHCPROBLEM2. After Step 1, each group has one item, and the data is replicated after Step 3. Steps 1 and 3 take one optical move each, and Step 2 takes $\log n$ electronic moves. (See Exercise 8.16).

Algorithm 8.8 OTISHCPROBLEM2

1. For all p, $0 \leq p \leq n-1$, processor p of group k sends its item to processor k of group p using one optical move.
2. Each group replicates its item in all of its processors by broadcasting it to all processors.
3. For all p, g, $0 \leq p, g \leq n-1$, processor p of group g sends its item to processor g of group p using one optical move.

8.16. Illustrate your solution to Exercise 8.15 for replicating the numbers $\{1, 7, 3, 4\}$ in group 2 in an OTIS-Hypercube with four groups.

The contents of the processors will be represented by a set of four sets, each representing a group of processors. Initially, the contents of the processors are

$$\{\{x, x, x, x\}, \{1, 7, 3, 4\}, \{x, x, x, x\}, \{x, x, x, x\}\},$$

where x stands for anything. In the first step, processor p of group 2 sends its item to processor 2 of group p. Following this step, we obtain

$$\{\{x, 1, x, x\}, \{x, 7, x, x\}, \{x, 3, x, x\}, \{x, 4, x, x\}\},$$

Now, each group replicates its item in all of its processors by broadcasting it to all processors in its group. The contents become

$$\{\{1, 1, 1, 1\}, \{7, 7, 7, 7\}, \{3, 3, 3, 3\}, \{4, 4, 4, 4\}\},$$

Finally, each processor p of group g sends its item to processor g of group p. After this final step, we obtain

$$\{\{1, 7, 3, 4\}, \{1, 7, 3, 4\}, \{1, 7, 3, 4\}, \{1, 7, 3, 4\}\}.$$

8.17. Outline a deterministic algorithm for routing on the OTIS-Hypercube.

Use one of the paths shown in the solution of Exercise 8.1 to route the source packet to its destination. For example, use the sequence

$$(g_1, p_1) \xrightarrow{e^*} (g_1, g_2) \xrightarrow{o} (g_2, g_1) \xrightarrow{e^*} (g_2, p_2).$$

Here, $\xrightarrow{e^*}$ is a sequence of zero or more electronic moves and $\xrightarrow{o}$ is an optical move. For routing within the hypercubes, use the greedy algorithm of Section 3.6.1.

8.18. Discuss the drawbacks of the deterministic algorithm for routing in the OTIS-Hypercube in Exercise 8.17.

The major drawback is that many packets may pile up at intermediate processors. In particular, all processors from group g_1 may want to send to all processors in group g_2. In this case, $\Theta(n)$ packets may accumulate at processor (g_1, g_2) before transmitting the packets along the optical link between processors (g_1, g_2) and (g_2, g_1). This implies that the delay, and hence the total number of steps, is $O(n)$.

Algorithm 8.9 OTISSTARBROADCAST
Input: x stored in processor (g, p).

Output: Broadcast x to all other processors.

1. Processor (g, p) broadcasts x to all processors in its group, group g.
2. Perform an OTIS move. That is, all processors in group g send their data to processors in other groups using optical links.
3. Processor (g', p') in every group g' broadcasts its data to all processors within its group.

8.19. Outline an algorithm for broadcasting a datum in processor (g, p) in the OTIS-Star.

The algorithm is similar to that in Section 8.2.2 for broadcasting in the mesh. It is shown as Algorithm OTISSTARBROADCAST. The algorithm for broadcasting in the star discussed in Section 7.7 may be used to broadcast in individual stars.

8.20. What is the degree of OTIS-MOT?

The degree of OTIS-MOT is 5, as can be seen from Fig. 8.6. In this figure, the degree of node 00 in group 10 is 5, and it is maximum.

8.21. What is the diameter of OTIS-MOT with n^2 processors? Assume the mesh of trees depicted in Fig. 8.5.

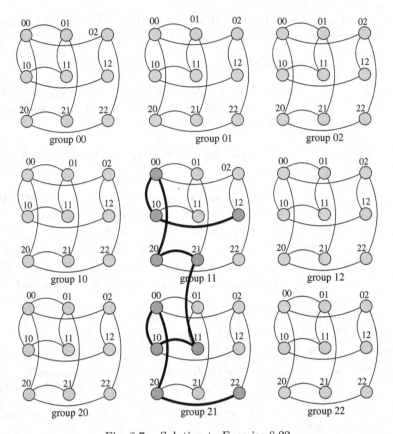

Fig. 8.7. Solution to Exercise 8.22.

The underlying mesh is of size n, and each binary tree has $\sqrt{n}$ nodes (see Fig. 8.5). Thus, the height of each binary tree is $\lfloor \log \sqrt{n} \rfloor$. It follows that the diameter of the mesh of trees is $4\lfloor \log \sqrt{n} \rfloor$, and hence the diameter of the OTIS-MOT with n^2 processors is $8\lfloor \log \sqrt{n} \rfloor + 1 = \Theta(\log n)$.

8.22. Give two nodes in the OTIS-MOT shown in Fig. 8.6 that realize the diameter derived in the solution to Exercise 8.21

The two nodes $(11, 12)$ and $(21, 22)$ realize the OTIS-MOT diameter. The distance between these two nodes is $8\lfloor \log \sqrt{9} \rfloor + 1 = 9$. The path between these two nodes is shown in thick lines in Fig. 8.7.

Chapter 9

Systolic Computation

9.1 Introduction

Systolic computation refers to one in which the processors, usually called processing elements (PE's), are arranged in a very regular way (most often, as one or two-dimensional arrays), and so the data moves through them in a regular fashion. Processors are usually primitive, and perform very simple operations on the data they receive, e.g., computing the maximum and minimum of two items. A systolic array is an on-chip multi-processor architecture. It was proposed as an architectural solution to the anticipated on-chip communication bottleneck of modern, very large-scale integration (VLSI) technology. A systolic array features a mesh-connected array of identical, simple PE's. In a systolic system, data flows from the computer memory in a rhythmic fashion, passing through many processing elements before it returns to memory. A systolic array is often configured into a linear array, a two-dimensional rectangular mesh array, or sometimes, a two dimensional hexagonal mesh array. In a systolic array, every PE is connected only to its nearest neighboring PEs through a dedicated, buffered local bus/dedicated, buffered local buses. This localized interconnects, and regular array configuration allow a systolic array to grow in size without incurring excessive on-chip global interconnect delays due to long wires. In the rest of this chapter, we will use the terms "PE" and "processor" interchangeably.

341

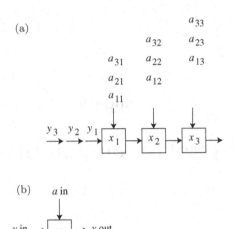

Fig. 9.1. Systolic matrix-vector multiplication.

9.2 Matrix-vector Multiplication

In this section, we present a simple example of systolic arrays. Consider performing the multiplication $\mathbf{y} = A\mathbf{x}$, where A is an $n \times n$ matrix, and $\mathbf{x}$ is an $n \times 1$ vector. One possible systolic array to solve this problem consists of n processors arranged in the form of a linear array. It is assumed that these processors are capable of performing scalar addition and multiplication of real numbers. Figure 9.1 shows an example of this array and arrangement of the input for $n = 3$. As shown in the figure, there are 3 processors, and data from the matrix A arrives in a systolic fashion, while the x_i's are preloaded to the processors. The initial arrangement and data movements of the $a_{i,j}$'s is such that column k is delayed by k cycles. The y_i's are initially set to zero, and their values are accumulated in the PEs. Thus, in the first cycle, y_1 is set to $a_{11}x_1$, in the next cycle, y_1 is set to $a_{11}x_1 + a_{12}x_2$ and y_2 is set to $a_{2,1}x_1$, and so on.

9.3 Computing the Convolution of Two Sequences

Let $\langle x_1, x_2, \ldots, x_n \rangle$ and $\langle w_1, w_2, \ldots, w_k \rangle$ be two sequences of real numbers. The *convolution* of these two sequences is defined as the sequence

$\langle y_1, y_2, \ldots, y_{n+1-k} \rangle$, where $y_i = w_1 x_i + w_2 x_{i+1} + \cdots + w_k x_{i+k-1}$. The elements of the sequence $\langle w_1, w_2, \ldots, w_k \rangle$ are called *weights*. The convolution of these two sequences can be expressed by the matrix-vector product

$$
\begin{pmatrix}
x_1 & x_2 & x_3 & \cdots & x_k \\
x_2 & x_3 & x_4 & \cdots & x_{k+1} \\
x_3 & x_4 & x_5 & \cdots & x_{k+2} \\
\vdots & \vdots & \vdots & \cdots & \vdots \\
x_{n+1-k} & x_{n+2-k} & x_{n+3-k} & \cdots & x_n
\end{pmatrix}
\begin{pmatrix}
w_1 \\
w_2 \\
w_3 \\
\vdots \\
w_k
\end{pmatrix}
=
\begin{pmatrix}
y_1 \\
y_2 \\
y_3 \\
\vdots \\
y_{n+1-k}
\end{pmatrix}.
$$

In what follows, we present two approaches for systolic computations to compute the convolution of two sequences, one semisystolic and the other systolic. The basic principles of these designs were previously proposed for circuits to implement a pattern matching processor and polynomial multiplication. For simplicity, we will assume in the rest of this section that $k = 3$.

9.3.1 *Semisystolic solution*

In this design, a bus is used for global data communication, and this is why it is referred to as "semisystolic". The x_i's are broadcast, results are moved, and weights stay in the PEs. The systolic array and its cell definition are depicted in Fig. 9.2. The weights are preloaded to the cells, one at each cell, and stay at the cells throughout the computation. The partial results y_i move systolically from cell to cell in the left-to-right direction during each cycle. At the beginning of a cycle, one x_i is broadcast to all the cells, and

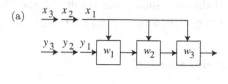

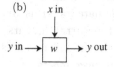

Fig. 9.2. Semisystolic convolution.

Table 9.1.   Convolution using the semisystolic design.

Cycle	y_1	y_2	y_3
1	w_1x_1	0	0
2	$w_1x_1 + w_2x_2$	w_1x_2	0
3	$w_1x_1 + w_2x_2 + w_3x_3$	$w_1x_2 + w_2x_3$	w_1x_3
4	Output y_1	$w_1x_2 + w_2x_3 + w_3x_4$	$w_1x_3 + w_2x_4$
5		Output y_2	$w_1x_3 + w_2x_4 + w_3x_5$
6			Output y_3

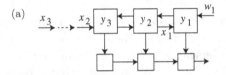

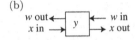

Fig. 9.3.   Systolic convolution.

one y_i, which is initialized as zero, enters the leftmost cell. Thus, during the first cycle, w_1x_1 is accumulated to y_1 at the leftmost cell, and during the second cycle, w_1x_2 and w_2x_2 are accumulated to y_2 and y_1 at the leftmost and middle cells respectively. Starting from the third cycle, the final values of $y_1, y_2, \ldots$ are output from the rightmost cell, one y_i per cycle.

Example 9.1   Table 9.1 shows the results of the computation of the convolution of the two sequences $\langle x_1, x_2, x_3, x_4, x_5 \rangle$ and $\langle w_1, w_2, w_3 \rangle$.   □

9.3.2   *Pure systolic solution*

An alternative to the semisystolic design is a pure systolic one in which each partial result y_i stays at a cell to accumulate its terms, and the x_i's and w_i's move in opposite directions. The systolic array and its cell definition are depicted in Fig. 9.3. Thus, in this design, the x_i's and w_i's move systolically in opposite directions such that when an x meets a w at a cell, they are multiplied and the resulting product is accumulated to the y staying at

Table 9.2. Convolution using the systolic design.

Cycle	y_1	y_2	y_3
1	w_1x_1	0	0
3	$w_1x_1 + w_2x_2$	w_1x_2	0
5	$w_1x_1 + w_2x_2 + w_3x_3$	$w_1x_2 + w_2x_3$	w_1x_3
7	Output y_1	$w_1x_2 + w_2x_3 + w_3x_4$	$w_1x_3 + w_2x_4$
9		Output y_2	$w_1x_3 + w_2x_4 + w_3x_5$
11			Output y_3

that cell. The difficulty with this design is that the x_i's and w_i's move twice as fast toward each other. The solution is to move data at half the speed. Thus, to ensure that each x_i is able to meet every w_i, consecutive x_i's on the x data stream are separated by two cycle times and so are the w_i's on the w data stream. In this design, a tag bit is associated with the first weight, w_1, to trigger the output and reset the accumulator contents of a cell. It can be easily checked that the y_i's will output from the systolic output path in the natural ordering $y_1, y_2, \ldots$. Specifically, when w_k leaves processor P_i ($k = 3$ in the figure), the final value of y_i is computed, and it can move out of the array through the data path below the array. Notice, however, that in this design only about one half the cells are doing useful work at any time.

Example 9.2 Table 9.2 shows the results of the computation of the convolution of the two sequences $\langle x_1, x_2, x_3, x_4, x_5 \rangle$ and $\langle w_1, w_2, w_3 \rangle$. It is similar to Table 9.1 except that the cycle numbers are incremented by 2 in this design. □

9.4 A Zero-time VLSI Sorter

Basically, this sorter consists of a linear array of $n/2$ cells, where n is assumed to be even. Each cell can store two items of the sequence to be sorted. Figure 9.4 depicts the block diagram of the sorter. As shown in the figure, there is only one connection between a cell and each of its upper and its lower neighboring cells. There are two phases: The up-down phase and the bottom-up phase. In both phases, after comparison, one of the two

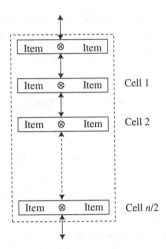

$\otimes$: Comparator

Fig. 9.4.   Block diagram of the sorter.

items moves to the next neighboring cell through this connection. Since the data flow is the same for all cells at any given time, this removed item occupies the newly-created space in the next cell; the removed item at the bottom cell is moved out of the array in a downward data flow, while the item at the top cell is moved out of the array in an upward data flow. The initial sequence to be sorted is entered into the sorter one item at each step. After the last item has been entered, the data flow direction is reversed, and the sorted sequence is then extracted as output, also serially. Each step, executed synchronously and simultaneously by all the cells, has two phases:

(1) Compare: The two items in each and every cell are compared to each other.
(2) Transfer: Subject to the result of the comparison, the desired sorting order (ascending or descending), and the sorting state (input or output), one or the other of the two items is transferred to a neighboring cell and the original cell receives an item from the other neighboring cell.

Example 9.3   Figures 9.5 and 9.6 show an example of sorting the sequence $\langle 4, 3, 1, 6, 2, 5 \rangle$ in ascending order. Here, ∞ represents the largest item possible. At the input stage (Fig. 9.5), the larger of the two items

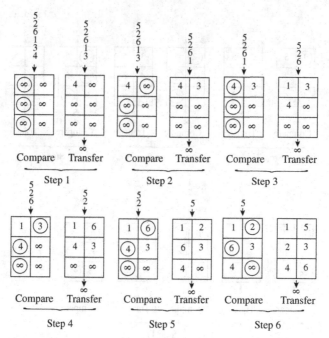

Fig. 9.5.   Input stage in the zero-time sorter: Larger items are circled and transferred.

in each cell is transferred down, while at the output stage (Figs. 9.6), the smaller of the two items is transferred up. ☐

Note that at the end of the input stage (step 6 in the above example), the smallest item must be in the top cell and the second smallest must be in either the top or the second cell. In general, the kth smallest item must be in one of the top k cells. This is why the output sequence is sorted.

9.5   An On-chip Bubble Sorter

The basic component of the bubble sorter is the compare/steer unit, which is shown in Fig. 9.7. It consists of four interconnected cells: A, B, C and D. The sorter consists of a stack of n comparators that work synchronously in one of two modes: downward and upward (see Fig. 9.8). In the downward mode, cell A in every unit receives its input from the unit above or from outside, the content of C is routed to B, and the content of D, which is

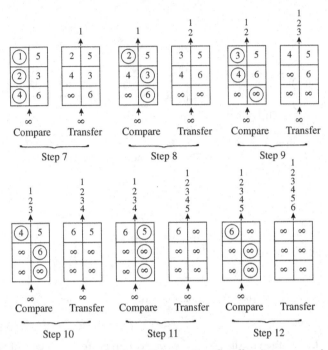

Fig. 9.6.   Output stage in the zero-time sorter: Smaller items are circled and transferred.

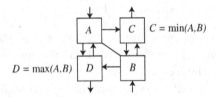

Fig. 9.7.   A compare/steer unit (comparator).

the larger of the two numbers, is moved to the next comparator below. Next, the contents of A and B are compared, and the minimum and maximum are delivered to C and D, respectively. That is, $C = \min\{A, B\}$ and $D = \max\{A, B\}$. In the upward mode, an outside key is loaded from the bottom into cell B of the unit, and an inside key previously at D is loaded into A. After loading, the comparison is executed, and the minimum is

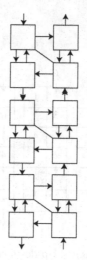

Fig. 9.8.   Sorter.

delivered to C and the maximum to D. Loading and comparing are executed almost simultaneously, so all these operations are performed in all comparators in every period, which we will take for convenience as one unit.

During the downward input phase, n keys are loaded into n units in $2n$ periods. During the upward output phase, each unit delivers the smaller key to its upper unit in every period, outputting one item per period from the sorted keys. The sorting time is completely absorbed into input/output time. So, it takes $2n$ periods to sort n numbers.

Example 9.4   Figures 9.9 and 9.10 illustrate the action of the sorter during the sorting of an input of six numbers, 4, 3, 1, 6, 2, and 5 in the downward and upward phases, respectively. Initially, at time t_0, the contents of the buffer cells in each comparator are all set to ∞. During the first cycle, the first number 4 is compared to ∞ and routed to the upper right cell. During the second cycle, the number 3 is loaded and compared to 4; then the number 3 is routed to the upper right cell and 4 is routed to the lower left cell of the first unit. During the third cycle, as the third number is being loaded into the first unit, the number 4 is loaded into the second unit. In other words, the larger of the two numbers will be pushed out of the comparator in which it resides. At the end of time t_3, the upper right cell of the first unit contains 1 and the lower left cell contains 3; and

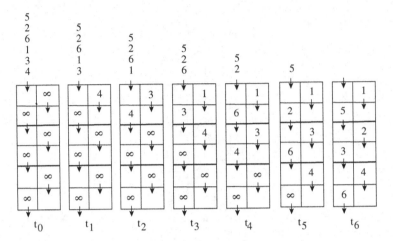

Fig. 9.9. Up-down sorter.

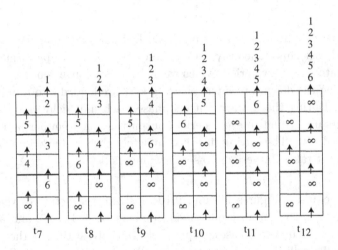

Fig. 9.10. Bottom-up sorter.

the upper right cell of the second unit contains 4 and the lower left cell contains ∞. At the end of time t_6, all the six numbers have been loaded into the sorter, thus completing the input downward phase. From time t_7 on, the output upward phase begins. Note that in the input phase the ∞'s are pushed out of the bottom of the sorter; in the output phase the ∞'s are pushed back into the sorter from the bottom. At the end of time t_7, the smallest number 1 is out and the second smallest 2 is in the upper right cell of the first unit awaiting to be output. In this output phase, the smaller of the two numbers within each comparator is popped up, leaving the unit it resides in and entering the unit on top of it. In the case of the top unit, the smaller number is delivered as output. Thus, the sorter continues to put out the numbers in order. At the end of time t_{12} all data in the sorter will have been output in ascending order as desired. At the same time, the sorter is automatically reset to its initial state (all ∞) and is ready to accept the next input sequence. □

Theorem 9.1 The sorter correctly sorts the input numbers.

Assume the elements to be sorted are distinct, and n is even. Let C_i and D_i denote the contents stored in cells C and D of the ith comparator. First, we show that $\min\{C_{i+1}, D_{i+1}\} \geq \min\{C_i, D_i\}$. It is the function of the ith comparator to push down the larger of its two keys in the input phase, and to pop up the smaller of the two keys in the output phase. In input phase, the keys C_{i+1} and D_{i+1} are obtained via comparator i. Hence, the pushed key C_{i+1} or D_{i+1} must be greater than or equal to the key in comparator i against which it was compared. Similarly, in the output phase, the popped up key C_i or D_i is obtained from comparator $i+1$, hence it must be smaller than or equal to the key in comparator $i+1$ against which it was compared. In both cases, it follows that $\min\{C_{i+1}, D_{i+1}\} \geq \min\{C_i, D_i\}$. Consequently, the kth smallest element is in one of the top k comparators. To see this, assume that the kth smallest element x is not in the first k comparators, that is, it is in comparator j for some $j > k$. Then, since $\min\{C_1, D_1\} \leq \min\{C_2, D_2\} \leq \cdots \leq \min\{C_j, D_j\} \leq x$, at least k elements are smaller than x, which is a contradiction. It follows that after n keys have been read into the sorter, the minimum must be in the top comparator, the second smallest must be either in the first or second comparator, and so on. Thus, the first element to be output must be the smallest, followed by the second smallest, etc.

9.6 Bibliographic Notes

Systolic array (Arnould, Kung, Menzilcioglu and Sarocky [12], Kung [50], Kung [51]) is an on-chip multi-processor architecture proposed by

H.T. Kung in late 1970's. It is proposed as an architectural solution to the anticipated on-chip communication bottleneck of modern very large-scale integration (VLSI) technology. For more on matrix-vector multiplication using less than n PEs, see Navarro, Llaberia and Valero [72], and Stojanovic, Milovanovic, Stojcev and Milovanovic [88]. Several variants of systolic architectures for the convolution problem can be found in Kung [50]. The zero-time sorter is due to Miranker, Tang and Wong [68]. Bubble sorter is from Lee, Hsu and Wong[54].

9.7 Exercises

9.1. Design another systolic array for the matrix-vector product such that $n = 4$.

9.2. How many steps are required to finish the computation in the systolic array for the matrix-vector product discussed in Section 9.2?

9.3. Design a systolic array for the matrix-vector product in which the x-values enter from the left of the array, and the product y-values stay. How many steps are required to finish the computation?

9.4. Design a two-dimensional systolic array for the problem of multiplying two 3×3 matrices A and B to produce the 3×3 matrix C. Assume that the products — that is, the $c_{i,j}$'s, will stay in the array.

9.5. How many steps are required to finish the computation in the systolic array for the matrix-matrix product in Exercise 9.4?

9.6. What is the main drawback of the systolic array design for convolution described in Section 9.3.1?

9.7. Design another semisystolic array for convolution similar to the one described in Section 9.3.1 in which the x_i's are broadcast, the results stay and the weights move.

9.8. What is the main drawback of the systolic array design for convolution described in Section 9.3.2?

9.9. Suggest a simple systolic array for sorting, and explain how it works.

9.10. Illustrate the operation of the zero-time sorter on the input sequence $\langle 3, 6, 2, 1, 3, 5 \rangle$.

9.11. Explain how the zero-time sorter can sort in descending order.

9.12. What modification should be done to the zero-time sorter algorithm if the sequence is entered and extracted from the bottom port?

9.13. Illustrate the operation of the bubble sorter on the input $\langle 3, 6, 2, 1, 3, 5 \rangle$.

9.14. Explain how to make the bubble sorter output the numbers in descending order.

9.8 Solutions

9.1. Design another systolic array for the matrix-vector product such that $n = 4$.

Similar to Fig. 9.1.

9.2. How many steps are required to finish the computation in the systolic array for the matrix-vector product discussed in Section 9.2?

It takes $2n - 1$ steps to produce the vector product **y**.

9.3. Design a systolic array for the matrix-vector product in which the x-values enter from the left of the array, and the product y-values stay. How many steps are required to finish the computation?

The systolic array is shown in Fig. 9.11. It takes $2n - 1$ steps to finish the computation.

9.4. Design a two-dimensional systolic array for the problem of multiplying two 3×3 matrices A and B to produce the 3×3 matrix C. Assume that the products, that is, the $c_{i,j}$'s, will stay in the array.

Arrange the rows and columns of A and B so that the ith row of A is input to the ith column of the array from the top, and the jth column of B is input to the jth row of the array from the left (see Fig. 9.12).

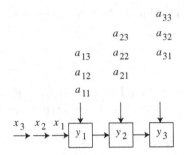

Fig. 9.11.   Systolic matrix-vector multiplication.

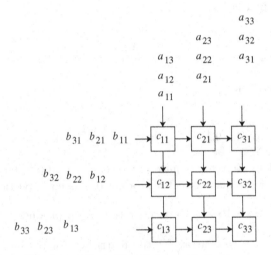

Fig. 9.12.   Systolic matrix multiplication.

The elements of A move downwards while the elements of B move in the left-to-right direction.

9.5. How many steps are required to finish the computation in the systolic array for the matrix-matrix product in Exercise 9.4?

It takes $3n - 2$ steps to finish the matrix-matrix multiplication.

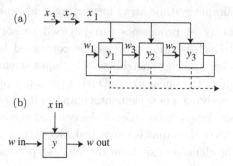

Fig. 9.13. Systolic convolution for Exercise 9.7.

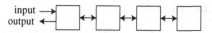

Fig. 9.14. Systolic sorting on linear array for Exercise 9.9.

9.6. What is the main drawback of the systolic array design for convolution described in Section 9.3.1?

The main drawback is that using the bus may be impractical for implementation. As the number of cells increases, wires become too long for the bus.

9.7. Design another semisystolic array for convolution similar to the one described in Section 9.3.1 in which the x_i's are broadcast, results stay and the weights move.

The x_i's are broadcast, results stay and the weights circulate around the array of cells. See Fig. 9.13. The first weight w_1 is associated with a tag bit that signals the accumulator to output and reset its contents.

9.8. What is the main drawback of the systolic array design for convolution described in Section 9.3.2?

The main drawback is that the computation of the y_i's takes twice as long, as input moves at half the speed.

9.9. Suggest a simple systolic array for sorting, and explain how it works.

A linear array of processors can be used to sort as follows (see Fig. 9.14). Each interior processor is connected by two-directional links to its left and right neighbors. The input stream enters from the leftmost end of the linear array. During the input phase, each processor, upon receiving a new element, compares its content with the current element, keeps the smaller of the two and passes the larger one to the right. After the input is consumed, the output phase commences, in which the elements exit from the leftmost processor one at a time.

9.10. Illustrate the operation of the zero-time sorter on the input sequence $\langle 3, 6, 2, 1, 3, 5 \rangle$.

Similar to Example 9.3.

9.11. Explain how the zero-time sorter can sort in descending order.

The same principle of sorting in ascending order applies to the descending sort; we only have to replace ∞ by $-\infty$, the smallest item, and interchange larger and smaller.

9.12. What modification should be done to the zero-time sorter algorithm if the sequence is entered and extracted from the bottom port?

In this case, the larger of the two items is moved up instead, and the smaller is moved down.

9.13. Illustrate the operation of the bubble sorter on the input $\langle 3, 6, 2, 1, 3, 5 \rangle$.

Similar to Example 9.4.

9.14. Explain how to make the bubble sorter output the numbers in descending order.

There are two possibilities. The first approach is to still use the same sorting mechanism, except that we add a multiplier on top of the sorter, which multiplies each input/output datum by -1. The second approach is to exchange the input and output ports. That is, to let the input data enter the sorter from the lower right end (i.e., where the number ∞ enters) and output data then comes out from the lower left end (i.e., where ∞ comes out). In addition to the I/O port exchange, the sorter must be initialized to contain a number known to be smaller than the input data.

Appendix A

Mathematical Preliminaries

A.1 Asymptotic Notations

A.1.1 *The O-notation*

Definition A.1 Let $f(n)$ and $g(n)$ be two functions from the set of natural numbers to the set of nonnegative real numbers. $f(n)$ is said to be $O(g(n))$ if there exists a natural number n_0 and a constant $c > 0$ such that

$$\forall\, n \geq n_0,\ f(n) \leq cg(n).$$

Consequently, if $\lim_{n\to\infty} f(n)/g(n)$ exists, then

$$\lim_{n\to\infty} \frac{f(n)}{g(n)} \neq \infty \text{ implies } f(n) = O(g(n)).$$

Informally, this definition says that f grows no faster than some constant times g. The O-notation can also be used in equations as a simplification tool. For instance, instead of writing

$$f(n) = 5n^3 + 7n^2 - 2n + 13,$$

we may write

$$f(n) = 5n^3 + O(n^2).$$

This is helpful if we are not interested in the *details* of the lower order terms.

A.1.2   *The Ω-notation*

Definition A.2   Let $f(n)$ and $g(n)$ be two functions from the set of natural numbers to the set of nonnegative real numbers. $f(n)$ is said to be $\Omega(g(n))$ if there exists a natural number n_0 and a constant $c > 0$ such that

$$\forall\, n \geq n_0, \;\; f(n) \geq cg(n).$$

Consequently, if $\lim_{n \to \infty} f(n)/g(n)$ exists, then

$$\lim_{n \to \infty} \frac{f(n)}{g(n)} \neq 0 \text{ implies } f(n) = \Omega(g(n)).$$

Informally, this definition says that f grows at least as fast as some constant times g. It is clear from the definition that

$$f(n) \text{ is } \Omega(g(n)) \text{ if and only if } g(n) \text{ is } O(f(n)).$$

A.1.3   *The Θ-notation*

Definition A.3   Let $f(n)$ and $g(n)$ be two functions from the set of natural numbers to the set of nonnegative real numbers. $f(n)$ is said to be $\Theta(g(n))$ if there exists a natural number n_0 and two positive constants c_1 and c_2 such that

$$\forall\, n \geq n_0, \;\; c_1 g(n) \leq f(n) \leq c_2 g(n).$$

Consequently, if $\lim_{n \to \infty} f(n)/g(n)$ exists, then

$$\lim_{n \to \infty} \frac{f(n)}{g(n)} = c \text{ implies } f(n) = \Theta(g(n)),$$

where c is a *constant strictly greater than 0*.

An important consequence of the above definition is that

$$f(n) = \Theta(g(n)) \text{ if and only if } f(n) = O(g(n)) \text{ and } f(n) = \Omega(g(n)).$$

Unlike the previous two notations, the Θ-notation gives an exact picture of the rate of growth of the running time of an algorithm.

A.1.4 The o-notation

Definition A.4 Let $f(n)$ and $g(n)$ be two functions from the set of natural numbers to the set of nonnegative real numbers. $f(n)$ is said to be $o(g(n))$ if for *every* constant $c > 0$ there exists a positive integer n_0 such that $f(n) < cg(n)$ for all $n \geq n_0$. Consequently, if $\lim_{n\to\infty} f(n)/g(n)$ exists, then

$$\lim_{n\to\infty} \frac{f(n)}{g(n)} = 0 \text{ implies } f(n) = o(g(n)).$$

Informally, this definition says that $f(n)$ becomes insignificant relative to $g(n)$ as n approaches infinity. It follows from the definition that

$$f(n) = o(g(n)) \text{ if and only if } f(n) = O(g(n)), \text{ but } g(n) \neq O(f(n)).$$

For example, $n \log n$ is $o(n^2)$ is equivalent to saying that $n \log n$ is $O(n^2)$ but n^2 is *not* $O(n \log n)$.

A.2 Divide-and-conquer Recurrences

Lemma A.1 Let a and c be nonnegative integers, b, d and x nonnegative constants, and let $n = c^k$, for some nonnegative integer k. Then, the solution to the recurrence

$$f(n) = \begin{cases} d & \text{if } n = 1 \\ af(n/c) + bn^x & \text{if } n \geq 2 \end{cases}$$

is

$$f(n) = bn^x \log_c n + dn^x \qquad\qquad \text{if } a = c^x,$$

$$f(n) = \left(d + \frac{bc^x}{a - c^x}\right) n^{\log_c a} - \left(\frac{bc^x}{a - c^x}\right) n^x \quad \text{if } a \neq c^x.$$

Corollary A.1 Let a and c be nonnegative integers, b, d and x nonnegative constants, and let $n = c^k$, for some nonnegative integer k. Then, the solution to the recurrence

$$f(n) = \begin{cases} d & \text{if } n = 1 \\ af(n/c) + bn^x & \text{if } n \geq 2 \end{cases}$$

satisfies

$$f(n) = bn^x \log_c n + dn^x \qquad \text{if } a = c^x,$$

$$f(n) \le \left(\frac{bc^x}{c^x - a}\right) n^x \qquad \text{if } a < c^x,$$

$$f(n) \le \left(d + \frac{bc^x}{a - c^x}\right) n^{\log_c a} \qquad \text{if } a > c^x.$$

Proof. If $a < c^x$, then $\log_c a < x$, or $n^{\log_c a} < n^x$. If $a > c^x$, then $\log_c a > x$, or $n^{\log_c a} > n^x$. The rest of the proof follows immediately from Lemma A.1. □

Theorem A.1 Let a and c be nonnegative integers, b, d and x nonnegative constants, and let $n = c^k$, for some nonnegative integer k. Then, the solution to the recurrence

$$f(n) = \begin{cases} d & \text{if } n = 1 \\ af(n/c) + bn^x & \text{if } n \ge 2 \end{cases}$$

is

$$f(n) = \begin{cases} \Theta(n^x) & \text{if } a < c^x. \\ \Theta(n^x \log n) & \text{if } a = c^x. \\ \Theta(n^{\log_c a}) & \text{if } a > c^x. \end{cases}$$

In particular, if $x = 1$, then

$$f(n) = \begin{cases} \Theta(n) & \text{if } a < c. \\ \Theta(n \log n) & \text{if } a = c. \\ \Theta(n^{\log_c a}) & \text{if } a > c. \end{cases}$$

Example A.1 Consider the recurrence

$$f(n) = \begin{cases} 1 & \text{if } n = 1 \\ f(n/2) + \sqrt{n} & \text{if } n \ge 2. \end{cases}$$

By Corollary A.1, since $a = b = 1, c = 2, x = 0.5$, we have

$$f(n) \le \frac{\sqrt{2}}{\sqrt{2} - 1} \sqrt{n} = \Theta(\sqrt{n}).$$ □

Example A.2   Consider the recurrence

$$f(n) = \begin{cases} 1 & \text{if } n = 1 \\ f(n/2) + h(n) & \text{if } n \geq 2. \end{cases}$$

Then,

$$f(n) = \sum_{i=0}^{n} h\left(\frac{n}{2^i}\right).$$

If we let $h(n) = \log n$, and $n = 2^k$, then the solution to the recurrence

$$f(n) = \begin{cases} 1 & \text{if } n = 1 \\ f(n/2) + \log n & \text{if } n \geq 2 \end{cases}$$

is

$$f(n) = \sum_{i=0}^{k} \log(n/2^i) = \sum_{i=0}^{k} (\log n - i) = \sum_{i=0}^{k} (k - i) = \frac{k(k+1)}{2} = \Theta(\log^2 n).$$

$\square$

A.3   Summations

The arithmetic series:

$$\sum_{j=1}^{n} j = \frac{n(n+1)}{2} = \Theta(n^2). \tag{A.1}$$

The sum of squares:

$$\sum_{j=1}^{n} j^2 = \frac{n(n+1)(2n+1)}{6} = \Theta(n^3). \tag{A.2}$$

The geometric series:

$$\sum_{j=0}^{n} c^j = \frac{c^{n+1} - 1}{c - 1} = \Theta(c^n), \quad c \neq 1. \tag{A.3}$$

If $c = 2$, we have

$$\sum_{j=0}^{n} 2^j = 2^{n+1} - 1 = \Theta(2^n). \tag{A.4}$$

If $c = 1/2$, we have

$$\sum_{j=0}^{n} \frac{1}{2^j} = 2 - \frac{1}{2^n} < 2 = \Theta(1). \tag{A.5}$$

When $|c| < 1$ and the sum is infinite, we have the infinite geometric series

$$\sum_{j=0}^{\infty} c^j = \frac{1}{1-c} = \Theta(1), \quad |c| < 1. \tag{A.6}$$

Differentiating both sides of Eq. (A.3) and multiplying by c yields

$$\sum_{j=0}^{n} jc^j = \sum_{j=1}^{n} jc^j = \frac{nc^{n+2} - nc^{n+1} - c^{n+1} + c}{(c-1)^2} = \Theta(nc^n), \quad c \neq 1. \tag{A.7}$$

Letting $c = 1/2$ in Eq. (A.7) yields

$$\sum_{j=0}^{n} \frac{j}{2^j} = \sum_{j=1}^{n} \frac{j}{2^j} = 2 - \frac{n+2}{2^n} = \Theta(1). \tag{A.8}$$

Differentiating both sides of Eq. (A.6) and multiplying by c yields

$$\sum_{j=0}^{\infty} jc^j = \frac{c}{(1-c)^2} = \Theta(1), \quad |c| < 1. \tag{A.9}$$

A.4   Probability

A.4.1   *Random variables and expectation*

A *random variable* X is a function from the sample space to the set of real numbers. For example, we may let X denote the number of heads appearing when throwing 3 coins. Then, the random variable X takes on one of the values 0, 1, 2, and 3 with probabilities

$\mathbf{Pr}[X = 0] = \mathbf{Pr}[\{TTT\}] = \frac{1}{8}$, $\mathbf{Pr}[X = 1] = \mathbf{Pr}[\{HTT, THT, TTH\}] = \frac{3}{8}$, $\mathbf{Pr}[X = 2] = \mathbf{Pr}[\{HHT, HTH, THH\}] = \frac{3}{8}$ and $\mathbf{Pr}[X = 3] = \mathbf{Pr}[\{HHH\}] = \frac{1}{8}$.

The *expected value* of a (discrete) random variable X with range S is defined as

$$\mathbf{E}[X] = \sum_{x \in S} x \mathbf{Pr}[X = x].$$

For example, if we let X denote the number appearing when throwing a die, then the expected value of X is

$$\mathbf{E}[X] = \sum_{k=1}^{6} k\mathbf{Pr}[X = k] = \frac{1}{6}(1 + 2 + 3 + 4 + 5 + 6) = \frac{7}{2}. \qquad (A.10)$$

$\mathbf{E}[X]$ represents the *mean* of the random variable X and is often written as μ_X or simply μ. An important and useful property is *linearity of expectation*:

$$\mathbf{E}\left[\sum_{i=1}^{n} X_i\right] = \sum_{i=1}^{n} \mathbf{E}[X_i],$$

which is always true regardless of independence.

A.4.2 *Bernoulli distribution*

A *Bernoulli trial* is an experiment with exactly two outcomes, e.g., flipping a coin. These two outcomes are often referred to as success and failure with probabilities p and $q = 1 - p$, respectively. Let X be the random variable corresponding to the toss of a biased coin with probability of heads $\frac{1}{3}$ and probability of tails $\frac{2}{3}$. If we label the outcome as successful when heads appear, then

$$X = \begin{cases} 1 & \text{if the trial succeeds} \\ 0 & \text{if it fails.} \end{cases}$$

A random variables that assumes only the numbers 0 and 1 is called an *indicator random variable*. The expected value and variance of an indicator random variable with probability of success p are given by

$$\mathbf{E}[X] = p \quad \text{and} \quad \mathbf{var}[X] = pq = p(1 - p).$$

A.4.3   *Binomial distribution*

Let $X = \sum_{i=1}^{n} X_i$, where the X_i's are indicator random variables corresponding to n *independent* Bernoulli trials with parameter p (identically distributed). Then, X is said to have the *binomial distribution* with parameters p and n. The probability that there are *exactly* k successes is given by

$$\mathbf{Pr}[X = k] = \binom{n}{k} p^k q^{n-k},$$

where $q = 1 - p$. The expected value and variance of X are given by:

$$\mathbf{E}[X] = np \quad \text{and} \quad \mathbf{var}[X] = npq = np(1 - p).$$

The first equality follows from the linearity of expectations, and the second follows from the fact that all $X_i's$ are pairwise independent.

For example, the probabilities of getting k heads, $0 \leq k \leq 4$, when tossing a fair coin 4 times are

$$\frac{1}{16}, \frac{1}{4}, \frac{3}{8}, \frac{1}{4}, \frac{1}{16}.$$

$\mathbf{E}[X] = 4 \times (1/2) = 2$, and $\mathbf{var}[X] = 4 \times (1/2) \times (1/2) = 1$.

A.4.4   *Chernoff bounds*

Let $X_1, X_2, \ldots, X_n$ be a collection of n independent indicator random variables representing Bernoulli trials such that each X_i has probability $\mathbf{Pr}[X_i = 1] = p_i$. We are interested in bounding the probability that their sum $X = \sum_{i=1}^{n} X_i$ will deviate from the mean $\mu = \mathbf{E}[X]$ by a multiple of μ.

A.4.4.1   *Lower tail*

Theorem A.2   Let δ be some constant in the interval (0,1). Then,

$$\mathbf{Pr}[X < (1 - \delta)\mu] < \left(\frac{e^{-\delta}}{(1 - \delta)^{(1-\delta)}} \right)^{\mu},$$

which can be simplified to

$$\mathbf{Pr}[X < (1 - \delta)\mu] < e^{-\mu \delta^2 / 2}$$

A.4.4.2 *Upper tail*

Theorem A.3 Let $\delta > 0$ Then,

$$\mathbf{Pr}[X > (1+\delta)\mu] < \left(\frac{e^{\delta}}{(1+\delta)^{(1+\delta)}}\right)^{\mu},$$

which can be simplified to

$$\mathbf{Pr}[X > (1+\delta)\mu] < e^{-\mu\delta^2/4} \quad \text{if } \delta < 2e - 1,$$

and

$$\mathbf{Pr}[X > (1+\delta)\mu] < 2^{-\delta\mu} \quad \text{if } \delta > 2e - 1.$$

Example A.3 We seek the probability that the number of heads in a sequence of n flips of a fair coin is at least $2n/3$.

Let $\mu = \mathbf{E}[X] = n/2$. Solving for δ,

$$(1+\delta)\mu = \frac{2n}{3}$$

gives $\delta = \frac{1}{3}$. We apply Chernoff bound of Theorem A.3. Since $\delta < 2e - 1$, we have

$$\mathbf{Pr}\left[X \geq \frac{2n}{3}\right] < e^{-\mu\delta^2/4}$$

$$= e^{-(n/2)(1/9)/4}$$

$$= e^{-n/72}.$$

So, we see that there is an exponential fall off. $\qquad\qquad\square$

Bibliography

[1] Akers, S. B., Harel, D. and Krishnamurthy, B., "The star graph: An attractive alternative to the n-cube", *Proceeding of the International Conference on Parallel Processing*, 393–400, 1987.

[2] Akers, S. B. and Krishnamurthy, B., "A group-theoretic model for symmetric interconnection networks", *IEEE Transactions on Computers*, **38**(4), 555–566, 1989.

[3] Akhgari, E., Ziaie, A. and Ghodsi, M., "Sorting on OTIS-Networks", In: Sarbazi-Azad, H., Parhami, B., Miremadi SG. and Hessabi, S. (eds.) *Advances in Computer Science and Engineering. CSICC 2008. Communications in Computer and Information Science*, Vol. 6. Springer, Berlin, Heidelberg, 871–875, 2008.

[4] Akl, S. G., *The Design and Analysis of Parallel Algorithms*, Prentice Hall, Englewood Cliffs, New Jersey, 1989.

[5] Akl, S. G., *Parallel Computation: Models and Methods*, Prentice Hall, Upper Saddle River, Florida, 1997.

[6] Akl, S. G., *Parallel Sorting Algorithms*, Academic Press, Englewood Cliffs, NJ, 1985.

[7] Akl, S. G., "An optimal algorithm for parallel selection", *Information Processing Letters*, **19**, 47–50, 1984.

[8] Akl, S. G. and Lyons, K. A., *Parallel Computational Geometry*, Prentice Hall, Englewood Cliffs, New Jersey, 1993.

[9] Akl, S. G., Qiu, K. and Stojmenovic, I., "Fundamental algorithms for the star and pancake interconnection networks with applications to computational geometry", *Networks, Special Issue: Interconnection Networks and Algorithms*, **23**, 215–226, 1993.

[10] Al-Sadi, J., Awwad, A. M. and AlBdaiwi, "Efficient routing algorithms on OTIS-Star network", *Proceedings of the IASTED International Conference on Advances in Computer Science and Technology*, Virgin Islands, U.S.A., ACTA Press, 157–162, 2004.

[11] Alsuwaiyel, M.H., "An efficient and adaptive algorithm for multi-selection on the PRAM", *Proceeding of the International Conference on Software Engineering, Artificial Intelligence, Networking and Parallel/Distributed Computing (SNPD01)* Nagoya, Japan, 140–143, 2001.

[12] Arnould, E., Kung, H., Menzilcioglu, O. and Sarocky, K., "A systolic array computer", *Proc. IEEE International Conference on Acoustics, Speech, and Signal Processing*, **10**, 232–235, 1985.

[13] Awwad, A. M., "OTIS-Star: An attractive alternative network", *Proceedings of the 4th WSEAS International Conference on Software Engineering, Parallel & Distributed Systems*, 37–41, 2005.

[14] Awwad, A. M. and Al-Sadi, J., "Investigating the distributed load balancing approach for OTIS-Star topology", *International Journal of Computer Science and Information Security (IJCSIS)*, **14**, no. 3, 163–171, 2016.

[15] Batcher, K., "Sorting networks and their applications", *AFIPS Spring Joint Computing Conference*, Atlantic City, NJ, 307–314, 1968.

[16] Blahut, R. E., *Fast Algorithms for Digital Signal Processing*, Addison Wesley, Reading, MA, 1985.

[17] Borodin, A. and Moenck, R., "Fast modular transforms", *Journal of Computer and System Sciences*, **8**, 366–386, 1974.

[18] L. E. Cannon, "A cellular computer to implement the Kalman filter algorithm", Ph.D. Thesis, Montana State University, 1969.

[19] Cantoni, V. and Levialdi, S., Eds. *Pyramidal Systems for Computer Vision*, Springer, Berlin, 1986.

[20] Chandran, S. and Rosenfeld, A., "Order statistics on a hypercube", *Information Processing Letters*, **27**, 129–132, 1988.

[21] Chaudhuri, P., *Parallel Algorithms: Design and Analysis*, Prentice Hall, Sydney, Australia, 1992.

[22] Chiang, W. K., "Topological properties of the (n, k)-star graph", *International Journal of Foundations of Computer Science*, **9**(2), 235–248, 1998.

[23] Chiang, W. K. and Chen, R. J., "The (n, k)-star graph: A generalized star graph", *Information Processing Letters*, **56**, 259–264, 1995.

[24] Christopher, T., "An implementation of Warshalls algorithm for transitive closure on a cellular computer, Technical Report 36, Institute for Computer Research, University of Chicago, Chicago, IL, 1973.

[25] Cinque, L. and Bongiovanni, G., "Parallel prefix computation on a pyramid computer", *Pattern Recognition Letters*, **16**, 19–22, 1995.

[26] Cole, R., "Parallel merge sort", *SIAM Journal on Computing*, **17**(4), 770–785, 1988.

[27] Cooley, J. M. and Tukey, J. W., "An algorithm for machine calculation of complex Fourier series", *Mathematics of Computation*, **19**, 297–301, 1965.

[28] Cook, S. A., "A taxonomy of problems with fast parallel algorithms", *Information and Control*, **64**, 2–22, 1985.

[29] Cosnard, M. and Trystram, D., *Parallel Algorithms and Architectures*, International Thomson Computer Press, London, 1995.

[30] Cypher, R. and Plaxton, G., "Deterministic sorting in nearly logarithmic time on the hypercube and related computers", In *Proceeding of the 22nd ACM Symp. Theory of Computing*, ACM Press, 1990.

[31] Day, K. and Al-Ayyoub, A., "Topological properties of OTIS-networks", *IEEE Transactions on Parallel and Distributed Systems*, **13**(4), 359–366, 2002.

[32] Day, K. and Tripathy, A., "Arrangement graphs: A class of generalized star graph", *Information Processing Letters*, **42**, 235–241, 1992.

[33] Dekel, E., Nassimi, D. and Sahni, S., "Parallel matrix and graph algorithms", *SIAM Journal on Computing*, **10**(4), pp. 307–315, 1981.

[34] Dietzfelbinger, M., Madhavapeddy, S. and Sudborough, I. H., "Three disjoint path paradigms in star networks", *Proceedings of the Third IEEE Symposium on Parallel and Distributed Processing*, 400–406, 1991.

[35] Durad, M. H., Akhtar, M. N. and Irfan-ul-Haq, "Performance analysis of parallel sorting algorithms Using MPI", *2014 12th International Conference on Frontiers of Information Technology*, Islamabad, pp. 202–207, 2014.

[36] Fiduccia, C. M., "Polynomial evaluation via the division algorithm:The fast Fourier transform revisited", In *Proceeding of the fourth ACM Symposium on Theory of Computing*, Denver, CO, 88–93, 1972.

[37] Gibbons, A. and Rytter, W., *Efficient Parallel Algorithms*, Cambridge University Press, London, 1990.

[38] Greenlaw, R., Hoover, J. and Ruzzo, W., *Limits to Parallel Computation: P-completeness Theory*, Oxford University Press, New York, 1995.

[39] Grama, A., Gupta, A., Karypis, G. and Kumar, V., *Introduction to Parallel Computing*, Addison-Wesley, New York, 2003.

[40] Gupta, A. and Sarkar, B. K., "Shortest path routing on OTIS hyper hexa-cell", *2017 8th International Conference on Computing, Communication and Networking Technologies (ICCCNT)*, pp. 1–6, 2017.

[41] Gupta, A., Singh, H. and Bhati, A., "Efficient parallel algorithm for mapping LaGrange's interpolation on OTIS and BSN hyper hexa-cell", *2020 International Conference on Emerging Smart Computing and Informatics (ESCI)*, AISSMS Institute of Information Technology, Pune, India, pp. 82–87, 2020.

[42] He, L., "Properties and Algorithms of the (n, k)-Star Graphs", Ms Thesis, Faculty of Mathematics and Science, Brock University, St. Catharines, Ontario, Canada, 2008.

[43] Horowitz, E., Sahni, S. and Rajasekaran, S., *Computer Algorithms*, Computer Science Press, Rockville, MD, 1998.

[44] JáJá, J., *An Introduction to Parallel Algorithms*, Addison-Wesley, Reading, MA, 1992.

[45] Jan, G. E. and Huang, Y. S., "A simple algorithm for optimal load balancing on hypercube multiprocessors, *Proceedings of 2001 International Conference on Parallel and Distributed Processing Techniques and Applications*, Las Vegas, Nevada, USA, 17, 2001.

[46] JáJá, J. and Ryu, K. W., "Load balancing on the hypercube and related networks", *The Proceeding of the 1990 International Conference on Parallel Processing*, pp. I203–I210, 1990.

[47] Kunde, M., "Ruting and sorting on mesh-connected arrays", *Proceeding of Third Agean Workshop on Computing: VLSI Algorithms and Architectures*, Vol. 319 of Lecture notes in computer science, pp. 423–433, Springer-Verlag, 1988.

[48] Kronsjo, L. *Algorithms: Their Complexity and Efficiency*, Wiley, New York, NY, 1987.

[49] Kruscal, C., "Searching, merging and sorting in parallel computation", *IEEE Transactions on Computers*, **C-32**(10), 942–946, 1983.

[50] Kung, H.T., "Why systolic architectures?", *IEEE Computers*, **15**, 37–46, 1982.

[51] Kung, S.Y., *VLSI Array Processors*. Prentice Hall, Englewood Cliffs, NJ, 1988.

[52] Lakshmivarahan, S. and Dhall, S. K., *Analysis and Design of Parallel Algorithms: Arithmetic and Matrix Problems*, McGraw-Hill, New York, 1990.

[53] Lakshmivarahan, S. and Dhall, S. K., *Parallel Computing Using the Prefix Problem*, Oxford University Press, New York, 1994.

[54] Lee, D.T., Hsu, C. and Wong, C. K., "An on-chip compare/steer bubble sorter", *IEEE Transactions on Computers*, c-**30**(6), 396–404, 1981.

[55] Leighton, F.T., *Complexity Issues in VLSI*, MIT Press, Cambridge, MA, 1983.

[56] Leighton, F.T., "Tight bounds on the complexity of parallel sorting", *IEEE Transactions on Computers*, c-**34**(4), 344–354, 1985.

[57] Leighton, F.T., *Introduction to Parallel Algorithms and Architectures: Arrays, Trees and Hypercubes*, Morgan Kaufmann Publishers, San Mateo, CA, 1992.

[58] Leighton, F.T., Makedon, F. and Tollis, I., "A $2n - 2$ step algorithm for routing in an $n \times n$ mesh", *Proceeding of the ACM Symposium on Parallel Algorithms and Architectures*, 328–335, 1989.

[59] Li, Y. and Qiu, K.,"Routing, broadcasting, prefix sums, and sorting algorithms on the arrangement graph", *2009 15th International Conference on Parallel and Distributed Systems*, 324–331, 2009.

[60] Lucas, K. T. and Jana, P. K., "An efficient parallel sorting algorithm on OTIS mesh of trees", *2009 IEEE International Advance Computing Conference (IACC 2009)*, 175–180, 2009.

[61] Lucas, K. T. and Jana, P. K., "Sorting and routing on OTIS mesh of trees", *Parallel Processing Letters*, **20**, no. 2, 145–154, 2010.

[62] Mahafzah, B. A., Sleit, A., Hamad, N. A., Ahmad, E. F. and Abu-Kabeer, T. M., "The OTIS hyper hexa-cell optoelectronic architecture", *J. Computing*, **94**(5), 411–432, 2012.

[63] Marsden, G., Marchand, P., Harvey, P. and Esener, S., "Optional transpose interconnection system architecture", *Optics Letters*, **18**(13), 1083–1085, 1993.

[64] McClellan, J. H. and Rader, C. M. *Number Theory in Digital Signal Processing*, Prentice Hall, Englewood Cliffs, NJ, 1979.

[65] Mendia, V. E. and Sarkar, D., "Optimal broadcasting on the star graph", *IEEE Transactions on Parallel and Distributed Systems*, **3**(4), 389–396, 1992.

[66] Miller, R. and Boxer, L., *Algorithms Sequential & Parallel*, Prentice-Hall, Englewood Cliffs, NJ, 2000.

[67] Miller, R. and Stout, Q. F., *Parallel Algorithms for Regular Architectures: Meshes and Pyramids*, MIT Press, Cambridge, MA, 1996.

[68] Miranker, G., Tang, L. and Wong, C. K., "A zero-time VLSI sorter", *IBM J. Res. Develop.*, **27**(2), 140–147, 1983.

[69] Najaf-abadi, H. H. and Sarbazi-azad, H., "Comparative evaluation of adaptive and deterministic routing in the OTIS-hypercube", *Proceeding of the 9th Asia-Pacific Computer Systems Architecture Conference (ACSAC)*, in LNCS 3189, pp. 349–362, 2004.

[70] Najaf-abadi, H. H. and Sarbazi-azad, H., "An empirical comparison of OTIS-mesh and OTIS-hypercube multicomputer systems under deterministic routing", *Proceeding of the 14th IEEE International Parallel and Distributed Processing Symposium*, p. 262-a, IEEE Press, New York, 2005.

[71] Nassimi, D. and Sahni, S., "Parallel permutation and sorting algorithms and a generalized interconnection network", *Journal of the ACM*, **29**(3), 642–667, 1982.

[72] Navarro, J., Llaberia, J. and Valero, M., "Partitioning: An essential step in mapping algorithms into systolic array processors", *Computer*, **20**(7), 77–89, July 1987.

[73] Osterloh, A., "Sorting on the OTIS-mesh", *19th IEEE International Parallel and Distributed Processing Symposium (IPDPS 2000)*, 269–274, 2000.

[74] Plaxton, C. G. "Load balancing, selection and sorting on the hypercube", *Proceeding of the 1989 ACM Symposium on Parallel Algorithms and Architectures*, 64–73, 1989.

[75] Rajasekaran, S., "Sorting and selection on interconnection networks", *DIMACS Series in Discrete Mathematics and Theoretical Computer Science*, **21**, 275–296, 1995.

[76] Rajasekaran, S. and Sahni, S., "Randomized routing, selection, and sorting on the OTIS-mesh", *IEEE Transactions on Parallel and Distributed Systems*, **9**(9), 833–840, 1998.

[77] Roosta, S. H., *Parallel Processing and Parallel Algorithms: Theory and Computation*, Springer-Verlag, New York, 2000.

[78] Rosenfeld, A., Ed. *Multiresolution Image Processing and Analysis*, Springer, Berlin, 1984.

[79] Sado, K. and Igarashi, Y., "Some parallel sorts on a mesh-connected processor array and their time efficiency", *Journal of Parallel and Distributed Computing*, **3**, 398–410, 1986.

[80] Sahni, S. and Wang, C-F., "BPC permutations on the OTIS-hypercube optoelectronic computer", *Informatica*, **22**, 263–269, 1998.

[81] Scherson, I., Sen, S. and Shamir, A., "Shear-sort: A true two-dimensional sorting technique for VLSI networks", *Proceeding of the International Conference on Parallel Processing*, 903–908, 1986.

[82] Shamos, M. I., "Computational Geometry", PhD Thesis, Department of Computer Science, Yale University, New Haven, CT, 1978.

[83] Shen, H., "Efficient parallel multiselection on hypercubes", *Proceeding of the 1997 International Symp. on Parallel Architectures, Algorithms and Networks (I-SPAN)*, IEEE CS Press, 338–342, 1997.

[84] Shen, H., "Optimal multiselection in hypercubes", *Parallel Algorithms and Applications*, **14**, 203–212, 2000.

[85] Sheu, J. P., Wu, C. T. and Chen, T. S., "An optimal broadcasting algorithm without message redundancy in star graphs", *IEEE Transactions on Parallel and Distributed Systems*, **6**(6), 653–658, 1995.

[86] Shi, H. and Schaeffer, J., "Parallel sorting by regular sampling", *Journal of Parallel and Distributed Computing*, **14**, 361–372, 1990.

[87] Shiloach, Y. and Vishkin, U., "Finding the maximum, merging and sorting in a parallel computation model", *Journal of Algorithms*, **2**(1), 88–102, 1981.

[88] Stojanovic, N. M. ,Milovanovic, I. Z.,Stojcev, M. K. and Milovanovic, E. I., "Matrix-vector Multiplication on a Fixed Size Unidirectional Systolic Array", *2007 8th International Conference on Telecommunications in Modern Satellite, Cable and Broadcasting Services*, 457–460, 2007.

[89] Stout, Q., "Sorting, merging, selecting, and filtering on tree and pyramid machines", *Proceeding of the 1983 International Conference on Parallel Processing*, 214–221, 1983.

[90] Szymanski, T., "Hypermesh optical interconnection networks for parallel computing ", *Journal of Parallel and Distributed Computing*, **26**, 1–23, 1995.

[91] Szymanski, T. and Hinton, H., "Architecture of a terabit free-space intelligent optical backplane", *Journal of Parallel and Distributed Computing*, **55**(1), 1–31, 1998.

[92] Thompson, C. and Kung, H., "Sorting on a mesh-connected parallel computer", *Communication of the ACM*, **20**(4), 263–271, 1977.

[93] Wagar, B., "Hyperquicksort: A fast sorting algorithm for hypercubes", in *Hypercube Multiprocessors*, M.T. Health, ed., SIAM, 292–299, 1987.

[94] Wang, C-F., "Algorithms for the OTIS optoelectronic computer", PhD thesis, Dept. of Computer Science, Univ. of Florida, 1998.

[95] Wang, C-F. and Sahni, S., "Basic operations on the OTIS-mesh optoelectronic computer", *IEEE Transactions on Parallel and Distributed Systems*, **9**(12), 1226–1236, 1998.

[96] Wang, C-F. and Sahni, S., "Image processing on the OTIS-mesh optoelectronic computer", *IEEE Transactions on Parallel and Distributed Systems*, **11**(2), 97–109, 2000.

[97] Wang, C-F. and Sahni, S., "Matrix multiplication on the OTIS-mesh optoelectronic computer", *IEEE Transactions on Computers*, **50**(7), 635–646, 2001.

[98] Winograd, S. *Arithmetic Complexity of Computation*, SIAM Publishers, 1980.

[99] Woo, J. and Sahni, S., "Load balancing on a hypercube", *1991 Proceedings of the Fifth International Parallel Processing Symposium*, 525–530, 1991.

[100] Valiant, L. G., "A scheme for fast parallel communication", *SIAM Journal on Computing*, **11**, 350–361, 1982.

[101] Valiant, L. G. and Brebner, G. L., "Universal schemes for parallel communication", *Proceedings of the 13th ACM Symposium on Theory of Computing*, Milwaukee, WI, 263–277, 1–9, 1981.

[102] Vishkin, U., "An optimal parallel algorithm for selection", *Advances in Computing Research*, JAI Press Inc., Greenwich, CT, 1987.

[103] Zane, F., Marchand, P., Pahuri, R. and Esener, S., "Scalable network architectures using the optical transpose interconnection system (OTIS)", *Proceeding of the Second International Conference Massively Parallel Processing Using Optical Interconnections (MPPOI' 96)*, 114–121, 1996.

[104] Xavier, C. and Iyengar, S. S., *Introduction to Parallel Algorithms*, John Wiley, New York, 1998.

Index

$\Theta(1)$ time, 11

A

acyclic graph, 210, 222
ARBITRARY, 8
area of a picture, 274, 277
arrangement graph, 296, 304, 307–308
array packing, 16–17, 77

B

balanced tree method, 8
Bernoulli distribution, 363
Bernoulli trial, 363
BFODDEVENMERGE algorithm,
    128–129, 132, 142, 146, 154
BFODDEVENMERGESORT algorithm,
    130, 132, 328
BFPARPREFIX algorithm, 126–127, 271
binomial distribution, 364
bipartite graph, 75, 92
bisection width, 95, 141, 151, 207,
    213, 274–277, 279
bisection width of a network, 4
bisection width of the butterfly, 141,
    151
bisection width of the hypercube, 95
bisection width of the mesh, 207, 213
bisection width of the torus, 207, 213

bit fixing, 106–107, 110, 144
bitonic merging, 39–40
bitonic merging and sorting, 35, 43
bitonic sequence, 35, 37
bitonic sort network, 71, 80
bitonic sorting, 40, 75, 92
BITONICMERGE algorithm, 39–42
BITONICSORT algorithm, 40–41
bottom-up merge sorting, 31
breadth-first spanning tree, 210, 222
Brent theorem, 10, 74, 90
broadcasting, 70, 78, 104, 138, 144,
    162, 207, 212, 294–295, 304, 307,
    316, 326, 332–334, 336, 339
broadcasting in OTIS-Mesh, 316, 332,
    334
broadcasting in the hypercube, 104,
    138, 144
broadcasting in the mesh, 162
broadcasting in the OTIS-Hypercube,
    326, 333, 336
broadcasting in the OTIS-Star, 333,
    339
broadcasting in the ring, 207, 212
broadcasting in the star network,
    294–295, 304, 307
BUCKETSORT, 139–140, 147–148
butterfly, 96, 98, 110

Printed in the United States
by Baker & Taylor Publisher Services